HEROIN, ORGANI
MAKING OF MODERN TURKEY

Heroin, Organized Crime, and the Making of Modern Turkey explores the history of organized crime in Turkey and the roles which gangs and gangsters have played in the making of the Turkish state and Turkish politics. Turkey's underworld, which has been at the heart of a number of devastating scandals over the last several decades, is strongly tied to the country's long history of opium production and heroin trafficking. As an industry at the centre of the Ottoman Empire's long transition into the modern Turkish Republic, as important as the silk road had been in earlier centuries, the modern rise of the opium and heroin trade helped to solidify and complicate long-standing relationships between state officials and criminal syndicates. Such relationships produced not only ongoing patterns of corruption, but helped fuel and enable repeated acts of state violence.

Drawing upon new archival sources from the United States and Turkey, including declassified documents from the Prime Minister's Archives of the Republic of Turkey and the Central Intelligence Agency, *Heroin, Organized Crime, and the Making of Modern Turkey* provides a critical window into how a handful of criminal syndicates played supporting roles in the making of national security politics in contemporary Turkey. The rise of the 'Turkish mafia', from its origins in the late Ottoman period to its role in the 'deep state' revealed by the so-called Susurluk and Ergenekon scandals, is a story that mirrors troubling elements in the republic's establishment and emphasizes the transnational and comparative significance of narcotics and gangs in the country's past.

Ryan Gingeras is the author of *Fall of the Sultanate: The Great War and the End of the Ottoman Empire 1908–1922* and *Sorrowful Shores: Violence, Ethnicity, and the End of the Ottoman Empire*, which received short list distinctions for the Rothschild Book Prize in Nationalism and Ethnic Studies and the British-Kuwait Friendship Society Book Prize. He has published on a wide variety of topics related to history and politics in such journals as *International Journal of Middle East Studies, Middle East Journal, Iranian Studies, Diplomatic History, Past & Present*, and *Journal of Contemporary European History*.

Heroin, Organized Crime, and the Making of Modern Turkey

RYAN GINGERAS

OXFORD
UNIVERSITY PRESS

OXFORD
UNIVERSITY PRESS

Great Clarendon Street, Oxford, OX2 6DP,
United Kingdom

Oxford University Press is a department of the University of Oxford. It furthers the University's objective of excellence in research, scholarship, and education by publishing worldwide. Oxford is a registered trade mark of Oxford University Press in the UK and in certain other countries

First published 2014
First published in paperback 2017

Published in the United States of America by Oxford University Press
198 Madison Avenue, New York, NY 10016, United States of America

British Library Cataloguing in Publication Data
Data available

Library of Congress Cataloging in Publication Data
Data available

ISBN 978–0–19–871602–0 (Hbk.)
ISBN 978–0–19–880419–2 (Pbk.)

For my mother

Preface

I have considered more than one title for this book over the last several years. Thinking the manuscript could use a name with some jazz or a hook, the first one I contemplated was *Sultans of Smack*. After some thought, I dispensed with that title, fearing it would undermine the earnestness of the work presented here. I then hoped to name the book *Patron*, a title that possesses an intended double meaning. In Turkish, *patron* is often used to refer to a boss, any boss. For a time however, it also specifically applied to major figures within Istanbul's heroin trade. A number of notorious, but today largely forgotten, figures bore the title: İhsan Sekban, Hüseyin Eminoğlu, Ahmet Soysal, Ali Osman Tüter, and perhaps others. The term appeared to have lost its significance during the 1970s when the more contemporary epithet, *baba*, entered popular diction. A *baba*, which generically means father, pays direct homage to *The Godfather*, a film that palpably changed global perceptions of organized crime. Arguably no one in contemporary Turkey would refer to a mafia figure simply as a *patron*. Since this book largely deals with the history of heroin and Turkish organized crime before 1980, the term *patron* seemed like a fitting choice for the title.

"Patron" possesses another obvious meaning in English. A patron is someone who protects and guards the interests of a client. Naturally, patron–client relations are found in realms beyond the confines of crime but in terms of the context of this study, such linkages are critical to understanding how and why heroin and organized crime are of critical significance to Turkish history. The heroin trade has influenced various levels of Turkish society and the Turkish state. A great host of Turkish smugglers, wholesalers, chemists, farmers, and business magnates have garnered immense profits from this trade in both legitimate and illegitimate terms. More importantly, the heroin trade has helped forge alliances, grounded in both financial gain and political interests, between criminal syndicates and elements of the country's political establishment. Success or failure within the Turkish heroin trade has often rested upon the ability of a trafficker or producer to court and maintain relations with powerful political allies. The wealth and clout of some *patrons*, such as the men cited earlier, often led to relations where they, the criminals, held greater authority over elected and appointed officials than one would normally expect.

This book explores the nature of patron–client relations in other ways. In order to understand the history of heroin and organized crime in Turkey, one must come to terms with how law enforcement officials, diplomats, and politicians perceived narcotics and criminal networks. The story of how we arrive at our contemporary understanding of the Turkish heroin trade necessitates greater appreciation of Turkey's relationship with the United States. A patrimonial system based upon security and structural and political development has long provided a basis for Ankara's ties with Washington. It is because of these ties that Turkish and American agents came to cooperate with one another in tackling and assessing the threat of organized crime and drug trafficking in Turkey today. Our modern perceptions of the structure, vitality, and influence of organized crime in Turkey is greatly indebted to the relationship formed between these two countries. Despite the closeness with which these two allies have worked on the challenge of heroin and organized crime over the course of the twentieth and twenty-first centuries, this has not always been a very happy, or functional, pairing.

After some convincing, I have opted for the book's present name in order to avoid unnecessary confusion and to emphasize the fundamental goal of my research. Heroin and organized crime *has* influenced the making of modern Turkey. In arriving at this conclusion, this book attempts to draw attention to broader historical points of comparison. The Republic of Turkey is by no means the only country impacted by development of the modern narcotics trade. Nor is it an exceptional state in terms of the political clout historically exercised by criminal syndicates. Yet to understand and contextualize the impact of drugs and gangsters in Turkish history, this book stresses the need to draw Turkish studies into a wider dialogue with works from other regional fields of history. I sincerely hope that this book is received, at least in part, as a work that is conscious of the trends and demands of comparative world history.

Five years of research preceded the production of this study. Many people directly and indirectly impacted the narrative and conclusions elucidated over the following pages. With that in mind, there are many people I wish to thank. First, I would like to extend my gratitude to my colleagues, past and present, at Long Island University, Lafayette College, and the Naval Postgraduate School who have supported me and encouraged me to write this book. In the last five years I have had the opportunity to regularly teach a comparative course on the history of organized crime, an opportunity that allowed me both the time and critical feedback necessary for the formulation of this study. The students at each of these institutions have given me much to think about and for that I am grateful. I wish to extend my sincerest thanks to the International Research and Exchange Program and the Woodrow Wilson Center for their invitation to take part in their Symposium on Transnational Crime and Corruption in Eastern Europe and Eurasia. Through this meeting I met many fine scholars in the field who contributed much to the way in which I now approach the history of organized crime.

The research invested in this book would not have been possible without the support and guidance of the staff at the National Archives in College Park, Maryland. This recognition is a small token of thanks for the hard, and often thankless, work the archivists expend in maintaining the records of the United States. I especially want to thank Burak Başaranlar for his assistance in exploring the Prime Minister's Republican Archive in Ankara. I am indebted to his time and patience.

There are several individuals who advised me, encouraged me, and critiqued the work presented here. Virginia Aksan, Robert Crews, Howard Eissenstat, Fatma Müge Göçek, Mark Galeotti, Peter Holquist, Reşat Kasaba, Hasan Kayalı, Mark Mazower, Jonathan Marshall, and Stefan Winter all played a role in making this book possible. Lastly, I want to thank my family. Mariana, Amaya, and Sebastian give me the inspiration, strength, and joy that keeps me going. Thank you.

Contents

List of Abbreviations

AKP	*Adalet ve Kalkışma Partisi*
ASALA	Armenian Secret Army for the Liberation of Armenia
BNDD	Bureau of Narcotics and Dangerous Drugs
CIA	Central Intelligence Agency
CNB	Central Narcotics Bureau
CUP	Committee of the Union and Progress
DEA	Drug Enforcement Administration
DDKD	*Devrimci Demokratik Kültür Derneği*
DP	Democratic Party
DPS	Directorate of Public Security
EIC	East India Trading Company
FBN	Federal Bureau of Narcotics
GAO	Government Accountability Office
ICA	International Cooperation Administration
IMRO	Internal Macedonian Revolutionary Organization
KOM	*Kaçakçılık ve Örgüt Suçlarla Mücadele Daire Başkanlığı*
MAS	*Muerte a Secuestraderos*
MHP	*Milliyetçi Hareket Partisi*
MİT	*Milli İstihbarat Teşkilatı*
NSP	National Salvation Party
NYPD	New York Police Department
OSI	Office of Special Investigations
OSS	Office of Special Services
PRC	People's Republic of China
PRI	Institutional Revolution Party
RPP	Republican People's Party
SELEC	Southeast European Law Enforcement Center
TADOC	Turkish Academy Against Drugs and Organized Crime
UNODC	United Nations Office of Drug Control

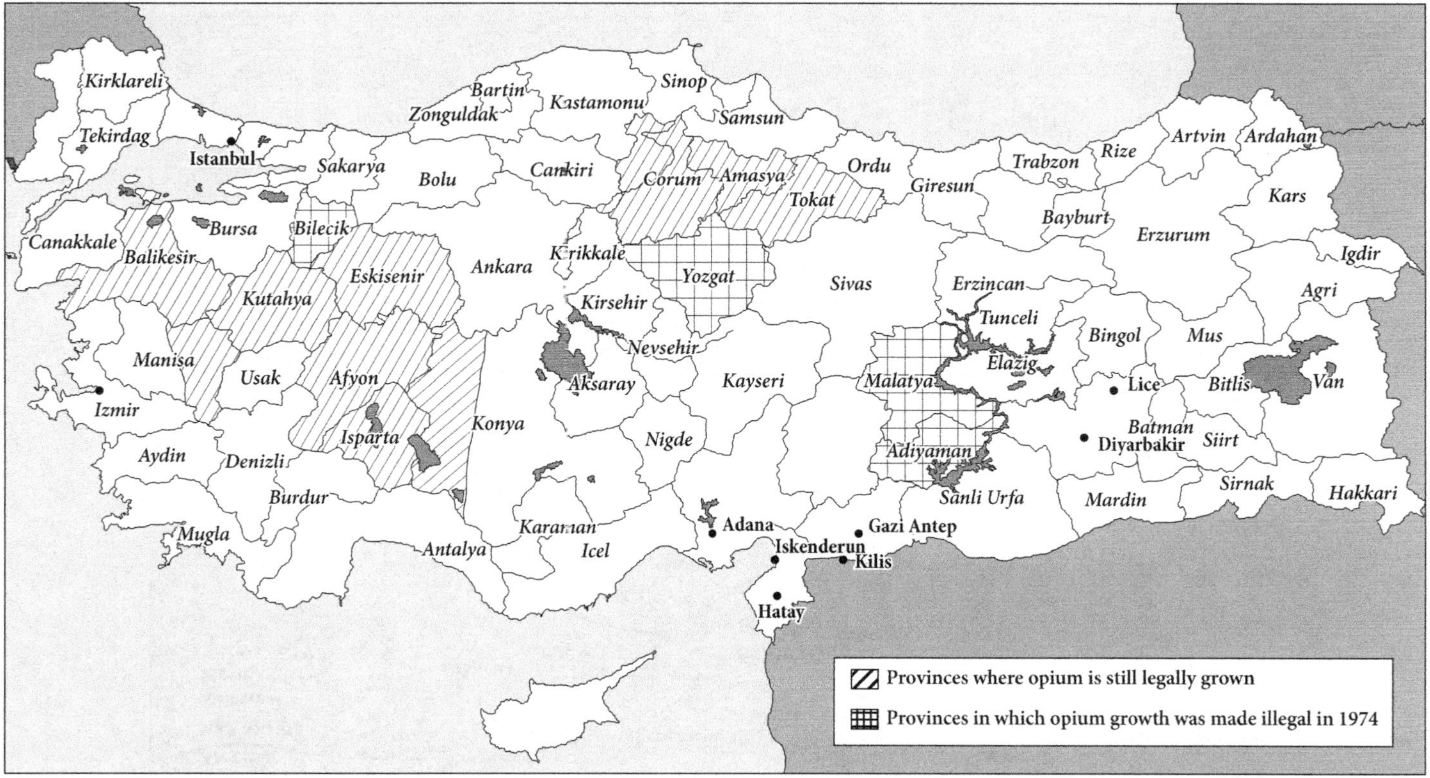

Map 1 Opium producing areas in Turkey, past and present.

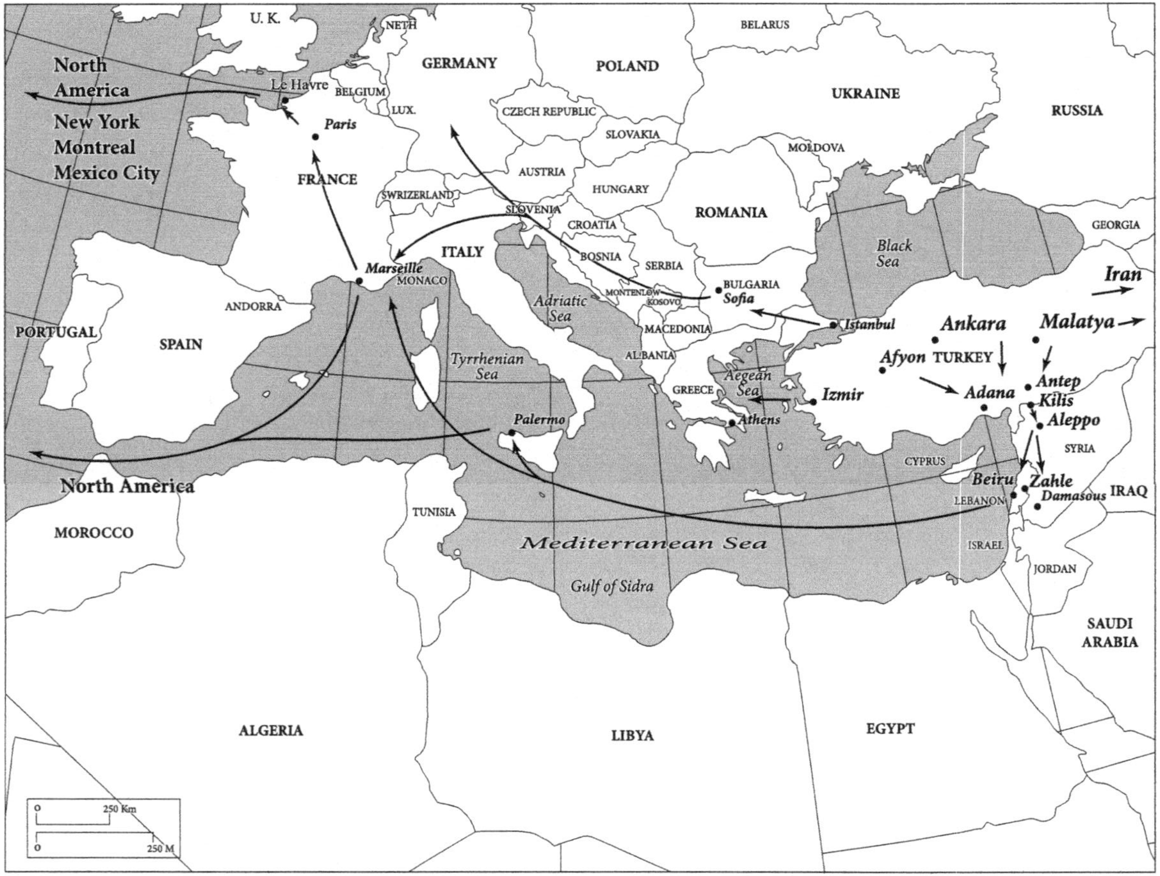

Map 2 Historical patterns of narcotics smuggling out of Turkey.

Introduction

Valley of the Wolves (*Kurtlar Vadisi*) first aired as a weekly television drama during the winter of 2003. The series had a two-year run on television and subsequently gave birth to a series of spin-off productions, including three major motion pictures. Superficially, one could categorize *Valley of the Wolves* as a prototypical action drama featuring a gallant but tough anti-hero who engages in daring secret missions against sinister, conspiratorial enemies. Critics and fans of *Valley of the Wolves* emphasize however that the show possesses deeper resonating qualities. *Valley of the Wolves*' main character, Polat Alemdar, epitomizes the virtues, as well as the responsibilities, of Turkish nationalism. Through each manifestation of *Valley of the Wolves*, the adventures Alemdar undertakes often represent not-so-subtle meditations on the supposed existential threats facing the Turkish nation. Plotlines, in turn, often derive from real events. As a secret agent working for a fictionalized version of the Turkish clandestine service, Alemdar's latest adventure (*Valley of the Wolves: Palestine*) takes him to Israel. After a series of twists and turns set in the Occupied Territories, Alemdar emerges victorious after taking revenge upon the general who ordered the storming of the real-life *Mavi Marmara*.

With each season of the series and with each film, viewers of *Valley of the Wolves* are entreated to think about the world in dark, conspiratorial terms. Headlines adorning daily newspapers, we are led to believe, only faintly allude to the secret cabals of powerful men who seek to violently shape the world around us. This tone is struck from the outset of the first season of *Valley of the Wolves*. The principal antagonist during the premiere season is a ruthless mob boss by the name of Süleyman Çakır. As Alemdar assumes a new identity and moves ever closer to apprehending Çakır, *Valley of the Wolves* introduces the viewer to the subterranean world of organized crime in Turkey. Instead of a country governed by laws and elected officials, the Turkish Republic is revealed to be secretly controlled by a "council of wolves" (*Kurtlar Konseyi*) of top mob bosses who manipulate the state behind the scenes. As Alemdar rises up the ladder of the mafia (particularly after Çakır's death), he discovers that many within the Turkish state actively collaborate with underworld figures from all over the world. His task, by the end of the series, is not simply to destroy the Turkish mafia from the inside, but to save the Turkish nation from a great host of threats and iniquities found both inside and out.[1]

[1] Zeynep Gültekin, "Irak'dan Önce: Kurtlar Vadisi Dizisi," *İletişim Kuram ve Araştırma Dergisi* 22 (Winter 2006), 9–36.

Organized crime appears to us, through the prism of *Valley of the Wolves*, as a kind of passkey to understanding the true nature of Turkish politics. Gangs and gangsters do not simply supply the subterfuge and corruption that may plague the state and soil the nation. Instead, the world of *Valley of the Wolves* would have us believe that organized crime *is*, at least in part, the state.

Such a premise, when viewed from the standpoint of Turkey's evolution over the last thirty years, contains certain elements of validity. Scandals and outrages involving participants in organized crime have regularly punctuated Turkish politics despite three military coups and many regular elections. The dark undertones that unfold in the *Valley of the Wolves* resonate most strongly with the real life Susurluk scandal of 1996.

On the morning of 4 November 1996, people around Turkey woke up to news of a car crash in the small town of Susurluk, just south of Istanbul. The crash in and of itself was nothing extraordinary; a new model Mercedes hits a truck on a dark country road. Inside were four passengers, three dead, one seriously injured. Counted among them was a former beauty pageant winner, an Istanbul police captain, a member of parliament and one of the most wanted men in the world, Abdullah Çatlı. Çatlı was a well-known drug trafficker, hit man and arms smuggler with both domestic and international arrest warrants to his name. The scandal that broke with the so-called Susurluk incident resulted in a parliamentary inquiry that would detail an ongoing alliance that had been formed between the Turkish military, members of the ruling party, domestic security officials, and members of organized crime. At the heart of this relationship was a shared concern over the domestic and international security of the Turkish state, wherein each member of the "Susurluk gang" (as it came to be called) worked together to suppress or liquidate dissident leftists, Kurdish guerrillas, or Armenian activists living abroad. The revelations that have emerged with the Susurluk investigation have resulted in a commonly held belief that such working relationships indeed typify, or perhaps dominate, the country.[2]

This book attempts to excavate the history of organized crime in Turkey and the roles gangs and gangsters have played in the making of the Turkish state and Turkish politics. An encyclopedic account of organized crime's origins and evolution is not intended here. Rather, what is presented over the following chapters is an attempt to situate a series of criminal syndicates within the context of Turkey's modern development. In focusing primarily upon the heroin trade, this book traces how and why gangs and gangsters came to be seen as a political force. Much of what will be discussed in this book will relate to perceptions of organized crime's political impact as opposed to some concrete reality.

The central chapters of this book span the years between the establishment of the so-called Young Turk regime, which presided over the very last decade of the Ottoman history, to the imposition of martial under law under General

[2] For a comprehensive review of the "Susurluk incident," see Human Rights Foundation of Turkey, *1998 Human Rights Report* (Ankara: Human Rights Foundation of Turkey Publications, 2000), 39–85.

Kenan Evren. Between 1908 and 1980, we see the full maturation of organized crime in Turkey. There is nothing inherently native to the culture of Turkey that gave birth to organized crime in the country. Rather, the development of politically powerful criminal syndicates is a result of a series of political, economic, and social factors, such as internal migration, urbanization, statist economic policies, the growth of illicit trades, and the development of Turkey's national security apparatus. Heroin trafficking, it is contended, is perhaps the most essential factor in Turkish organized crime's development during these years. As a product derived from the native poppy plants of Anatolia, heroin became a tool with which a growing collection of criminals amassed unprecedented amounts of material wealth and political clout.

Understanding the history of organized crime in Turkey also necessitates a closer look at how state officials comprehended and approached the policing of criminal syndicates. For much of the period under discussion in this book, American narcotics officers and politicians played a vital role in defining and assisting Ankara's fight against Turkish heroin traffickers. As a result, the records of American agencies and departments provide the bulk of the archival material used in this book. When coupled with available Turkish sources (which include newspapers, memoirs, and official documents), the composite archival record demonstrates the degree to which elements of the Turkish state both battled and collaborated with members of the Turkish underworld. American and Turkish sources make it quite clear that no all-powerful "council of wolves" existed between 1908 and 1980. Indeed the archival record assembled for this book adds excellent insights into the methods and ideological underpinnings that informed both American and Turkish investigations of narcotics and organized crime during this period of time. The available evidence also suggests that the heroin trade did help to forge alliances between criminals, lawmen, and politicians. As the trade in heroin and other opiates grew and evolved, particularly between 1930 and 1980, the relationships officers and officials constructed with gangsters grew in complexity. By 1980, bribes and shared material gains were not the only medium by which members on opposite sides of the law interacted. Instead, by 1980, we begin to see evidence of the kinds of common political and professional interests, particularly in matters of national security, that would eventually inform the basis of the "Susurluk incident" and other scandals involving organized crime in Turkey.

This book follows in the footsteps of several prominent scholars who have attempted to re-evaluate how narcotics have helped to shape the modern world. In approaching the development of the modern Turkish Republic, I wish to put the heroin trade at the center of this state's long transition from imperial core to nation-state. Rather than exile heroin to the margins of the historical development of state institutions, I intend to give the centrality of narcotics the same discursive legitimacy as other pivotal resources in the Middle East. Like the role of oil in constructing such states of Saudi Arabia, Iran, or Azerbaijan, one cannot fully understand the modern Republic of Turkey without gauging the local, national, and transnational forces related to the flow of heroin in, through, and out of Asia Minor.

This case study is also intended to contribute to the established body of scholarly and popular literature on the emergence of organized crime in the contemporary world. Organized crime, like so many relevant and impactful socio-political forces, is a modern artificial construct. Personal and ideological subjectivity often determine the criteria for defining who is a "gangster" and what constitutes "organized crime." To be more specific, it is quite clear that in the case of Turkey, as well as many other places around the world, American agencies and officials have historically provided the standards and diction used to define "organized crime." While one may be able to add organized crime to the ever-growing list of "invented traditions," it is nonetheless clear that individuals belonging to criminal syndicates often do play supporting roles in the building of modern states. While this book is not explicitly comparative in nature, the narrative presented over the coming chapters is certainly informed by studies exclusive of Turkey.

HISTORIOGRAPHY: GANGS, DRUGS, AND THE MAKING OF THE TURKISH STATE

There are several historiographical issues with which this book contends. Most fundamentally, this assessment of organized crime and heroin in Turkey upholds and expands upon the present critical trends in Turkish studies. Successive waves of scholarly works have done much to transform the field over the last fifty years. With the publication of Bernard Lewis's *The Emergence of Modern Turkey*, students and scholars alike have been challenged to think about the making of the modern Turkish Republic as the result of over 200 years of revolutionary changes. The debates over the origins, contours, and effects of the reforms that have shaped Turkey remained contested and unresolved.

Perhaps the most central theme that continues to define revisionist studies of Turkish history is the degree to which the republic's development is informed by its imperial past. For much of the last century, many scholars and statesmen have accepted the premise that Mustafa Kemal Atatürk's declaration of republican rule over the remaining territories of the Ottoman Empire in 1923 signaled a definitive break in the political, economic, and social evolution of Asia Minor. Although one may see a certain degree of continuity in the patterns of "top-down" reform in the decades immediately before and after the empire's collapse, some studies, such as those undertaken by Bernard Lewis and Stanford Shaw, have posed that Turkey's transformation into a Westernized, secular, and increasingly democratic state has all but eradicated the imperial, feudalistic, and theocratic facets of the region's historic composition.[3]

[3] Bernard Lewis, *The Emergence of Modern Turkey* (Oxford: Oxford University Press, 1968); Stanford Shaw, *History of the Ottoman Empire and Modern Turkey Volume II* (Cambridge: Cambridge University Press, 1977).

More recent generations of scholars have challenged both the fundamentals and particulars of how "unprecedented," "revolutionary," and "transformed" the Republic of Turkey actually is. Rather than see 1923 as the absolute turning point in Anatolia's history, many have suggested a new periodization for Turkish history, one that places the declaration of the republic at the midpoint of a crucial stage in the region's history. A more appropriate framing of the republic's history should instead begin at 1908 with outbreak of the Young Turk Revolution. Erik Jan Zürcher's many contributions to the study of the Young Turk regime suggests that we should see continuities between the final Ottoman regime and the governing Kemalist elite in terms not only of personnel but also in terms of policy. In the years between 1908 and 1938, a coherent (but ever-dwindling) cohort of officers, intellectuals, and administrators set out to radically transform Anatolian politics and society with increasing intensity and ruthlessness. Most fundamentally, the goal of these reform measures, as Zürcher and others argue, was to rationalize and consolidate political, economic, and social control over the remaining Ottoman lands. In other words, nationalism, secularism, and constitutionalism were not ends in themselves; rather, in the light of the Ottoman Empire's recent struggles with rebellion, invasion, and partition, the many reforms undertaken during the "long" Young Turk era were meant to enable the state to mobilize, re-engineer, and modernize the peoples and physical resources of Anatolia into a coherent, governable whole.[4]

It now seems reasonably clear that the efforts of the Young Turk/Kemalist regime were only partially successful. Since 1938, Turkey's evolving democratic tendencies have given voice to larger swaths of peoples previously ignored or repressed. While it seems that many popular movements and inclinations are rooted in the Ottoman past, many scholarly studies of contemporary civil society and politics in modern Turkey are careful to point out the degrees to which the post-Ottoman transformation of Anatolia shapes contemporary rhetoric and actions. Hakan Yavuz, for example, has carefully documented the evolution of Islamist politics in Turkey since the republic's establishment. Through his many works, Yavuz convincingly demonstrates that the cornerstones of modern-day Islamism were set during the late Ottoman era. However, while contemporary reformist and fundamentalist movements may hark back (both literally and figuratively) to the Ottoman Empire, Yavuz emphasizes the degree to which Islamists have operated within the parameters of Turkey's secular political and legal structures.[5]

[4] Reşat Kasaba (ed.), *The Cambridge History of Turkey, Volume 4: Turkey in the Modern World* (Cambridge: Cambridge University Press, 2008); Erik Jan Zürcher, "The Ottoman Legacy of the Turkish Republic: An Attempt at a New Periodization," *Die Welt des Islams*, 32 (1992), 237–253; Erik Jan Zürcher, *Turkey: A Modern History* (London and New York: I.B. Tauris, 1993).

[5] See e.g. Amit Bein, *Ottoman Ulema, Turkish Republic: Agents of Change and Guardians of Tradition* (Palo Alto, CA: Stanford University Press, 2011); Esra Özyürek, *Nostalgia for the Modern: State Secularism and Everyday Politics in Turkey* (Chapel Hill, NC: Duke University Press, 2006); Hakan Yavuz, *Islamic Political Identity in Turkey* (Oxford: Oxford University Press, 2005); Hakan Yavuz, *Secularism and Muslim Democracy* (Cambridge: Cambridge University Press, 2009).

Among the more innovative revisionist studies of Turkish history are those that have dwelt upon provincial society. Michael Meeker's *A Nation of Empire* stands as a particularly fine demonstration of the Ottoman Empire's continued resonance in everyday life at the local level. *A Nation of Empire* excels at examining the imperial legacies found in provincial family, factional, and ethnic politics.[6] Ethnic politics and culture in general loom large within contemporary studies of Turkey. Ankara's ongoing struggle with the country's Kurdish minority has helped to inspire many historical works dealing with political activism, violence, and cultural survival in eastern Anatolia. Many scholars have persuasively argued that current efforts to pacify and reform Turkey's eastern borderlands at times represent a continuation of the violent, and often genocidal, policies enacted during the Young Turk/Kemalist era.[7]

This book situates itself within Turkish historiography in two general ways. First and foremost, this work seeks to fill a sizable void found within Turkish studies. While gangsters and drugs are certainly topics of popular enjoyment and debate in Turkey, no work yet exists that attempts to present an archivally based account of these two phenomena in Turkey. Moreover, I would argue that organized crime and heroin trafficking during the twentieth century are not topics that can be approached in isolation. Instead, in telling the story of how smugglers, politicians, policemen, thugs, spies, diplomats, and hitmen helped to construct the world of drug trafficking and organized crime in Turkey, this book also foregrounds the ways in which Turkey's development directly and indirectly shaped the underworld of the modern republic.

The second historiographical contribution of this book is to present a somewhat different take on the history of the Turkish state and its imperial roots. Both gangs and narcotics have been of considerable political and social significance since the reign of the Young Turks. However, the perceptions and effects of drugs and gangs in Turkey have changed dramatically over time. On the basis of the archival evidence available to us, I would argue that criminal syndicates, particularly those that emerged out of the heroin trade of the mid-twentieth century, assumed important positions of political influence in both opposition to and in collaboration with elements of the Turkish state.

[6] Michael Meeker, *A Nation of Empire: The Ottoman Legacy of Turkish Modernity* (Berkeley: University of California Press, 2002).

[7] Sabri Ateş, "Empire at the Margins: Towards a History of the Ottoman-Iranian Borderland and the Borderland Peoples" (Ph.D. Dissertation: New York University, 2006); David Gaunt, *Massacres, Resistance, Protectors: Muslim-Christian Relations in Eastern Anatolia During World War I* (Piscatway, NJ: Gorgias, 2006); Hans-Lukas Kieser, *Der Verpasste Friede: Mission, Ethnie und Staat in den Ostprovinzen der Türkei* (Zürich: Chronos Verlag, 2000); Janet Klein, *Power in the Periphery: The Margins of Empire* (Palo Alto, CA: Stanford University Press, 2011); Uğur Ümit Üngör, *The Making of Modern Turkey* (Oxford: Oxford University Press, 2011).

HISTORIOGRAPHY: TURKEY AND THE WIDER WORLD OF ORGANIZED CRIME

Decades of research and debate has not led to a general consensus on what delineates organized crime. Opinions vary among scholars and law enforcement agencies. The Federal Bureau of Investigation, for example, opts for a simple and concise definition. Organized crime is:

> any group having some manner of a formalized structure with the primary objective is to obtain money through illegal activities. Such groups maintain their position through the use of actual or threatened violence, corrupt public officials, graft or extortion, and generally having significant impact on the people in their locales, region or the country as a whole.[8]

More scholarly approaches towards the meaning of organized crime tend to be more expansive in citing core characteristics or patterns of behavior. Stephan Mallory, in surveying how several noted criminologists have defined organized crime, presents a list of eighteen traits critical to understanding the nature of modern day crime syndicates.[9] As a book grounded in the practice of history, and not criminology, the narrative presented here does not offer new insights or seek to contest the technical parameters of organized crime. This book describes and analyzes organized crime in much more colloquial terms. For the sake of continuity and simplicity, organized crime, as portrayed in the narrative to follow, applies to a variety of groups and actors engaged in illicit trades.

Organized crime, in differing respects, is both a recent and well-worn topic of scholarly investigation. Conceptually, "organized crime" is a modern neologism that emerged out of the United States at the turn of the twentieth century. According to Michael Woodiwiss, state investigators in New York first coined the phrase in 1896.[10] Before the 1950s, American scholars and officials used the term "organized crime" to describe a select number of criminal enterprises operated by networks of individuals (be it theft, prostitution, or smuggling). Organized crime gradually took on a new meaning with the advent of the Cold War. In an era that featured rising waves of hysteria over the threat of Communist infiltrators lurking within the folds of American politics and society, law enforcement officials increasingly adopted the concept of organized crime as a term describing discrete bands of individuals perpetrating national and international criminal conspiracies.[11] In other words, as Michael Woodiwiss puts it, *who* was committing crimes took on greater significance than *what* crimes were being committed.[12]

[8] Howard Abadinsky, *Organized Crime* (Belmont, CA: Wadsworth Publishing, 2009), 2.

[9] Stephan Mallory, *Understanding Organized Crime* (Boston, MA: Jones and Bartlett Publishers, 2011), 8–9.

[10] Michael Woodiwiss, *Organized Crime and American Power: A History* (Toronto: University of Toronto Press, 2001), 177.

[11] Lee Bernstein, *Greatest Menace* (Boston: University of Massachusetts Press, 2009).

[12] Michael Woodiwiss, "Organized Crime—The Dumbing of Discourse," *The British Criminology Conference: Selected Proceedings*. Volume 3. Papers from the British Society of Criminology Conference, Liverpool (July 1999), 1–10.

Present-day criminology, as a field of study, seems to embrace both connotations of organized crime. Standard textbooks on the subject, such as the volumes produced by Howard Abadinksy, Michael Lyman, Stephan Mallory, Gary Potter, and others, present students with concise chapters identifying patterns of organized criminal behavior as well as discussion of specific past and present criminals and organizations associated with organized crime. Within the confines of general criminological studies, theoretical approaches towards organized crime deal with both the comparative structural nature of criminal syndicates as well as the psychological or social precepts that compel individuals to join gangs and other criminal conspiracies.[13]

Many contemporary scholars seem at ease with including "banditry" within the historical and contemporary framework of organized crime studies.[14] In the field of history, understanding the evolution of banditry provides more than just a prologue to contemporary organized crime. Recent research on an assorted array of highwaymen, robbers, and brigands (as well as pirates, privateers, and other "bandits" on the high seas) has provided a number of revisionist insights into the development of states. Eric Hobsbawm's classic work *Bandits* sets a series of benchmarks for contemporary historians interested in the relationship between power, politics, and the subaltern. Through the many editions and modifications of *Bandits*, Hobsbawm has concluded that the phenomenon of banditry represents a fundamental challenge to the "economic, social and political order by challenging those who hold or lay claim to power, law and control of resources."[15] Banditry represents physical (and to some degree existential) realms that exist outside the ever-expanding reaches of the state. Physical or political distance from power, as well as the experience of social or economic inequities, makes bandits intrinsically marginal characters.[16] Yet, in his acknowledgement of a series of critiques levied by Anton Blok, Hobsbawm also posits that particularly successful bandits may not be so physically or politically marginal as he had previously supposed. Instead, individuals of political, economic, or social standing seeking to challenge authority, or to benefit materially from a gang's crimes, tend to stand behind the careers of successful bandits.[17]

The rise of the modern industrialized nation-state, it appears at present, seems to mark the end of banditry as an all-pervasive global phenomenon. With the

[13] Abadinsky, *Organized Crime*, 1–16; Jay Albanese, *Organized Crime in Our Time* (Burlington, MA: Elsevier, 2011), 1–16; Peter Lupsha, "Transnational Crime versus Nation-State," *Transnational Organized Crime* 2.1 (Spring 1996), 21–48; Michael Lyman and Gary Potter, *Organized Crime* (New York: Prentice Hall, 2010), 4–15; Mallory, Understanding Organized Crime, 1–11, 32–37; Letizia Paoli and Cyrille Fijnaut, "Introduction to Part I: The History of the Concept," in Cyrille Fijnaut and Letizia Paoli (eds.), *Organised Crime in Europe* (Dordrecht, The Netherlands: Springer, 2004), 21–46.

[14] For an expansive historical approach to the long history of organized crime, see Mark Galeotti (ed.), *Organized Crime in History* (New York: Routledge, 2009).

[15] Eric Hobsbawm, *Bandits* (London: Abacus, 2007), 7.

[16] Hobsbawm, *Bandits*, 7–18.

[17] Anton Blok, "The Peasant and the Brigand: Social Banditry Reconsidered," *Comparative Studies in Society and History* 14.4 (September 1972), 494–503.

development of more powerful and effective levers to exert control over the countryside, modern states have greatly reduced the ability of rural bandits to hide or seek support of provincially powerful figures. In this regard, Charles Tilly suggests, with a hint of irony, that the state's monopoly on power and violence, with the intent to extract services and resources from the population, possesses similar features to organized crime.[18] Industrialization has also had an effect upon banditry's gradual shift towards extinction in the modern world. Urbanization, new modes of production, and the establishment of standardized police forces, courts, and modern means of communication have reduced the bandit's historically rural domain. One could also consider that the rise of a more urbanized, monetized, and proletarianized world changes the nature of crime in general. In other words, crime no longer plagues the modern countryside since people, as well as loot or spoils, are found in greater amounts in town.

That is not to say history has only recently given birth to urban gangs. It is quite clear that predatory groups of people prowled the streets and alleys of cities as early as the classical era. Banditry's gradual demise, coupled with the steady growth of cities worldwide, seems now to amplify the overall prevalence and significance of urban criminal syndicates.[19] Nevertheless, many of the factors that contributed to the longevity and vitality of rural banditry continues to define the historical and contemporary evolution of urban gangs. Cities today, like various corners of the countryside, harbor vast numbers of politically, economically, and socially "marginal peoples" (such as immigrants, minorities, or the working class). Like distant highlands or dense forests, densely packed neighborhoods and city quarters afford a potential criminal a degree of anonymity, camouflage, and concealment from the law. Criminal groups have profited from the city's transformation into man's principal habitat in other ways. In addition to offering more individuals to rob or kidnap, the city can easily be transformed into a central market for a variety of illicit trades. As we will see in the case of the heroin trade, the emergence of modern national and international regimes that target certain types of economic (and largely urban) exchange has been a key factor in the development of modern organized crime.[20]

Contemporary organized crime's relationship with power and politics differs little from the historical roles played by many bandits. Like banditry over so many

[18] Charles Tilly, "War Making and State Making as Organized Crime," in Peter Evans et al. (eds.), *Bringing the State Back In* (Cambridge: Cambridge University Press, 1985), 173–174.

[19] Florike Egmond, "Multiple Underworlds in the Dutch Republic of the Seventeenth and Eighteenth Century," in Cyrille Fijnaut and Letizia Paoli (eds.), *Organised Crime in Europe* (Dordrecht, The Netherlands: Springer, 2004), 77–109; Katrin Lange, "'Many a Lord is Guilty, Indeed for Many a Poor Man's Dishonest Deed': Gangs of Robbers in Early Modern Germany," in Cyrille Fijnaut and Letizia Paoli (eds.), *Organised Crime in Europe* (Dordrecht, The Netherlands: Springer, 2004), 109–150; Julius Ruff, *Violence in Early Modern Europe, 1500–1800* (Cambridge: Cambridge University Press, 2001), 216–247.

[20] Abdul Qaiyum Lodhi and Charles Tilly warn us, however, not to see urbanization, in and of itself, as a principal cause of criminality in the modern era. See Abdul Qaiyum Lodhi and Charles Tilly, "Urbanization, Crime, and Collective Violence in 19th-Century France," *The American Journal of Sociology* 79.2 (September 1973), 296–318.

centuries, modern urban mafias and gangs embody existential threats to political and socio-economic orders. Even the United Nations has taken up the issue. According to General Assembly Resolution 55/25, the United Nations not only expressed deep concern for "the negative economic and social implications" of organized crime, but considered "the growing links between transnational organized crime and terrorist crimes" a potential violation of the organization's founding charter.[21] However, despite the growing number of national and international agencies and laws aimed at counteracting the influence of criminal syndicates, examples of collaboration between governments and gangsters abound. It is without dispute that many of the most powerful and notorious organized crime figures of the last century, such as Al Capone or Pablo Escobar, courted their respective political establishments and forged close relations with politicians, judges, and legitimate businessmen alike. Moreover, as we will see in this book, corruption was not the only link binding public officials to members of organized crime. The modern gangster can also be a savvy political actor and serve as a conductor and a tool of political change.

There are two countries that stand out among all others where organized crime features as a prominent theme of popular and scholarly study: Italy and the United States. We find in Italian studies a great many fine examples of historical research on the origins, evolution, and impact of criminal syndicates. The Camora of Naples, Calabria's "Ndrangheta," and the notorious mafia of Sicily, Cosa Nostra, are critical institutions in the development of provincial politics, economy, and society of the Mezzogiorno (a development that is strikingly different from the more industrial and prosperous north of Italy). Through the passage of the twentieth century, each of these criminal syndicates has carved out an economic niche rooted in either extortion or in legal or illicit trade (be it lemons, sulfur, heroin, or cigarettes). Organized crime's impact upon Italy, both in terms of the crimes of gangs as well as the power wielded by past and present mafia chieftains, reflects Rome's ongoing struggle to integrate and govern its southern provinces.[22]

Gangs and gangsters are equally essential in the retelling of American history. Generations of novelists, journalists, and government investigators have cast the mafia thug of the twentieth century into a stock character reflecting multiple positive and negative tropes and values deemed essentially American; he is simultaneously the embodiment of the self-made man, the menacing immigrant, the shrewd, merciless capitalist, and the vigilante gunslinger.[23] Both scholars and popular

[21] United Nations Office on Drugs and Crime, *United Nations Convention Against Transnational Organized Crime and the Protocols Thereto* (New York: United Nations, 2004), 2.

[22] See John Dickie, *Cosa Nostra: A History of the Sicilian Mafia* (New York: Palgrave Macmillan, 2004); Gianluca Fulvetti, "The Mafia and the 'Problem of the Mafia': Organised Crime in Italy, 1820–1970," in Cyrille Fijnaut and Letizia Paoli (eds.), *Organised Crime in Europe* (Dordrecht, The Netherlands: Springer, 2004), 47–76; Letizia Paoli, *Mafia Brotherhoods: Organized Crime, Italian Style* (Oxford: Oxford University Press, 2008); James Walston, "See Naples and Die: Organized Crime in Campania," in Robert Kelly (ed.), *Organized Crime: A Global Perspective* (Totawa, NJ: Rowman & Littlefield, 1986), 134–158.

[23] Lee Bernstein, "The Greatest Menace: Organized Crime in U.S. Culture and Politics, 1946–1961," (Ph.D. Dissertation: University of Minnesota, 1997), 13–16.

writers have weaved gangs and criminal outfits into the building of the economies, neighborhoods, and machine politics of Chicago, Los Angeles, New Orleans, New York, and Boston.[24] Here and there we do see glimpses of organized crime's influence on the American state (most notably in terms of Washington's policies toward Cuba and the Kennedy assassination).[25] However, as Michael Woodiwiss and Lee Bernstein argue in their respective works, organized crime has also served as a convenient boogeyman and scapegoat for elected and unelected officials seeking to deflect attention from far more egregious issues of crime and insecurity.[26]

Evidence presented from Mexico, Japan, China, and Russia affirms many of the collective claims submitted by researchers in the United States and Italy regarding the historic legacies of organized crime. Groups like the Yakuza and the northern cartels of Mexico derive from a similar state of provincial and political marginalization found in the cases of the Camora or the Outfit of Chicago.[27] Men of low standing, particularly migrants, populate such criminal gangs. An evolving system of political economy has informed the gradual shift from banditry to urban organized crime in Mexico and Russia, as well as China, a shift that features not only extortion and criminal extraction but also smuggling and racketeering (particularly drug trafficking).[28] The emergence of modern organized crime in each of these states also showcases specific forms of rituals and rites of passage that are

[24] Herbert Asbury, *Barbary Coast: An Informal History of the San Francisco Underworld* (New York: Basic Books, 2002); Herbert Asbury, *The French Quarter: An Informal History of the New Orleans Underworld* (New York: Basic Books, 2003); Herbert Asbury, *Gangs of Chicago: An Informal History of the Chicago Underworld* (New York: Basic Books, 2002); Herbert Asbury, *Gangs of New York* (New York: Vintage, 2008); Alan Block, *East Side West Side: Organizing Crime in New York: 1930–1950* (New Brunswick, NJ: Transaction Publishers, 1999); David Pietrusza, *Rothstein: The Life, Times and Murder of the Criminal Genius Who Fixed the 1919 World Series* (New York: Basic Books, 2004); Selwyn Raab, *Five Families: The Rise, Decline and Resurgence of America's Most Powerful Mafia Empires* (New York: St. Martins Griffin, 2006).

[25] Howard Jones, *The Bay of Pigs* (Oxford: Oxford University Press, 2008), 23–26; David Kaiser, *Road to Dallas* (Cambridge, MA: Harvard University Press, 2009), 53–74.

[26] This thesis has been further expanded upon in Michael Woodiwiss, *Gangster Capitalism: The United States and the Globalization of Organized Crime* (New York: Basic Books, 2005).

[27] Ana Maria Alonso, *Thread of Blood: Colonialism, Revolution, and Gender on Mexico's Northern Frontier* (Tucson: University of Arizona Press, 1997); Luis Astorga, "Organized Crime and the Organization of Crime," in John Bailey and Roy Godson (eds.), *Organized Crime and Democratic Governability* (Pittsburgh: University of Pittsburgh Press, 2001), 58–82; Peter Hill, "The Changing Face of the *Yakuza*," in Mark Galeotti (ed.), *Global Crime Today: The Changing Face of Organised Crime* (London: Routledge, 2005), 97–117; Peter Hill, *The Japanese Mafia: Yakuza, Law, and the State* (Oxford: Oxford University Press, 2003); David E. Kaplan and Alec Dubro, *Yakuza: Japan's Criminal Underworld* (Berkeley: University of California Press, 2003); Eiko Maruko Siniawer, *Ruffians, Yakuza, Nationalists: The Violent Politics of Modern Japan, 1860–1960* (Ithaca, NY: Cornell University Press, 2008); James A. Sandos, "Northern Separatism during the Mexican Revolution: An Inquiry into the Role of Drug Trafficking, 1910–1920," *The Americas* 41.2 (October 1984), 191–214.

[28] See e.g. Phil Billingsley, "Bandits, Bosses and Bare Sticks: Beneath the Surface of Local Control in Early Republican China," *Modern China* 7.3 (July 1981), 235–288; Phil Billingsley, *Bandits in Republican China* (Stanford, CT: Stanford University Press, 1988); Yakov Gilinski and Yakov Kostjukovsky, "From Thievish Artel to Criminal Corporation: The History of Organised Crime in Russia," in Cyrille Fijnaut and Letizia Paoli (eds.), *Organised Crime in Europe* (Dordrecht, The Netherlands: Springer, 2004), 181–202; W. C. Wang, "Tu Yueh-Sheng (1888–1951): A Tentative Political Biography," *Journal of Asian Studies* 26.3 (May 1967), 433–455.

quite similar to syndicates found in Italy and the United States. More importantly, organized crime's development in Japan, China, Mexico, and Russia are intimately intertwined with modern state-building. Simply put, gangsters, politicians, and law enforcement officials (as well as spies) have played elemental roles in the construction of critical state institutions in both the capital and the provinces.

A typical Turkish bookstore offers a great many books on organized crime in the contemporary republic.[29] Most of these works are written by journalists and present insider accounts of notorious bosses or offer analysis of how gangs have influenced recent political scandals. With few exceptions, there are virtually no books in print that attempt to treat organized crime in historical terms. Among these exceptions, the bulk of which deals with criminal conspiracies and gangs before 1900, only one directly confronts organized crime during the twentieth century. In 2007, two Dutch scholars, Frank Bovenkerk and Yücel Yeşilgöz, published an English language edition of their groundbreaking study on the origins of Turkish organized crime.[30] While this book contains a great many insights into some the earliest features of twentieth-century gang culture (specifically during the late Ottoman period), most of the research marshaled by Bovenkerk and Yeşilgöz dwells on more contemporary manifestations of organized crime (particularly with respect to the "deep state" relationships forged between gangsters and state actors since the 1970s).

This book addresses more than the gaps yet to be filled by other works on gangs and crime in Turkey. In looking specifically at the years between 1908 and 1980, the story presented here interweaves organized crime into a critical history of the Turkish Republic's birth and development. Three discrete periods of Turkish history are at the heart of this study: the Young Turk/Kemalist era (1908–38), the reign of Adnan Menderes and the years surrounding the rise of the Justice Party (1950–70), and the violent decade preceding Kenan Evren's 1980 coup (1970–80). Organized crime's development takes a crucial turn during each of these periods. With the passage of each phase, we see the emergence of ever more sophisticated crime groups in Turkey. In profiling the gangsters and the state officials who helped to define these eras, we achieve more than just a better understanding of Turkey's underworld. A closer look at both the perpetrators of crime and their pursuers reveals subtle insights into fundamental features of Turkish politics and society. In other words, one cannot gauge or discuss organized crime in Turkey's history without also broaching such topics as state-building, modernization, the legacy of empire, immigration, and Turkey's relationship with the West (especially the United States). No understanding of Turkey's mafia, and its place in the country's history, can be achieved without gauging how power and politics have bound together, and divided, both outlaws and officials.

[29] For examples of more popular books on organized crime, see Hasan Cem, *Türkiye'de Babalar ve Mafya* (Istanbul: Geçit Kitabevi, 2004); Mehmet Eymür, *Çeteler, Mafya ve Siyaset* (Istanbul: Birey Yayıncılık, 2001); İsmail Oğuz, *Babalar Vadisi* (Istanbul: Ares Kitap, 2006).

[30] Frank Bovenkerk and Yücel Yeşilgöz, *The Turkish Mafia: A History of the Heroin Godfathers* (Lancs, United Kingdom: Milo Books Ltd., 2007).

HISTORIOGRAPHY: TURKEY AND THE WIDER WORLD OF NARCOTICS

Narcotics are at the foundation of a great many histories. The production, trade, and consumption of a variety of intoxicants, be they stimulants or depressants, are complex facets of human history dating back millennia. Heroin trafficking, which is at the core of this study, possesses a far more recent history. Heroin is a product born out of the initial stages of the nineteenth-century medical revolution. As a derivative of morphine, heroin was first hailed as one in a series of wonder drugs used to combat severe or chronic pain. It also amplified the already thriving transnational trade in opium, a trade that was a harbinger of the global ascendency of European and American mercantile interests during the nineteenth century. Mass recreational use of opium in both the colonized world, as well as in imperial metropoles, eventually gave birth to the prohibition regime that also now governs heroin. The advent of the twentieth century global order barring the production, sale, and consumption of opium, and the parallel clandestine trade in heroin, are forces that have greatly shaped states worldwide. In looking at Turkey, this book admittedly goes to no great lengths in evaluating its economic impact upon the history of the republic. Nor does this book offer new insights into the social effects of the heroin trade. Rather what is at stake in this book are the ways in which heroin contributed to the evolution of gangs, legitimate political factions, and political negotiations during the course of Turkey's development.

Like the case of organized crime, broader historiographical trends related to the drug trade offer a number of signposts this book intends to follow. General political and social histories of narcotics (be it heroin, marijuana, or cocaine) tend to dwell upon the passage of the last 200 years.[31] The birth of "new imperialism" during the nineteenth century, we are told, transformed narcotics in a number of ways. Modern imperialism, in a sense, gave birth to the contemporary parameters of the drug trade. In the aftermath of the First Opium War, a vast cadre of largely Western shippers, wholesalers, and manufacturers dominated the trade in raw opium. European scientists and manufacturers first isolated and clinically extracted morphine from opium sap. A second generation of European scientists similarly derived heroin in 1875, a drug that synthesized an admixture of morphine and acetic anhydride. While representatives and interests stemming from the major powers of Europe and North America enjoyed the bulk of the profits of the trade, a gathering wave of hysteria in the West regarding the social effects of heroin and opium soon took hold.

Like past campaigns targeting piracy and the trafficking of slaves, imperial politics informed the first global agreement prohibiting the unlicensed trade in opium. A series of embellishments outlining this emerging global order followed in the wake of the Hague Convention of 1912. Since the end of the

[31] Martin Booth, *Cannabis: A History* (New York: St. Martin's Press, 2003); Martin Booth, *Opium: A History* (New York: St. Martin's Press, 1999); Dominic Streatfeild, *Cocaine* (London: Virgin Books Limited, 2002).

First World War, the United States has been at the forefront in compelling other states to adopt stringent laws which criminalize not only the production, but also the illicit sale and use, of narcotics. It is now abundantly clear that prohibition has categorically failed on all fronts (despite steady increases in funding and manpower deployed to police the narcotics trade). Moreover, more localized studies of the drug trade suggest that the shifting patterns of the drug trade have progressively benefited larger numbers of states and actors who would have been marginalized during the imperial heyday of the nineteenth century.

Mexican and Chinese historians have arguably been at the vanguard in documenting how Western attempts at prohibition have empowered new local elites and given rise to new political dynamics. In the case of China, several scholars have presented convincing portrayals detailing how the interwar opium trade transformed politics and law enforcement in Shanghai. In the early stages of China's post-imperial civil war, opium trafficking in Shanghai provided a platform from which a small cohort of native Chinese traffickers were able to seize control of the city. At the center of many of these studies is the gangster Du Yueu Shang, one of the principal leaders of the notorious Green Gang. Research conducted by Brian Martin and Frederic Wakeman conclusively depicts the degree to which opium politics helped to forge a close working relationship between Du's gang and Chiang Kai-shek's Nationalist party (a relationship which sealed Nationalist control over Shanghai until the Japanese invasion in 1938).[32]

Even more expansive examples of how the drug trade has laid the foundation for modern national political orders can be found in Mexico. Opium trafficking, according to many scholarly studies, was an important dynamic in the political restoration of order and governance following the Mexican Revolution.[33] Early on during the reign of the Institutional Revolutionary Party, regional power brokers seized control of local opium networks (as well as alcohol production and cocaine distribution) as a means of solidifying their political base. Luis Astorga's studies of power, politics, and drugs provide a compelling case for the degree to which narcotics trafficking has historically blurred the dividing lines between legitimate and illegitimate sources of authority. Like in China, as well as in many other countries, the extent to which narcotics trafficking has corrupted both local and national institutions in Mexico has greatly compromised American efforts to combat the trade.

Turkey, like other states, suffers from a critical lack of studies on how narcotics have shaped local and national politics. F. Cengiz Erdinç's work stands alone in

[32] Brian Martin, "The Green Gang and the Guomindang State: Du Yuesheng and the Politics of Shanghai," *The Journal of Asian Studies* 54.1 (February 1995), 64–92; Kathryn Meyer and Terry Parssinen, *Web of Smoke: Smugglers, Warlords, Spies and the History of the International Drug Trade* (Lanham, MD: Rowman and Littlefield Publishers, 1998), 235–266; Edward R. Slack, *Opium, State and Society: China's Narco-Economy and the Guomindang, 1924–1937* (Honolulu: University of Hawaii Press, 2001); Fredric Wakeman, "Licensing Leisure: The Chinese Nationalists' Attempt to Regulate Shanghai, 1927–1949" *The Journal of Asian Studies* 54.1 (February 1995), 19–42.

[33] Luis Astorga, *Drogas Sin Fronteras* (Mexico City: Grijalbo, 2003).

terms of research on the history of the heroin trade from the late Ottoman period to the end of the twentieth century.[34] While he is often very effective in gauging the political repercussions of the drug trade upon Turkish politics, Erdinç's *Overdose Türkiye*, which employs few archival resources, provides an overview of opium and heroin trafficking with only minimal discussion of the individuals and networks that conducted the trade inside of Turkey. This book hopes to build upon Erdinç's revelations by not only presenting new, unexplored sources, but also by providing an examination of the means and motivations of those who both promoted and policed Turkey's heroin trade.

A NOTE ON SOURCES AND AN OUTLINE OF CHAPTERS

For better or for worse, this book does not possess an exceedingly strong Turkish voice. While Ankara has endeavored to provide greater access to both native and foreign researchers to the records of the Ottoman Empire, access to the republic's archives remains fairly limited. The Directorate for Public Security (*Genel Emniyet Müdürlüğü*), for example, has denied access to its archives despite a formal request submitted for information and documents relevant to this study. That is not to say, however, that official reports drawn from the Ottoman Empire and the Republic of Turkey were absent during the writing of this book; here and there, we do receive invaluable insights from the internal governmental correspondence available today in Turkey. The memoirs and press clippings garnered for this work do provide a decent amount of augmentation in eliciting local perceptions of organized crime and the heroin trade.

In lieu of the lack of Turkish sources, papers drawn from the National Archives of the United States provide the archival backbone for this study. Between 1930 and 1980, American diplomats, law enforcement officials, journalists, and intelligence agents authored hundreds of pages of reports and correspondences related to organized crime and heroin trafficking in Turkey. We receive a sustained and detailed account of American activities for much of this era (although the quality of this archival record begins to decline, in terms of both length and detail, by the beginning of the 1960s). For reasons that remain unclear, the Department of Justice still has not furnished the records of the Bureau of Narcotics and Dangerous Drugs and the Drug Enforcement Administration to the National Archives (records that would greatly aid in illuminating the years after 1967). Moreover, the Central Intelligence Agency has repeatedly denied several Freedom of Information Act requests related to key figures detailed in the book for reasons related to "national security." Aside from raising suspicions, such denials serve to

[34] F. Cengiz Erdinç, *Overdose Türkiye: Türkiye'de Eroin Kaçakçılığı, Bağımlılğı ve Politikalar* (Istanbul: İletişim Yayınları, 2004).

hamper our understanding of how the premier American intelligence agency perceived and at times benefited from the policing of narcotics trafficking in Turkey.

The single greatest challenge confronting this book is found in the failings and ignorance of the American observers who served in Turkey between 1930 and 1980. Many key American officials profiled in this book spoke no Turkish and demonstrably possessed a limited knowledge about Turkish society or politics both before and after their tours in-country. Equally challenging are some of the suppositions and blinders that undergird American perceptions of Turkey during this period. Chief among these suppositions is the very notion of organized crime. Per their experiences back in the United States, Americans came to Turkey looking for gangs and mafias (particularly ones that comprised exclusive ethnic cliques). Worse still, American drug enforcement priorities in Turkey precluded much investigation into political corruption or ancillary crimes committed by heroin traffickers (such as arms trafficking or the smuggling of other forms of contraband).

These shortcomings, as troublesome as they may be, are at times both walls as well as windows separating us from the past. Considering the pervasiveness with which American law enforcement models and methods are employed all over the world today, a closer analysis of the American archival record related to Turkey allows us an opportunity to understand and critique the origins and applicability of American notions of organized crime in real time. To put it another way, a work of this nature, despite a lack of certain critical resources, still allows us to raise questions and pose answers to several fundamental questions: is there a Turkish mafia? If so, what are its origins and how has it historically functioned? If no singular Turkish mafia ever existed, how do we describe the criminal syndicates of Turkey's recent past? More broadly put, how did American experiences and theories related to combating organized crime obscure and lucidate the activities, functionality, and organizational structure of criminal syndicates in Turkey?

This book follows a basic linear narrative. Chapter 1 surveys multiple manifestations of organized crime in the Ottoman Empire and the Republic of Turkey between 1908 and 1938. Organized crime in Turkey does not derive from a singular root. In looking closely at this period, this chapter surveys the evolution and impact of three early manifestations of organized criminal activity in Anatolia: banditry (including paramilitary gangs), smuggling, and urban gangs (*kabadayı*). A critical understanding of how these early three forms of organized crime informed later syndicates cannot be fully appreciated without also gauging a variety of political, social, and economic trends that defined the final years of the Ottoman Empire and the founding of the Turkish Republic. This chapter poses that organized crime, as well as state reactions to organized crime, was shaped in large measure by the shifts in transnational migration, the formation of modern state institutions, patterns of warfare and counterinsurgency, party politics, trade, and Western economic intervention. Even at this early stage of Turkish history, we see the degree to which both provincial and urban gangs both clashed and cooperated with elements of Ottoman and Republican political authority.

Chapter 2 focuses upon two intertwining historical threads. The primary purpose of this chapter is to provide a brief survey of early American counter-narcotics policies and approaches. In particular, it addresses the origins of the Federal Bureau of Narcotics and how this bureau's principal founder, Harry Anslinger, laid the groundwork for a global campaign to interdict the flow of narcotics into the United States. This discussion of early American counter-narcotics strategies is complemented by a survey of the history of opium trade in Anatolia from the early nineteenth century to the outbreak of the Second World War. In particular, this element of the chapter takes up the way in which Ottoman and Turkish politicians and merchants interacted with Western traders in constructing the networks and markets that came to define the production and transshipment of Anatolian opium and heroin. It is during this period that the United States first came to see Turkish narcotics as a leading source for American narcotics consumers. By the outbreak of the Second World War, we witness the first demonstrations of American intervention into Turkish policing of opium and the initial formulation of modern drug trafficking syndicates in the Republic of Turkey.

Chapter 3 of this book undertakes a detailed analysis of Turkey's maturation as a central purveyor of opium and heroin in the greater Middle East in the postwar era. A central feature of this chapter is an exploration of the origins of the so-called French Connection, an elaborate network of wholesalers, manufacturers, and traffickers that linked Turkey into the wider world of the transatlantic heroin trade. In addition to discussing how Turkish, Lebanese, French, and American narcotics traffickers funneled large amounts of opium, morphine, and heroin into the European and American markets, this chapter surveys Turkey's impact upon narcotics use and governmental prohibitions in Iran.

Chapter 4 undertakes specific discussion of early American and Turkish counter-narcotics operations during and after the Menderes era (1950–70). It is during this period that American law enforcement officials first set foot in Turkey. As guests of the Menderes government, agents from the Federal Bureau of Narcotics worked closely with their Turkish counterparts in their efforts to detect, understand, and apprehend the gangs they believed to be responsible for a rising tide of heroin flowing into the United States. The revelations of these American agents tell us much about the politics of crime and heroin during this seminal period of democratization in Cold War Turkey. While a military coup may have brought Turkey's first decade of multi-party rule to an abrupt end, neither the Turkish military, nor American and Turkish law enforcement officials, were able to undermine the growing power and influence of Istanbul's heroin underworld. More to the point, it is during this period of time that we see substantial evidence for the close collaborative ties criminal syndicates and state officials would forge over the course of the coming decades.

Chapter 5 addresses the conflicting currents of heroin, organized crime, and politics during the 1970s. This era features Turkey's unprecedented attempt to ban the cultivation of opium. Ankara's prohibition against opium would only last from 1971 to 1974, much to Washington's dismay. Despite the travails of the heroin trade during this period, many of the old organized criminal syndicates in

Turkey remained undaunted. Moreover, we see the rise of new figures from within Istanbul's underworld, individuals who would have a far greater impact upon politics than any gangster since the fall of the Ottoman Empire. Worse still, we see the emergence of Turkish mobsters as a global force in crime and politics, a phenomenon that would be first revealed with the attempted murder of Pope John Paul II.

The concluding chapter seeks to underscore the contemporary significance of the heroin trade and organized crime in Turkey through discussion of the Susurluk and Ergenekon investigations, two pivotal scandals that have marked the turn of the twenty-first century. Unlike past periods in the development of criminal syndicates and drug trafficking, these two scandals have received copious amounts of attention from the Turkish government and the popular press. This chapter admittedly does not present an exhaustive survey of these respective investigations. Rather, the object of this conclusion is to highlight the continuities and discontinuities between Susurluk, Ergenekon, and the earlier stages of organized crime's emergence in Turkey. In doing so, this chapter calls into account the notion of Turkey's "deep state," a catchphrase often used to encapsulate the long-standing relationship between the country's civilian government, its security apparatus, and unlawful actors. While the concept of the deep state is helpful in providing a basic framework for identifying and debating how gangsters, politicians, and security officials have collaborated with one another at various points in the nation's history, political relations between official and criminal parties are by no means unique to Turkey. As seen throughout this work, shared security interests, based upon a mutually acceptable socio-political or economic status quo, has forged alliances between governments and gangs in various corners of the world at different points in early modern and modern history.

1

The Imperial Origins of the "Turkish Mafia"

Hasan Basri Çantay was among the first voices to herald the dawning of the Republic of Turkey. As a journalist and editor based in the northwestern Anatolian town of Balıkesir, Çantay ranked amongst the most notable and impactful figures to first champion the rise of Mustafa Kemal Atatürk. In 1964 he republished a personal collection of articles representing the "black days (*kara günler*)" as he called them, of war and insecurity that preceded Atatürk's ascendency and the establishment of the republic. His choice of articles, which are mostly reprinted editorials from his newspaper *The Voice* (or *Ses*), are telling representations of his concerns and anxieties from the period. The first article Çantay included in this collection was an essay entitled the "Scourge of Banditry (*Eşkiyalık Derdi*)." Written two weeks before the Ottoman Empire's surrender to the Entente alliance in late 1918, Çantay recounts how banditry had become among the worst afflictions, "a pestilence" in his words, plaguing society. The pervasiveness of roving bandits in the countryside had grown to such an extent that there were often few things left to steal in many villages. One could not be blind to the fact, Çantay argued, that bandits had become a governing force on their own.[1] In an editorial on the "security issue (*asayış meselesi*)" written one week later, he made a more direct appeal to bandits to lay down their arms and end their acts of "vengeance." "What a great anguish it is to see our fields unharvested," he explained, "the barns empty, our hometowns deprived because of [the lack of] security and to see the martyrs from our villages who have fought the wildest bands for years now."[2]

Hasan Çantay's lamentations exemplify a central element of Turkish history that often escapes outside observers. The modern Turkish Republic, like all of the states that succeeded that Ottoman Empire, is a state born out of violence and disorder. War, separatism, and intercommunal conflict laid the foundation for the borders and internal politics that defined Anatolia during the decades preceding and ensuing the First World War. Battles and massacres, however, were not the only manifestations of violence during these years of conflict. More banal forms of violence, particularly banditry, tainted the lives and the memories of Turkey's first citizens.

In the years preceding the First World War, the general prevalence of organized criminal activity in both town and country typified the sort of failures

[1] Hasan Basri Çantay, *Kara Günler ve İbret Levhaları* (Istanbul: Ahmet Said Matbaası, 1964), 41–43.
[2] Çantay, *Kara Günler ve İbret Levhaları*, 43–45.

and impediments threatening to topple the Ottoman state. At the dawn of the nineteenth century, the problem of banditry, as well as smuggling, paramilitarism, and other forms of crime, was among the many challenges prompting the imperial government in Istanbul to initiate an expansive agenda of reform aimed at securing and policing the population. The outbreak of war in 1914, as well as the seemingly intractable problems of poverty, mass displacement of refugees, and state bankruptcy, would prove fatal to these reforms. The crisis posed by the ever-expanding power of criminal gangs reached such a threshold during the last years of the Ottoman Empire that imperial officers and officials often chose to incorporate thugs and lawbreakers into state service. Such steps did not simply serve as a means of controlling or minimizing the activities of criminal syndicates. As we shall see, the synthesis forged between criminal groups and the state allowed elements of the Ottoman and early republican regimes a violent and uncompromising instrument with which they could impose their political authority.

The power and influence wielded by the gangs of the late Ottoman period ultimately did not survive long into the first years of the Turkish Republic. By the mid-1920s, many of the more powerful criminal networks that had dominated the countryside (and whose influence had permeated the ranks of the state) vanished. While banditry faded, but did not disappear, as both a political and social concern, other forms of crime, such as smuggling, achieved a new degree of relevance.

To understand the origins of organized crime in Turkey one must look first at the context and the significance of crime and violence in Anatolia during the first three decades of the twentieth century. While innumerable criminal enterprises may be found over the many centuries of history preceding the Ottoman Empire's collapse and the subsequent birth of the Republic of Turkey, organized crime in the years between 1908 and 1938 introduced several paradigms that remained significant over the remainder of the twentieth century. Although never coined in such terms, at least during the first half of the century, organized crime was a source of both political concern and reform in the young Turkish Republic. Nevertheless, many events during this era of crisis and transformation highlight the degrees to which gangs play a role in the making and executing of state of policy. Later chapters will return to this particular trope in the evolution of organized crime.

The years spanning the reign of the Young Turks and Atatürk's Republican People's Party pose important points of discontinuity in the history of organized crime as well. The physical demise of bandit groups following the establishment of the republic signaled the beginning of new criminal cultures and new networks of crime. While some aspects of Ottoman and early Kemalist organized crime have remained relevant, what we will see over the course of later chapters is a gradual, and almost total, reinvention of gangs in Turkey in the decades following Atatürk's death in 1938.

CONTEXTUALIZING CRIMINAL SYNDICATES AND THE (UN-)MAKING OF THE OTTOMAN EMPIRE

Hasan Basri Çantay's observations in 1918 would have sounded familiar to an untold number of subjects, statesmen, and sovereigns living in the Ottoman Empire during the course of its six centuries of existence. Banditry and piracy plagued virtually all corners of the Ottoman world at different points in time and with various degrees of intensity. The Ottoman state itself was in part born out of the raiding of Byzantine lands by horsemen loyal to Osman Bey, founder of the Ottoman household. The slow transformation of Osman's petty fiefdom bordering Byzantine Constantinople into a massive state residing on three continents naturally did not leave the Ottoman Empire immune from the marauding the first Ottomans were initially known for. Yet from epoch to epoch, it is clear that the root causes and significance of differing forms of organized criminal activity (such as banditry) changed dramatically. In searching for the origins of organized crime in Turkey in the twentieth century, it is therefore essential to understand both the nature and socio-political context of the criminal syndicates that preceded the Turkish Republic's establishment.

Eric Hobsbawm reminds us that banditry, to some degree or another, plagued even the strongest of empires.[3] Before the dawning of modern bureaucracies, courts, militaries, systems of taxation, police departments, and networks of transport, it was simply impossible for even the most wealthy, sophisticated, and stable of imperial governments to extend its rule evenly and efficiently over long periods of time. Harsh topography and long distances particularly bedeviled early modern empires. High mountains, barren deserts, thick woods, and isolated bays and inlets were usually where one could find the most stubborn of bandits, pirates, and other bands of lawbreakers. During times of profound imperial crisis, such as war and famine, those forms of organized law-breaking that were most commonly associated with out-of-the-way corners of the realm could appear even within the walls of the capital.

Other historians have documented further examples of organized criminal behavior that plagued early modern and late empires in history. Bands of smugglers have long traversed borders and high seas, eating into personal profits and state treasuries alike.[4] Urban centers, both big and small, contended with gangs of young men starting fights and exploiting hapless shop owners.[5]

The advent of the modern nation-state provided some solutions to these and other types of criminal activity. Modern law enforcement institutions, such as courts, urban police departments, rural gendarmeries, coast guards, and prisons,

[3] Hobsbawm, *Bandits*, 16.

[4] Alan Karras, *Smuggling: Contraband and Corruption in World History* (Lanham, MD: Rowman & Littlefield, 2011).

[5] See e.g. Keith Hopwood (ed.), *Organised Crime in Antiquity* (London: The Classical Press of Wales, 1998); John McMullan, "Organization in Sixteenth and Seventeenth Century London," *Social Problems* 29.3 (February 1982), 311–323.

became ever more refined tools of imposing order.[6] It is fitting here to call to mind the comparison Charles Tilly draws between state-building and organized crime; with the gradual diminution (but not elimination) of banditry, purveyors of the state, like a supreme set of bandit chieftains, are able to exploit and extract the monetary wealth and personal loyalties of the population at large with greater ease.[7]

To paraphrase Hobsbawm, to understand how the Ottomans experienced the evolution of organized crime (both in terms of its causes and its impact), one must pay close attention to the history of imperial power and sovereignty within the Ottoman lands. During the first two-and-a-half centuries of the Ottoman sultans, a period in which the empire's borders grew by leaps and bounds, civil and judicial institutions slowly took on permanent, settled, and consistent qualities.[8] Joshua White's work on piracy in the Aegean during the sixteenth century hints at the limited degree to which Istanbul could regularly command and govern affairs within its domain.[9] The dawning of the seventeenth century may have brought about the maturation of the "sedentary" Ottoman state (again, one with more fixed frontiers and with more defined and predictable civil/judicial institutions) but it did not lead to any mitigation of marauding bands on the land or sea.

As the Ottoman Empire entered the 1600s, a perfect storm of political, economic, and ecological conditions (conditions which included rising population levels, ongoing border conflicts, higher taxes, inflation, landlessness, and climate change) helped produce sustained waves of banditry and peasant rebellion. Against the backdrop of these so-called *celali* rebellions, administrators in the Ottoman Empire established several important precedents with respect to the politics and the policing of criminal groups like bandits.[10]

It is in the seventeenth century that we see the initial signs of state decentralization in the Ottoman lands. Unlike the classic cases of France or Great Britain, two states that developed more consolidated, centralized forms of governance during the early modern period, Ottoman governance instead relied increasingly upon locally rooted power brokers as the main arbiters of imperial administration. The question of who would serve in such a capacity was largely the outcome of local competition between regional political factions. The decentralized structure of Ottoman imperial rule became ever more entrenched during the eighteenth

[6] To understand the long evolution of how police enforcement and internal state security evolved, one has to appreciate the general shift from agrarian to industrial forms of governance. See e.g. Ernest Gellner, *Nations and Nationalism* (Ithaca, NY: Cornell University Press, 1983), 8–38.

[7] Tilly, "War Making and State Making as Organized Crime," 172.

[8] For greater discussion of the fluidity of early Ottoman state development, see Daniel Goffman, *The Ottoman Empire and Early Modern Europe* (Cambridge: Cambridge University Press, 2002), 27–58; Cemal Kafadar, *Between Two Worlds* (Cambridge, MA: Harvard University Press, 1996).

[9] Joshua White, "Easy Targets: The Illegal Enslavement of Ottoman Subjects in the Aegean (Late 16th C.)," paper presented at New York University Ottoman Studies Workshop on Violence in Anatolia (4–5 March 2011).

[10] On the broader causes and effects of the crises of the seventeenth century, see Geoffrey Park, "Crisis and Catastrophe: The Global Crisis of the Seventeenth Century Reconsidered," *American Historical Review* 113.4 (October 2008), 1053–1079; Sam White, *The Climate of Rebellion in the Early Ottoman Empire* (Cambridge: Cambridge University Press, 2011).

century. By 1800, the collective authority, military potential, and even financial might of local lords (*ayan*) vastly overshadowed the sultan's court in Istanbul.[11]

Political and administrative decentralization in the Ottoman Empire, beginning in the seventeenth century, was arguably both a consequence and an expression of a second important precedent: the growing visibility and the politicization of banditry. Karen Barkey has convincingly demonstrated that, unlike in many of the emerging nation-states of Europe, a series of short-term, as opposed to long-term, strategies defined Istanbul's responses to banditry and peasant rebellion during the seventeenth century. Among the strategies employed by the Ottoman capital was the recruitment of *celali*s, bandits, and would-be bandits into both the military and the provincial administration.[12] Militarily, such a policy did hold certain immediate benefits. As the Ottoman Empire engaged in grander military campaigns, campaigns that demanded larger numbers of foot soldiers equipped with firearms, employing bandits and peasant rebels provided a stopgap resource for filling the ranks. In an empire where the capital exerted increasingly less influence in local affairs, bandits and rebels emerged to become the sort of provincial power brokers that became synonymous with this age of decentralization.[13] Men such as Ali Pasha of Jannina, the great *ayan* of the western Balkans at the turn of the eighteenth century, assumed such heights through his earlier career as a bandit in what is today the borderlands of Albania and northern Greece.[14]

In addition to the political fortunes amassed by bandits between the seventeenth and eighteenth centuries, the pervasiveness of banditry was indicative of the physical and economic degradation witnessed in various corners of the Ottoman countryside. Decades of conflict with Russia and Austria had a particularly acute effect in instigating continual outbreaks of banditry in the southern Balkans. In addition to the poverty, high taxes, and social dislocation that accompanied long periods of warfare, mass migration was among the chief causes that contributed to lawlessness in this key region of the Ottoman Empire. Among the areas most hard hit by the rise in brigandage of the eighteenth century were in the Albanian highlands of the western Balkans. Beginning in the mid-eighteenth century, Albanian mountaineers, already hard-pressed to make a substantive living in one of the most ecologically and topographically desperate regions of southeastern Europe, regularly raided villages in the low-lying regions to the south and east.[15] By the end of the 1700s, particularly with the loss of the Crimea at the hands of imperial Russia, the Ottoman Empire would also experience the first of many refugee

[11] Fikret Adanir, "Semi-Autonomous Provincial Forces in the Balkans and Anatolia," in Suraiya Faroqhi (ed.), *The Cambridge History of Turkey: Volume 3, The Later Ottoman Empire, 1603–1839* (Cambridge: Cambridge University Press, 2006), 157–185.

[12] Karen Barkey, *Bandits and Bureaucrats: The Ottoman Route to State Centralization* (Ithica, NY: Cornell University Press, 1994).

[13] Virginia Aksan, "War and Peace," in Suraiya Faroqhi (ed.), *The Cambridge History of Turkey: Volume 3, The Later Ottoman Empire, 1603–1839* (Cambridge: Cambridge University Press, 2006), 81–117.

[14] Katherine Fleming, *The Muslim Bonaparte* (Princeton, NJ: Princeton University Press, 1999).

[15] Fredrick Anscombe, "Albanians and 'Mountain Bandits'," in Fredrick Anscombe (ed.), *The Ottoman Balkans, 1750–1830* (Princeton, NJ: Markus Wiener Publications, 2006), 87–113.

crises. The arrival of hundreds of thousands of Crimean Tatar refugees during the first half of the nineteenth century foreshadowed even larger waves of migrants destined to settle within the confines of the Ottoman Empire.[16] The political and social evolution of many of these immigrant communities (Tatars as well as many others), as we will see, are crucial to understanding both the nature and the perceptions of organized crime up to the present.

While banditry certainly plagued large portions of the Ottoman realm, lawlessness in the countryside was only one indication of graver physical threats to the survival of the state. As the nineteenth century commenced, the threat of war and political dismemberment confronted both imperial officials and provincial notables. Repeated failures upon the battlefield during the last quarter of the 1700s (first in the Balkans and then in Egypt), as well as a weak treasury, compelled many inside and outside of the capital to contemplate reform. Meanwhile, the outbreak of rebellion in Serbia (and then later in Greece) offered further evidence of administrative degradation (particularly as a result of capricious *ayan*). There was also a growing sense of cultural and technological malaise among elements of the Ottoman elite, a phenomenon perhaps best illustrated by the experiences of Ottoman Egyptians during France's brief occupation at the close of the 1700s.[17]

The ascendency of Mahmud II to the Ottoman throne in 1808 signaled a decisive turn in the nature of Ottoman governance. It is during his reign that reform first became a permanent byword of imperial politics. As the nineteenth century progressed Istanbul steadily reclaimed its place as the absolute center of imperial politics and sovereignty. This drive towards state centralization, and state-run reform, resulted in the mass elimination or suppression of provincial *ayan* lords, rebellious janissaries, and recalcitrant tribes in various corners of the empire. In the place of local notables and lords, reform-minded officials in Istanbul began to assemble a regularized professional bureaucracy. Reform era schools and professional academies provided the expanding ranks of the bureaucracy and military with graduates who fostered a new spirit of state service and positivist thought. As the state grew in sophistication and size, personal and communal notions of law, belonging, and citizenship were transformed.[18]

Banditry, as well as other forms of organized criminal behavior, did not subside with the rise of the modern Ottoman state. Arguably lawlessness in the countryside remained as pervasive in the Ottoman lands as it had been a century earlier. Yet the empire's evolution into an increasingly centralized, rationalized, and

[16] Kemal Karpat, *Ottoman Population, 1830–1914: Demographic and Social Characteristics* (Madison: University of Wisconsin Press, 1985), 65–66; Hakan Kırımlı, *National Movements and National Identity Among the Crimean Tatars, 1905–1916* (Leiden: E.J. Brill Press, 1996), 7–8.

[17] *Al-Jabarti's Chronicle of the First Seven Months of the French Occupation of Egypt, June-December 1798/Muharram-Rajab 1213* (Princeton, NJ: Markus Wiener Publishing, 1993), 19–48.

[18] Fredrick Anscombe, "Islam and the Age of Ottoman Reform," *Past & Present* 208 (August 2010), 159–189; Carter Vaughn Findley, *Bureaucratic Reform in the Ottoman Empire: The Sublime Porte, 1789–1922* (Princeton, NJ: Princeton University Press, 1980); Carter Vaughn Findley, "The Tanzimat," in Reşat Kasaba (ed.), *The Cambridge History of Turkey, Volume 4: Turkey in the Modern World* (Cambridge: Cambridge University Press, 2008), 11–37.

"modernizing" polity had a profound impact upon the nature and the perception of criminal networks and syndicates.

THE POLITICS OF OTTOMAN MACEDONIA AND THE ORIGINS OF THE MODERN "ÇETE"

Ottoman administrators and commentators had long used the term bandit (*eşkiya* or *şaki*) to describe a great host of lawbreakers. "Bandit" applied equally to highwaymen, kidnappers, marauding tribesmen, rebelling cavalrymen, and dissident provincial elites. A new series of regional crises during the nineteenth and early twentieth century infused the concept of banditry with a new connotation: nationalist revolutionary. The role of bandits in fomenting nationalist revolution in the Balkans remains a topic of intense interest and debate.[19] While one may doubt the national consciousness of Serb, Greek, or Bulgarian bandits before or during the commencement of the national revolutions of the nineteenth century. Ottoman administrators applied that term *eşkiya* to ostensibly apolitical brigands as well as to organized revolutionary groups. Labeling armed groups (be they of the political or apolitical sort) as bandits remained a trend into the early twentieth century. Even with the complete breakdown of Ottoman authority after the First World War, provincial Greek and Armenian fighters were all termed bandits by Istanbul regardless of whether or not they were committing random acts of violence against Muslim civilians, defending their homes, or laying some irredentist claim to a territorial portion of Anatolia.[20]

Arguably, out of all of the empire's remaining territorial holdings left at the turn of the twentieth century, "political banditry" was most synonymous with the Ottoman provinces of Macedonia. This central portion of the Balkans, comprising what is today the Republic of Macedonia, northern Greece, and southwestern Bulgaria, became the subject of intense regional competition following the signing of the Treaty of Berlin in 1878. Over the next thirty-four years, Istanbul labored vigorously to defend its Macedonian provinces against the irredentist interests of Greece, Bulgaria, and Serbia. The contest over Macedonia's incredibly diverse population of Orthodox Christians, Muslims, and Jews entailed a propaganda war as all sides attempted to open competing schools, churches, and public offices meant to sway locals' loyalties.[21] This contest between the Ottoman Empire,

[19] Hobsbawm, *Bandits*, 77–90; Barbara Jelavich, *History of the Balkans Volume I* (Cambridge: Cambridge University Press, 1983), 61–62.

[20] See e.g. Adnan Sofuoğlu, *Kuva-yı Milliye Döneminde Kuzeybatı Anadolu, 1919–1921* (Ankara: Genelkurmay Basım Evi, 1994), 31–36.

[21] İpek Yasmanoğlu, "The Priest's Robe and the Rebel's Rifle: Communal Conflict and the Construction of National Identity in Ottoman Macedonia, 1878–1908," (Ph.D. diss., Princeton University, 2005).

Greece, Bulgaria, and Serbia turned violent in the 1890s with the introduction of armed gangs into the conflict.

Ironically, the first faction to successfully utilize armed gangs (or *çetes* in Turkish) as a means of projecting political control over the region was an indigenous movement with no official ties to any of the competing states in the Balkans. Founded in 1890 in the port city of Salonika, the Internal Macedonian Revolutionary Organization (IMRO) principally advocated the creation of an autonomous state in Macedonia that was largely outside of the control of Istanbul. The early leaders of this organization, who were inspired by past violent uprisings in the Balkans, organized their armed bands predominantly from Macedonia's Slavic-speaking Orthodox Christian population (even though the IMRO, officially at least, did not claim to speak in the name of any single ethnic group in the region). Through the support of scores of village *çetes*, which were largely financed by local and international donations, the IMRO created a virtual "state within a state" within ten years of its founding. In the summer of 1903, *çetes* loyal to the IMRO rose in rebellion throughout Macedonia, gambling that such an act would arouse the sympathies of the Great Powers of Europe. Despite some early successes, the insurrection failed, leaving the IMRO weakened and fractured. In the wake of the 1903 rebellion, the states of Greece, Bulgaria, Serbia, and Romania appropriated the IMRO's model and raised their own national *çetes*. Between 1904 and 1908, law and order in Macedonia virtually collapsed as rival gangs (many composed of fighters recruited from outside the region) burned villages, looted homes, and massacred civilians in the name of "national liberation."[22]

Despite the great weight and effort invested in reforming imperial and local institutions in the region, Ottoman officers and officials tasked with administering Macedonia were hard-pressed to defeat, let alone engage, the various bands roaming the countryside. Istanbul's failure to subdue rival *çetes* in Macedonia, coupled with general frustrations both inside and outside the ranks of government regarding the rule of then Sultan Abdülhamid II, resulted in revolution. The Young Turk Revolution of 1908, which induced the reinstitution of parliamentary rule under a constitutional monarchy, did bring some respite to the violence (since many local factions in Macedonia, including remnants of the IMRO, came to support a return to constitutional rule).[23] However, within four years after the rise of the so-called Young Turks, *çete* violence slowly returned to Macedonia with a

[22] Fikret Adanır, *Die Makedonische Frage: Ihre Entstehung und Entwicklung bis 1908* (Wiesbaden: Steiner Verlag, 1979); Douglas Dakin, *The Greek Struggle in Macedonia, 1897–1913* (Thessaloniki: Institute for Balkan Studies, 1966); Dimitar Dimeski, *Makedonskoto Nacionalnoosloboditelno Dvizhenje vo Bitolskiot Vilaet (1893–1903)* (Skopje: Studentski Zbor, 1981); Ryan Gingeras, "'Scores Dead in Smerdesh': Communal Violence and International Intrigue in Ottoman Macedonia," *Balkanistika* 25 (2012), 75–98; Duncan Perry, *The Politics of Terror: The Macedonian Liberation Movement 1893–1903* (Durham, NC: Duke University Press, 1988); Nadine Lange-Akhund *The Macedonian Question, 1893–1908, From Western Sources* (Boulder, CO: East European Monographs, 1998); Steven Sowards, *Austria's Policy of Macedonian Reform* (Boulder, CO: East European Monographs, 1989).

[23] Şükrü Hanioğlu, *Preparation for a Revolution: The Young Turks, 1902–1908* (Oxford: Oxford University Press, 2001), 244–249.

vengeance. Finally, in the fall of 1912, the armies of Greece, Bulgaria, Serbia, and Montenegro marched into Macedonia with the support of local Christian armed bands, resulting in the final dismemberment of the Ottoman Balkans.

To be sure, the IMRO was no mafia. More importantly, one cannot find an Ottoman official who conceived of Macedonian militants as gangsters or members of some discrete organized crime outfit. Nevertheless, *çete* violence in Macedonia would have a lasting imprint upon future perceptions and interpretations of organized crime. The word *çete*, which is of Slavic and not Turkish origin, eventually became the staple term applied to contemporary gangs and criminal syndicates in the Republic of Turkey. Yet like the more historical usage of *eşkiya, çete* may still be applied more loosely to groups and activities exclusive of crime. *Çete* and *çetecilik*, for example, may be used to describe a "guerrilla" or "paramilitary activity," two forms of behavior that could just as easily be undertaken by legitimate or official actors.

Çete violence in Macedonia had a direct effect upon many of the leaders of the late Ottoman state, as well as many of the founders of the Turkish Republic. Erik Jan Zürcher has convincingly demonstrated that the Young Turk generation of officers and bureaucrats were rooted in the events that transpired in Macedonia between the 1870s and 1912. A majority of the seminal members of the Committee of the Union and Progress (CUP), the clandestine party that secretly organized the 1908 revolution, were born in the southern Balkans. A great many more officers and officials who came to lead or serve the Young Turk state had experienced the violence first hand as local administrators or military commanders.[24]

CUP officials, both in the Balkans and in the capital, appear to have drawn two critical, but conflicting, lessons from dealing with the *çetes* of Macedonia. The partisan fighting in Macedonia indelibly tainted the way many Ottoman officials came to view non-Muslims (particularly Christians). *Çete* violence embodied the inherent threat posed by Orthodox Christian nationalism. Although it was the regular armies of Serbia, Greece, and Bulgaria that were responsible for the partitioning of Ottoman Macedonia, local *çetes*, after years of terrorizing local administrators, security personnel, and civilians, appeared to have helped blaze their path to victory. As the empire limped towards the outbreak of the First World War, the apparent strength of and threat posed by Greek and Armenian *çetes* weighed heavily upon the minds of many within the capital.[25]

CUP adherents in the military and in the imperial administration drew a more technical, but equally profound, lesson from the *çetes* of Macedonia. While much of the violence that plagued the Ottoman Balkans at the turn of the twentieth century was largely associated with local and foreign Orthodox Christian militants, provincial Muslim civilians were not opposed to forming

[24] Erik Jan Zürcher, "Young Turks—Children of the Borderlands?," in Kemal Karpat and Robert W. Zens (eds.), *Ottoman Borderlands: Issues, Personalities and Political Changes* (Madison: University of Wisconsin Press, 2003), 279–282.

[25] See Donald Bloxham, "Terrorism and Imperial Decline: The Ottoman-Armenian Case," *European Review of History* 14.3 (2007), 301–324.

their own *çetes*. Muslim bands, more commonly known outside of the empire as *başıbozuks*, were most notoriously utilized at times of civil insurrection (the Bulgarian rebellion of 1876 and the Macedonian insurrection of 1903 being the most well-known cases of *başıbozuk* violence against Christian civilians). Ongoing fighting between Greek, Bulgarian, Serb, and IMRO *çetes* between 1904 and 1908 once again compelled local Muslims to form their own armed militias in Macedonia. In setting the stage for the revolution of 1908, the CUP appropriated or formed *çetes* of local Muslims during the spring and summer of 1908. It was at the head of their own bands of Muslim (mostly Albanian) paramilitaries that such heroes of the Young Turk Revolution as Ahmet Niyazi and Enver were launched into fame and political prominence.[26] When Abdülhamid reneged in 1909 upon his initial reinstatement of the constitution, bands loyal to the CUP once again rallied throughout Macedonia and formed a part of the advancing army that resulted in the sultan's removal from power.

The CUP did not cease in their reliance upon their *çete* networks of Macedonia following Abdülhamid's removal from power. As Young Turk loyalists gathered greater amounts of power in a restored Ottoman parliament (as well as within the ranks of the military and bureaucracy), Muslim *çetes* became a more regular feature of the Macedonian political landscape. Unlike past gangs, which were formed in response to open revolt, many Muslim *çetes* operating in Macedonia after 1908 served as an extension of the CUP's political base. Even though many of the older Orthodox Christian bands (including elements of IMRO) had demobilized following the Young Turk Revolution, evidence suggests that Muslim *çetes* continued to target individuals suspected of past or present acts of insurrection.[27]

Like the IMRO, it would be grossly inaccurate to consider the CUP's *çetes* in Macedonia anything like organized crime (even though their acts were still officially considered criminal). Yet, unlike the IMRO, it is clear that many within the ranks of the CUP considered the formation of state-backed gangs to be a legitimate and effective tool in combating a similar foe. In an era when the empire seemed beset on all sides by uncompromising and violent adversaries both inside and outside the imperial borders, fighting separatists and irredentists (both real and imaginary as it would turn out) with their own methods was deemed warranted.

Such sentiments, despite radically changing circumstances, have endured over the course of the Ottoman Empire's long evolution into the Republic of Turkey. Since the formal collapse of the Young Turk regime in 1918, organizing, facilitating, supporting, and praising the activities of pro-government gangs persists in the contemporary Republic of Turkey. Even the use of the term *çete* has remained consistent. What has changed, perhaps, is the nature or character of the modern "*çeteci*." While a member of a CUP-sponsored gang may have been a shepherd, an unemployed field hand, or refugee pressed into service, a *çeteci* in contemporary

[26] Hanioğlu, *Preparation for a Revolution: The Young Turks, 1902–1908*, 221–232.

[27] In the town of Florina, a paramilitary group of Muslim *çetecis* was maintained to check the influence of the remnants of the Macedonian insurgent movement even after 1908. See PRO/FO 294/47/27, 9 May 1911; PRO/FO 294/47/32, 31 May 1911; PRO/FO 294/47/35, 9 June 1911.

parlance denotes an individual who is nothing less than a thug or a gangster. A *çeteci* today would almost certainly engage in a criminal trade like arms or drug trafficking. While CUP *çete* leaders certainly recruited men without criminal pedigrees for service, one may argue that the modern Turkish *çeteci* comes to serve as an agent or armed guardian of the Turkish state precisely because he is a drug smuggler or a killer.

PORTRAIT OF A BANDIT: MIGRATION, ETHNICITY, AND THE OTTOMAN ROOTS OF TURKISH ORGANIZED CRIME

Bandit gangs and *çetes* without any visible political goal were found in various corners of the Ottoman Empire during the nineteenth and early twentieth centuries. In a variety of localities, banditry was a seemingly intrinsic feature of the provincial socio-economic landscape. At the turn of the twentieth century for example, bands of Turkmen brigands plagued the immediate hinterland of Anatolia's Aegean coastline.[28] Ottoman officials in eastern Anatolia regularly complained of the suffering caused by the marauding of Kurdish tribesmen. Bedouin nomads posed a similar danger to settled agricultural communities in various corners of Ottoman Syria and Jordan.[29]

As stewards of a reforming and modernizing state, Ottoman officials and officers in the nineteenth century perceived, as well as imagined, a great host of threats and challenges to the survival of the empire. Arguably, in the minds of many Ottoman reformers, the greatest challenge to the future of the state was, to put it baldly, its people. From the perspective of Istanbul, the sultan's subjects suffered from a wide-ranging number of impediments. Before the dawn of the reform age, there was no single institution that served to unite or mobilize the empire's diverse population. Enforcement of civil and criminal law depended upon one's confessional background or perhaps where one lived in the empire. The vast majority of the empire's population was illiterate and only a sliver of the sultan's subjects possessed full command of Ottoman Turkish as a written or even a spoken lingua franca.

In the "modern" age, Ottoman statesmen were increasingly troubled by what they saw as archaic or reactionary patterns of behavior among segments of the empire's population. In particular, bureaucrats and officers soured upon the continued prevalence of nomadism and tribal authority in various corners of the state.[30] Moreover, as the empire entered the twentieth century, the economic and cultural disparities between town and country were growing ever starker. Whether

[28] Sabri Yetkin, *Ege'de Eşkıyalar* (Istanbul: Tarih Vakfı Yurt Yayınları, 2003).

[29] See e.g. Eugene Rogan, *Frontiers of the State in the Late Ottoman Empire: Transjordan 1850–1921* (Cambridge: Cambridge University Press, 1999).

[30] Reşat Kasaba charts the earliest stages of Ottoman settlement policies towards nomads in the empire as early as the seventeenth century. See Reşat Kasaba, *A Moveable Empire: Ottoman Nomads, Migrants & Refugees* (Seattle: University of Washington Press, 2009).

one assumes the perspective of the imperial capital of Istanbul or a market town in the hinterland, the growing economic and cultural sophistication and materialism of urban centers clashed with the endemic poverty, provincialism, and generally uncouth behavior of people residing outside of town. The archetypal urbane Ottoman officials tended to fear the common villager. As one studies the policies enacted by the reforming Ottoman state during the nineteenth and early twentieth centuries, it is clear that the emerging imperial bureaucracy sought both to control and remold the Ottoman populace at large. Reengineering the Ottoman "volk" was not a task done for the good of the people; it was instead perceived as a matter of national survival.

Fighting both the prospective causes and the actual manifestation of banditry, which was an endemic trait of provincial Ottoman society at large, gradually became infused into the reforming agenda of the modernizing Ottoman elite. Beginning with the so-called "Tanzimat" period (1839–76), Istanbul placed a new emphasis upon settling and governing nomadic tribes. Officials throughout the empire instituted a series of policies meant to win the political loyalties of tribesmen as well as to punish nomads who exercised unbridled amounts of autonomy. One of these measures included the recruitment of loyal tribesmen into special tribal militias tasked with maintaining domestic security (such as the Hamidye in eastern Anatolia). New civil and criminal courts, disarmament programs, schools, and internal migration laws (particularly those targeting vagrants or *serseri*) were still other methods used to mitigate the causes of banditry and, generally speaking, civilize the Ottoman masses.[31]

Trained bodies of rural gendarmes and urban policemen, separate from the army, could eventually be found throughout the empire by the turn of the twentieth century. The destruction of the janissary corps, which had traditionally maintained law and order in the capital, paved the way for the establishment of a professional police force in Istanbul in 1845. Abdülhamid II's ascendency to the throne quickened the pace of policing reform. In 1879, reformers established a rural gendarmerie that would operate separately from urban police forces. Like other aspects of the Ottoman reform movement, European models (particularly from France) critically influenced the organization and methods of police and gendarmerie. While both policemen and gendarmes were tasked with overseeing the civil and moral behavior of Ottoman citizens, the chief assignment of law enforcement personnel during the reign of Abdulhamid II was to combat potential centers of dissent and physical disorder.[32]

Despite the unprecedented extent to which the Ottoman criminal justice system was reformed during the long nineteenth century, banditry remained an

[31] Ferdan Ergut, "State and Social Control: The Police in the Late Ottoman Empire and the Early Republican Turkey, 1839–1939" (New School for Social Research Ph.D. Thesis, 1999), 118–120.

[32] Noemi Levy, "Une Institution en Formation: La Police Ottomane a l'époque d' Abdülhamid II," *European Journal of Turkish Studies* 8 (2008); Nadir Özbek, "Policing the Countryside: Gendarmes of the Late 19th Century Ottoman Empire (1876–1908)," *International Journal of Middle East Studies* 40 (2008), 47–67.

obstinate problem. Although one could cite a multiplicity of factors hindering the government's ability to fight criminal *çetes* and *eşkiya* throughout the countryside (such as the lack of training and funds for security personnel), Ottoman officials tended to place particular blame upon the problem of migration and settlement.

Internal migration and the arrival of new immigrants were standing features of Ottoman politics and society before the nineteenth century. Year-in and year-out, waves of migrants took to the road or embarked upon ships in search of skilled and unskilled work throughout the empire. Be they sailors or fishermen from the Aegean islands, shepherds from the Albanian highlands, masons from Romania, or silk spinners from western Anatolia, such migrants were long the lifeblood of the empire's work force. When out of work, stranded migrant laborers often turned to crime. During the eighteenth century, the threat of unemployed Albanian migrants proved so grave that local officials in Salonika and Istanbul forbade all Albanians from entering or settling in their cities.[33]

Beginning in the late eighteenth century, war and the breakdown of provincial law and order transformed patterns of migration throughout the empire in dramatic and violent ways. Continued conflict with the Russian Empire after the annexation of the Crimea induced even greater numbers of refugees to seek asylum in the Ottoman Empire. Between 1860 in 1864, it is estimated that up to two million refugees from the North Caucasus fled their homes in the wake of the Russian annexation of the region. The outbreak of hostilities between Russia and the Ottoman Empire in 1877 produced yet another massive wave of Caucasian refugees (this time numbering perhaps as many as 500,000).[34] The final shock wave came in 1912 with the close of the First Balkan War. While official reports compiled immediately after the conflict estimated the number of Balkan refugees seeking asylum in Anatolia at around 500,000, it is clear that ongoing campaigns of ethnic cleansing and oppression in the former Ottoman territories of Macedonia would compel still many more to flee their homes.[35]

The various refugee crises of the long nineteenth century did more than levy further financial and material strains upon the imperial government.[36] The arrival of Muslim refugees from the Balkans and the Caucasus in the hundreds of thousands served to radically change the demographic complexion of what remained of the Ottoman Empire the dawn of the twentieth century. Most of these new

[33] See Eyal Ginio, "Migrants and Workers in an Ottoman Port: Ottoman Salonica in the Eighteenth Century," in Eugene Rogan (ed.), *Outside In: On the Margins of the Modern Middle East* (London: I.B. Taurus, 2002), 136–138; Christoph Herzog, "Migration and the State: On Ottoman Regulations Concerning Migration Since the Age of Mahmud II," in Ulrike Freitag et al. (eds.), *The City in the Ottoman Empire: Migration and the Making of Urban Modernity* (New York: Routledge, 2011), 117–134.

[34] Arsen Avagyan, *Osmanlı İmparatorluğu ve Kemalist Türkiye'nin Devlet-İktidar Sisteminde Çerkesler* (Istanbul: Belge Yayınları 2004), 23–36; Karpat, *Ottoman Population, 1830–1914: Demographic and Social Characteristics*, 66–70.

[35] BCA 272.14.75.24.6.21, September 1920.

[36] David Cuthell, "The Muhacirin Komisyonu: An Agent in the Transformation of Ottoman Anatolia, 1860–1866," (Ph.D. diss., Columbia University, 2005).

immigrants came to settle in dense community among their fellow kin and countrymen throughout various corners of Anatolia. Virtually all of these newcomers arrived with no possessions or any means to carry on their former livelihoods. While Istanbul was able to offer some degree of economic support to a minority of these newly settled refugees, the overwhelming majority spent their first years in exile living in poverty.

It did not take long for many newcomers to garner a reputation for lawlessness, banditry, and violence. At a time when many natives living in the countryside were already hard-pressed to maintain a subsistent living, the settlement of Caucasian and Balkan refugees quickly provoked tension and competition over land, labor, and other resources. Ottoman records show repeated outbreaks of violence through the late nineteenth century between locals and refugees.[37] The government was able to mitigate some of the local tensions by recruiting newly arrived refugees (particularly those with reputations as bandits) into the ranks of the military and gendarmerie (a tactic again dating back several centuries).[38] Nevertheless, in locales ranging from Sivas to Edirne to Urfa to Izmir, the scourge of violent, thieving refugees became an indelible feature of provincial life.

The perceived links between banditry and refugees deeply influenced official Ottoman discourse and policy related to culture and ethnicity in the provinces. As one pages through official reports or even newspaper clippings from the turn of the twentieth century, it appears that certain ethnicities acquired a particularly acute reputation for criminal behavior. Time and again, it is difficult to find examples of provincial banditry without running across the names of men specifically identified by their ethnic background. In the absence of a paternal name, using ethnic epithets served as a proper way of distinguishing a Muslim man's identity (for example, *Arnavut* Mehmet, Mehmet the Albanian or *Çerkes* Ahmet, Ahmet the Circassian). As one scans printed official and public accounts from the turn of the twentieth century, the repeated listing of men deriving from some kind Balkan or Caucasian ethnic background indicates that such crimes were not simply indicative of the Ottoman Empire's refugee problem. One instead gets the impression that a bandit typically possessed the accent, costume, or name of an immigrant or refugee.[39]

Of the empire's profoundly diverse population, several specific migrant groups arguably stood out as being among the most prone towards banditry and other forms of crime. Albanians, for example, were considered to be among the most notorious constituents the empire. The continued prevalence of Albanian banditry, from the eighteenth century through to the end of the empire, seemed to reinforce

[37] Nedim İpek, *Rumeli'den Anadolu'ya Türk Göçleri (1877–1890)* (Ankara: Türk Tarih Kurumu, 1994), 187–200.

[38] Avagyan, *Osmanlı İmparatorluğu ve Kemalist Türkiye'nin Devlet-İktidar Sisteminde Çerkesler*, 99–104; Ehud R. Toledano, *Slavery and Abolition in the Ottoman Middle East* (Seattle: University of Washington Press, 1998), 102–104.

[39] See Ryan Gingeras, *Sorrowful Shores: Violence, Ethnicity and the End of the Ottoman Empire* (Oxford: Oxford University Press, 2009), 29–30, 33–34.

both official and popular impressions that Albanians were quick to violence and disposed to joining gangs.[40]

Imperial officials, as well as significant segments of the Ottoman public, perceived North Caucasian immigrants through a similar lens. Like Albanians living in the western highlands of the Balkans, poor Circassian (or Adige), Abkhazian and Chechen refugees were considered "tribal" people with inherently warlike qualities. Also like Albanians, their supposed warlike nature made them predisposed to both military service as well as a life of crime. Western observers commenting from abroad, as well as from within the empire, affirmed such stereotypes.[41] In proposing a series of administrative reforms tailored to Eastern Anatolia, the Treaty of Berlin, for example, made explicit note of the threat to peaceful Armenians posed by Circassian brigands.[42]

A last ethnic group that became especially associated with banditry in the late Ottoman Empire was the Laz. The Laz, a predominantly Muslim group closely related to the Mingrelian branch of the Georgian peoples, possess a long history of labor migration within the context of the Ottoman Empire (as well as the Turkish Republic). Evliya Çelebi, the famed Ottoman travel writer, notes the presence of these Black Sea migrants in the imperial capital as early as the seventeenth century.[43] Their status as one of many migratory groups changed radically with the wars of the nineteenth century. As a result of the Russo-Ottoman War of 1877–78, hundreds of thousands of Laz were evicted from their homes, forcing large numbers to resettle within the vicinity of Istanbul.[44] Although many would find work on the docks or as seamen sailing up and down the straits or the coast of the Sea of Marmara, impoverished Laz men became equally notorious as Albanians or Circassians in terms of official depictions of banditry and brigandage.[45]

With the establishment of a Young Turk dictatorship in 1913, Istanbul would enact a variety of imperial laws and statutes premised upon this perceived correlation between ethnic refugees and crime. In the wake of the Balkan wars, the CUP government instituted a new empire-wide policy related to migration and settlement. According to these new regulations, certain ethnicities, namely Albanians, Bosnians, and Laz, were categorically forbidden to settle in several key strategic zones (for example, the capital and its immediate surroundings). Rather than have them congregate in densely packed communities in the countryside or in town, Istanbul mandated that these and other ethnic refugees be scattered throughout Anatolia. Wherever they were settled, it was deemed crucial to the total number of the settled refugee community total no more than 10 percent of the local

[40] Anscombe, "Albanians."
[41] H.N. Brailsford, *Macedonia: Its Races and their Future* (London: Methuen & Co., 1906), 221.
[42] Vahakn N. Dadrian, *The History of the Armenian Genocide: Ethnic Conflict from the Balkans to the Caucasus* (Providence, RI: Berghahn Books, 1995), 106.
[43] Doğan Yurdakul, *Abi: Kabadayıler-Mafya Derin Devlet İlişkilsi* (Istanbul: Positif Yayınları, 2007), 22.
[44] Justin McCarthy, *Ölüm ve Sürgün: Osmanlı Müslümanlarına Karşı Yürülten Ulus Olarack Temizleme İşlemi* (Istanbul: İnkılap Kitapevi, 1998), 123–124.
[45] PRO/FO 371/4161/49194, 19 March 1919.

population.[46] In the case of Albanians, the Young Turk administration itemized a series of motives for such a drastic and ambitious policy. Among the reasons listed for the prohibitions placed upon Albanian refugees was the Albanian propensity for violence and banditry.[47]

The outbreak of world war in 1914 made the implementation of the CUP resettlement policy difficult, and at times impossible, to implement. In addition to the lack of resources and resistance on the part of migrants themselves, Russian armies advancing through eastern Anatolia created fresh waves of refugees and migrants.[48] Further losses on the battlefield, as well as the overall degenerative state of the Ottoman armies, further exacerbated the empire's refugee problem as hundreds of thousands of demobilized and deserting soldiers fled the frontlines.[49] All in all, the years between 1912 and 1923 can truly be considered an age of displacement. When the fighting finally ended with the establishment of the Republic of Turkey, virtually no corner of Anatolia was left untouched by the refugee crisis.

Banditry achieved a near pandemic state in the midst the refugee crisis of the First World War. In lamenting his empire's "blackest days," Hasan Basri Çantay contemplated the fact that Anatolia had achieved a state of lawlessness and violence rivaling that of the lost provinces of Macedonia.[50] Istanbul's absolute inability to police the countryside and enforce the law at war's end essentially left large swaths of the Anatolian hinterland in the hands of bandit chieftains. At the end of 1918, with no other means within the government's grasp, the sultan issued a decree pardoning all those alleged or imprisoned for taking part in bandit activity.[51] Naturally, the extension of the sultan's good graces did little to persuade past and current brigands to abide by the law. During those final years of Ottoman governance, whole towns and counties in Anatolia were transformed into bandit fiefdoms.[52]

The truly dismal state of law and order in Anatolia during the closing years of the empire's history is exemplified in the case of Istanbul and its immediate vicinity. From the outset of the First World War, the capital was already awash in homeless, impoverished refugees. As world war gave way to the Turkish War of Independence, the number of displaced persons living in Istanbul and its surrounding counties swelled into the hundreds of thousands. The influx of refugees did not end with the imposition of a British and French occupation of the city in 1920. Gendarmerie reports from the period make it clear that Ottoman efforts to police and control the movements of criminally suspect ethnic groups remained

46 Fuat Dündar, *İttihat ve Terakki'nin Müslümanları İskan Politikası (1913–1918)* (Istanbul: İlestişim Yayınları, 2001), 118.

47 Dündar, *İskan Politikası*, 113–14.

48 McCarthy, *Ölüm ve Sürgün: Osmanlı Müslümanlarına Karşı Yürülten Ulus Olarack Temizleme İşlemi*, 257–266.

49 Ahmed Emin Yalman, *Turkey in the World War* (New Haven, CT: Yale University Press), 259–263.

50 Çantay, *Kara Günler ve İbret Levhaları*, 45.

51 Zühtü Güven, *Anzavur İsyan: İstiklâl Savaşı Hatıralarından Acı Bir Safha* (Ankara: Türkiye Iş Bankası, 1965), 23.

52 Güven, *Anzavur İsyan: İstiklâl Savaşı Hatıralarından Acı Bir Safha*, 24–26.

fruitless. As late as 1922, the Interior Ministry mandated that all unemployed men of Laz descent be expelled from the confines of Istanbul. Citing the proliferation of marauding gangs on both sides of the Bosphorus, reporting officials declared that Laz, as well as Albanians, were using the capital as a place of refuge from war and conscription and therefore had to be remanded back to their points of origin.[53]

The declaration of the Republic of Turkey in 1923 did not lead to an official change in policy towards immigrants seen as having violent or criminal proclivities. Efforts to limit the ability of immigrants to congregate together in densely packed communities were reinitiated immediately following the conclusion of the War of Independence. Under the auspices of newly imposed immigration laws, Ankara officially banned Albanians from entering the country. North Caucasian groups, like Circassians, were permitted entry only after the written consent of the Interior Ministry.[54] Even though most Laz lived within Turkish territory as citizens, large numbers appear to have been forcibly relocated from the Black Sea territories to areas further west in the hopes, it appears, to wean them away from their "tribal" predilections.[55] In general, as the research of Söner Çagaptay clearly illustrates, Ankara imposed a variety of measures to monitor and police the movements and behavior of several immigrant and native minorities in Turkey.[56]

Several scholars have correctly cited such steps as manifestations of Ankara's unwavering commitment to nationalize and "Turkicize" Anatolia's diverse population. Indeed, Mustafa Kemal (Atatürk), as well as many of his supporters and retainers, argued with great vigor that it was essential to stamp out any variance in identity other than Turkish nationalism.[57] Yet, in considering the Ottoman roots of Kemalism, one could argue that Ankara's drive towards "Turkification" also served, at least in the minds of Turkish officials, a more practical purpose. Singling out Albanians, Circassians, and Laz (as well as, to different degrees, Kurds, Bosnians, Cypriots, Cretans, Arabs, Armenians, and Greeks) as suspect groups helped to ensure the physical security of the state. From the perspective of officials in the new capital, limiting or prohibiting Circassians or Albanians from freely migrating or settling in Turkey allowed the government both to maintain the façade of national unanimity as well as to stymie the criminal potential of such groups. The logic of Turkish nationalism dictated that once settled properly (that is in localities separate from large numbers of their ethnic kin) and closely monitored, so-called "non-Turks" would assimilate into the new cultural and political norms of the republic. They would simply become proper Turkish-speaking citizens who would not steal, kidnap, behave violently, or, worst of all, rebel.

[53] BOA.DH.KMS 62/23, 9 June 1922.

[54] Soner Çagaptay, "Crafting the Turkish Nation: Kemalism and Turkish Nationalism in the 1930s," (Ph.D. diss., Yale University, 2003), 190.

[55] "Nakledilen Aşiretler: Son Kafile Perşembeye Trabzon'dan Ayrılacak," *Cumhuriyet* 25 November 1931.

[56] Çagaptay, "Crafting the Turkish Nation: Kemalism and Turkish Nationalism in the 1930s," 220.

[57] Ayşe Afetinan, *Medeni Bilgiler ve M. K. Atatürk El Yazıları* (Ankara: Türk Tarih Kurumu, 1968), 23.

In the wake of Mustafa Kemal's rise to power, official organs of the Turkish government would eventually abandon even the use of minority terms or epithets (such as Laz, Albanian, or Kurd) with respect to the population.[58] Even with the postwar relaxation of some of the nationalist tendencies imposed by the Kemalist government, newspapers in the 1950s and 1960s rarely mentioned ethnic minorities (particularly among Muslims) in their day-to-day reporting. This was even the case with the reporting of crimes in such diverse metropoles as Istanbul, Izmir, or Ankara. From an official standpoint, Turkey was Turkish and nothing more.

Nevertheless, behind closed doors, Turkish officials in the post-Ottoman era continued to view crime in part through the prism of ethnicity. Although the nature of crimes and gangs would change, the ethnic character of the suspects remained somewhat consistent. As will become clear later on, men of Laz, Albanian, and Kurdish descent continued to be counted among Turkey's most notorious criminals.

PARAMILITARISM AND THE POLITICS OF OTTOMAN WARTIME SECURITY

It is abundantly clear that officials and officers in the service of the Ottoman Empire were greatly concerned with the threats posed by bandits lurking in the countryside. But for all of the steps taken by the imperial government to minimize the supposed root causes of brigandage, it is also clear that Muslim bandits were not viewed as the sole or perhaps most paramount threats to the absolute security and existence of the state. In the aftermath of the Balkan Wars, a conflict which resulted in the loss of the empire's principal territories in the Balkans, the danger of Christian separatism loomed far larger in the minds of the empire's principal leaders and policymakers.[59]

In the minds of many Young Turks, past terrorist acts committed by Armenian nationalist groups like the Dashnaktsutiun appeared to point to the possibility that similar conditions which led to the loss of the Balkans would occur in Anatolia in the future.[60] As Istanbul lurched towards the outbreak of world war in 1914, the CUP government reasoned that the prospect of future revolts among Anatolia's Christian populations (namely Armenians, Greeks, and Assyrians) could not be countered reflexively or passively. Aggressive, proactive steps had to be taken in order to stave off the kind of disaster that befell Ottoman Macedonia. Assuring the survival of the empire meant eradicating these potentially disloyal

[58] Erik Jan Zürcher, "Young Turks, Ottoman Muslims and Turkish Nationalists: Identity Politics 1908–1938," in Erik Jan Zürcher (ed.), *The Young Turk Legacy and Nation Building: From the Ottoman Empire to Atatürk's Turkey* (London: I.B. Tauris, 2010), 232.

[59] See George Gawrych, "The Culture of Violence in Turkish Society, 1903–1914," *Middle Eastern Studies* 22.3 (1986), 307–330.

[60] Dikran Kaligian, *Armenian Organization and Ideology Under Ottoman Rule, 1908–1914* (New Brunswick, NJ: Transaction Publishers, 2011).

segments of the Ottoman population before they took up arms.[61] In prosecuting such a bloody, and ostensibly illegal, stroke of action, elements of the CUP government recruited and utilized gangs and bandits as effective, but disposable, instruments of state violence.

As mentioned earlier, elements of the CUP state (that is, members found in both the military and the bureaucracy) came to see the use of Muslim gangs as an effective tactic in their war against Orthodox Christian separatists in Macedonia. Although bandits could be found within the ranks or at the head of gendarmerie outfits throughout the empire, the outright mobilization or appropriation of *çetecis* seems to have been an ad hoc strategy largely localized to the Ottoman Balkans before 1912. The outcome of the first Balkan war, however, seems to prompted a change in approach among some Young Turk strategists. In the wake of the Bulgarian occupation of Western Thrace, a cabal of CUP commanders, led by the hero of the Young Turk Revolution, Enver Pasha, drew together a small host of junior officers in a clandestine attempt to reassert Ottoman control over this strategically vital region. Dubbed the Special Organization (*Teşkilat-ı Mahsusa*), this paramilitary unit, it was hoped, would provide a vanguard for Muslim resistance to the Bulgarian occupation. Aside from a few engagements and scattered propaganda efforts, the Special Organization ultimately failed to preempt the loss of Western Thrace.[62]

Nevertheless, an important precedent was established with the creation of the Special Organization. Rather than a regional tactic meant to amplify local counterinsurgency efforts, the deployment of a unified body of paramilitaries would allow the central government to take the fight to provincial guerrillas and dissidents without involving regular elements of the Ottoman security establishment. Considering the seeming intractable nature of Armenian nationalist guerrillas in eastern Anatolia, or the prospect of an uprising among Anatolian Greeks in western Anatolia, individuals within the inner circle of the CUP reasoned that more drastic measures needed to be taken in order to safeguard the empire from partition. A clandestine paramilitary arm of the state operating outside the confines of the official chain of command allowed the Young Turk leadership leverage to realize such measures, if need be, without legal constraints.[63]

The Special Organization was not simply an expression of creative or desperate military planning. Rather, as one looks more closely at the organizational and interpersonal linkages of the CUP, the Special Organization reflected the socio-political nature of the Young Turks as a political party. Professional service and experience, be it fighting Christian *çetes* in Macedonia or attending the imperial military academy, generally formed close ties between supporters of the CUP. Through these

[61] Ronald Grigor Suny, *Looking Towards Ararat: Armenia in Modern History* (Bloomington: Indiana University Press, 1993), 113–114.

[62] Tevfik Bıyıklıoğlu, *Trakya'da Milli Müdadele* (Ankara: Türk Tarıh Kurumu, 1992), 84–86; Philip Hendrick Stoddard, "The Ottoman Government and the Arabs, 1911 to 1918: A Preliminary Study of the Teşkilat-ı Mahsusa," (Ph.D. diss., Princeton University, 1963), 52–54.

[63] See Feroz Ahmad, "War and Society under the Young Turks, 1908–1918," *Review* 11.2 (1988), 265–286.

experiences, each Young Turk, be they an officer, a bureaucrat, a merchant, or a journalist, shared a deep-seeded devotion to the Ottoman state.[64] Shared ethnic bonds, as well as personal and ideological ties, made the men who formed the CUP, and in the Special Organization in particular, an even more tightly knit unit. Officers and officials of Circassian descent (and to a lesser degree of Albanian descent) were found at various levels of the Special Organization.[65]

None of the sources related to the Special Organization gives us direct clues as to why Circassian migrants played such prominent roles in the Special Organization. However, in looking at memoirs and biographies from the period, the available evidence suggests that senior Circassian officers with close ties to the CUP functioned as recruiters for Circassians with experiences as bandits and *çetecis*. Some of the most noted, and notorious, members of the Special Organization, such as Çerkes Reşit and Mehmet Reşit, were personally connected with provincial gangs in Anatolia.[66] While one can assume that diasporic ties may have facilitated such relationships, internal correspondence is explicit in what purpose such bandits and *çetecis* were to serve once recruited into the Special Organization. Wartime telegrams and commands dictated to the provinces state clearly that Circassians, as well as criminals in general, were to be used in a paramilitary (*çetecilik*) capacity. While it appears that some of the Special Organization units would be used to raise rebellion among their ethnic kind in Russian territory, the documentary record also suggests that Circassian *çetecis* would be used behind Ottoman lines.[67]

An air of official secrecy helped to shield the bloody nature of the Special Organization's work. In addition to maintaining a clandestine budget and command structure headed by the Minister of War, Enver Pasha, the existence of the Special Organization was held in secret from the Ottoman parliament and public at large. It was only with the conclusion of the war, and the imposition of a foreign occupation, that crimes committed by the Special Organization came to light. Testimony heard at the Istanbul war crimes trials during the immediate aftermath of the war tells of Special Organization *çetecis* used to summarily kill Armenian civilians in such areas as Yozgat and Trabzon (sometimes, although not always, with the assistance of local gendarmes or volunteer auxiliaries).[68]

The course of events following the empire's capitulation to the Entente in 1918 prevents us from achieving a full understanding of how the CUP foresaw the future of the Special Organization, and the foot soldiers they employed. With the departure of the CUP principal leadership in late 1918, the Special Organization

[64] Erik Jan Zürcher, *The Young Turk Legacy and Nation Building: From the Ottoman Empire to Atatürk's Turkey* (London: I.B. Tauris, 2010), 95–109.

[65] Gingeras, *Sorrowful Shores*, 56–65.

[66] Gingeras, *Sorrowful Shores*, 78–79; Hans-Lukas Kieser, "Dr. Mehmed Reshid (1873–1919): A Political Doctor," in Hans-Lukas Kieser and Dominik J. Schaller (eds.), *Der Völkermord an den Armeniern und die Shoah/The Armenian Genocide and the Holocaust* (Zurich: Chronos, 2003), 245–280.

[67] Taner Akçam, *Armenien und der Völkermord: Die Istanbuler Prozesse und die türkische Nationalbewegung* (Hamburg: Hamburger Edition, 1996), 318–319.

[68] Akçam, *Armenien*, 167–364.

formally ceased to exist. Nevertheless, in anticipation of the arrival of foreign troops upon Ottoman lands, exiled CUP officials, together with officers left behind, did not completely dismiss or abandon the Organization's men or its administrative structure outright. In the months preceding the landing of Greek troops on the port of Izmir (an event which formally marked the beginning of the Turkish War of Independence), many officers and men previously affiliated with the Special Organization remained furtively in the field. In the absence of a regular imperial army (which had largely been demobilized at war's end), CUP officers and officials remaining in Anatolia reconstituted the Special Organization as the vanguard of the national resistance movement against foreign occupation. For the first two years of the conflict, *çetes* loyal to Mustafa Kemal Atatürk's National Forces comprised the backbone of armed fighters bent upon evicting the foreign expeditionary armies (as well as their supposed local Christian allies).[69]

The consolidation of power under Mustafa Kemal and his immediate followers would eventually lead to the abandonment of paramilitary activity and dissolution of the remaining CUP *çetes*. Following a 1921 decree stipulating the full integration of armed resistance forces under one unified, regular command, paramilitary activity of any kind became formally (but still not categorically) illegal. Those *çete* leaders who disobeyed this command were deemed rebels and traitors. Greece's defeat in the Turkish War of Independence would not only entail the mass departure of Orthodox Christians from Anatolia, but also the eviction of thousands of individuals (many of them Circassian veterans of the Special Organization) accused of banditry and rebellious behavior.[70]

At war's end, several of the most important officials who had been responsible for the construction of the Special Organization remained firmly rooted in the upper echelons of the young Turkish state. As Erik Jan Zürcher has shown, several of these individuals, such as Rauf Orbay, *Kara* Kemal and *Kara* Vasıf, were among a cohort of former high-ranking Special Organization operatives to organize against the Mustafa Kemal's nascent dictatorship. An attempt upon Mustafa Kemal's life in 1926 signaled the demise of these Special Organization operatives. Through a series of show trials targeting those who opposed or dissented from the rule of Mustafa Kemal and his Republican People's Party (RPP), many of the last major Special Organization figures were imprisoned, executed, or driven into exile.[71]

The 1926 show trials represent a foundational moment in the making of the Turkish Republic for a number of reasons. Mustafa Kemal's authority knew few bounds following the elimination of his chief rivals in 1926. Ataturk's RPP monopolized power for nearly quarter of a century after the Izmir trials and initiated an era of fiercely radical reform. Although a great many continuities may be found between the Kemalist period and the reign of the Young Turks, the Izmir show trials obliterated the CUP as a political party and as an autonomous element of the

[69] Gingeras, *Sorrowful Shores*, 68–80.

[70] Gingeras, *Sorrowful Shores*, 134–135.

[71] Erik Jan Zürcher, *The Unionist Factor: The Role of the Committee of Union and Progress in the Turkish Nationalist Movement, 1905–1926* (Leiden: Brill, 1984), 142–156.

post-Ottoman elite. "Resurrecting Unionism" became a crime unto itself (a charge levied against many during the subsequent show trials). Following Mustafa Kemal's vilification of the CUP in his famous thirty-six-hour speech before a congress of RPP members in 1927, the official narrative of the Turkish Republic formally dismissed the CUP as one of many discarded vestiges of Turkey's imperial past.

The CUP's inglorious downfall in 1926 concomitantly marks a critical juncture in the relationship between the state, paramilitarism, and clandestine activities. In looking at the names of those condemned following the Izmir plot, it is clear that the show trials simultaneously eliminated the CUP as both a party and a paramilitary organization. The fact that so many of those accused of "resurrecting Unionism" were prominent figures within the Special Organization was no coincidence. Considering the events that led to the emergence of Mustafa Kemal and the establishment of the Republic of Turkey, there is no question that the Special Organization militated the return of so many CUP officers and officials to power. Integrating the *çete* formations into the regular army of the National Forces was only one step in defanging Mustafa Kemal's political opponents. The show trials of 1926 saw to it that the clique of individuals who formed and maintained this clandestine array of armed bands would equally meet its end.

It must be noted that the destruction of the Special Organization, and the elimination of its principal leaders, was not a consequence of any aversion to paramilitarism as a political or military tactic. Mustafa Kemal himself employed one of the most notorious *çetecis* of the wartime era, *Topal* Osman, as his personal bodyguard during the closing days of the Turkish War of Independence.[72] Nevertheless, what is clear is that the RPP leadership no longer permited the formation of a clandestine organization within the government exclusive of Mustafa Kemal's control. One year following the Izmir trials a modest clandestine service entitled the National Security Service (*Milli Emniyet Hizmeti*) came into existence. The first commander of Turkey's first spy agency, Şükrü Ali Ögel, did serve as a junior officer in the First World War and the Turkish War of Independence, but possessed no apparent experience in clandestine operations.[73] More importantly, according to official accounts, the National Security Service did not appear to revive the use of paramilitaries as a core practice.

The purging of remnants of the CUP and Special Organization from the Turkish state also suggests a fundamental shift in the nature of governance and statecraft in the aftermath of the Ottoman Empire. Mustafa Kemal's ascendancy and the establishment of a one-party state represents a crucial sea change in the nature of governmental authority and security in Anatolia. The near complete eradication of Armenian and native Greek society, coupled with the suppression of Kurdish resistance, greatly reduced the possibility of partition or sedition along ethnic lines in Anatolia. Atatürk's commitment to neutrality and his rejection of territorial

[72] Dadrian, *The History of the Armenian Genocide: Ethnic Conflict from the Balkans to the Caucasus*, 369–370.

[73] <http://www.mit.gov.tr/tarihce/ikinci_bolum_G1.html#ogel> (accessed 16 March 2012); Tuncay Özkan, *MİT'in Gizli Tarihi* (Istanbul: Afla, 2003), 162–163.

expansion into lost Ottoman lands would help ensure Turkey's safety from foreign invasion well into the Second World War.

The creation of a more confident and tenable Turkey under a more regularized and unitary system of government tells us much about the insecure and byzantine nature of the Young Turk state. One could pose that a "deep state" existed at the end of the Ottoman Empire in part due to the profound anxieties felt by members of the CUP. As a party that emerged secretly for fear of state suppression, the CUP continued to maintain its furtive roots after the revolution of 1908 out of fear of losing power. Much of the party's activities and deliberations were kept secret because of distrust for the public at large. With the commencement of what they saw as a life and death struggle in 1914, the CUP opted to utilize clandestine, brutal, and extralegal means in the hopes of eliminating all potential threats to the empire's survival.

The Special Organization is critical in understanding both the paranoia of the Young Turks' state and the role played by criminal bands in maintaining that state. The Special Organization served an important purpose in bringing together various parties interested in or committed to the empire's preservation. It provided an added tool, beyond the CUP itself, for forging alliances between elements of state and society. Its clandestine nature allowed for military officers, bureaucrats, landowners, intellectuals, and paramilitary leaders to meet and function in unison without official or public oversight. *Çetes* provided the muscle to do this cabal's dirty work. As proven in Macedonia (and to a far lesser degree Thrace), paramilitary gangs, it was hoped, could succeed in crushing centers of opposition in areas where elements of the regular administration and military had previously failed. Once the raw, bloody work was done, *çetecis*, it seems, could just as easily be disbanded or disowned.

In historical terms, the Special Organization serves an important precedent in the making of modern Turkey. While it is not clear if the Turkish bureaucracy or military continued to retain any specific institutional memory of the Special Organization, many of the conditions that prompted the CUP state to form a secret paramilitary arm can be found in Turkey during the latter decades of the twentieth century. It is during this time that the tactical practice of recruiting and arming criminals and gangs reemerges with a vengeance.

SMUGGLERS, NEIGHBORHOOD TOUGHS, AND OTHER FOUNDATIONAL ELEMENTS OF TURKISH ORGANIZED CRIME

Banditry and paramilitarism were not the sole forms of organized criminal activity in the late Ottoman Empire. In considering the roots of modern day organized crime in Turkey, one must recognize the history and impact of two other criminal occupations. Aside from bandits and *çetecis*, smugglers were among the most pervasive and problematic lawbreakers found in the late Ottoman state. The evolution of the smuggling economy in the Ottoman Empire during the nineteenth and early twentieth centuries reflects two critical trends essential to understanding both the making of modern Turkey and the origins of Turkish organized crime. Like banditry, Ottoman smugglers posed a direct challenge to the creation of a reformed, modern state. Moreover, debates surrounding the prevalence of smuggling in the Ottoman Empire reflected both the Ottoman Empire's place within the making of the world economy in the nineteenth century and, more pointedly, the growing influence of European capital and trade throughout the Ottoman lands.

Like the bandit, the smuggler plagued the earliest manifestation of the Ottoman state. Even though Ottoman economic policies remained relatively fluid through much of the early modern era, Istanbul's attempts at regulating and monitoring taxable trade posed a difficult challenge.[74] As the empire entered the nineteenth century, and the first reforms of the *Tanzimat* era were implemented, maintaining tight control over the flow of goods in and out of the Ottoman Empire achieved new significance. Istanbul's insatiable demand for tax revenue (revenue to be used to finance the expansion of state services and institutions) forced officials to rely more heavily upon the collection of import and export duties. However, customs officers could not regulate the legal and illegal flow of goods out of the empire alone. Borders, previously unmarked and uncontrolled, needed to be clearly delineated and monitored.[75] The movement of peoples, both within and across borders, also had to be limited and regularized. Like the fight against banditry, government efforts towards "fixing" or settling peoples and borders particularly affected nomads, immigrants, and refugees.[76]

A myriad of economic and political obstacles helped to thwart or constrain the implementation of countermeasures against smuggling. The chief factor in limiting the Ottoman Empire's ability to combat smuggling, as well as its ability to profit from tighter protectionist regulations, was the expanding role of European diplomats, merchants, and bankers in the imperial economy. Although European actors had long traded with Ottoman merchants, events and trends in the nineteenth century would tip the balance of power in Ottoman and European relations westward. As the empire shrank and greater sums of money were required to fund both wars on the frontiers and reforms on the home front, the Ottoman Empire increasingly looked to European lenders for financial assistance. Age-old trade regulations (called the capitulations, or *ahidname*) that awarded lower tariffs and extraterritorial privileges to the empire's closest trading partners increasingly worked against the interests of the Ottoman state. With the passage of the eighteenth century, European traders and investors took great advantage of past capitulation agreements (which were consummated at a time when the Ottoman

74 Halil Inalcik and Donald Quataert, *Economic and Social History of the Ottoman Empire, Volume I* (Cambridge: Cambridge University Press, 1997), 199–202.

75 Isa Blumi, "Contesting the Edges of the Ottoman Empire: Rethinking Ethnic and Sectarian Boundaries in the Malësore, 1878–1912," *International Journal of Middle East Studies* 35.2 (May 2003), 237–256.

76 Kasaba, *A Moveable Empire*, 84–122.

Empire was in a far more stable and prosperous state) to dominate large portions of the empire's domestic consumer market and foreign trade.[77] Istanbul's ability to resist the increasingly invasive nature of European capital was greatly offset by the empire's weak military and diplomatic standing. To make matters worse still, the ability of European merchants, diplomats, and missionaries to employ Ottoman citizens (and thereby extend the same privileges granted to foreign nationals) opened up large rifts in the communal and economic fabric of Ottoman society.[78] By the end of the nineteenth century, the imperial budget itself fell into foreign hands with the creation of the Ottoman Public Debt Administration.

It is against this backdrop that various components of both the state and society confronted the phenomenon of smuggling. Isa Blumi's study of Albania and Yemen demonstrates, for example, the degree to which imperial attempts to limit smuggling were only one facet of the overall project of building modern (and invasive) state institutions on the Ottoman periphery. Demarcating the imperial border in the Albanian highlands and building roads in the southern Arabian peninsula served not only to regularize the movement of people and goods within and across the empire's borders but, more importantly, helped to establish greater state control over regions and peoples previously unexposed to regular governmental control. An ever-expanding regime of taxation and juridical control ignited popular indignation and resistance in these two desperate corners of the empire. Local producers and merchants in both Albania and Yemen labored to circumvent imperial and foreign restrictions on a variety of trades (including weapons, slaves, salt, and tobacco). Provincial smuggling networks, which often operated under the patronage of petty officials, at times proved to be so successful and lucrative that both Ottoman and European agents were compelled to abet elements of the contraband trade in an effort to maintain a semblance of order and regularity.[79]

Perhaps the greatest, and most universal, example of smuggling found in the Ottoman Empire at the turn of the twentieth century was the tobacco trade. Tobacco cultivation spanned large portions of the empire's holdings in the Balkans, Anatolia, and Arab lands. Increased consumer demand for tobacco both inside and outside of the empire during the course of the nineteenth century prompted both Ottoman and European officials to take greater interest in monopolizing the trade. Following the imposition of the Ottoman Public Debt Administration, European pressure in 1884 compelled Istanbul to form the Tabac Régie, an imperial company designed to monopolize the production, sale, and transport of tobacco products inside of the Ottoman Empire. The imposition of the Régie, which channeled all proceeds into the financing of the empire's debts, imposed the greatest of burdens upon tobacco cultivators throughout the empire. Not only would the monopoly

[77] Edhem Eldem, "Capitulations and Western Trade," in Suraiya Faroqhi (ed.), *The Cambridge History of Turkey: Volume 3, The Later Ottoman Empire, 1603–1839* (Cambridge: Cambridge University Press, 2006), 283–325.

[78] Fatma Müge Göçek, *Rise of Bourgeoisie, Demise of Empire: Ottoman Westernization and Social Change* (New York: Oxford University Press, 1996).

[79] Isa Blumi, "Illicit Trade and the Emergence of Albania and Yemen," in I. William Zartman (ed.), *Understanding Life in the Borderlands* (Atlanta: Georgia State Press, 2010), 58–84.

entail restrictions upon who could plant and where and how much tobacco could be grown, it would also necessitate the placing of price controls upon the selling of the product when brought to market. While some farmers, fearing higher taxes and lower earnings, simply abandoned the tobacco trade altogether, a great many more planted and sold tobacco illegally. Smuggling tobacco became nearly universal in the Ottoman Empire by the end of the twentieth century. Much to the chagrin of European investors, Ottoman officials at various levels of government proved themselves to be both incapable and, at times, unwilling to put an end to smuggling activities.[80]

No single ethnic group or region in the Ottoman Empire dominated the smuggling trade or the black market. The proceeds from smuggling lined the pockets of a variety of groups, ranging from semi-nomadic Zeybek Turkmen in Anatolia's Aegean highlands to Armenian militants active along the empire's border with Iran.[81] Despite the widespread nature of the practice, smugglers did occasionally incur the wrath of the Ottoman state. It is estimated, for example that over 2,000 people died every year in clashes between tobacco smugglers and security forces during the fourteen years following the Régie's establishment.[82]

The long transition between the Young Turk and post-Young Turk era produced a massive change in the economic policy towards the shrinking territories of the empire. Under the auspices of creating a "national economy," CUP officials endeavored to create an economic climate that favored native, particularly Muslim, industrialists, traders, and entrepreneurs throughout Anatolia. This change in state policy was in part conceived as a means of thwarting the invasive presence of Europeans in the empire (as demonstrated by the abrogation of the capitulations in September 1914).[83] The main thrust of the CUP's nationalist policies focused upon reversing the economic fortunes of Ottoman Christians (whom the Young Turks uniformly painted as collaborators with European imperialists and native separatists). With the mass deportations of both native Greeks and Armenians from their homes during the course of the First World War, for example, imperial officials auctioned off vast tracks of abandon land (as well as homes and industrial equipment) to local Muslims.[84] The nationalization and consolidation of the Anatolian economy continued after the onset of Kemalist rule. In addition to initiating a policy of import substitution as a means of fostering native industrial

[80] William H. Hall, *Reconstruction in Turkey* (New York: American Committee of Armenian and Syrian Relief, 1918), 226; Reşat Kasaba, "Migrants, Refugees and Smugglers: The Impact on Border-Crossers," *Turkish Studies Association Bulletin* 17 (1993), 88–91; Donald Quataert, "Ottoman Resistance to European Economic Penetration: Tobacco Smugglers, the Regie and the Ottoman Government," *Turkish Studies Association Bulletin* 7.1 (1983), 25–27.

[81] Halil İnalcık, "The Yürüks: Their Origins, Expansion and Economic Role," *The Middle East and the Balkans under the Ottoman Empire: Essays on Economy and Society* (Bloomington: Indiana University Press, 1993), 97–136.

[82] Necia Geyikdağı, *Foreign Investment in the Ottoman Empire* (London: I.B. Tauris, 2011), 130.

[83] Turgay Akkuş, "Bir İktisadi Siyasa Projesi: Milli İktisat ve Bursa," *Çağdaş Türkiye Tarihi Araştırmaları Dergisi* 8.16–17 (2008), 103–141.

[84] Bedross Der Matossian, "The Taboo within the Taboo: The Fate of 'Armenian Capital' at the End of the Ottoman Empire," *European Journal of Turkish Studies* (2011).

development, Ankara abolished the old Tabac Régie in favor of a new national (and exclusively Turkish) monopoly over tobacco cultivation in Anatolia.[85]

Ankara's renewed commitment to economic nationalism did little to mitigate the prevalence of smuggling in what remained of the old Ottoman territories of Anatolia. Many of the old staples of the Ottoman smuggling trade, such as tobacco, guns, nuts, salt, and, as we will see, opium, remained sought after black market commodities. Contextually, however, smuggling in the post-Ottoman era diverged from its imperial roots in one critical respect. The dissolution of the empire into the respective states of the contemporary Middle East created new, more truncated borders for security personnel to police. While this new reality certainly liberated Turkish officials from the previously impossible task of monitoring the flow of goods and people over the vast expanse of the old empire, it did not eliminate the long-established trade networks that crisscrossed Anatolia's new national frontiers.[86] Buyers, sellers, and transporters in Turkey continued to foster and maintain ties with their counterparts residing on the other side of the Greek, Bulgarian, Syrian, Iraqi, and Iranian border. The fact that many of these clandestine trading networks comprised individuals belonging to the same ethnic and filial kin (such as Kurds and Arabs) made the task of penetrating and apprehending smuggling rings that much more difficult for Turkish officers and officials. Above all, in the minds of Turkish officials in Ankara, the general correlation between the state's principal minorities and the scourge of smuggling underscored the notion that law enforcement on the border could not be separated from the grander, and still ongoing, undertaking of consolidating state control over Anatolia's diverse population. For this reason, as we shall see, smuggling in the post-Ottoman era took on increasingly "ethnic" dimensions. In addition to viewing the activities of Kurdish smugglers as evidence of sedition in eastern Anatolia, Turkish security officials would come to paint contraband traders as primarily a "minority" trait.

There is one final pattern of criminal behavior that transcends the late Ottoman and early Republican era that is critical to the future evolution of organized crime in Turkey. This last trend emerges out of the still relatively obscure history of urban crime in the Ottoman Empire. Recent scholarship from the early modern period suggests that criminals plied a wide variety of schemes and trades in Ottoman Istanbul. The expected array of "usual suspects" populated Istanbul's underworld: pimps, prostitutes, pickpockets, burglars, brawlers, thieves, and cutthroats are characters that one can easily find during various periods of history in the city. Aside from these examples of criminal behavior, residential neighborhoods within the capital, at least by the nineteenth century, often came under the control of local strongmen, or *kabadayı*.

[85] Ebru Kayaalp, "From Seed to Smoke: The Re-Making of the Tobacco Market in Turkey," (Ph.D. diss., Rice University, 2009), 227.

[86] Cyrus Schayegh, "The Many Worlds of 'Abud Yasin; or, What Narcotics Trafficking in the Interwar Middle East Can Tell Us about Territorialization," *American Historical Review* 116.2 (April 2011), 273–306.

Kabadayı culture, according to Roger Deal, was in large measure a remnant of the janissary corps.[87] Before the dissolution of this elite class of Ottoman soldier in 1826, janissaries residing in the capital (as well as in the provinces) equally established themselves as constables, local despots, and bandits. While the Beneficent Event of 1826 may have formerly eliminated the janissaries as a *de facto* military force, Deal poses that the parochial violence and patriarchal authority long associated with janissaries did not vanish. *Kabadayıs*, like janissaries before them, were known for their fighting ability and their casual willingness to resort to violence in disputes.[88]

Violence was intrinsic to a *kabadayı*'s behavior and his livelihood. His reputation was made through fights with other strongmen of his caliber. The act of fighting ultimately served two purposes in the making of a neighborhood *kabadayı*. As a man of violence, a *kabadayı* was fundamentally an extortionist. A young man seeking to make his reputation as a local tough often used his muscle to shakedown shops and weddings. A *kabadayı* also solidified his reputation as a man of "respect" and "honor" through besting other *kabadayıs* and bringing order to a neighborhood. His position within an Istanbul neighborhood could become further rooted, and perhaps valued, through his ownership of, or mere presence at, a local café, restaurant, or bar. His greatest service to a community was a *kabadayı*'s ability to mediate problems (often termed *racon*) between local residents and even other neighborhood strongmen.[89]

No single ethnicity, or social class, was associated with *kabadayı* culture. Through his analysis of the Istanbul press from the late nineteenth century, Roger Deal asserts that *kabadayıs* could equally be Muslims, Christians, or Jews. Poor and elite individuals and communities fell under the influence of neighborhood *kabadayıs*. Nevertheless, like the phenomenon of banditry in the provinces, Deal notes that Laz and Albanians were strongly associated with *kabadayı* culture.[90] Bandits and *kabadayı* also shared a similarly ambivalent relationship with the local administration of the capital. A neighborhood *kabadayı* assisted in the policing of his district by keeping other rough men (like himself) in line.[91] Deal also argues that *kabadayı* culture may have existed to various degrees in towns and cities throughout the Ottoman Empire (including in the Balkans and the Arab lands).[92]

The historical significance of *kabadayı* culture and its relationship to more contemporary figures found in Turkey's underworld seems to possess more symbolic

[87] *Kabadayı* culture also is rooted in other urban subcultures in Istanbul. Men characterized as *külhanbeys* (individuals who slept and worked in bathhouses) as well as local firefighters (*tulumbacıs*) also were associated with urban gang behavior and petty crimes. See Roger Deal, "The Kabadayis of Istanbul," (Masters Thesis, University of Utah, 2000), 9–15; Mehmet Demirtaş, "XVIII Yüzyılda Osmanlıda Bir Zümrenin Alt-Kültür Grubuna Dönüşmesi: Külhanbeyleri," OTAM 19-20 (January 2006), 113–141.

[88] Deal, "Kabadayis of Istanbul," 44–50.

[89] Deal, "Kabadayis of Istanbul," 15–32.

[90] Deal, "Kabadayis of Istanbul," 28–29.

[91] Deal, "Kabadayis of Istanbul," 40.

[92] Deal, "Kabadayis of Istanbul," 47–48.

than actual value. *Kabadayıs* in nineteenth-century Istanbul at times did belong to a gang or pursue a collective criminal enterprise. However, Deal and Tanilli pose that *kabadayı* gangs, as well as most independent *kabadayıs*, disappeared for a time in the aftermath of the Young Turk Revolution (particularly after the passage of laws targeting "vagrants (*serseri*)" in 1909).[93] As the twentieth century progressed, men associated with organized crime in Istanbul staked a claim to the traditions, virility, and popular stature of the *kabadayı*. Dündar Kılıç, for example, took exception to being called a member of the "mafia." Despite being one of the most notorious figures in the Istanbul underworld during the second half of the twentieth century, Kılıç claimed he, like the *kabadayı* of old, was a "humanist" and a man of the people. The mafia, he added, were rough sorts and cared nothing for the common man.[94]

THE IMPERIAL ROOTS OF TURKISH ORGANIZED CRIME IN A GLOBAL CONTEXT

With the death of Mustafa Kemal Ataturk in 1938, no one in the Republic of Turkey spoke of organized crime as a singular phenomenon that typified or dominated any criminal trade in the country. The term organized crime itself did not become a part of the Turkish lexicon until decades after the passing of Turkey's founder and first president. Nevertheless, many of the criminal enterprises cited in this chapter endured during and after the end of the Kemalist period. *Kabadayıs* of various stripes continued to assert control over many Istanbul neighborhoods. Smugglers and black marketeers remained a fixture of different ports and crossing points throughout Anatolia. Even under the iron fist of the Republican Peoples' Party, banditry still manifested itself in the Turkish countryside (although, from an official standpoint, *eşkıya* activity was most often associated with rural Kurds).

No single subculture emerges out of the wreckage of the Ottoman Empire that would provide the principal framework or basis for the criminal syndicates in the republican era. In looking at the imperial past, this chapter has attempted to expand upon key criminal enterprises that would influence, to one degree or another, the establishment, and outside perceptions, of more contemporary Turkish organized crime outfits. Any reading of the history of crime in the Ottoman Empire, and the implication this history would have upon the development of Turkey, cannot be separated from modern state-building efforts in Anatolia and elsewhere. The evolution of organized criminal enterprises have long been contingent upon the ways in which state actors understood, discussed, and interacted with the criminals themselves.

By no means is the Ottoman/early Republican experience with organized crime unique. In thinking about the broader imperial roots of Turkish organized crime,

[93] Deal, "Kabadayis of Istanbul," 33–43; Sever Tanilli, "Geçen Yüzyılda İstanbul'de Kabadayılar ve Külhanbeyleri," in François Georgeon and Paul Dumont (eds.), *Osmanlı İmparatorluğunda Yaşamak* (Istanbul: İletişim, 2003), 145.

[94] Yurdakul, *Abi: Kabadayıler-Mafya Derin Devlet İlişkilsi*, 36.

the cases and patterns of criminal behavior cited earlier affirm more general trends seen in the making of modern day organized crime the world over. Existing scholarship from a variety of contexts points to similar social, political, and economic factors in the ways in which gangs of criminals are formed and the way they operate. Moreover, the story of how the late Ottoman and early Republican statesmen approached issues like smuggling, banditry, and urban crime is indicative of broader challenges and patterns of development among states and state institutions throughout the world in the nineteenth and early twentieth centuries. In other words, in seeking the origins of modern day organized crime in Turkey and elsewhere, one must specifically lend a critical eye to still prevailing forms of state governance.

Nineteenth-century patterns of state centralization lay at the foundation of contemporary perceptions of organized crime. The need for states to consolidate unitary control over its core territories and establish stable, predictable, and efficient levers of governance in both town and country placed supreme emphasis upon eliminating parochial resistance. Banditry, a phenomenon long associated with wayward or peripheral regions of states, represented a prime example of the sort of tests modernizing states were forced to confront. Regions like Sicily or Corsica, which the Italian and French states respectively laid claim to in 1860 and 1769 respectively, were synonymous with banditry even as late as the early twentieth century. The attention that both Rome and Paris dedicated to rooting out rural brigandage on these two islands was not only indicative of the prevalence of the lawlessness to be found in these relatively new territories. Rather, from the perspective of elites residing in both of these capitals, the sheer act of bringing order to these otherwise "backward" islands exemplified the unquestionable authority and uncompromising civility of the Italian and French states.[95]

American and Mexican attempts to subdue and consolidate their respective frontiers offer further points of comparison to the Ottoman experience in dealing with banditry. Life in the American west and the Mexican north during the nineteenth century shared much in common with different portions of the Ottoman Empire in the decades preceding the *Tanzimat* reforms: varying degrees of autonomy exercised by local elites, a high prevalence of violence and brigandage outside of urban centers, and fluctuating degrees of local resistance to centralized governance. At the turn of the nineteenth century, American and Mexican officials labeled all forms of armed activity on its frontiers "banditry" regardless of whether it was rooted in political resistance or not. Geronimo, Jesse James, Malverde (if he ever existed), Pancho Villa, and other provincial rebels were no less than thieves and bandits according to government accounts.[96]

[95] Steven Hughes, "Brigands, Mafiosi and Others: Italy," in Clime Emsley and Louis A. Knafla (eds.), *Crime History and Histories of Crime* (Westport, CT: Greenwood Press, 1996), 139–159; Alison Jamieson, "Mafia and Political Power 1943–1989," *International Relations* 10.13 (1990), 13–30; Jack Reece, "Fascism, the Mafia and the Emergence of Sicilian Separatism, 1919–1943," *The Journal of Modern History* 45.2 (June 1973), 261–276; Stephen Wilson, "Banditry in Corsica: The Eighteenth to Twentieth Centuries," in Cyrille Fijnaut and Letizia Paoli (eds.), *Organised Crime in Europe* (Dordrecht, The Netherlands: Springer, 2004), 151–180.

[96] James Creechan and Jorge de la Herran Garcia, "Without God or Law: Narcoculture and Belief in Jesus Malverde," *Religious Studies and Theology* 24.2 (2005), 5–57; Richard White, "Outlaw Gangs

However, in the Mexico case (and others as well), we see patterns of state–bandit cooperation that are striking similar to the trends seen in the late Ottoman Empire. As a state frequently racked by instability in the capital and foreign invasion, Mexico habitually struggled to sustain unified control over its constituent territories (most notably those in the rugged, remote north). In keeping with colonial practices, Mexico City regularly relied upon local political bosses (*caciques*) to supervise provincial affairs in the nineteenth century. In the absence of a professional and independent bureaucracy, day-to-day law enforcement outside of the capital often fell to bandits or former bandits employed by local benefactors. Ana Maria Alonzo specifically documents this process in her study of nineteenth-century Chihuahua (maintaining that the Mexican Revolution of 1910, at least in this portion of northern Mexico, was born out of local rage towards the suppression of the state's unique culture of militancy and vigilantism).[97]

China experienced similar trends during eras of profound crisis. Following the collapse of the Qing state and the establishment of a republic under Sun Yat Tsen, vast swaths of Chinese territory fell under the sway of local warlords (many of whom were common bandits before ascending to such political heights).[98] As mentioned in the introduction, several scholars have highlighted the fascinating case of interwar Shanghai, where Chiang Kai-shek's Nationalist government closely coordinated with the region's most powerful criminal syndicate, the Green Gang, in maintaining control over vital sectors of the city. Yet, with Mao Tse-tung's victory in 1949, a strong Chinese state eventually rebounded and took great pains to eliminate (at least overt) demonstrations of bandit/rebel/criminal authority in the Chinese countryside.[99] Post-revolutionary Mexico, unlike Communist China, has experienced only limited success in eradicating the influence of violent criminal syndicates in local political life. Both Luis Astorga and James Sandos have utilized the example of Esteban Cantú Jiménez, the post-revolutionary governor of Baja Califonria Norte, as a formative case where legitimate members of the local political establishment collaborated with drug smugglers and thugs (from both the American and Mexican sides of the border) in order to maintain a semblance of law and order and enrich themselves at the expense of state authority.[100]

Where the late Ottoman Empire perhaps differs most from states during this period of time was in its policy of recruiting armed bands of criminals and bandits for

of the Middle Border: American Social Bandits," *The Western Historical Quarterly* 12.4 (October 1981), 387–408.

97 Alonso, *Thread of Blood: Colonialism, Revolution, and Gender on Mexico's Northern Frontier*, 15–50; Chris Fraser, *Bandit Nation: A History of Outlaws and Cultural Struggle in Mexico, 1810–1920* (Lincoln: University of Nebraska Press, 2006), 20–57; Paul Vanderwood, *Disorder and Progress: Bandits, Police, and Mexican Development* (Wilmington, DE: A Scholarly Resources Inc., 1992), 5–13.

98 Billingsley, "Bandits, Bosses, and Bare Sticks," 235–288.

99 He Bingsong, "Organized Crime: A Perspective from China," in Jay Albanese et al. (eds.), *Organized Crime: World Perspectives* (Upper Saddle River, NJ: Prentice Hall, 2003), 279–297.

100 Astorga, "Organized Crime," 62–65; Nicole Mottier, "Drug Gangs and Politics in Ciudad Juarez: 1928–1936," *Mexican Studies* 25.1 (Winter 2009), 19–46; Sandos, "Northern Separatism during the Mexican Revolution: An Inquiry into the Role of Drug Trafficking, 1910–1920," 191–214.

clandestine service. While the employment of local militias made up of runaways, tribes, and rebels is a phenomenon steeped in history worldwide (the Cossacks and other border units in such places as China and the Habsburg Empire being among the most well-known examples), it is difficult to find an analogous unit similar to that of the Ottoman Special Organization.[101] Nevertheless, the utilization of individuals with violent pedigrees for the purposes of clandestine, extrajudicial actions (such as assassinations and mass murder operations) can be found in a number of locales after the First World War. John Paul Newman, Julia Eichenburg, and Robert Gerwarth do point to some similar patterns of paramilitary mobilization among marginalized (although not necessarily criminally inclined or experienced) individuals in central Europe in the aftermath of the Great War.[102]

Another strong basis of comparison between the Ottoman Empire and other states during the late nineteenth and early twentieth centuries is in respect to the ways in which patterns of migration and notions of ethnicity influenced perceptions of organized criminal behavior. Mass migration was an integral aspect of world history during the long nineteenth century. Refugees and fortune seekers flooded virtually every continent during this age. Moreover, in a period that witnessed rapid changes in modes and means of production, empires and states great and small contended with the massive movement of their own citizens (a phenomenon that most often entailed the mass migration of rural migrants to expanding urban centers). The arrival of newcomers to the city or to foreign shores tended to greatly upset the established socio-economic order and the political status quo of towns, states, or regions. Crime in the nineteenth century city tended to be universally synonymous with resident aliens. Local officials in major American cities categorically associated Sicilians, Mexicans, Irishmen, Jews, African Americans, and Chicanos with criminal behavior. Chinese and Russian authorities perceived similar links between newly arriving peasants and crime. One also cannot forget the ways in which certain imperial states, such as the British Raj and Russia, scripted certain native groups as inherently "warlike" peoples prone towards crime (such as Chechens and the *thugs* of central India).[103] Italian criminologist Cesare Lombroso gave further credence to popular and elite perceptions of criminality,

[101] Perhaps the best study of the inclusion of particularly ethnically based militias and units is Wayne Lee (ed.), *Empires and Indigenes: Intercultural Alliance, Imperial Expansion and Warfare in the Early Modern World* (New York: NYU Press, 2011).

[102] Julia Eichenberg, "The Dark Side of Independence: Paramilitary Violence in Ireland and Poland after the First World War," *Journal of Contemporary European History* 19.3 (2010), 231–248; Robert Gerwarth and John Horne, "The Great War and Paramilitarism, 1917–1923," *Journal of Contemporary European History* 19.3 (2010), 267–273; John Paul Newman, "Post-Imperial and Post-war Violence in the South Slav Lands, 1917–1923," *Journal of Contemporary European History* 19.3 (2010), 249–265.

[103] Robert Anthony, "Demons, Gangsters and Secret Societies in Early Modern China," *East Asian History* 27 (June 2004), 71–98; Mark Galeotti, "Brotherhoods and Associates: Chechen Networks of Crime and Resistance," *Networks, Terrorism and Global Insurgency* 1 (2005), 171–182; Peter Holquist "To Count, to Extract, and to Exterminate: Population Statistics and Population Politics in Late Imperial and Soviet Russia," in Ronald Grigor Suny and Terry Martin (eds.), *A State of Nations: Empire and Nation Making in the Age of Lenin and Stalin* (New York: Oxford University Press, 2001), 111–144; Kim A. Wagner, "The Deconstructed Stranglers: A Reassessment of Thuggee," *Modern Asian Studies* 38.4 (2004), 931–963.

ethnicity, and class through his study of the association between criminality and human anatomy.[104] While contemporary scholarship does not deny the prevalence of criminal behavior among politically and economically marginalized groups (particularly migrants), it is clear nineteenth-century criminal anthropologists were incorrect in seeing violence and law-breaking as somehow racially or ethnically inborn or genetic. Rather than expressions of an absolute reality, contemporary scholars posit that such rationalizations reflect the socio-political apprehensions of nineteenth-century elites and the emergence of modern scientific methods of law enforcement and criminal prevention.[105]

Ottoman and early republican officials did reserve specific attention for certain ethnicities and migrants (namely Albanians, Laz, Circassians, and Kurds) when discussing or reporting criminal activity. However, it must be kept in mind that unlike the United States or other industrialized states, the total preponderance of organized criminal behavior in the Ottoman Empire occurred outside of urban centers (be it banditry or smuggling). Turkey's largest city, Istanbul, numbered no more than a million and a half residents as late as the 1920s (a population which far outpaced any other urban center in the young Turkish Republic).[106] Cities of comparable political and economic significance, such as London, St. Petersburg, or Paris, were considerably bigger in the postwar years. This disparity in urban growth fed into important differences in the ways in which the Ottoman and Turkish states approached the issue of ethnicity and crime. While elites in the United States, Great Britain, and the Soviet Union tended to place heavier emphasis upon the threats of street gangs and other forms of urban crime, the Ottoman and Turkish officials continued to view "ethnic" crime as an essentially rural phenomenon. Nevertheless, Ottoman and Turkish elites made an important distinction between the ethnicities most often deemed inclined towards crime. Muslim groups, like Albanians, Laz, and Kurds, did pose a threat to law and order. But, under the right conditions (such as through forced settlement and population distribution), the criminal tendencies of certain Muslim groups could be mitigated. Christian groups such as Greeks and Armenians, while not necessarily predisposed to pedestrian crimes, represented an existential danger to the state as potential sources of separatism and collaboration with foreign enemies. Therefore,

[104] Peter D'Agostino, "Craniums, Criminals, and the 'Cursed Race': Italian Anthropology in American Racial Thought, 1861–1924," *Comparative Studies in Society and History* 44.2 (April 2002), 319–343.

[105] Malcolm Gaskill, "The Displacement of Providence: Policing and Prosecution in Seventeenth- and Eighteenth Century England," *Continuity and Change* 11.3 (1996), 341–374; Rene Levy, "Crime, the Judicial System and Punishment in Modern France," in Clime Emsley and Louis A. Knafla (eds.), *Crime History and Histories of Crime* (Westport, CT: Greenwood Press, 1996), 87–108; Alf Lüdke and Herbert Reinke, "Crime, Police and the 'Good Order': Germany," in Clime Emsley and Louis A. Knafla (eds.), *Crime History and Histories of Crime* (Westport, CT: Greenwood Press, 1996), 109–138; Jeffrey Scott McIllwain, "Organizing Crime in Chinatown: New York City's Chinatown and the Social System of Organized Crime during the Progressive Era," (Ph.D. diss., Pennsylvania State University, 1997).

[106] In 1914, according to imperial sources, Istanbul officially possessed a population of just over 900,000. See Karpat, *Ottoman Population*, 170–171.

both Ottoman and early Turkish statesmen were far more inclined to deal more harshly with these potentially dire domestic threats.

All in all, it must be emphasized again that the various trends from the history of the Ottoman Empire and early Turkish Republic do not form, nor do they go on to comprise, a singular subculture or tendency that can rightly be identified as the source of modern day organized crime in Turkey. In looking at the global picture, one sees few specific subcultures or organizations formed in the prewar era that continue to thrive or evolve into the postwar era (such as Cosa Nostra, the Camorra, and a select number of *tong* brotherhoods found in the Chinese diaspora). With that said, one should ask why the Ottoman or early Republican era matters at all in understanding the origins of organized crime in Turkey. In other words, if the bandits or the *kabadayıs* of the late Ottoman era do not ultimately form the core for the crime syndicates in modern Istanbul or Diyarbakir, what relevance do they hold for the present day?

An understanding of the various forms of organized criminal activity in the nineteenth and early twentieth century offers important glimpses and insights into later patterns of behavior among both criminals and the state officials tasked with policing their crimes. The prism of ethnicity remains essential to Turkish depictions of organized crime. Even as the Turkish state matured into the twentieth century, politicians and law enforcement officials find themselves compelled to abet and cooperate with elements of the Turkish underworld. Moreover, we also see continued patterns of resistance to centralized political control over the periphery of the Turkish state (resistance that manifests itself both in terms of popular defiance and institutional opposition within the Turkish state itself).

A complete understanding of the origins of Turkish organized crime, however, necessitates other factors not necessarily found within geographic confines of the Ottoman Empire or early Turkish Republic. As will become clearer in the next chapter, the emergence of the United States is a critical contributor to the comprehension and delimitation of the Turkish underworld as it is understood today. In particular, it is through American policies and domestic debates with regards to narcotics, particularly heroin, that earlier criminal tendencies (and state policies towards crime) in the Ottoman and early Turkish contexts take on greater significance.

2

Turkey, the United States, and the Birth of the Heroin Trade

In the summer of 1943, prosecutors in a Brooklyn federal court brought to trial the two most notorious drug traffickers in the world. The two men, George and Elias Eliopoulos, had arrived in the United States two years earlier and were living in respectively upscale hotels located around Manhattan's Central Park. As scions of one of the wealthiest shipping families in Greece, the Eliopoulos brothers had been suppliers to the Greek army and held claims to bauxite and gold mines back in Greece. Both came to reside in New York after Germany's invasion and occupation of Greece in 1941.[1]

According to the prosecution, the Eliopoulos brothers were the masterminds of a narcotics smuggling operation that spanned the entire globe. The extent of their network was of such weight and significance that the League of Nations had earlier intervened in the hopes of coordinating an end to their dealings. The indictment filed in the Brooklyn court, according to the *Washington Post*, was the result of a collective effort by law enforcement agents in the United States, Canada, Great Britain, Holland, France, China, Switzerland, and Egypt.[2] Although one federal agent would not speculate as to the millions of dollars in profits gleaned by the two Greek men, the indictment filed in Brooklyn specifically charged Elias and George Eliopoulos with smuggling two million dollars- (later downgraded to one million dollars-) worth of morphine into the port of Hoboken back in 1931. An eleven-day trial of the two men led to their conviction on all charges. Success, however, quickly turned to defeat for federal prosecutors. After four months of the deliberations, the presiding judge, Matthew T. Abruzzo, set aside the verdict after declaring that the statute of limitations had been exceeded in the case. Further confusion and delays on the part of the government's attorneys rendered the indictments as null and void four years after Abruzzo's findings.[3] By the end of 1947, Elias Eliopoulos, the most notorious of the two brothers, had returned to a liberated Greece in order to resume the family businesses (which at the time included narcotics and arms smuggling).[4]

1 "2 Held as Leaders of a Narcotic Ring," *New York Times*, 23 November 1941; "2 Held in Narcotics Case," *New York Times*, 22 November 1941; Robert Rice, *The Business of Crime* (New York: Farrar, Straus & Cudahy, 1956), 140–6; "Two Greek Refugees Indicted as Smugglers of $1,000,000 of Narcotics into the U.S. in 1930," *New York Times*, 5 May 1943.

2 Eric Friedheim, "Greek 'Mystery Man' is Jailed as Head of Huge Dope Ring," *Washington Post*, 22 November 1941.

3 "2 Brothers Freed in Narcotics Case," *New York Times*, 9 October 1943; Rice , The Business of Crime, 146–147.

4 Martin Pera to Charles Siragusa, 30 April 1951; Martin Pera's File; FBN Files, 1916–70; DEA Records; RG 170, NAB.

The effort to try and convict the Eliopoulos brothers represents a key moment in the early history of America's confrontation with the global drug trade. The trial itself, which concluded in the midst of the Second World War, reflected a rising consciousness within both Washington and the American population at large regarding the use, sales, and trafficking of narcotics. While federal laws regulating the consumption and exchange of opiates had been on the books since 1914, Washington was slow to develop the means to enforce these new mandates. It was only in 1930 that lawmakers allowed for the creation of a small agency to deal specifically with narcotics violations. Housed within the Department of Treasury, the Federal Bureau of Narcotics (FBN) was the brainchild of its founder, Harry J. Anslinger. Anslinger would preside over the FBN for thirty-two years as its commissioner and oversaw the bureau's expansion into a law enforcement body with both domestic and international reach and clout.

Anslinger's personal investment into bringing Elias and George Eliopoulos to justice reflected a crucial aspect of the FBN's interests during the years preceding the Second World War. While the two Eliopoulos brothers imported opium, as well as other narcotics, into various ports across the globe, these two pioneers of the drug trade were most reliant upon the production and refinement capabilities of farmers, chemists, and wholesalers based in the Republic of Turkey. Turkey, as Anslinger and others would have it, ranked among the chief opium suppliers for the world narcotics market during the interwar period. Despite Ankara's hesitant steps towards curbing domestic production and sales of illicit opiates, the FBN grew increasingly wary of the impact Turkish narcotics had upon the United States. As the Second World War drew to a close, Anslinger's FBN sought to establish a more fixed and engaged American presence in Turkey in the hopes of fighting the Turkish narcotics trade at its source.

This chapter traces the evolution of two separate, but interlinking, historical threads. It surveys the origins of Washington's prohibitionist stance towards narcotics and the construction of the Federal Bureau of Narcotics. In profiling state efforts to halt narcotics consumption in the United States and the development of the FBN between the years between 1930 and 1950, this chapter reflects upon America's development as a rising hegemon on the world stage. It is with this understanding of America's expanding global ambitions in the prewar and wartime eras that this chapter also turns to the development of Turkey's opium industry. Anatolia has long been a source for the production and trade of opium within the eastern Mediterranean. During the nineteenth century, demand for Ottoman opium grew by leaps and bounds. However, Western imperial domination greatly diminished the Ottoman state's ability to directly benefit economically from this rise in demand. The gradual imposition of global prohibitions upon opiates after 1909 ironically served to heighten the economic importance and political impact of narcotics within Republican Turkey. America's emergence as a chief enforcer of the international embargo placed upon opium and other drugs would help to bring the United States to engage more closely in Turkish affairs. As American interests in Turkey expanded to other areas of concerns (most notably in matters of security and diplomacy), opium production and illicit drug trafficking became a greater source of both cooperation and tensions within Turkish–American relations. The synergy generated by the interaction between Turkish and American officials, agents, and criminals in turn deeply influenced the evolution of Turkey's modern underworld.

THE OTTOMAN EMPIRE AND THE MAKING OF THE MODERN OPIUM TRADE

The trade and consumption of opium, the raw sap drawn from the poppy plant, appears to have followed lockstep with the development of organized society since antiquity. Its presence within the grand Mediterranean marketplace can be dated back to as early as the Bronze Age.[5] One may say, with a tinge of irony, that the cornerstone of the Ottoman Empire rests somewhere within a field of poppies. Osman Gazi, the empire's titular founder, was born in the town of Söğüt, a sleepy place lying within a day's travel from the lush fields surrounding modern-day Afyon (meaning poppy in Turkish). By the time of his great grandson, Bayezit I, the state Osman had engendered would encompass much of the Anatolian lands best suited for the production of opium. In addition to the territory lying between Afyon and Yozgat, peasants and traders have made the poppy a staple crop in the environs of Aydın, Balıkesir, Kütahya, Konya, İsparta and elsewhere in western and central Anatolia.

Opium appeared to have no great impact upon the Ottoman Empire until the nineteenth century. Contrary to the popular images favored by Orientalist artists and writers (i.e. a moderately stoned Ottoman effendi relaxing casually with his waterpipe), consumption of opium as a narcotic was limited. Both the seed and the sap from the poppy were instead used for a variety of purposes, such as for cooking oil, flavoring (such as in bread), and medicinal purposes. Although neither Muslim nor Christian farmers monopolized the harvesting of opium, trade in poppy-related products became associated with Armenians by the nineteenth century.[6]

Events half a world away transformed opium's status in Anatolia at the turn of the nineteenth century. From their vast holdings in Bengal, agents of the East India Trading Company (EIC) conceived of a radical plan to penetrate and subvert the Chinese marketplace. British demand for tea through the course of the eighteenth century had created a lopsided balance in accounts for EIC merchants. Recognizing the historic demand for raw opium in southern China, EIC officials

[5] Alfred McCoy, *The Politics of Heroin: CIA Complicity in the Global Drug Trade* (Chicago, IL: Lawrence Hill Books, 2003), 3; Booth, *Opium*, 15–34.

[6] İbrahim İhsan Poroy, "Expansion of Opium Production in Turkey and the State Monopoly of 1828–1839," *International Journal of Middle East Studies* 13.2 (May 1981), 196; A. Üner Turgay, "The Nineteenth Century Golden Triangle: Chinese Consumption, Ottoman Production, and the American Connection, II," *International Journal of Turkish Studies* 3.1 (1984–85), 65–66.

and traders utilized their newly founded hold over Bengal to resurrect the old Mughal monopoly over opium. The fact that the Qing government in Beijing forbade the sale and importation of opium did not deter EIC agents from introducing incrementally larger amounts of opium into the Chinese marketplace. The illicit trafficking of British-Indian opium reaped a significant windfall of profit for the East India Company (and other foreign merchants) at the expense of addicts along China's southern coast. When the ruling Qing dynasts attempted to thwart further sale of British opium to its population, war was declared. The outcome of the First Opium War promptly transformed the nature of trade, diplomacy, and society in East Asia. The war laid bare any political and legal barrier that could inhibit European and American mercantile interests in China, leading to over a century of Western domination of the Chinese state and economy. During the ensuing decades, China would be transformed into the global epicenter of opium consumption. With over a quarter of China's adult male population using opium on a regular basis by 1906, the Chinese domestic market required tens of thousands of tons of opium to fulfill demand.[7]

China's rapidly growing population of addicts had a magnetic effect upon traders and producers of opium throughout the world. Southern China's seemingly insatiable demand for opium compelled governments and private interests to foster native opium production or to seek new sources of the drug. Since opium was indigenous to only a narrow belt of land stretching from east to west across the Eurasian landmass, much of the lands best suited for cultivation were in the possession of three imperial states: British India, Qajar Iran, and the Ottoman Empire. Following the Bengalese model, Ottoman and Qajar farmers and merchants responded quickly to the lure of high profits, transforming opium into a vital cash crop.[8]

Istanbul was far from ignorant of opium's growing importance within the world economy. In 1828, the Ottoman government responded to the dramatic rise in demand for opium by instituting a state monopoly (*yed-i vahet*) on the drug. Under the *yed-i vahet*, poppy production and profits soared. Although never rivaling the sort of production capabilities of Bengal, Ottoman opium would at one point account for 10 percent of China's overall consumption of the drug.[9] The monopoly placed on the opium trade provided a needed financial lifeline to the imperial treasury. For much of the eighteenth century and into the nineteenth century, Istanbul struggled to maintained stable sources of revenue. In an

[7] For further reference on this subject, see Gregory Blue, "Opium for China: The British Connection," in Timothy Brook and Bob Tadashi Wakabayashi (eds.), *Opium Regimes: China, Britain and Japan, 1839–1952* (Berkeley: University of California Press, 2000), 31–54; Alfred McCoy, "The Stimulus of Prohibition: A Critical History of the Global Narcotics Trade," in Michael K. Steinberg et al. (eds.), *Dangerous Harvest: Drug Plants and the Transformation of Indigenous Landscapes* (New York: Oxford University Press, 2004), 37; Alfred McCoy, "Heroin as a Global Commodity: A History of Southeast Asia's Opium Trade," in Alfred McCoy and Alan Block (eds.), *War on Drugs: Studies in the Failure of U.S. Narcotics Policy* (Boulder, CO: Westview Press, 1992), 237–279.

[8] For the Qajar case, see Rudi Matthee, *The Pursuit of Pleasure: Drugs and Stimulants in Iranian History 1500–1900* (Princeton, NJ: Princeton University Press, 2005), 207–218.

[9] Poroy, "Expansion of Opium Production in Turkey and the State Monopoly of 1828–1839," 192.

era that featured incessant clashes with the empire's Russian and Austrian rivals, much of the funds secured by the imperial purse were spent upon war-making. Yet a gradual shift towards a more decentralized system complicated and limited the sultan's ability to maximize and monitor the amount funds gleaned from taxation. While local *ayan* families in Anatolia and the Balkans enriched themselves at the expense of the peasantry, state-licensed tax farmers skimmed large portions of the tax revenue that otherwise would have benefited the welfare of the empire. The first separatist movements of the nineteenth century in Serbia and Greece only further dampened Istanbul's ability to manage its fiscal affairs.[10]

The ascendency of Mahmud II in 1808 marked a decisive turn away from the impotency of past Ottoman governments. With the smashing of the empire's praetorian guard, the janissary corps, in 1826, the *ayan* of the Ottoman countryside were gradually brought to heel or eliminated outright. In the place of these two sources of the empire's military establishment, Mahmud sought the establishment of a conscripted army drilled and outfitted in the mold of Western soldiers. To pay for this reformed military, as well to provide for the expanding bureaucracy that governed it, older, less efficient forms of taxation (such as tax farming) were gradually done away with. Proceeds gleaned from the state's control over various trades, including opium, flowed directly into the newly reformed Ottoman military.[11]

Direct state control over the production of Ottoman opium did not last long. As mentioned in the previous chapter, the erosion of empire's economic sovereignty was a gradual process. The gradual marginalization of the Mediterranean economy and the expanding production capacity of states in Western Europe served to exacerbate the military and diplomatic defeats Ottoman Empire suffered during the eighteenth century.[12] Military failures during the early nineteenth century further aggravated the empire's retention of its sovereign rights. When Mehmet Ali, governor of Egypt, rebelled and laid claim to Ottoman Syria, Mahmud II's new army of conscripts proved incapable of meeting the challenge. After Mehmet's troops routed the sultan's forces at the Battle of Konya in 1833, Mahmud II sought the intercession of Russia and other European Powers in order to save his throne and state. The offer of British support for the territorial solvency of the Ottoman Empire came, in part, at a price. In 1838, a year before the sweeping Tanzimat reforms undertaken by Sultan Abdülmecid I, Great Britain compelled Istanbul to sign the Treaty of Balta Limanı, which stipulated the abrogation of Istanbul's monopoly over all agricultural products and a reduction in duties on foreign goods.

[10] Linda Darling, "Public Finance: The Role of the Ottoman Center," in Suraiya Faroqhi (ed.), *The Cambridge History of Turkey: Volume 3, The Later Ottoman Empire, 1603–1839* (Cambridge: Cambridge University Press, 2006), 118–131; Eldem, "Capitulations and Western Trade"; Suraiya Faroqhi, *The Ottoman Empire and the World Around It* (London: I.B. Tauris, 2006), 70–72.

[11] Poroy, "Expansion of Opium Production in Turkey and the State Monopoly of 1828–1839," 198–202.

[12] Immanuel Wallerstein et al., "The Incorporation of the Ottoman Empire into the World Economy," in Huri Islamoglu-Inan (ed.), *The Ottoman Empire and the World Economy* (Cambridge: Cambridge University Press, 1987), 88–100.

British demands for free trade within the Ottoman Empire radically changed the political and economic significance of the opium trade. No longer would the expanding proceeds of foreign opium sales be transferred to state coffers or invested in institutional reform. In lowering the barriers to foreign exports and investment, the Treaty of Balta Limanı allowed Western merchants and manufacturers to swarm over Anatolia's poppy crop. For the next century, the bulk of the opium trade (and its profits) in Anatolia fell into foreign hands.[13] Growing sectarian divisions within Ottoman society further impacted the local character of the West's growing influence in the opium trade. Anecdotal evidence suggests that Jews and Christians (particularly Armenians and Greeks) tended to be more conspicuously involved in exporting opium. Western merchants and diplomats, who overwhelmingly preferred to deal with Christians and Jews, abetted the dominance of non-Muslims within the opium trade. From the perspective of Ottoman Muslim nationalists, particularly after the rise of the Committee of Union and Progress (CUP), the fact that Christians and Jews held the heights of trade and industry (such as in the case of opium) and collaborated so closely with Western commercial interests seem to suggest that non-Muslims were equally complicit in the West's plans to subjugate and control the Ottoman state and its economy.

Sales of Ottoman opium appeared to have remained steady well into the First World War. With the opening of the Great War, the tonnage of Ottoman opium exports dropped to about half of the pre-1912 levels. Exports out of Anatolia remained a fraction of their prewar totals well into the 1930s.[14] Nevertheless, a series of new conditions governed the region's position within the global opium trade after 1912. With the gradual expansion of the pharmaceutical industry in both the United States and Europe, demand for Anatolian opium, which was prized for its higher morphine content, increased over its Indian, Iranian, and Chinese competitors. This increase in demand roughly coincided with the commencement of the Young Turk movement and the establishment of the CUP government in 1913. With the outbreak of the First World War, the Young Turk administration abrogated the old system of capitulations, definitively marking a radical turn towards the building of a "national economy" free of Western (as well as native Christian) influence.[15] Lastly, it is in 1912 that the first international accord restricting the transnational sale of opium was signed. Each of these shifts would have dramatic effect upon the underpinnings of the Republic of Turkey's relationship with opium. In the years that followed, opium gradually ceased to be a freely traded commodity strictly dominated by European, American, and local non-Muslim actors. While significant numbers of native Jews and Christians continued to operate in conjunction with foreign opium traders during the immediate aftermath of the war, the establishment of the Republic of Turkey in 1923

[13] Poroy, "Expansion of Opium Production in Turkey and the State Monopoly of 1828–1839," 202–203.

[14] Erdinç, *Overdose Türkiye: Türkiye'de Eroin Kaçakçılığı, Bağımlılğı ve Politikalar*, 46.

[15] Zafer Toprak, *İttihad-Terakki ve Cihan Harbi: Savaş Ekonomisi ve Türkiye'de Devletçilik* (Istanbul: Homer Kitabevi, 2003).

gradually led to greater state involvement in the opium trade in Anatolia. As the twentieth century progressed further, larger numbers of native Muslim Turks would assume control over both the legal and illegal export of opium and its morphine and heroin derivatives.

THE VANGUARD OF PROHIBITION: THE UNITED STATES, OPIUM, AND THE BUILDING OF THE FEDERAL BUREAU OF NARCOTICS

Ottoman politics or economy generated minimal interest in the United States during the course of the nineteenth century. While the United States had established diplomatic relations with the empire in 1831, Washington remained fairly aloof from the Great Power politics that defined European and Ottoman negotiations over the so-called "Eastern Question." American foreign policy during its first-century history was instead transfixed upon political, economic, and diplomatic matters in the Western Hemisphere and East Asia. Washington's general indifference towards the future of the Ottoman Empire did not preclude the involvement of private American citizens. Throughout the nineteenth century, American missionaries were at the forefront of Western efforts to proselytize Christianity among the empire's diverse population. In addition to the establishment of hospitals and churches, American missionaries constructed schools in various corners of the Ottoman world. Several of these schools survived the fall of the empire and remain pillars of education in the contemporary Middle East.[16]

Although Latin America and China were arguably the focal points of American diplomacy and foreign trade, some nineteenth-century merchants and traders looked to the Ottoman Empire as a market for Yankee exports and investment.[17] While Ottoman tobacco ranked as the most lucrative commodity sold in the United States, Americans particular came to see the Ottoman Empire as a valued source of opium.[18] Sales of Ottoman opium to American buyers skyrocketed in the aftermath of the Civil War.

David Courtwright's research into narcotics use in the nineteenth century provides many examples for the medicinal and recreational uses of opium. Doctors and pharmacists frequently proscribed morphine for pain (a trend amplified by the Civil War and its aftermath). Opiates, according to nineteenth-century practices, provided relief from such diverse ailments such as asthma, depression, cholera, dysentery, and

16 Ussama Makdisi, *Artillery of Heaven: American Missionaries and the Failed Conversion of the Middle East* (Ithaca, New York: Cornell University Press, 2009).

17 Leland James Gordon, *American Relations with Turkey, 1830–1930* (Philadelphia: University Pennsylvania Press, 1932), 49. Mineral oils (petroleum), cotton goods, firearms, and distilled spirits were among the more profitable American exports to the Ottoman Empire between 1862 and 1892.

18 Gordon, *American Relations with Turkey, 1830–1930*, 83–86; Turgay, "The Nineteenth Century Golden Triangle: Chinese Consumption, Ottoman Production, and the American Connection, II," 93. By the turn of the twentieth century, Ottoman opium accounted for anywhere between 66% and 89% of American consumption.

malaria.[19] Recreational opium smoking was also a practice that became increasingly more commonplace in various corners of the United States. The proliferation of opium dens through the United States (especially in the nascent Chinatowns of various American cities) was complemented by the incremental introduction of heroin to American consumers. Both the popular press and medical journals reported during the turn of the twentieth century increasingly common sights of young men sniffing small quantities of heroin in multiple urban centers. In an era that featured long hours of backbreaking working in cold, dangerous factories and sweatshops, heroin most certainly provided some comfort to workers confronted with the physical and physiological challenges of modern life.[20]

Dependency upon opiates for both medicinal and recreational reasons attracted the attention of American reformers well before the turn of the twentieth century. Supporters of the temperance movement saw in opium, morphine, and heroin use many of the socially and economic corrosive traits that accompanied the consumption of alcohol. Men and women who partook in opiates became lethargic, distracted, and ill-disciplined workers, fathers, mothers, and Christians. Narcotics consumption, in the eyes of many, also amplified the perils posed by racial minorities and the underclass. Like the "gin epidemics" of the early nineteenth century, opiates, cocaine, and marijuana brought out the very worst in Asian, African American, and Chicano users, transforming them into alternatively lazy, depraved, or violent characters (depending upon the drug and the user). While researchers discovered opiate consumption to be particularly pervasive among Southern white men and women in the early twentieth century, fears of miscegenation and the loss of supremacy gradually drove local and state governments across the United States to take a firmer line upon the supposed threat of narcotics use and addiction.[21]

Affairs outside of the United States also impacted domestic opinions of opiate use. American and European missionaries grew increasingly concerned at the rapid spread of addiction across China, as well as other parts of Asia, during the latter half of the nineteenth century. Concerns over the social, economic, and moral ramifications of opium addiction created alliances that spanned across Christian denominations and drew in British and Chinese imperial officials to the cause of halting the transnational opium trade. In 1906, after thirty years of public pressure, the British House of Commons moved to abolish the opium trade in India. Public and state-led anti-opium campaigns also intensified within China both before and after the fall of the Qing dynasty in 1911 (although with little definitive success).[22] In 1903, the recently established American colonial administration

[19] David T. Courtwright, "The Hidden Epidemic: Opiate Addiction and Cocaine Use in the South, 1860–1920," *The Journal of Southern History* 49.1 (February 1983), 63–65.

[20] Jill Jonnes, *Hep-cats, Narcs and Pipe Dreams: A History of America's Romance with Illegal Drugs* (Baltimore, MD: Johns Hopkins University Press, 1999), 38.

[21] Douglas Clark Kinder, "Shutting Out the Evil: Nativism and Narcotics Control in the United States," in William O. Walker III (ed.), *Drug Control Policy: Essays in Historical and Comparative Perspective* (University Park, PA: Pennsylvania State University Press, 1992), 117–142.

[22] McCoy, "Heroin as a Global Commodity," 250; Arnold H. Taylor, *American Diplomacy and the Narcotics Traffic, 1900–1939* (Durham, NC: Duke University Press, 1969), 20–46.

in the Philippines also took up the issue of opium sales and consumption. Under the advice of a commission led by Charles Brent, an Episcopal bishop and missionary, the American colonial government outlawed the smoking of opium across the Philippines in 1906.[23] Continued opium smuggling out of China spurred Brent and other American officials to seek a broader diplomatic approach towards the broader challenge of narcotics use in the Philippines and the rest of Asia. In 1909, representatives from thirteen countries convened in Shanghai to discuss the possibility of imposing restrictions upon the transnational sale of opium. After a month of deliberations, the Shanghai Opium Commission unanimously recommended the "gradual suppression" of opium as a global commodity. A second larger convention, again spearheaded by the United States, was convened two years later in The Hague. The International Conference on Opium followed in the footsteps of the Shanghai agreement in securing a legally binding resolution that stipulated that all signatory countries draft domestic legislation overseeing the "manufacturing, importing, selling, distribution and exporting of opium, morphine, cocaine and their respective derivatives." Only eleven nations (Germany, the United States, China, France, Iran, Italy, the Netherlands, Russia, Thailand, Japan, and Portugal) consented to this 1912 agreement. Yet, with the ending of the First World War, language from the Hague Convention was incorporated into the Treaty of Versailles, thereby widening the number of international signatories.[24]

The First World War did not dull American desires to see further legislative prohibitions placed upon the sale and use of opiates. Before the outbreak of the war, various states in the union had outlawed opium smoking (a policy that was used to target Chinese migrants and citizens living along the west coast).[25] In December 1914, Congress passed the Harrison Narcotics Tax Act. According to this new law, all dispensers of opium and its derivatives were required to register with the federal government. While the law allowed for the continued exploitation of opium for medicinal purposes, this landmark piece of legislation made the majority of opiate users and traders subject to federal prosecution.

Ratification of the eighteenth amendment in 1919 further amplified Washington's role in monitoring and policing the recreational consumption habits of American citizens. Federal officers from multiple agencies, alongside state and local police, were tasked with upholding both the prohibition upon alcohol and narcotics. Through the 1920s, this grand spectrum of policing agencies categorically failed at their work. In the case of beer, wine, and spirits, citizens around the country flouted the prohibition on alcohol at will. Local government officials, as well as federal agents, equally strove to circumvent the law, gleaning untold profits in the process. With the onset of the Depression, prohibition was swiftly repealed

[23] Anne Foster, "Prohibiting Opium in the Philippines and the United States: The Creation of an Interventionist State," in Alfred McCoy and Francisco Scarano (eds.), *Colonial Crucible: Empire in the Making of the Modern American State* (Madison: University of Wisconsin Press, 2009), 95–105.

[24] Taylor, *American Diplomacy and the Narcotics Traffic, 1900–1939*, 46–81.

[25] Kinder, "Shutting Out the Evil," 122.

in 1931. As the Prohibition era passed on into oblivion, the Harrison Act stood firm.[26]

Through the Roaring Twenties, federal enforcement of the Harrison Act largely fell to the Narcotics Division, a subset of the Internal Revenue Service's Prohibition Unit. The profound levels of corruption that plagued the ability of the IRS to enforcement of the eighteenth amendment and the Volstead Act prompted a new approach towards both domestic and international restrictions on opium. In June 1930 the Department of Treasury created a new agency entitled the Bureau of Narcotics (more colloquially known as the FBN). In establishing the FBN, President Herbert Hoover accepted the recommendations of Congressional Representative Stephen Porter, and newspaper magnate William Randolph Hearst, and appointed Harry J. Anslinger to head this new agency.[27]

Anslinger, aged thirty-eight at the time of his appointment, began his career working on the railroads of his native Pennsylvania. Anslinger's personal writings provide interesting clues regarding the origins of his views and approaches towards his work within the FBN. According to his memoirs, Anslinger was exposed to the evils of both opium and organized crime as a young man. In one of the opening passages of his 1961 book, *The Murderers*, Anslinger tells of a young man he knew while growing up in Altoona who had made a name for himself as crack pool player (yet who also sang in a local choir). The young man, however, ultimately met his demise after two years of addiction to smoking opium. It was also while growing up in Pennsylvania that he first witnessed the violence of the mafia. As a labor boss overseeing work gangs on the railroad, Anslinger claims to have seen the aftermath of a brutal murder of young Sicilian migrant. A local *mano nera*, or black hand, was surmised to be behind the young man's death.[28] Considering Anslinger's future crusades, it is tempting to see these anecdotes from his past as purposeful melodramatic embellishments. His choice to include them early on in his memoirs is nonetheless revealing of the origins of his desire to represent his earnestness and commitment to his fight against narcotics and crime.

In 1918 Harry Anslinger entered the Foreign Service. Over the next eight years, he would serve as a consular official in Germany, Venezuela, and the Bahamas. According to his own account of these years, Anslinger worked closely with British intelligence circles after personally observing communist activists attempting to plant agents in the United States. His tour in Venezuela and the Bahamas also exposed him to the varieties of smuggling that occurred within the Caribbean. Upon returning to the United States in 1926, he entered the Treasury Department

26 See Norman Clark, *Deliver Us From Evil: An Interpretation of American Prohibition* (New York: W.W. Norton Press, 1976); On the Harrison Act, see John McWilliams, "Through the Past Darkly: The Politics and Policies of America's Drug War," in William O. Walker III (ed.), *Drug Control Policy* (University Park, PA: Pennsylvania State University, 1992), 9–13.

27 Douglas Valentine, *The Strength of the Wolf* (London: Verso, 2004), 15.

28 Harry J. Anslinger and Will Oursler, *The Murderers: The Story of the Narcotics Gang* (New York: Farrar, Straus and Cudahy, 1961), 8–10. For discussion of the "mano nero" in America and its relationship with the rise of the American mafia, see Dickie, *Cosa Nostra: A History of the Sicilian Mafia*, 171.

and ultimately rose to head the Prohibition Unit's elite Flying Squad. His record of service, coupled with his personal connections to several politically powerful families, secured him his appointment to head the FBN at the outset of the 1930s.[29]

Anslinger's original mandate as commissioner of the FBN included the establishment and management of fourteen offices located within the United States. While there is very little empirical research devoted to the conduct and utility of the FBN during the prewar era, it appears that much was asked of Anslinger's agents.[30] The demands of the job seemed to have attracted headstrong, resourceful, and energetic men. While the nuts and bolts of the FBN's first investigations inside of the United States remains relatively obscure, it appears clear that several of Anslinger's early recruits had an indelible impact upon the FBN and the future of America's war on drugs. Two of these early recruits, George H. White and Charles Siragusa, play specifically important roles in defining the FBN's involvement in investigating narcotics trafficking and organized crime in Turkey. Like their boss, their personalities and their formative experiences in state service greatly influenced their perceptions and approaches over the course of their career.

George White was born in Los Angeles, the son of the city manager of the suburban city of Alhambra. Before entering the FBN, he first covered crime as a beat reporter for the *San Francisco Bulletin* and the *Los Angeles Daily News*. In 1933, the twenty-five-year old White served one year as a border patrol agent in the Immigration and Naturalization Service but soon transferred into Anslinger's still relatively fledgling Bureau of Narcotics.[31] Charles Siragusa, by contrast, was the son of Sicilian immigrants and was raised in the Bronx. Like White, Siragusa graduated from university and held odd jobs before entering the Immigration and Naturalization Service as a typist. After four years of tedious deskwork, he received an offer to join the FBN (however, from his memoirs, it is unclear under what circumstances he came to choose law enforcement as his new line of work).[32]

Early on in their careers in the FBN, both White and Siragusa made names for themselves as undercover agents. As the child of Sicilian immigrants, Charles Siragusa repeatedly and convincingly posed as a mafioso with a tough Bronx accent. White, it appears, took on multiple alter egos (such as a gangster or sailor) while infiltrating various criminal rings. By the outbreak of the Second World War, both professed a strong familiarity with the American underworld. According to his memoirs, Siragusa's knowledge and experience with the Italian gangsters was rooted in his family's history in Sicily. His grandfather, he claimed, was murdered upon the orders of a mafia don in the town of Messina before his family emigrated to the United States. His hatred for the mafia grew more personal through his

[29] Anslinger and Oursler, *The Murderers: The Story of the Narcotics Gang*, 10–20; Valentine, *Strength of the Wolf*, 16.

[30] Kinder, "Shutting Out the Evil," 130–131.

[31] "Guide to the George White Papers, 1932-1970," Stanford University Library (<http://findingaids.stanford.edu/xtf/view?docId=ead/mss/m1111.xml;query=;brand=default>), accessed 25 May 2012; Valentine, *Strength of the Wolf*, 27.

[32] Charles Siragusa and Robert Wiedrich, *Trail of the Poppy* (Englewood Cliffs, NJ: Prentice Hall Inc., 1966), 36–45.

exposure to youth gangs and wiseguys growing up in the Bronx.[33] White's experiences with criminal syndicates grew out of his first years as an agent in the FBN. In 1936, he famously infiltrated the inner circle of the Seattle chapter of the Hip Sing Tong, a Chinese fraternal organization suspected of drug trafficking. His investigation, which resulted in over thirty arrests, dealt a serious blow to the Hip Sing, which had long been a notorious source of gang violence and opium smuggling dating back to the turn of the twentieth century.[34]

After the outbreak of the Second World War, both men sought commissions in the United States military. White entered the army in 1942, eventually rising to the rank of colonel. Siragusa followed suit two years later, joining the navy as an ensign. Before war's end, both men were recruited into the Office of Special Services (OSS), the premier intelligence agency of the United States military. Under the auspices of their duties as intelligence operatives, Siragusa and White undertook extended tours in the Mediterranean theater. In 1944, Siragusa was stationed in Rome and at one point served under James Jesus Angleton, future counterintelligence chief for the Central Intelligence Agency (CIA).[35] In addition to advising research by the OSS on a potential "truth drug" (an initiative that eventually culminated in the CIA's MKULTRA program), White's clandestine duties also took him to Egypt, Palestine, Syria, Iraq, Iran, and Libya between 1942 and 1943.[36]

The service White and Siragusa performed on the behalf of the American war effort was not irrelevant to the concerns or plans of their boss, Harry Anslinger. Anslinger himself actively advised the OSS. As a resident expert in narcotics issues, he played a supporting role in developing a potential "truth drug" for interrogation purposes. In the grander scheme of OSS operations in the Second World War, Anslinger played, in the words of John McWilliams, a largely "inconsequential role."[37] Beyond the war itself however, the FBN contribution to the OSS had a profound impact upon both the future of counter-narcotics operations at home and abroad. The training Siragusa and White specifically received as members of the uniformed military in counter-intelligence operations ultimately augmented the skills and experiences the two agents gleaned as undercover agents before the war. As time progressed in the years that followed the close of the war, their service in the OSS provided both men with an early introduction to undertaking investigations abroad. Through the personal connections and field experiences White and Siragusa incurred while in the Middle East and Italy respectively, both of these men laid the foundation for an intimate network of foreign informants and officials that would become invaluable to FBN operations in the postwar era.

33 Siragusa and Weidrich, *Trail of the Poppy*, 33–36.

34 Valentine, *Strength of the Wolf*, 27. Ko-Lin Chin, *Chinatown Gangs: Extortion, Enterprise and Ethnicity* (Oxford: Oxford University Press, 2000), 119.

35 Siragusa and Wiedrich, *Trail of the Poppy*, 58–63.

36 George White Diary, Entries 22 November 1942–6 March 1943, George H. White Papers, Box 7, Special Collections Department, Stanford University; Valentine, *Strength of the Wolf*, 131–132.

37 John McWilliams, *The Protectors: Harry J. Anslinger and the Federal Bureau of Narcotics, 1930–1962* (Newark: University of Delaware Press, 1990), 159.

The FBN's association with the US intelligence community did not end with the transformation of the OSS into the Central Intelligence Agency in 1948. Both White and Siragusa, with the full knowledge of Harry Anslinger, remained closely tied to CIA activities both at home and abroad. Through Anslinger, White, Siragusa, and others, a working relationship between the FBN and the CIA was consummated, a relationship that would grow and thrive as the Cold War commenced. Both the FBN and the CIA grew to benefit from this relationship. The CIA's partnership with the FBN helped to cloak US-led intelligence operations abroad. Both Siragusa and White, as well as agents later hired by the bureau, often wore two hats; while ostensibly assigned to coordinate counter-narcotics activities in various host countries, FBN agents stationed outside the United States also undertook clandestine missions commissioned by Langley (missions that were never documented within the files of the bureau). For an agency that remained relatively small and underfunded for much of its history (particularly compared to J. Edgar Hoover's FBI), the FBN found in the CIA a useful ally willing to share intelligence and provide other logistical support.

When viewed within the broader political context of the era, the development of the Federal Bureau of Narcotics is emblematic of deeper currents which defined the evolution of the United States. The gradual construction of Anslinger's bureau mirrored Washington's growing obsession with national security in the early twentieth century. Policing narcotics use at home did not simply serve the betterment of public health; rather, from the outset of the prohibitionist era, fighting drug use was used as a means to suppress and counteract (in the minds of Anslinger and others) intrinsically subversive and degenerate elements in American society (principally, although not exclusively, ethnic and racial minorities). Anslinger contended early on that America's physical borders should not limit the struggle against narcotics. Halting the flow of narcotics into the United States was a struggle that had to be taken to the sources of production found abroad.

THE FIRST FRENCH CONNECTION: TURKEY, THE UNITED STATES, AND THE PREWAR OPIUM TRADE

The Ottoman Empire refused to partake in any negotiations over opium production until well after the end of the First World War. Istanbul first claimed that participation in the Shanghai Commission of 1909 was deemed impossible due to the domestic troubles that followed a coup led by Abdülhamid II in March of that year.[38] Two years later, the Young Turk government again refused to take part in negotiations at The Hague, this time stating an anti-opium convention would harm the state's financial interests.[39] Anti-Western and nationalist sentiments, as

[38] Wie Tsain Dunn, *The Opium Traffic in its International Aspects* (New York: Columbia University Press, 1920), 75; Taylor, *American Diplomacy and the Narcotics Traffic, 1900–1939*, 63.

[39] Taylor, *American Diplomacy and the Narcotics Traffic, 1900–1939*, 114.

well as the outbreak of the Great War itself, further compounded Istanbul's refusal to participate in any international accord on the opium trade. In an era that featured the construction of a "national economy" free of European imperialist interests, the Young Turk government showed little concern for the misgivings of the world's great powers. It was only after the conclusion of the conflict that Istanbul's obstinacy began to fade. In the midst of an Allied occupation of the capital, the Ottoman government finally conceded to the terms of the Hague Convention with the signing of the Treaty of Sèvres in 1920. Atatürk's great victory over Greece in 1922, followed by the abolition of the sultanate in 1923, rendered Ottoman acquiescence to the Hague consensus null and void.[40]

Turkish Interior Ministry records from the interwar period suggest that smuggling was not considered an exceptionally serious crime. General security (*asayış*) summaries from the 1920s and 1930s instead largely detail Ankara's ongoing struggles with "bandits" (*şakiler*, or *eşkiya*) in the Anatolian interior. As the 1930s progressed, most reports entail brief accounts of mass thefts (such as animal stealing) or violent crimes in central and eastern Anatolia.[41] Virtually no document makes mention of the ethnicity of criminal perpetrators (in keeping with the era's moratorium on discussion of the country's cultural diversity) in spite of the ongoing Kurdish opposition to Ankara's nationalizing policies.[42] One report would only go as far as to say that policemen in Artvin and Erzincan had to contend with local populations of Kızılbaş (perhaps Azeris or Shi'ite Turcomans) that spoke Turkish and non-Turkish languages.[43] Of the documents that do mention acts of smuggling, Interior Ministry records only mention the numbers of individuals arrested during the course of a confrontation with police. Between November 1932 and February 1933, the Interior Ministry arrested only six individuals for smuggling.[44] Articles surveying the problem of smuggling within the young republic published in this period are also similarly vague.[45]

[40] Mr. Henderson to the Marquis Curzon of Kedleston, 25 August 1923, PRO/FO 87/2454/2607, in *The Opium Trade, 1910–1941, Volume 5—1922–1926* (Wilmington, DE: Scholarly Resources, Inc., 1974), 30–31.

[41] BCA 30.10.0.0.128.923.2, 9 November 1932; BCA 30.10.0.0.128.923.3, 21 December 1932; BCA 30.10.0.0.128.923.4, 25 February 1933. In this special series of general security reports from the winter of 1932–33, the reporting officer emphasizes that most events of law breaking (*asayış bozan muhim sayılacak vak'alar*) occurred most notably in Diyarbakır, Erzurum, Muş, Van, Elazığ, Mardin, and Urfa. None of the reports make any mention of Kurds or Kurdish resistance. Instead, each account presents a province by province catalogue of crimes (mostly violent crimes such as theft, acts of banditry, and murder) with attention paid to the names of individuals who headed notorious bands (*çetes*). For specific discussion of animal theft in Malatya, see BCA 30.10.0.0.88.580.9, 27 January 1929.

[42] In some sense we see evidence of official recognition of Kurdish resistance in specific Interior Ministry accounts from late 1929 with a detailed report of banditry activities in region of Ağrı Dağı in the province of Bayazit. In this particularl case, a group of 160 mounted men under the command of individuals close to a former general (Kör Hüseyin Paşa) fled across the border to Iran out of fear of air attacks (presumably by the Turkish Air Force) See BCA 30.10.0.0.112.753.14, 3 September 1929.

[43] BCA 30.10.0.0.88.380.19, no date, 1931.

[44] BCA 30.10.0.0.128.923.3, 21 December 1932.

[45] "Kaçakcılık Başladı!," *Cumhuriyet*, 24 November 1931.

With the establishment of republican rule in 1923, Turkey entered the global community of nations as an opium producing state free from any international obligations. While Greece's invasion and occupation of Anatolia left multiple opium regions devastated, it appears that Turkey lost little time in supplying the European marketplace with both legal and illicit opiates.[46] According to statistics compiled by Alan Block, Turkey produced an annual bounty of 200 to 480 tons of opium in the years between 1925 and 1930. A portion of this annual total found its way to Chinese markets where it was either consumed locally or sold on to buyers in the Western Hemisphere. Perhaps the lion's share was shipped to France. While other cities in Europe boasted centers of legal and illicit morphine and heroin production (such as Basel and Sofia), Paris emerged during the immediate postwar years as the global epicenter for the refinement of opium into its principal derivatives. According to Block, French traders imported over a quarter of a million tons of Turkish opium in 1928 alone, a total that was nearly three times greater than the rest of the world's consumption of Turkish opium. French oversight of this trade, according to League of Nations sources, was lax.[47]

A 1935 criminal case lodged against a prominent Parisian restaurant owner offers some insight into the complexity and influence of French narcotics traffickers during the interwar era. According to US sources, Louis Lyon used his popular restaurant as a front for his narcotics and gambling activities in the city. Under the protection of elements of the *Sûreté Nationale*, the French National police, as well as prominent national politicians, Lyon also operated a series of illegal factories used to process opium.[48] Traffickers and thugs based in Marseille were among the early contributors to Lyon's operations. Among the most noted collaborators of Lyon's trafficking network was an Egyptian-born Corsican gangster by the name of Paul Carbone. Alongside François Spirito, Carbone's role as an enforcer for Lyon's smuggling operation help to solidify his standing as the most powerful figure in the Marseille underworld. Like Lyon, Carbone also possessed powerful friends within the local political elite. The strength of Marseille's so-called "Corsican mafia" grew in the aftermath of Lyon's prosecution in 1935.[49] In advance of the Second World War, Marseille slowly became the focal point of clandestine heroin and morphine processing in France (and perhaps in Europe as well).[50] Spirito and Carbone's personal ties to Corsican immigrants living in the Western Hemisphere further amplified the global reach of the Marseille underworld.[51]

46 Gordon, *American Relations with Turkey, 1830–1930*, 94.

47 Alan Block, "European Drug Traffic and Traffickers between the Wars: The Policy of Suppression and its Consequences," *Journal of Social History* 23.2 (Winter 1989), 321–322.

48 Meyer and Parssinen, *Web of Smoke: Smugglers, Warlords, Spies and the History of the International Drug Trade*, 256–257.

49 Block, "European Drug Traffic," 328.

50 Sir G. Clerk to Mr. A Henderson, 3 July 1930, PRO/FO 87/88/3778, in *The Opium Trade, 1910–1941, Volume 5—1922–1926* (Wilmington, DE: Scholarly Resources, Inc., 1974), 30–31.

51 Pierre Galante and Louis Sapin, *The Marseilles Mafia: The Truth Behind the World of Drug Trafficking* (London: W.H. Allen, 1979), 8–15. Galante and Sapin tell the story, e.g., of Auguste Ricord, someone who "hovered around Carbone and Spirito" in the 1920s in Marseille. During the war, he came to Paris where he collaborated with the German occupation forces. With the end of the

The Lyon network, as well as other smuggling syndicates in Western Europe and China, provided Turkish opiates to an equally small circle of high profile traffickers and gangsters based in the United States. Much has been written about the impact of Arnold Rothstein, arguably the most powerful figure in the New York underworld during the Roaring Twenties. As one of the premier bootleggers of the era (as well as the man who fixed the 1919 World Series) Rothstein first imported narcotics into the United States early on in the 1920s.[52] Several of his initial partners in the trade, such as Jacob "Yasha" Katzenberg, "Legs" Diamond, Dutch Schultz, and Salvatore "Lucky" Luciano, assumed controlling interests over drug trafficking in to the port of New York after Rothstein was assassinated in 1929. Under the protection of Luciano and Louis "Lepke" Buchhalter (leader of the notorious "Murder Incorporated" gang), the New York narcotics trade continued to take root in the 1930s. Two events however served to hinder the evolution of New York's prewar narcotics networks. Before the outbreak of war in Europe, prosecutors indicted Luciano, Katzenberg, and Buchhalter in separate cases, resulting in long prison sentences.[53] Washington's declaration of war on the Axis powers in December 1941 had an even more profound impact. With intense fighting on the high seas, opiates from both the Mediterranean and Asia ground to a sudden halt.

Luciano, Rothstein, and other New York gangsters were not the sole purveyors of Turkish opium in the United States. Raids and inspections carried out by the FBN in San Francisco and elsewhere did uncover small quantities of Turkish opium (often mixed in with opium derived from Iranian and Chinese sources). FBN reports suggest that a significant portion of illicit Turkish opium often passed through American ports in the hands of individual merchant seamen who, at least according to government sources, appeared to have possessed no immediate connection to the budding criminal syndicates of the prewar era.

Of all of the figures to emerge during the interwar period, Elie Eliopoulos stands as the most notorious and prolific of the smugglers who traded in Turkish opium. Elie (or Elias) was born to a prominent family in the Greek port city of Piraeus in 1894. Like many ambitious, affluent young men both inside and outside of the Ottoman Empire, he attended Roberts College, an elite American university located up the Bosphorus from the old city of Istanbul. Although it is clear Eliopoulos had already established himself as an importer of military wares in advance of his career as a smuggler, it is not clear exactly when or how Eliopoulos first entered the drug trade. Whatever the exact circumstances, Elie Eliopoulos did forge partnerships with individuals who had made their mark upon the trade before the 1930s. An early confederate of the Eliopoulos brothers, David Gourievidis, an ethnic Greek from the Russian town of Novgorod, had exported opium into France after having

war, Ricord fled to Buenos Aires where he involved himself with other Corsican gangsters involved in the Argentinian underworld.

52 Pietrusza, *Rothstein: The Life, Times and Murder of the Criminal Genius Who Fixed the 1919 World Series*.

53 Raab, *Five Families: The Rise, Decline and Resurgence of America's Most Powerful Mafia Empires*, 13–57.

spent several years living in China.[54] By the early 1930s, Eliopoulos, in partnership with Louis Lyon, Gourievidis, and other traffickers, had established a network of buyers, smugglers, and suppliers across Europe, Asia, and North America. His influence over the global narcotics trade particularly came to light with arrest of August "Little Augie" Del Gracio, a New York gangster with connections to Lucky Luciano. Del Gracio's arrest at the hands of German police in 1931 attracted the attention of both the United States and the League of Nations, leading to an expansive investigation of various transnational traffickers (including Eliopoulos). One witness interviewed by League of Nations sources suggested that Elie's dealings in France alone during the early 1930s netted him over £400,000.[55]

Elie Eliopoulos made it clear to investigators that he was a man with powerful friends. In a 1932 interview conducted by British officers in Egypt, Eliopoulos offered a lengthy autobiographical account of his activities, detailing both his methods and the accomplices who aided him along the way. In addition to his collaboration with Louis Lyon (who possessed his own connections to men of influence), he claimed that his operations in France were protected by a chief inspector of the *Sûreté* in Paris. Politicians in Athens similarly abetted his activities in Greece.[56] Even a Peruvian diplomat based in Oslo became a client, smuggling large quantities of heroin to the United States in his official luggage. It was only in the wake of the Del Gracio case that the protection proffered by officers in *Sûreté Nationale* began to evaporate. His expulsion from France in 1931 was sealed, he claimed, after Eliopoulos refused to pay one last bribe to a retired inspector.[57]

Elie Eliopoulos, it appears, rarely laid a hand upon the narcotics he was often credited with smuggling. Instead, he acted as a creditor, investor and middleman for both producers and shippers involved in the opium trade. One of his clients, whose name features prominently in the early "narcotics suspect" files of the United States Department of the Treasury, was Georges Baklacoğlu (often spelled Bakladjoglou). Born in Istanbul, Baklacoğlu's career began in the Egyptian Market (*Mısır Çarşı*), a neighborhood located within the old city of Istanbul. Alongside his brother-in-law (who operated an opium factory in Istanbul), he had made his name as an international smuggler by the early 1930s. In October 1930, he was implicated (although never imprisoned) in a case that involved the sale of forty kilos of heroin in the Egyptian port city of Alexandria.[58] Three years later, his name was mentioned in an investigation of Nessim Calderon, another Istanbul-based trafficker who serviced heroin markets in France, Egypt and Ethiopia.[59]

54 "Advisory Committee on Traffic in Opium and Other Dangerous Drugs: Activities of the Eliopoulos-Del Gratio Gang of Traffickers," 8 June 1933, Eliopoulos File, Narcotics Suspect Files, 1927–42, RG 59, NAB.

55 Harry Anslinger to Fuller, 29 December 1932, Box 4536, CD Files, 1930–39; RG 59, NAB.

56 Harry Anslinger to Fuller, 29 December 1932, Box 4536, CD Files, 1930–39; RG 59, NAB.

57 Harry Anslinger to Fuller, 29 December 1932, Box 4536, CD Files, 1930–39; RG 59, NAB.

58 Central Narcotics Intelligence Bureau, Cairo Egypt: Georges Bakladjoghlou, 20 April 1934, Bakladjoglou File, Narcotics Suspect Files, 1927–42, RG 59, NAB.

59 See PRO/FO 371/17171/6136, 21 September 1933; Report no. 1, George Bacladjoglou or Pacladjoglou, 25 July 1935, Bakladjoglou File, Narcotics Suspect Files, 1927–42, RG 59, NAB.

The Baklacoğlu case further highlights the complexity of the interwar drug trade and foreshadows Turkey's growing prominence within the emerging heroin market. According to an informant contracted by American investigators, Georges Baklacoğlu operated a series of narcotics factories in the southern Balkans. From his string of processing centers in Greece, Bulgaria, and Albania, Baklacoğlu capitalized upon both his connection to raw Anatolian opium as well as local (and significantly rich) opium sources in the Balkans. His ties to French traffickers implicated Baklacoğlu in the sale of heroin and morphine to various European and American wholesalers (including Eliopoulos).[60] Even with greater governmental restrictions placed upon the outflow of Turkish opium, he was able to maintain his operations into the mid-1930s from Greece. American inquiries into Baklacoğlu's activities appeared to have come to an abrupt halt in 1935, leaving the impression that Baklacoğlu may have never seen the inside of a prison for his crimes. Whatever the case, if the story of Elie Eliopoulos serves as any precedent, it is probable that the Nazi invasion of Greece in 1941 perhaps brought his smuggler efforts to an end regardless of his past successes.[61]

The League of Nations, which initially took up the mantel of enforcing the Hague Convention, began to shift attention in 1930 towards Turkey's role in the international opium trade. Harry Anslinger, who assumed command of the FBN that same year, also directed his attention towards Turkey's intransigence. With the aid of State and Treasury Department personnel, Anslinger took particular interest in three factories that openly and freely produced heroin and morphine for both the legal and illicit markets. One factory located in Kuşkuncuk on the Asian side of the city, entitled the "Societe Anonyme Turque de Produits Pharmaceutiques et Chimiques," was operated by a consortium of directors which included four Turkish citizens (two Muslims and two Armenians), a Mexican national and Belgian citizen by the name of Paul Mechelaere, who was well known in the international drug trade.[62] A second, far smaller factory operating under the name "Oriental Products Company" was established in Taksim, just north of the old city center. Alongside his Turkish co-signer named Hovsep Gelanian, a Japanese national by the name of Hite Sakan claimed ownership of the Oriental Products Company. According to Cengiz Erdinç, Sakan arrived to Istanbul in 1926 after years of living in cities such as New York, Hamburg, and Paris. Unlike his European competitors, Sakan and his chemists exported solely to the growing Japanese market in East Asia (which in the early 1930s supplied narcotics to consumers in Korea, China, and Japan).[63]

[60] Re: Bakladjoglou and Eliopoulos, 3 April 1935, Bakladjoglou File, Narcotics Suspect Files, 1927–42, RG 59, NAB.

[61] According to a Greek report, the 1935 coup in Greece (organized by former prime minister Eleutherios Venizelos) resulted in even greater amounts of trafficking through Greek ports. However, it is not clear how the rise of Metaxas' military government in 1936 affected the narcotics trade during the lead-up to the Nazi invasion of 1941. See Report no. 1, George Bacladjoglou or Pacladjoglou, 25 July 1935, Bakladjoglou File, Narcotics Suspect Files, 1927–42, RG 59, NAB.

[62] Charles Allen to Secretary of State, 25 November 1931, 1930–34; FBN Files, 1916–70; DEA Records; RG 170; NAB; "Report on the Narcotics Factories of Turkey," 16 January 1931, 1930–34; FBN Files, 1916–70; DEA Records; RG 170, NAB.

[63] Erdinç, *Overdose Türkiye: Türkiye'de Eroin Kaçakçılığı, Bağımlılğı ve Politikalar*, 68; "Report on the Narcotics Factories of Turkey," 16 January 1931, 1930–34; FBN Files, 1916–70; DEA Records; RG 170, NAB.

The third factory identified by Harry Anslinger's sources was perhaps of greatest interest to American and European observers. The Etkim Factory, established in Eyüp (just west of the old city walls), was owned and operated by three individuals, Albert, Richard, and Leon Taranto.[64] Little is known about the origins of the Taranto family's wealth aside from the suggestion that the patriarch of the family, Nesim, was a prominent merchant (*tuccar*) from the city of Istanbul who had engaged in the opium trade from the outset of the twentieth century.[65] Ancillary sources suggest that the Taranto name carried considerable political clout in the final years of the Ottoman Empire. One member of the family, Isaac Taranto, was an official within the Ottoman Foreign Ministry during the years preceding the First World War. With war engaged in January 1915, the Committee of Union and Progress attempted to utilize Leon Taranto, Nesim's son and Isaac's cousin, as an intermediary between the Ottoman government and Great Britain in the hopes of sealing a separate peace between the two states.[66] The failure of Leon's overtures did not, however, dull the family's financial or political fortunes. In addition to personal relations with several high-ranking ministers in Ankara, Leon Taranto and his Etkim factory also received support and investment from Yunus Nadi, founder and editor of the ruling Republican People's Party's most loyal newspaper, *Cumhuriyet*.[67] American interest in the activities of the Taranto family was particularly peaked following revelations that the Etkim factory was a source of the Eliopoulos smuggling network.[68]

Before the League of Nations and in personal conversations with ambassadors and consular officials, Turkish officials did profess concern regarding the illicit trade of Turkish opium.[69] Yet even as the League of Nations in Geneva called for a renewed commitment to the Hague Convention in 1925, no law or government body regulated the production, processing, or export of opiates in Turkey before 1930. Economic nationalism continued to govern Ankara's approach towards narcotics. As Mazhar Bey, Turkey's representative to the League of Nations, explained:

> Present-day Turkey could never agree to such a restriction on her economic growth. Nor could she rest content with the part which is proposed to allot to her in this

[64] "Report on the Narcotics Factories of Turkey," 16 January 1931, 1930–34; FBN Files, 1916–70; DEA Records; RG 170, NAB.

[65] Abraham Galante, *Türkler ve Yahudiler: Tarihî, Siyasî Tetkik* (Istanbul: Tan Matbaası, 1947), 48–49.

[66] Feroz Ahmad, "The Special Relationship: The Committee of Union and Progress and the Ottoman Jewish Political Elite, 1908–1918," in Avigdor Levy (ed.), *Jews, Turks, Ottomans: A Shared History, Fifteenth Through the Twentieth Century* (Syracuse: Syracuse University Press, 2002), 230.

[67] Charles Allen to Secretary of State, 15 February 1932, 1930–34; FBN Files, 1916–70; DEA Records; RG 170, NAB.

[68] Burton Berry to Secretary of State, 23 September 1931, 1930–34; FBN Files, 1916–70; DEA Records; RG 170, NAB. It should be noted that Richard Taranto, a member of the Taranto family in Istanbul, also was suspected of having dealings with George Baklacoğlu. See Re: George Bakladjoglou, 19 June 1934, Bakladjoglou File, Narcotics Suspect Files, 1927–42, RG 59, NAB; "Advisory Committee on Traffic in Opium and Other Dangerous Drugs: Activities of the Eliopoulos-Del Gratio Gang of Traffickers," 8 June 1933, Eliopoulos File, Narcotics Suspect Files, 1927–42, RG 59, NAB.

[69] See quote from Russel Pasha in "Re: Turkey: Memorandum for Division of Foreign Control," undated, 1930–34; FBN Files, 1916–70; DEA Records; RG 170, NAB.

> business, viz., to remain forever a country which produces raw material, but is refused the right to convert it into manufactured goods.[70]

Boasting a strain of opium with among the highest morphine content in the globe, Mustafa Kemal's government demanded that Turkish opium command a large share of the global market share in the otherwise legitimate trade in morphine. Short of this demand, Turkish diplomats insisted, Ankara would not enter into negotiations on the Hague Convention or other restrictive treaties upon the opium trade.[71]

In the first half of 1931, Harry Anslinger, as well as United States Ambassador Joseph Grew, took dramatic steps to force a change in Ankara's policy. In December 1930, under the leadership of New York Congressman Fiorello LaGuardia, the United States House of Representatives introduced legislation banning the purchasing of opium derivatives from nations that failed to comply with the prohibitions outlined in the Hague Convention.[72] As the American representative to the International Opium Convention (the body that succeeded the Hague Convention), Anslinger personally delivered a letter outlining the threat now posed by the LaGuardia bill to his Turkish counterpart. Turkish officials in Geneva, after communicating with Ankara, soon switched tack and informed Anslinger that a change in Turkish policy would be forthcoming.

In February 1931, Turkish authorities shuttered the three principal factories that had been at the focus of Anslinger's initial investigations.[73] These steps ultimately proved "provisional" as production was allowed to progress into the following year with limited governmental oversight. In December 1932, Ambassador Grew continued to apply pressure upon Ankara, meeting personally with Mustafa Kemal as well as other high-ranking officials in the hopes that Turkey would craft more definitive legislation on the opium issue. In addressing the Foreign Minister, Tevfik Rüştü, Grew insinuated that according to rumors in Paris, "several people in authority in Turkey were financially benefiting by this nefarious and illicit opium smuggling." Grew explained of course that he did not believe such rumors. Nevertheless, "the best way to answer them," Grew suggested, "would be to annihilate or greatly diminish the traffic, and thus show the world that little or no profit was left there in."[74]

After a cabinet meeting on Christmas Day 1932, Mustafa Kemal announced that Turkey would accede to the Hague Convention and the 1925 Geneva revisions.[75]

[70] "London Conference: Statement by Turkish Delegate Regarding the Reasons for Maintaining Alkaloid Factories in Turkey," 7 November 1930, 1930–34; FBN Files, 1916–70; DEA Records; RG 170, NAB. Also see William McAllister, *Drug Diplomacy in the Twentieth Century* (London: Routledge, 2000), 99–100.

[71] Taylor, *American Diplomacy and the Narcotics Traffic, 1900–1939*, 244.

[72] For a draft of the bill see Harry Anslinger to Fiorello LaGuardia, 3 January 1933, 1930–34; FBN Files, 1916–70; DEA Records; RG 170, NAB.

[73] "Turkey Restricts Narcotic Output," *The New York Times*, 23 February 1931; "Turk Urges Action on Seizures," *The New York Times*, 30 June 1931.

[74] Charles E. Sherrill to Secretary of State, 1 November 1932, 1930–34; FBN Files, 1916–70; DEA Records; RG 170, NAB.

[75] "Fırka Grupunda Afyon Mes'elesi Görüşülüyor," *Cumhuriyet* 27 December 1932; "Fırka Grupu: Uyuşturcu Maddeler İçin Yaptığı Müzakereyi Dün Bitirdi," 28 December 1932.

The number of provinces and districts would also gradually be limited, permiting only a handful of regions in the center of Turkey. In doing so, Ankara would establish in 1938 the Land Production Office (*Toprak Mahsulları Ofisini*), which, in addition to other forms of agrarian output, would oversee and limit opium production strictly for medicinal purposes.[76]

Dissent towards this shift in policy manifested itself throughout Ankara's deliberations following Anslinger's ultimatum. According to American sources, several of Mustafa Kemal's close confidants, including Şükrü Kaya, Hasan Saka, and Yunus Nadi, privately opposed any restriction upon opium production. In the lead up to the Christmas decree, one member of the Taranto family (presumably Leon) journeyed to Ankara in the hopes of reopening the Etkim facilities. In addition to attempting to meet with American ambassador Joseph Grew, Taranto called upon his "friends," the Ministers of Foreign Affairs, Hygiene and Interior, claiming that his factory did not concern itself with illicit trading.[77] However, following the passage of a new opium law in early 1933, the Etkim factory remained shuttered.

Despite the seemingly definitive nature of Ankara's actions in 1932, it is clear that the flow of illicit narcotics did not cease with Mustafa Kemal's Christmas Day announcement. In 1934, League of Nations officials interviewed George Baklacoğlu on a wide range of issues related to narcotics trafficking in Europe. According to Baklacoğlu, there were "not tens, but hundreds of small clandestine drug plants operating in Turkey without fear of interference." He further posited that a close confident of Mustafa Kemal, Ekrem Necip, had personally intervened on the behalf of opium merchants, making it clear to government officials that the profits from the trade outweighed any effort to try to stem illegal opium exports.[78]

The Taranto family's fortunes flagged in the years immediately following the new regime on opium. Years later, in August 1950, Charles Siragusa paid a visit to Leon Taranto in his office in Istanbul. Having recently arrived in Istanbul as a part of broader effort to gather intelligence on the state of heroin trafficking in the eastern Mediterranean, Siragusa anticipated that Taranto would be willing to aid American anti-narcotics efforts in the region. Instead, Leon treated his visitor to a long tale of woe. Again, the ageing merchant insisted that he was innocent of any past wrong doings, suggesting instead that he had manufactured heroin at a time when there were no laws prohibiting its production. Twenty years later, Taranto remained deeply embittered towards the United States for forcing Turkey to eliminate the free trade in opium and imposing the state monopoly. Since the closure of the Etkim factory, the Taranto family, he explained, had fared poorly. Following the 1931 closure order, owners of the Oriental Products Company burned their factory to the ground in order to collect the insurance

[76] Erdinç, *Overdose Türkiye: Türkiye'de Eroin Kaçakçılığı, Bağımlılğı ve Politikalar*, 140–141.

[77] Joseph Grew to Secretary of State, 18 November 1931, 1930–34; FBN Files, 1916–70; DEA Records; RG 170, NAB.

[78] Re: Bakladjoglou, Turkey, 31 October 1934, Bakladjoglou File, Narcotics Suspect Files, 1927–42, RG 59, NAB. Ekrem Necip was also accused of being involved in the Del Gracio/Eliopoulos case made in Germany in 1931. See Erdinç, *Overdose Türkiye: Türkiye'de Eroin Kaçakçılığı, Bağımlılğı ve Politikalar*, 102–103, 121.

money. Meanwhile, the owners of the Kuşkuncuk facility were allowed to strip their factory bare and liquidate their equipment. Leon Taranto, however, had never been compensated for the closing of the Etkim factory, and insisted that the United States (due to their support of the restrictions on opium) owed him between $100,000 and $200,000 in "reparations."[79]

Further misfortunes befell the Taranto family following the outbreak of the Second World War. In 1942, Ankara passed the draconian "wealth tax (*Varlık Vergisi*)," a punitive measure which specifically targeted non-Muslim business owners throughout Turkey. Under threat of exile to the Black Sea coast, Leon was forced to pay a tax bill of 875,000 lira.[80] Taranto continued to sue former business partners and and government officials in open court over losses well into the mid-1950s.[81] When Siragusa found him in 1950, the old merchant sat in an office belonging to his nephew. Taranto, it appeared to Siragusa, was doing very little trading or business. When asked if he had any knowledge regarding the present state of the Turkish heroin trade, Taranto replied that the only thing he knew was "that the Turkish police undoubtedly knew all the personalities involved." However, he quipped that "the lack of police enforcement" in the postwar era "only indicates the obvious—the police realize huge sums of protection money."[82]

Leon's hardships, as well as the scant information he did provide, seem to have elicited little sympathy or pity from Charles Siragusa. In 1955, Siragusa earnestly endeavored to block and discredit the activities of an Italian chemical company, UVADO (later renamed Assofio), which employed Leon Taranto as its Turkish representative.[83] According to one letter from one of the company's representatives, Taranto had acted as a middleman in negotiations with the Land Production Office in Ankara.[84] With news of Leon's checkered past, and the allegations that his cousin Victor was still involved in illicit opiate trafficking, the company moved to sever all ties with the former narcotics producer.[85] Leon Taranto passed away on 4 December 1965, leaving behind an extended family that spanned Turkey, Western Europe, the United States, and South America.[86]

[79] Charles Siragusa to Harry Anslinger, 18 August 1950, Turkey, 1950; FBN Files, 1916–70; DEA Records; RG 170, NAB.

[80] Metin Toker, "Varlık Vergisini Ödemeyen Çalışma Kampına Gidiyor," *Milliyet* 8 January 1984. Also see Ayhan Aktar, *Varlık Vergisi ve "Türkleştirme" Politikaları* (Istanbul: İletişim Yayınları, 2001).

[81] "Taranto Meselesi," *Milliyet* 22 January 1955; "Yüce Divana Sevki İstenen Eski Bakanlar," *Milliyet* 22 January 1952.

[82] Charles Siragusa to Harry Anslinger, 18 August 1950, Turkey, 1950; FBN Files, 1916–70; DEA Records; RG 170, NAB.

[83] Charles Siragusa to Harry Anslinger, 29 July 1955, Turkey, 1955–56; FBN Files, 1916–70; DEA Records; RG 170, NAB.

[84] Filippo Carpi to Charles Siragusa, 29 September 1955, Turkey, 1955–56; FBN Files, 1916–70; DEA Records; RG 170, NAB.

[85] Charles Siragusa to Harry Anslinger, 19 September 1955, Turkey, 1955–56; FBN Files, 1916–70; DEA Records; RG 170, NAB.

[86] "Vefat—Leon Taranto Türarslan," *Milliyet* 5 December 1965. According to the obituary of a relative roughly a year earlier, Leon Taranto possessed relatives living in Portugal, Switzerland, the United States, and Uruguay. See "Ölüm—Bay Vitali Taranto," *Milliyet* 16 January 1965.

TURKEY IN THE CONTEXT OF THE INTERWAR DRUG TRADE

Leon Taranto's death in 1965 sealed the end of an era with regard to the history of drug trafficking and organized crime in the Republic of Turkey. His experiences, enterprises, and misfortunes embodied many of the trends that defined the evolution of opium and heroin trafficking during the interwar period. The Taranto family did not enter into the opium trade as criminals. Instead, whether under the patronage of Nesim or Leon, a case of opium sold to either an American, British, or Dutch merchants would probably have been officially logged or registered as an Ottoman export or commodity. As dealers in opium, the Taranto family clearly played a small but noted role in the makings of the modern pharmaceutical industry. It may equally be said that they impacted the broader revolution in the consumption of depressants for recreational purposes. While Leon as well as other members of the Taranto family did grow rich from the sales of opiates, both before and after the onset of global prohibition, neither they nor the workers who harvested or brought the opium to market saw the lion's share of the profit. Once the opium or heroin was loaded on ships bound for France, America, or China, Western traders, refiners, and retailers arguably came to enjoy far wider profit margins. Western financial gains also came at the expense of the Ottoman and, to a lesser extent, Turkish governments. British pressure to open the Anatolian market to free trade, and the gradual loss of state sovereignty over the empire's ability to tax and collect duties, made it impossible for Istanbul to profit fully from the opium trade. Ankara clearly internalized this historical lesson. Yet, even with the imposition of the state monopoly in 1938, Turkish officials continued to struggle to set the terms of Turkey's role in the modern opium trade.

At a crucial stage in the interwar period, Leon Taranto was personally and professionally connected to a wider world of traffickers and dealers who dominated the Mediterranean and North Atlantic heroin trade. As Alan Block quite correctly notes, the Taranto and Eliopoulos families embodied certain continuities in eastern Mediterranean trade that dated back to earlier periods in Ottoman history. Non-Muslim citizens, be they Orthodox, Armenian, or Jewish, were long conspicuous in their roles as middlemen and merchants in the region. Large extended families, like in the Taranto case, or perhaps shared cultural or ethnic ties, like in the Eliopoulos case, added to the durability of these networks even in the aftermath of the empire's fall. Moreover, Leon and Elie's ability to communicate in multiple languages, as well as their generally cosmopolitan pedigrees and demeanors, made them ideal facilitators in a complex and economically vibrant region. Perhaps the most crucial privilege both individuals enjoyed (at least for some extended period of time) was the high-level political protection both men were able to secure. The police inspectors, politicians, and other notables who sheltered and profited from their dealings were instrumental in forming and maintaining both of these networks. By the demise of both Elie and Leon's dealings by the early 1950s, neither man had ever been subjected to extended periods of jail time.

Beyond the Mediterranean dealings of Leon Taranto and Elie Eliopolous, we see during this period the emergence of a trans-Atlantic system of trafficking that came to define much of the twentieth century. By the outbreak of the Second World War, two interlocking networks of traffickers formed, each consolidating and dominating the majority of the North Atlantic heroin trade. Although Paris did serve as the focal point for much of the interwar European drug trade, the rise of Paul Carbone and the so-called "Corsican mafia" would lead to a forty-year period of dominance by groups based in Marseille. Marseille's ascendency as a center for heroin processing and transshipment occurred precisely as New York's underworld was experiencing a revolution in organization and leadership. It was in the aftermath of the so-called Castellemamarese Wars (1928–31) that the city's Five Families came into existence. This realignment of power into the hands of a relatively younger, American-born set of gangsters would lead to a long era of stability and control over the importing and distribution of heroin into the port of New York City. Lucky Luciano, who emerged from the Castellemamarese Wars as one of the most powerful figures of the era, also laid the foundation for greater coordination and cooperation among crime syndicates across the United States. To what degree Luciano's "National Commission" was successful in harmonizing the interests and activities of organized crime in America is unclear. What does appear certain is that the dominance of the New York crime families beginning in this period impacted (and was influenced by) the importance of New York as a center for heroin distribution.[87]

While citing and highlighting the importance of Marseille and New York in retelling the origins of the modern heroin trade (which has been recounted in numerous venues), one must keep in mind that the first "French Connection" was not the only means Turkish opiates arrived to the American market. Smalltime dealers trading in Turkish opium did manifest themselves in ports of call aside from New York. More importantly, as will be explained in the next chapter, the flow of Turkish opium did not only favor points west; illicit opium exports from Turkey had a profound effect upon Iran, China and, much later, Afghanistan as well.

Leon Taranto's name was etched into diplomatic cables and reports because of the Hague Convention of 1912. It is perhaps helpful to think about the Shanghai and Hague accords as remnants of the age of high imperialism. The notion of imposing a global ban on opium is indebted to the transnational authority wielded by the "Great Powers" of Europe and the United States. If one even looks at the participants and non-participants (like the Ottoman Empire) invited to both the Shanghai and the Hague conventions, there is a clear differential in power, responsibility, and enforcement between the countries that largely produced raw opium and the countries that largely consumed its derivatives. The prohibition on opium is also indebted to the mechanics and structures of empire. With the seven seas patrolled by Western navies, and much of the world governed

[87] Tim Newark, *Lucky Luciano: The Real and the Fake Gangster* (New York: St. Martin's Press, 2010), 71.

by European imperial representatives and administrators, the conceit of being able to enforce a global ban on narcotics trafficking appeared, at face value, possible. Lastly, one must grasp the imperial roots of opium prohibition as an expression of the civilizing norms embraced by modern Western states. The pressure levied by Anslinger and Grew upon the government of Mustafa Kemal, and the resulting Christmas Day decision to suppress the opium trade, is just one example of a broader Western effort to compel both colonial regimes and independent states to join the post-Hague consensus on narcotics trafficking. Like in the Philippines, China, Iran, and elsewhere, Turkey's compliance in "the international narcotics war" was framed in Western discussions and reporting in highly moralistic and developmental terms. Mustafa Kemal's leadership on opium issues, in the estimation of many, solidified Turkey's place within the community of nations as well as saving "Turkish youth" and "innocent farmers" from the evils of opium addiction and production.[88]

Washington's direct intervention in Turkish affairs in matters related to narcotics cannot be divorced from two fundamental shifts in America's development as a state. On the one hand, America's proactive policies on narcotics trafficking were indicative of the emergence of the United States as a global power. Despite overarching "isolationist" tendencies, the United States became an increasingly active and invasive actor on the world stage during the interwar period. It is during this period that one begins to see an ever-clearer articulation of Washington's "national security" interests with respect to maintaining domestic tranquility as well as preserving or promoting state and private American interests abroad. William O. Walker's work on the opium trade in interwar Asia emphasizes this point in discussing Washington's concerns over the relationship between drug trafficking and instability in China and mounting Japanese aggression in the region.[89] With the establishment of the FBN, we also see evidence of the physical construction of what many have called America's "national security state." Harry Anslinger, with the support of multiple administrations, conceived of his bureau as having an ever-expanding purview of authority in both domestic and global affairs. While small and relatively underfunded, the FBN complemented and supported other facets of American authority both at home and abroad.

On the other hand, in considering how and why American officials came to engage with Turkey on narcotics issues, it is important to recognize a radical shift in how lawmakers, law enforcement officials and the public at large perceived criminal syndicates and organized crime in the United States and elsewhere. Passage of the Eighteenth Amendment and the Volstead Act arguably gave birth to the modern American gangster. More than creating a means for shadowy underworld

[88] "Radio broadcast delivered February 24, 1934 by Gen. Charles H. Sherrill, Layton Bassett as Turkey, over WABC network under the auspices of the World Narcotic Defense Association as part of the eighth annual observance of Narcotic Education Week," 1930–34; FBN Files, 1916–70; DEA Records; RG 170, NAB.

[89] William O. Walker III, *Opium and Foreign Policy: The Anglo-American Search for Order in Asia, 1912–1954* (Chapel Hill: University of North Carolina Press, 1991), 140–141.

figures to glean massive profits through the smuggling and wholesaling of alcohol, the Prohibition era introduced the American public (not to mention local, state, and federal government officials) to the violent capabilities, political influence, and social mystique of prominent gangsters like Al Capone and Lucky Luciano. This golden age of the American gangster indelibly affected the construction and evolution of the FBN. The interwar experiences accrued by Harry Anslinger, as well as his chief lieutenants, George White and Charles Siragusa, shaped how FBN agents described and combated organized crime both at home and abroad over the subsequent decades. In the case of Turkey and the wider web of narcotics trafficking networks in the Mediterranean, individuals such as Elie Eliopoulos and Leon Taranto were not simply smugglers or producers of illicit goods; they were "drug barons" at the head of treacherous "gangs."[90] In citing Taranto and Eliopoulos as chief culprits in the international illicit drug trade, Anslinger and others, both inside and outside of the United States, made easy associations between these men and other infamous violators of the day (such as Rothstein, Katzenberg, "Legs" Diamond, and Paul Carbone). While it remains to be seen if Taranto or Eliopoulos saw themselves as gangsters or as integral members of a gang, American narcotics agents in the postwar era continued to describe and rationalize patterns of drug trafficking as expressions of some integral and centrally coordinated criminal conspiracy. As the postwar era progressed, FBN agents ventured abroad in the hunt for gangsters and mafias, regardless of whether they existed or not.

In thinking about Turkey's wider evolution with respect to its relationship to opium and the origins of America's crusade against narcotics smuggling, it is important to keep the broader global context in mind. As we shall see in the postwar period, Anatolia was not the only source of the illicit opiates that found its way to the world market. The trade in contraband opium from China, for example, posed an even greater challenge to policymakers and law enforcement officials in the United States and Europe. By the 1930s, surplus Chinese opium gradually dwarfed other sources of the drug (such as Turkey, Iran, and India). The smuggling networks based in China, such as Du Yu Sheng's notorious Green Gang, arguably possessed greater influence over local, national, and international affairs than any single trafficking syndicate based in Turkey or in the greater Mediterranean. Jonathan Marshall's research emphasizes that while Anslinger and other American officials were conscious of the power and scope of Du's hold over illicit opium trafficking in East Asia, diplomats and military officers were compelled to overlook the Green Gang's activities so long as the Kuomintang, Washington's principal ally in the region, maintained its alliance with this Shanghai syndicate. American support for powerful figures and movements associated with the East Asian opium trade, Marshall explains, continued into the postwar period. In addition to harboring individuals like Yoshio Kodama, a radical Japanese intelligence agent with ties to the Chinese and Japanese underworlds, the United States actively supported

[90] In his memoirs, Anslinger more than once refers to Eliopoulos as a "baron" of narcotics. See e.g. Anslinger and Ousler, *The Murderers: The Story of the Narcotics Gang*, 58, 59, 61.

elements of the Kuomintang that utilized the Burmese highlands as a base for exporting opium and maintaining their struggle against the Communist government in Beijing.[91]

A more analogous case to Turkey's interwar struggles with the opium trade can be found in early Pahlavi Iran. After the ascendency of Reza Shah to the throne in 1925, Tehran labored to monopolize opium production in the country. With the direct support and guidance of American officials, Reza Shah set in motion a series of policies to centralize both the collection of raw opium as well as to consolidate the delivery of Iranian opium to foreign markets. Both policies failed miserably. Although state revenue gleaned from the monopolization of the crop did rise during the interwar period, opium smuggling remained rampant by the outbreak of the Second World War. Iran's large opium-consuming population further complicated state efforts to reign in the sale and movement of opium within the confines of the country itself.[92]

Opium and heroin production in interwar Mexico appears that much more complicated. Poppy cultivation arrived to Mexico in conjunction with the settlement of large numbers of Chinese migrants to the north states of Sinaloa, Chihuahua, and elsewhere. Up until the passage of the Harrison Narcotics Tax, the greater availability of Turkish and Chinese opium seems to have overshadowed the sales and consumption of Mexican opiates in the United States. The outbreak of revolution in Mexico in 1910, as well as passage of the Eighteenth Amendment, irrevocably changed both the Mexican narcotics market and the power relationship between traffickers and politicians in Mexico's border states. As the Roaring Twenties progressed, towns like Ciudad Juarez and Tijuana were transformed into havens of vice and illicit consumption for American tourists. Meanwhile, the construction of a new state under the auspices of the Institutional Revolution Party (PRI) brought about a consolidation of narcotics trafficking and other industries under the control of politicians and notables attached to the post-revolutionary order. These "persistent oligarchs," in the words of Mark Wasserman, helped to displace older ethnic Chinese networks and functionally supported a state-backed reorganization of "native" smuggling syndicates.[93] Unlike Turkey, Iran, or China, illicit trafficking into the United States during the interwar period was governed by more direct connections between Mexico and American organized crime syndicates. Individuals such as Bugsy Siegel and Harold "Happy" Meltzer forged personal relationships with Mexican officials with direct ties to the country's drug

[91] Jonathan Marshall, "Opium, Tungsten, and the Search for National Security, 1940–1952," in William O. Walker III (ed.), *Drug Control Policy: Essays in Historical and Comparative Perspective* (University Park: Pennsylvania State University Press, 1992), 89–116.

[92] Bradley Hansen, "Learning to Tax: The Political Economy of the Opium Trade in Iran, 1921–1941," *The Journal of Economic History* 16.1 (March 2001), 95–113.

[93] Elias Castillo and Peter Unsinger, "Mexican Drug Syndicates in California," in John Baily and Roy Godson (eds.), *Organized Crime and Democratic Governability: Mexico and the U.S.—Mexico Borderlands* (Pittsburgh, PA: University of Pittsburgh Press, 2000), 199–200; Mark Wasserman, *Persistent Oligarchs: Elites and Politics in Chihuahua, Mexico 1910–1940* (Durham, NC: Duke University Press, 1993).

trade.[94] Members of the Cuban political establishment shared a similar relationship with American narcotics consumers and criminal syndicates during this period as well. Cuba remained, well into the 1950s, either a transit point for narcotics imported from abroad or a vacation destination for American tourists seeking to indulge in illicit sex, drugs, and alcohol.[95]

Opiate consumption and trafficking appears to have received the lion's share of attention from American and European officials tasked with monitoring and policing the international drug trade. Nevertheless, this is an era that featured the early development of networks that would introduce cocaine to the wider global market. Paul Gootenberg's enterprising work on the history of the Andean cocaine trade illustrates that a rich tapestry of merchants, scientists, and smugglers from Europe, the United States, and Japan dominated foreign exporting routes from South America. Like Turkish opium, while some of the cocaine that found its way to foreign markets was consumed for medicinal or scientific purposes, interwar smugglers did trade in increasing quantities of contraband cocaine. Like the trade in Turkish and other sources of opium, Gootenberg emphasizes that even during this seminal period, the networks that brought Andean cocaine to market were vast in scope despite the relatively small amounts of cocaine brought to market.[96]

The Second World War marks a definitive turn in the history of the drug trade. As war raged on the high seas and in various opium-cultivating countries (such as Iran, China, and India), transoceanic opiate trafficking came to a virtual halt. The reported numbers of addicts in the United States, according to FBN accounts, dropped dramatically with the suspension of trade across both the Atlantic and Pacific.[97] In lieu of European or Asian sources, legal and illicit opium from Mexico provided an alternative for the American medical field and the illicit marketplace alike.[98] Turkish neutrality in the Second World War allowed both British and German agents an opportunity to procure morphine as supplies waned during the course of the war.[99]

It is possible to find multiple continuities in the history of narcotics that followed Japan's formal surrender in August 1945. Prewar syndicates and gangsters that traded in narcotics in New York would reconnect to new and former partners lying on the other side of the Atlantic. Despite changes in domestic

[94] Astorga, "Organized Crime," 65.

[95] Eduardo Saenz Rovner, *The Cuban Connection: Drug Trafficking, Smuggling and Gambling in Cuba from the 1920s to the Revolution* (Chapel Hill: University of North Carolina Press, 2008), 17–44.

[96] Paul Gootenberg, *Andean Cocaine: The Making of a Global Drug* (Chapel Hill: University of North Carolina Press, 2008), 105–142.

[97] According to FBN statistics, 602 kilograms of prepared opium was seized in the United States in 1938. A year later, that number dropped to 116 kilograms. Only 29 kilograms were seized in 1941. Trade in opium, it appears, quickly picked up, with the FBN reporting total seizures between 1945 and 1946 rising from 101 and 127 kilograms respectively. *Traffic in Opium and Other Dangerous Drugs for the Year Ended December 31, 1946* (Washington DC: U.S. Treasury Department, Bureau of Narcotics, 1947), 14.

[98] McCoy, "Stimulus of Prohibition," 42.

[99] PRO/FO 44/120/5379, 5 April 1944.

law and official adherence to the Hague principles, Turkey remained a source of illicit opium for wholesalers, traders, and consumers residing in North America, Europe, and Southwest Asia. As one looks beyond 1945, two particular trends would come to define our broader understanding of the global heroin trade (and Turkey's specific position within the trade). First and foremost, the postwar era would witness steady increases in the amount of heroin produced on a yearly basis. Paired with these increases was a steady rise of heroin users and addicts residing in various corners of the world (but most notably in the United States). The second trend that would come to define the global heroin trade in the postwar era was the steady rise in official interest in the global drug trade among policymakers and law enforcement officials in Washington. American engagement in counter-narcotics efforts both at home and abroad expanded dramatically in the first twenty-five years following the surrender of the Axis powers. While the fight against Communism and left-wing subversion monopolized much of Washington's attention during this period, Harry Anslinger and his officers in the FBN slowly laid the foundation for an official American declaration of war on narcotics in 1969. Recasting narcotics trafficking as a threat to America's national security was only partially indebted to the physical construction and augmentation of federal and international law enforcement entities during this period of time. Central to the postwar perception of the heroin trade was the identification of specific gangsters, mafias, and syndicates as the main purveyors of narcotics in the world at large. With the recognition of key individuals and groups, the notion that narcotics indeed threatened the integrity of the state became more tangible and immediate.

In hindsight, the "personification" of the heroin trade, in the form of suspected masterminds and thugs, also offers us insights, intended or not, into the functioning of politics and power during this era. In the case of Turkey, the numbers and names of actors involved in narcotics trafficking grew rapidly in the postwar era. With the opening of the FBN files to researchers, it is now possible to analyze the impact of narcotics trafficking beyond the official statements and studies Washington and Ankara issued to their respective publics. Internal FBN correspondence detailing key traffickers and syndicates, as well as the routes and partners that enabled their participation in the heroin trade, sheds a good deal of light upon their roles in local, national, and international politics. Moreover, in gauging the limitations of American perceptions and investigations of narcotics activity in Turkey and beyond, one also gets a sense of the prejudices and misperceptions that guided FBN officials to construct their views of the underworlds they confronted.

3
The French Connection

In late July 1963, Harry Anslinger took a seat before Senator John L. McClellan of Arkansas. As chairman of a permanent senate subcommittee investigating organized crime and illicit trafficking in narcotics, McClellan extended the seventy-one-year old former head of the Federal Bureau of Narcotics the warmest of welcomes. Anslinger had retired from the bureau a year early after thirty-two years of service as its head. After Anslinger cited his long years of working in the federal government, McClellan stipulated for the record that "there is no one in the United States who is possessed of [*sic*] greater experience in this field than you are."[1] Anslinger's testimony before McClellan's subcommittee lasted two days. His exchanges with committee members complemented the testimony of several agents still employed by the FBN (including then commissioner, Henry Giordano). Topics touched upon by the committee that July were expansive in scale and breadth. Testimony offered by FBN agents extended to such issues as hemp production in Lebanon, the role of Communist China in heroin trafficking, the organization of the Canadian drug trade, and the methods used to smoke cocaine. Also entered into the official record was a series of documents largely compiled by the FBN. In the finalized bound edition of the proceedings, the reader is presented with indices detailing court cases and seizures, biographies of suspected traffickers, and abridged surveys of how narcotics are produced and what routes smugglers used to bring their contraband to market.

The findings of the McClellan Subcommittee, in spite of the wealth of knowledge it produced, were not entirely unprecedented. Senator Estes Kefauver's hearings in 1951 tread over similar ground in their investigation of organized crime within the United States. As a televised event, the Kefauver Commission is perhaps best known for the appearance of several of America's most notorious underworld figures from the period: Sam Giancana, Vito Genovese, Willy Morretti, and others. While none of the mobsters brought before the committee offered to divulge any secrets or confessions, FBN agents (with Anslinger in the lead) proved more than willing to expand upon their investigations into the American mafia. FBN revelations on the nature of organized crime in the United States drew a sharp contrast with opinions of FBI director J. Edgar Hoover, who had long maintained that no mafia existed in the country.[2]

[1] U.S. Senate, Permanent Subcommittee on Investigations, *Organized Crime and Illicit Traffic in Narcotics*, Part 3 (Washington DC: U.S. Government Printing Office, 1964), 679.

[2] It has long been surmised that Hoover may have established a rapport with key mafia figures within the United States before the Second World War. One newspaper columnist suggested that Hoover used the organized crime figures as sources of information in exchange for protection. In exchange, Hoover purportedly directed a cohort of FBI agents to document the non-existence of the

Turkey featured prominently in the FBN's public and confidential accounts of the global drug trade in the years immediately after the Second World War. While Anslinger publicly decried the People's Republic of China (PRC) as the chief source of heroin consumed in the United States during the 1950s, FBN investigators labored in earnest to understand, document, and counteract the influence Turkish opium had upon the American drug market. By the end of the 1960s, Turkey would displace the PRC, as well as all other opium-producing states, as the central focus of American counter-narcotics efforts.

Turkey, in the FBN's estimation, was at the heart of a tangled web of smuggling routes emanating across the Mediterranean and North Atlantic. Long before the adventures of "Popeye" Egan were regaled in books and films, FBN agents had come to think of the "French Connection" as a bureau priority.[3] While the phrase itself did not appear in FBN or State Department correspondence until well after the first publication of the *French Connection* in 1969, it is clear that American and local narcotics officers in the eastern Mediterranean had conceived of an intricate web of traffickers that pipelined Turkish heroin via Marseille into North America soon after the end of the war. It was only after intensive diplomatic efforts in the early 1970s that law enforcement officials in the United States claimed victory in its struggle against the French Connection.

While the rise and fall of the French Connection garnered much attention in the American popular media, Iran figured prominently in a far less successful front in American counter-narcotics efforts during the Cold War. Following 1945, the United States pressed Tehran to take more progressive action on opium trafficking, production, and consumption. This enterprise bore fruit in 1955 with Mohammad Reza Shah's declaration of a total prohibition upon opium cultivation in the country. While the State Department and the FBN rejoiced in the support the "king of kings" lent to America's global vision of a world without illicit narcotics, continued production and smuggling of opium from Turkey ultimately helped to offset these gains. The resumption of opium production in Iran in 1967, in the eyes of American officials, was as much the fault of Turkey's intransigence as it was the result of the shah's lack of political will.

In situating Anatolia within the history of heroin trafficking between the years 1945 and 1971, this chapter seeks to highlight a variety of themes critical to understanding and contextualizing the broader evolution of narcotics and organized crime in Turkey. Admittedly the individual Turks described within FBN files and Turkish newspaper accounts from this period comprised a very small and relatively obscure portion of the entangled groups of individuals making up the French Connection. Yet the major Turkish traffickers to emerge during this period were undoubtedly trendsetters and mentors to men who have more recently come to direct narcotics trafficking and other illicit trades from within Turkey. Moreover, in this and subsequent chapters, it is abundantly clear that elements of Turkey's underworld

mafia. Burton Hersh, *Bobby and J. Edgar* (New York: Carroll & Graf Publishers, 2007), 49; Stephen Fox, *Power and Blood* (New York: William Morrow and Company, Inc. 1989), 337.

[3] See Robin Moore, *The French Connection* (Guilford, CT: Lyons Press, 2003).

gathered increasing amounts of influence among local and national representatives of country's political and economic establishment.

This chapter does not intend to deal with the postwar Turkish underworld, and its role within the global trade in illicit opiates, in isolation. The connections between Turkish and foreign criminals were indeed often tenuous, passing, or far removed at best. It is also clear that the French Connection, let alone Turkish trafficking into Iran, did not conform to a single, uniform, and integrated criminal conspiracy. Understanding how Turkish traffickers did and did not interact with counterparts in Syria, Lebanon, Iran, France, Italy, Canada, or the United States does offer important insights into the conditions that governed how and why Turkish drug trafficking networks continued to flourish following the breakdown of the French Connection.

Official and classified FBN reports, as well as a variety of journalistic and diplomatic commentaries, account for the bulk of the source material that informs the following discussion of heroin trafficking across Turkey's western and eastern borders. However, what is intended in this chapter is less a detailed analysis or critique of these various reports and press accounts as it is an effort to survey and contextualize the overall mechanics of the French Connection and the Turkish/Iranian drug trade. Through first exploring the methods and men associated with this period of the Turkish heroin trade, it will then be possible to approach how investigators came both to comprehend the trade and target (or perhaps ignore) the men and networks who gave life to this element of the international heroin trade.

THE FIRST *BABAS*: THE WHOLESALERS AND CHEMISTS OF ISTANBUL

Revelations regarding the origins of İhsan Sekban's career in organized crime emerged piecemeal during the first few years of the FBN's presence in the Republic of Turkey. Official police files state unequivocally that he was born in Rize, a small port located on the northeastern coast.[4] Rumor had it, according to one informant, that Sekban was an Armenian but had converted to Islam and had changed his name. How he came into a life of crime was also a matter of conjecture. The same informant, a Greek trafficker named Michael Kalogrides, proffered that Sekban had dealt in hashish in Egypt before striking it rich in the Istanbul underworld.[5] One source close to the CIA had heard that Sekban had operated as a "poor, ordinary taxi driver" in the city up until 1942.[6] Still other unnamed sources posed that *Laz* İhsan arrived in Istanbul as a penniless migrant from the Black Sea who had

[4] International List No. 309, undated, Turkey, 1951–52; FBN Files, 1916–70; DEA Records; RG 170, NAB.

[5] Martin Pera to Charles Siragusa, 30 April 1951, Turkey: Martin Pera File; FBN Files, 1916–70; DEA Records; RG 170, NAB.

[6] Charles Siragusa to Harry Anslinger, 25 July 1950, Turkey, 1950; FBN Files, 1916–70; DEA Records; RG 170, NAB.

found employment as a petty dope dealer and gradually learned the manufacturing and smuggling side of the trade. In the mid-1930s, he served almost two years in prison in connection with a murder-for-hire plot. He was arrested again in 1942 and 1950 on narcotics charges but escaped any lengthy prison terms either through acquittal or on appeal.[7]

In July 1950, Charles Siragusa arrived at the US consulate to meet with Istanbul's CIA station chief, G. Joseph Zogby. In Zogby's possession was a two-year-old report the Agency had compiled on İhsan Sekhban (which, considering the date, suggests that much of the information had been gleaned by OSS operatives). The content of this report remains classified. However, according to Siragusa, the CIA had ascertained in early 1948 that İhsan was among the most prominent heroin traffickers in the country.[8] Siragusa's contacts in the Istanbul underworld later contended that he and his gang operated anywhere between thirty to forty factories in the environs of the city.[9] It was suggested in more than one report that İhsan Sekban was among the wealthiest men in Istanbul during the early 1950s. In addition to driving around town in his American automobile and consorting with a famous local nightclub singer, he also owned a multi-million dollar apartment complex on İstiklal Boulevard, one the city's main thoroughfares.[10] Most importantly, Sekban was a man with friends in high places. Politicians, policemen, and journalists in both Istanbul and the port city of Izmir could be counted upon to protect him from prosecution and to keep his name out of the newspaper.

Turkish and American investigators took note of İhsan Sekban's activities at a time when there appeared to have been a profound shift in the nature of the heroin trade in Turkey and in the wider Mediterranean world. From the vantage point of American narcotics officers, and their Turkish interlocutors, İhsan Sekban represented the upper ranks of a small cohort of narcotics wholesalers based in the city of Istanbul at the mid-point of the twentieth century. His pedigree, as well as his patterns of behavior, appears to have mirrored the emergence of other powerful drug traffickers in the city in the aftermath of the Second World War. Although far less is known about the biographies of other men who helped shape the Istanbul

[7] Translation: "The Arrest of Ihsan Sekban, A Trafficker," *Istanbul* 26 July 1950, Turkey, 1950; FBN Files, 1916–70; DEA Records; RG 170, NAB; International List No. 309, undated, Turkey, 1951–52; FBN Files, 1916–70; DEA Records; RG 170, NAB.

[8] Charles Siragusa to Harry Anslinger, 24 July 1950, Turkey, 1950; FBN Files, 1916–70; DEA Records; RG 170, NAB. On 29 June 2009, I submitted a Freedom of Information Act request to the CIA for files related to İhsan Sekban. On 15 July 2009, the Office of the Information and Privacy Coordinator informed me that my request was denied on the basis of b(1) and b(3) of the FOI. While "the CIA can neither confirm nor deny the existence," any release of information was exempt due to the "interest of national defense or foreign policy" and to "protect from disclosure of intelligence sources and methods."

[9] Charles Siragusa to Harry Anslinger, 6 August 1950, Turkey, 1950; FBN Files, 1916–70; DEA Records; RG 170, NAB.

[10] Translation: "The Arrest of Ihsan Sekban, A Trafficker," *Istanbul* 26 July 1950, Turkey, 1950; FBN Files, 1916–70; DEA Records; RG 170, NAB; International List No. 309, undated, Turkey, 1951–52; FBN Files, 1916–70; DEA Records; RG 170, NAB; Newsday, *The Heroin Trail* (New York: New American Library, 1973), 36. In the early 1970s, reporters from the daily *Newsday* identify Sekban under the alias of "İhsan Seymenoglu."

heroin market in the years and decades after 1945, it seems clear that Sekban's story resonated in the lives and the practices of other powerful underworld figures in the city.

The clandestine trade in heroin in Istanbul remained an industry largely dominated by non-Muslim citizens of the city at the close of the Second World War. In addition to Leon Taranto, whose family purportedly continued to deal in illicit opium after the closure of the Etkim factory in Eyüp, Turkish and American officials also took note of other prominent Christian and Jewish dealers active in postwar Istanbul.[11] One name that appears with great frequency within the pages of American postwar reporting from Turkey is Vasil Arcan (or Artin). Vasil was born in Istanbul in 1898 to Greek Orthodox parents.[12] When George White met him during a 1948 investigation in Istanbul, Arcan introduced himself as the former owner of the *Piccadilly Bar* in Tepebaşı, a neighborhood traditionally known for its bars, coffeehouses, and nightlife.[13] According to one of the first informants hired by the FBN, Vasil used this unassuming establishment near the Galata docks as the base of a sophisticated narcotics dealing and manufacturing empire. As late as the summer of 1950, an underworld informant suggested to Charles Siragusa that he possessed more opium conversion labs and employed more men than İhsan Sekban, making him the largest heroin dealer in all of Turkey.[14]

While Vasil Arcan may have been among the most prominent narcotics traffickers in the immediate postwar era, the era of powerful non-Muslim drug merchants was quickly coming to an end. İhsan Sekban, one informant claimed, was tougher and more ruthless than Arcan. While Arcan may have maintained a lower profile than Sekban in terms of their outward appearances and character, the Laz gangster from Rize arguably maintained stronger ties with local law enforcement officials. In exchange for protection from prosecution, İhsan gladly offered information on his competitor's activities to officers in the Istanbul narcotics bureau.[15]

Vasil Arcan's name gradually vanished from the FBN's reporting from the city of Istanbul. His eventual absence from the Bureau's internal records coincided with the abrupt disappearance of other non-Muslim suspects involved in the Turkish heroin trade. In 1951, one informant came to reveal the underlying cause in this shift in the nature of the Istanbul underworld. The informant, who was interviewed by Agent Martin Pera, had observed that Armenians and Greeks in the city were being "squeezed out" of the heroin market. While upstart Muslim

[11] Translation, Legal Note(?), "Accused of Selling Heroin," Turkey 1943–48; FBN Files, 1916–70; DEA Records; RG 170, NAB.

[12] Translation, Legal Note(?), "Accused of Selling Heroin," Turkey 1943–48; FBN Files, 1916–70; DEA Records; RG 170, NAB.

[13] For Commissioner of Narcotics Anslinger from White #9, 4 June 1948, George H. White Papers, Box 1, Folder 7, Special Collections Department, Stanford University; For Commissioner of Narcotics Anslinger from White #10, 10 June 1948, George H. White Papers, Box 1, Folder 7, Special Collections Department, Stanford University.

[14] Charles Siragusa to Harry Anslinger, 6 August 1950, Turkey, 1950; FBN Files, 1916–70; DEA Records; RG 170, NAB.

[15] Charles Siragusa to Harry Anslinger, 8 August 1950, Turkey, 1950; FBN Files, 1916–70; DEA Records; RG 170, NAB.

competitors were naturally the chief beneficiaries of this sea change, the informant suspected that "law enforcement organizations" were "part and parcel" of such a dramatic shift in the nature of the city's local color. Martin Pera, in reporting this information, affirms that he had heard similar rumors that year.[16]

Pera's revelations, knowingly or not, fall into line with the grander transformation of the Turkish economy in the years succeeding the establishment of the Kemalist state. Beginning with the "great exchange" of populations between Greece and Turkey in 1923–24, the sizable presence of Greek Orthodox Christians within the fledgling Turkish economy quickly evaporated. Passage of the punitive "wealth tax" during the Second World War further staggered the economic clout of non-Muslims at large in the republic, an event that further crippled the business dealings of Leon Taranto and others in the aftermath of the closure of the main Istanbul heroin factories in 1931. The building of a "national economy" premised upon Muslim ownership and entrepreneurialism did not end with the conclusion of one-party Kemalist rule in 1950. Anti-Christian sentiments continued, with an increasingly violent edge with the rise of the Democratic Party under Adnan Menderes. In September 1955, false rumors concerning the bombing of Mustafa Kemal's birthplace in Salonika sparked mass pogroms against both Christian and Jewish businesses in the city of Istanbul, leaving thousands of shops damaged throughout the city. While Ankara was quick to lay blame for the violence upon police incompetence, subsequent accounts and investigations of the 1955 riots suggested that officials in the city of Istanbul (and perhaps Ankara as well) had a hand in organizing the attacks. Informants close to the CIA were confident, for example, that the attacks were "well-planned and organized from their inception" to the point that it was impossible for them to be spontaneous. While CIA analysts initially suspected that Turkish suspicions towards Greek intentions towards Cyprus were critical in spawning the riots, it is clear that Ankara's longer-term desire to purge Turkish society of non-Muslims played an indelible role in the violence.[17] If one accepts the intelligence gathered by Martin Pera at face value, official efforts towards reordering and "Turkifying" economy extended into the black market as well.

The men who came to replace Vasil Arcan and Leon Taranto as the chief architects of the postwar Turkish drug trade were recent immigrants to the city of Istanbul. By and large, the greatest beneficiaries of this change in management were middle-aged men from Turkey's Black Sea coast. While İhsan Sekban was one of the few traffickers pointedly identified as Laz (even though he may in fact have been of Armenian origin), it is clear that many of the individuals who collaborated

[16] Martin Pera to Charles Siragusa, 5 March 1951, Turkey, 1951–52; FBN Files, 1916–70; DEA Records; RG 170, NAB.

[17] "Subject: 1. Anti-Menderes Group Among DP Deputies in the Grand National Assembly, 2. Anti-Greek Riots in Turkey," 4 October 1955, Report number blacked out, Central Intelligence Agency, attained via FOIA request, released 12 July 2011; Speros Vyronis, *The Mechanism of Catastrophe: The Turkish Pogrom of September 6–7, 1955, and the Destruction of the Greek Community of Istanbul* (Greekworks.com, 2008).

with him or competed against his interests came from towns and villages within close proximity of his hometown of Rize.

An individual considered by many to be Sekban's equal in weight and influence in Istanbul's postwar drug underworld was a prominent smuggler named Hüseyin Eminoğlu. Born around 1898 in Rize, Hüseyin was working as an errand boy at a quayside café in the Galata area of Istanbul when he was first introduced to the narcotics trade.[18] By the time he was fifty, local police came to identify him as a major trafficker of opiates out of the city. In 1948, Eminoğlu served four months in prison (followed by a six-month term "in exile" in Trabzon) after being convicted on drug trafficking charges.[19] At some point before 1950, he established a close business partnership with Ali Osman Tüter, a former officer in the Turkish military police. Unlike Eminoğlu, Ali Osman established his career in the narcotics trade as a chemist and processor of heroin (a craft he learned from a Greek trafficker, Michael Kalogrides).[20] FBN records unfortunately reveal little regarding the internal workings of the organization founded by Eminoğlu and Tüter. Random pieces of intelligence and assorted criminal cases filed against Hüseyin suggest however that the scope of the two men's trafficking network was expansive in terms of the amount of narcotics the two shipped out of Turkish ports.[21]

The prominence of Laz (or more generally Black Sea) migrants in the Istanbul narcotics trade was an issue that was first raised in FBN correspondence towards the end of the 1950s. Paul Knight, an agent who eventually served with distinction in both Turkey and Lebanon, pointedly argued that "Lasi" merchant seamen staffed several of the steamers often used to ship illicit opiates out of the port of Istanbul. One officer expressly warned Knight that it was useless for him to attempt to approach one trafficker on his own since all of those surrounding the suspect were Laz.[22]

Knight's characterization of the Istanbul drug underworld as an almost exclusively Laz domain (similar to that of the Corsicans of Marseille, as he put it) is belied by the presence of more minor figures active in the city during the 1950s and 1960s. İhsan Sekban, for example, closely cooperated with a Greek trafficker named Mavromatis (or more formally known as Nickli Eftimyadis), who operated a factory outside of Istanbul and supplied morphine base and heroin to wholesalers

[18] Newsday, *The Heroin Trail*, 32; Untitled photo array sheet (Turkish version), 1948, Turkey, 1943–48; Subject Files of the Bureau of Narcotics and Dangerous Drugs, 1916–70; Records of the Drug Enforcement Administration, Record Group 170; National Archives Building II, Silver Spring, MD.

[19] M. Sicot to Charles Siragusa, 3 March 1956, Turkey, 1955–56; FBN Files, 1916–70; DEA Records; RG 170, NAB.

[20] Martin Pera to Charles Siragusa, 30 April 1951, Turkey: Martin Pera File; FBN Files, 1916–70; DEA Records; RG 170, NAB.

[21] Charles Siragusa to John Cusack, 9 July 1952, Turkey, 1951–52; FBN Files, 1916–70; DEA Records; RG 170, NAB.

[22] Memorandum Report, 22 October 1958; Turkey, 1957–59; FBN Files, 1916–70; DEA Records; RG 170, NAB.

in Greece.[23] Sekban's gang, who supposedly all came from Rize, included an individual who was apparently Albanian in origin.[24]

Another major exception to the apparent grip that Black Sea smugglers, chemists, and dealers had on the city's narcotics industry is found in the influence wielded by the Soysal family. According to Turkish authorities, the family had migrated to Turkey from the town of Vodina (or Edessa) in northern Greece. Like Sekban, Turkish authorities labeled the Soysal brothers, Hüsnü, Ahmet and Mehmet, "first hand (*birinci el*)" or major bosses (*patronlar*) who supplied refined opium to smaller dealers in the city.[25] In the summer of 1950, Charles Siragusa arranged for a meeting with Hüsnü through an informant arrested in an FBN related case from two years earlier. Siragusa found the Greek-born trafficker forthcoming and talkative regarding his past in the narcotics industry and the nature of the Istanbul drug trade. Hüsnü claimed that his career as a chemist and wholesaler dated back to the 1930s. While he did not state how he entered the trade, Hüsnü's arrest record suggests that his skills as a chemist and his access to opium produced in Afyon provided him entrée into the circles of İhsan Sekban, Hüseyin Eminoğlu, Vasil Arcan, and others major smugglers in postwar Istanbul.[26] After retiring from the industry in 1944, he resumed his work in narcotics after losing all his money in "legal but unsound" investments. An Istanbul policeman, he claimed, provided him with his first connection in his renewed career, giving him two kilos of acetic anhydride in exchange for a regular bribe of 100 liras a week. After four years under the protection of this official, police raided Hüsnü's laboratory and home as a result, he claimed, of a dispute over an increase in bribe money demanded by Hüsnü's police contact.[27] His arrest in May 1950, and his subsequent employment as an FBN informant, did not deter him, or his brother Ahmet, from continuing their occupation.[28]

While Hüsnü appeared to have left the trade after attempting suicide in 1959, his younger brothers Ahmet and Mehmet Fahrettin remained a fixture of the Istanbul underworld well into the 1970s.[29] The two were arrested on multiple

[23] Elmore Gross to Charles Siragusa, 7 April 1955, Turkey, 1955–56; FBN Files, 1916–70; DEA Records; RG 170, NAB.

[24] Frank Sojat to Harry Anslinger, 5 February 1952, Turkey, 1951–52, FBN Files, 1916–70; DEA Records; RG 170, NAB.

[25] Frank Sojat to Harry Anslinger, 1 October 1951, Turkey, 1951–52; FBN Files, 1916–70; DEA Records; RG 170, NAB. American documents are a bit confused on this point. Hüsnü Soysal purportedly introduced himself as "Selanikli Hüsnü" or Hüsnü from Salonika, the largest port city in Greek Macedonia. Yet according to information related to the McClellan Commisson, Ahmet Soysal was identified as a smuggler born in the Turkish/Syrian border town of Kilis. While it is possible that the family may have had roots in Aegean Macedonia, it may be the case that Hüsnü considered himself a native of Solanika (perhaps a mark of status or a reference to where he had lived, grown up, or was educated) while his brother is referenced as a native of Kilis due to his business dealings with smugglers in the region. See U.S. Senate 951.

[26] Charles Siragusa to H. J. Anslinger, 10 August 1950; Turkey, 1950; FBN Files, 1916–70; DEA Records; RG 170, NAB.

[27] Charles Siragusa to H. J. Anslinger, 10 August 1950; Turkey, 1950; FBN Files, 1916–70; DEA Records; RG 170, NAB; "50,000 Liralık Eroin Bulundu," *Milliyet* 3 May 1950.

[28] Memorandum Report, 22 October 1958; Turkey, 1957–59; FBN Files, 1916–70; DEA Records; RG 170, NAB.

[29] "Boşandığı Karısının Evini Ateşe Verdi," *Milliyet* 21 July 1959; "Karısının Evini Yakan Eroinci Tevkii Edildi," *Milliyet* 22 July 1959.

occasions between 1950 and 1980 and were accused of smuggling narcotics as well as coffee, weapons, ammunition, tobacco, gold, and other goods. [30] If their arrest record from this period stands as an indication of their importance within the Istanbul underworld, it seems clear that Ahmet and Fahrettin, like their brother Hüsnü, operated and moved within influential circles. In 1964, Istanbul prosecutors arrested the two Soysal brothers alongside Hüseyin Eminoğlu on charges of attempting to smuggling ninety kilos of morphine into Marseille. As late as 1980, Fahrettin was charged with illegally importing cigarettes, ammunition, firearms, and foreign currency into Turkey. Counted among the twenty-seven other suspects in the case was Dündar Kılıç, arguably one of the most powerful gangsters in Istanbul between the 1970s and the 1990s.[31]

Two of the other suspects arrested in this case from December 1980 were a set of brothers who possessed a very different sort of pedigree to most of Istanbul's major traffickers. The two men, Ziya and Savaş, were relatives of Nazim Kalkavan, one of the founders of Kalkavan Holdings, one of the most influential shipping companies in Turkey. Nazim was born in Istanbul in 1914 but like other other major traffickers in the city, his roots, too, stemmed from the Black Sea coast. Despite the company he may have kept as a result of his more nefarious interests, Nazim Kalkavan was a graduate of both Roberts College and Oxford University and was an acquaintance of Ian Fleming, famed writer of the James Bond series.[32] In 1955, however, the FBN asserted that he had used ships belonging to his company in a conspiracy to smuggle morphine and heroin to Marseille in collaboration with Hüseyin Eminoğlu and Ali Osman Tüter. The FBN further contended that Kalkavan's connections extended directly to Sami al-Khoury, one of the most prominent smugglers in Lebanon, and to Antoine Guerini, a powerful figure within the Marseille underworld.[33] Official Turkish denials of Nazim's involvement in narcotics trafficking did not put to rest the connections between Kalkavan Holdings and Mediterranean drug trade.[34] In 1970, American narcotics officials again charged the company with complicity in the Turkish heroin trade, this time singling out Ziya Kalkavan as the primary culprit.[35] Despite his arrest in 1980 on drug-related charges, Ziya Kalkavan's name now adorns an Istanbul professional high school devoted to navigation and shipping (Ziya Kalkavan Denizcilik Meslek Lisesi).

[30] "Eroin Kaçakçılığı Sanıklarından İkisi Dün Teslim Oldu," *Milliyet* 5 December 1962; Newsday, *The Heroin Trail*, 34, 36; "Kahve Kaçakçılığı Duruşması Başladı," *Milliyet* 4 September 1959; "150 Ton Tütün Motorla Triyeste'ye Kaçırıldı," *Milliyet* 30 June 1960.

[31] "Toplu Kaçakçılık Sanığı 28 Kişi Daha Tutuklandı," *Milliyet* 25 December 1980.

[32] John Pearson, *The Life of Ian Fleming* (London: Jonathan Cape, 1966), 273–274; "Kalkavan Yalı 2.7 Trilyon Liraya Kalkavanlar'a Kaldı," *Hürriyet* 29 May 1999. It should be noted that Ian Fleming, during the time he became acquainted with Kalkavan in Istanbul, was a member of MI6.

[33] Elmore Gross to Charles Siragusa, 7 April 1955, Turkey, 1955–56; FBN Files, 1916–70; DEA Records; RG 170, NAB; Elmore Gross to Charles Siragusa, 17 March 1955; Turkey, 1955–56; FBN Files, 1916–70; DEA Records; RG 170, NAB.

[34] Azai Yumak to Charles Siragusa, 12 November 1955; Turkey, 1955–56; FBN Files, 1916–70; DEA Records; RG 170, NAB.

[35] Newsday, *The Heroin Trail*, 33.

Another unlikely family that stood accused of involvement in the Istanbul drug trade was that of the Akar brothers. Necip and Cemil Akar were born in 1904 in the town of Nezip, located close to the southern Turkish town of Gaziantep. After moving to Istanbul and graduating from a local pharmacy school, the two founded one of the first companies in the young Turkish Republic to produce toothpaste.[36] According to a source close to George White, a journalist named Riza Çandır, the trademark production of *Radyolin* toothpaste was not the only source of the family's newly acquired wealth. Before the outbreak of the Second World War, the two supposedly used their toothpaste bottles to smuggle significant quantities of heroin to Egypt. With the start of the Second World War, the Akar brothers further expanded their illicit dealings after entering into partnership with a German supplier of quinine. At a time when shortages of quinine plagued both the general public and the Turkish military, both Necip and Cemil, Çandır explained, knowingly syphoned off signficant quantities from their German supplier, selling solutions that comprised 40 percent chalk to local buyers. Neither brother was ever arrested for either scheme. Moreover, as Riza Çandır later explained, an undersecretary in the Turkish Ministry of Health actively collaborated with the Akars despite prior knowledge of the two's duplicitous dealings.[37]

No single method or means of negotiation or delivery defined the way major Istanbul wholesalers interacted with potential buyers. While some such as Hüseyin Eminoğlu and Ali Osman Tüter were capable of negotiating in a foreign language (French and English in their case), most Istanbul traffickers appeared to have known no other language than Turkish.[38] Foreigners who sought opium, morphine base, or heroin in Istanbul could at times meet in person with a major wholesaler to negotiate the sale of narcotics. Those transactions that did take place in the city were often conducted in the open at nightclubs or cafés.[39] On other occasions, large transactions of opium were handled outside of the city, usually close to villages where the product was housed or processed. While smaller transactions of a kilo or less happened with great regularity in alleys and cafés throughout the city, the purchase of large amounts of opium (for processing into heroin or morphine) and the exchange of money for such sales, usually occurred in isolated corners of the countryside.

The elite of the Istanbul drug trade tended to deal directly with European and Lebanese buyers. Ahmet Soysal, Hüseyin Eminoğlu, and Nazim Kalkavan were among the few to directly supply Marseille- and Beirut-based traffickers with processed heroin and morphine intended for transshipment to Western Europe or

[36] Gürkan Hacır, "'Bir Gripin Al, Bir Şeyin Kalmaz,'" *Akşam* 19 September 2009.

[37] Riza Chandir to George White, 30 June 1948, Turkey, 1943–48; FBN Files, 1916–70; DEA Records; RG 170, NAB.

[38] Sal Vizzini et al., *Vizzini: The Secret Lives of America's Most Successful Undercover Agent* (New York: Arbor House, 1972), 102, 110.

[39] For Commissioner of Narcotics Anslinger from White #10, 10 June 1948, George H. White Papers, Box 1, Folder 7, Special Collections Department, Stanford University; Alvin Moscow, *Merchants of Heroin* (New York: Dial Press, 1968), 5–7; Vizzini, *Vizzini: The Secret Lives of America's Most Successful Undercover Agent*, 10–11.

North America.[40] The vast majority of Istanbul traffickers, it appears however, operated as middlemen for farmers and smugglers located in the Anatolian interior. The sale of this raw opium often did not pass through Istanbul, but was usually traded overland through Syria and Lebanon for processing and packaging. For much of the history of the French Connection, the personal dealings of a major wholesaler like Sekban or Eminoğlu largely began and ended within Istanbul's city limits.

As one reads the full breadth of FBN field reports from the 1950s and 1960s, it is clear that there was no singular figure, gang, or cartel that monopolized Istanbul's heroin trade. American investigations, as well as internal Turkish documents supplied to the FBN, do list the names of numerous traffickers active in the city other than those cited earlier. Most reports offer few details aside from the names of these individuals or the descriptions of their specific crimes.[41] Agent Paul Knight, for example, cites a "chief trafficker" by the name of Hasan Turan, who supposedly led a gang of Laz smugglers who operated several ships based in Istanbul.[42] A search of FBN files and the Turkish press however has yet to yield any information supporting this claim, let alone any insights into who Hasan Turan was. Considering the extent to which the sale of opiates was a trade plied by individuals and collectives of various degrees of significance, there appears reason to doubt one FBN agent's claim that the "Istanbul underworld was fairly small."[43] Moreover, if FBN revelations regarding the activities of the Kalkavans and Akars are indeed correct, it may be equally difficult to delineate the city's underworld from Istanbul's otherwise legitimate "overworld."

The divide between drug trafficking and other legitimate and illegitimate trades grows more indistinct when one considers the additional investments of several of Istanbul's major smugglers. İhsan Sekban's dealings in the Istanbul real estate market were complemented by his purported interests in the illicit trade of weapons.[44] Hüseyin Eminoğlu's business ventures appear even more expansive. In addition to smuggling a variety of contraband goods into Turkey, Eminoğlu also had established a fine arts school in Istanbul. Both he and his partner Ali Osman also owned apartment buildings in the city, as well as farms and a cinema back in Eminoğlu's hometown of Rize.[45] Ahmet Soysal similarly invested heavily

[40] Moscow, *Merchants of Heroin*, 5–7; Elmore Gross to Charles Siragusa, 7 April 1955; Turkey, 1955–56; FBN Files, 1916–70; DEA Records; RG 170, NAB; Elmore Gross to Charles Siragusa, 17 March 1955; Turkey, 1955–56; FBN Files, 1916–70; DEA Records; RG 170, NAB.7114.

[41] See e.g. Elmore Gross to Charles Siragusa, 12 February 1955; Turkey, 1955–56; FBN Files, 1916–70; DEA Records; RG 170: Elmore Gross to Charles Siragusa, 23 February 1955; Turkey, 1955–56; FBN Files, 1916–70; DEA Records; RG 170.

[42] Memorandum, 10 March 1959; Turkey, 1957–59; FBN Files, 1916–70; DEA Records; RG 170, NAB.

[43] Elmore Gross to Charles Siragusa, 17 February 1955; Turkey, 1955–56; FBN Files, 1916–70; DEA Records; RG 170.

[44] Charles Siragusa to Mr. H. J. Anslinger, 25 July 1950; Turkey, 1950; Subject Files of the Bureau of Narcotics and Dangerous Drugs, 1916–70; Records of the Drug Enforcement Administration, Record Group 170; National Archives Building II, Silver Spring, MD.

[45] Arai Yumak to Charles Siragusa, 4 May 1956; Turkey, 1955–56; FBN Files, 1916–70; DEA Records; RG 170; Elmore Gross to Charles Siragusa, 17 March 1955; Turkey, 1955–56; FBN Files, 1916–70; DEA Records; RG 170, NAB.

in legitimate businesses, eventually claiming ownership of a watch store, an apartment complex, and an auto parts store.[46]

Understanding the diversity of business ventures undertaken by these traders and others is essential to comprehending both the economic and political clout wielded by elements of Turkey's criminal underworld. At a time when the country was only recently emerging from the shadows of war, intercommunal conflict, and economic devastation, men like Sekban and Eminoğlu stood out as individuals possessing exceptional wealth. The affluence accrued by these men afforded them more than just money with which officials could be bribed. The legitimate businesses they owned, as well as the contraband goods they supplied to the broader Turkish public, allowed them to enter the upper ranks of the Turkish political and economic establishment.

A closer look at the positions Sekban, Eminoğlu, and Soysal occupied within the Turkish economy (and the international drug trade) also demands a greater appreciation of the broader black market found within the country in the aftermath of the Second World War. Opiate trafficking in Istanbul comprised only one component of a more generalized industry of illicit production, consumption, and transshipment that was found throughout the republic. The vast majority of those involved in buying, selling, and smuggling illicit goods did not glean great financial rewards or hold sway over politicians and policemen. They constituted an incredibly rich array of cultivators, processors, and smugglers located in multiple corners of the Anatolian interior. No great patron of the Istanbul drug trade was capable of maintaining their success without tapping into the ingenuity and sophistication of these vast rural networks.

FARMERS AND SMUGGLERS: RURAL OPIUM AND THE TURKISH BLACK MARKET

At some point in the 1920s, an internal memo discussing the serious nature of the Turkish smuggling trade circulated within confines of the Ministry of the Interior in Ankara. Solving the problem of illegal smuggling was, in the words of the memo's author, an effort that demanded the attention of "officers, administration, administrators and from all of us." The principal point of concern identified in the short memo was the issue of illegal coffee imports. "The broad networks" carrying out these "ingenious enterprises" were part of a larger culture of smuggling that not only comprised the illicit exchange of money but also the exchange of domestic goods (namely, hazelnuts) on a one-for-one basis.[47]

As mentioned in the last chapter, crimes related to "banditry" or other acts of violence or resistance remained the principal concern for security personnel

[46] Newsday, *The Heroin Trail*, 54.

[47] BCA 30.01.00.00.41.246.17, undated. It can be surmised from the document that it was written in the era immediately following Turkey's language reform laws since the report is produced in both Latin letters and in the late Ottoman script.

in central and eastern Anatolia.[48] Nevertheless, the "seriousness" with which the author speaks of the smuggled coffee reflects deeper trends in the evolution of the Turkish economy following independence in 1923. As seen in the Turkish defense of the opium trade during the early Kemalist era, the economic nationalism that defined late Ottoman politics remained at the core of the republic's economic policy. High tariffs continued to be levied on foreign goods following the Great Depression and into the postwar period. Under the post-Kemalist Democratic government of the 1950s, Ankara readily endorsed import substitution policies in the hopes of both boosting domestic industries as well as further minimizing demand for foreign goods. Beginning with the Kemalist period, significant portions of Turkey's industrial or agricultural capacity were owned or monopolized by appendages of the state. While the Democratic Party initially favored greater amounts of foreign direct investment in the country during the early 1950s, the Menderes government ultimately reinstated tighter controls over imports and foreign exchange towards the end of the decade. By the late 1950s, Turkey's flagging economic prospects brought about the imposition of price controls over domestic commodities and goods, as well as a fixed exchange rate for the lira. The fall of the Menderes government and the establishment of a new constitution in 1960 further amplified the statist tendencies seen in the preceding decades. The new constitution stipulated the creation of a "State Planning Organization (*Devlet Planlama Teşkilatı*)," which forecast and initiated economic growth on the state's behalf. While the post-1960 economic regime did bring about greater improvements to the country's industrial sector, inefficiencies and dysfunction continued to plague state-run or supported industries into the 1970s. Meanwhile, the Turkish agricultural sector, which continued to comprise the bulk of Turkey's economy and labor force in the immediate postwar era, witnessed only moderate gains and improvements following the reforms enacted during the Democratic era.[49]

It is against this backdrop that several black market industries took shape and developed in Turkey. An internal report surveying the causes and dynamics

[48] While the period between 1945 and 1980 is often depicted as a dormant era in the history of Kurdish resistance in Turkey, documents from the Prime Minister's Republican Archive do point to ongoing acts of localized violence. In 1959, e.g. the governors of Erzincan and Tunceli (Dersim) report fighting between specific tribes over grazing rights. Other reports from Diyarbakir and Rize discuss outbreaks of blood feuds (while one does not find mention of the ethnic nature of the perpetrators or victims in either case, the murder of a man Diyarbakir in 1958 was deemed significant since he belonged to a family that supported the Democratic Party). American Embassy Ankara to Department of State, "A Report on the Kurds in Southeastern Turkey," 8 December 1952, 882.41/12-852, Central Decimal Files, 1950–54, RG 59, NAB; BCA 30.1.00.00.69.435.2, 7 August 1959; BCA 30.1.00.00.69.435.4, 20 September 1958; BCA 30.1.00.00.69.438.2 7 August 1959; BCA 30.1.00.00.72.460.8, 27 August 1969.

[49] Şevket Pamuk, "Economic Change in Twentieth Century Turkey: Is the Glass more than Half Full," in Reşat Kasaba (ed.), *The Cambridge History of Turkey: Volume 4, Turkey in the Modern World* (Cambridge: Cambridge University Press, 2008), 266–300; Erik Jan Zürcher, *Turkey: A Modern History* (London: I.B. Tauris, 1997), 202–209, 234–240, 278–280.

of smuggling in Turkey in 1965 gives an even clearer indication of how various portions of the Turkish bureaucracy viewed the nature and extent of illicit economic activity. First and foremost, both the Ministry of the Interior and the Foreign Ministry agreed that smuggling was a problem most associated with the country's eastern and southeastern borders. Many causes lay at the heart of Turkey's struggle with cross-border smuggling in these regions. On economic grounds, smuggling was driven by "high taxes," import restrictions, and rising prices within the Republic of Turkey. Meanwhile, foreign demand for certain Turkish commodities (such as livestock and olive oil) goaded smugglers to cross into Iraq, Iran, and Syria to sell their goods. Unemployment (and promises of a steady income of 50 to 200 lira per shipment) and the desire for higher rates of exchange also had an effect upon the motivations of individuals to participate in smuggling.[50]

Opium and its derivatives comprised only a portion of illicit goods flowing out of the Republic of Turkey in the postwar era. In addition to opiates, Turkish authorities seized contraband animals (especially sheep), tobacco, olive oil, dried fruit, and wood.[51] Between 1954 and 1959 alone, for example, Turkish authorities interdicted over 56,000 kilos of illegally exported tobacco along the Turkish border.[52] Flowing across the border into Turkey were equally large numbers of illicit goods such as clothing (particularly nylons and silk), gold, Turkish and foreign currency, natural gas (especially from Iran), tires, coffee, razors, and watches.[53] Turkish archival sources again provide an exceptional glimpse into this traffic during the years between 1954 and 1959. Between November 1954 and April 1959, Interior Ministry officials counted a grand total of at least 10,980 "incidents (*olaylar*)" of trafficking encountered by border authorities. As a result of these incidents, 7,639 people were apprehended.[54] Both American and Turkish sources noted that such encounters often resulted in firefights between border security forces and

[50] BCA 30.0.001.000.000.39.235.4, 21 August 1965. Interior Ministry officials also associated smuggling as a byproduct of specific agreements with Syria and Iran in terms of the use of territory on either side of the border as grazing land for local pastoralists. Under the auspices of this regime (*pasavan rejimi*) both legal and illicit traders in livestock and other goods were able to move across the frontier with relative ease.

[51] BCA 30.0.001.000.000.39.235.4, 21 August 1965.

[52] BCA 30.1.0.0.67.423.7, 4 July 1955; BCA 30.1.0.0.58.428.4, 1 February 1957; BCA 30.1.0.0.68.428.2, 18 January 1957; BCA 30.1.0.0.68.432.10, 1957; BCA 30.1.0.0.69.433.2, 7 January 1958; BCA 30.1.0.0.69.433.3, 10 January 1958; BCA 30.1.0.0.69.433.5, 15 February 1958; BCA 30.1.0.0.69.433.8, 8 March 1958; BCA 30.1.0.0.69.433.12, 12 April 1958; BCA 30.1.0.0.69.434.5, 9 May 1958, BCA 30.1.0.0.69.434.8, 7 June 1958; BCA 30.1.0.0.69.434.13, 12 July 1958; BCA 30.1.0.0.69.434.16, 8 August 1958; BCA 30.1.0.0.69.435.2, 13 September 1958; BCA 30.1.0.0.69.435.15, 10 December 1958; BCA 30.1.0.0.69.435.15, 10 December 1958; BCA 30.1.0.0.69.436.2, 7 February 1959; BCA 30.1.0.0.69.436.6, 13 March 1959; BCA 30.1.0.0.69.437.2, 6 May 1959; BCA 30.1.0.0.69.437.6, 9 June 1959.

[53] BCA 30.0.001.000.000.39.235.4, 21 August 1965.

[54] Memorandum: District #17, 24 November 1955; Turkey, 1955–56; FBN Files, 1916–70; DEA Records; RG 170, NAB; Memorandum Report, 6 January 1957, Iran Miscellaneous File; FBN Files, 1916–70; DEA Records; RG 170, NAB; Memorandum Report, 22 October 1958; Turkey, 1957–59; FBN Files, 1916–70; DEA Records; RG 170, NAB.

smugglers.[55] During this same period of time, 295 smugglers were killed in border clashes (with 108 losing their lives in 1957 alone). In order to deter smuggling, Ankara sought to mine large swaths of the Turkish/Syrian frontier (an effort that appeared to do little to inhibit the activities of smugglers in the region).[56] Locals in the border town of Kilis, according to one American official, had a saying, "If you see a young man in Kilis with a limp, he's a smuggler; if you see an old man with a limp, he fought with Atatürk."[57]

FBN agents could at best estimate the total amount of opiates smuggled out of the country in the postwar period. As early as 1952, Turkish officials confidentially informed American officials that an estimated 15 percent of legitimate opium production in Anatolia was diverted to illicit sources.[58] In 1959, Harry Anslinger personally informed one State Department official that "accurate figures on Turkey's opium production have never been obtained. We can only estimate the huge quantities which peasant producers do not sell to the government monopoly, all of which is fed to the underworld."[59] Inclement weather, poor roads, and the threat of rural banditry made regular monitoring of provincial sources of trafficking hazardous in many regions of the country.[60] The sheer range of territory associated with opium production in Turkey also inhibited both American and Turkish officials from locating and tracking the amount of licit and illicit harvested in the country. By the early 1960s, the Land Production Office permitted opium production in only seven provinces: Afyon, Eskişehir, Amasya, Kütahya, Malatya, Denizli, and Konya.[61] Nevertheless, cases made before and after the reduction in opium producing provinces suggests that illicit opium harvesting continued in areas outside of the official appointed districts.[62]

[55] BCA 30.1.0.0.67.423.7, 4 July 1955; BCA 30.1.0.0.58.428.4, 1 February 1957; BCA 30.1.0.0.68.428.2, 18 January 1957; BCA 30.1.0.0.68.432.10, 1957; BCA 30.1.0.0.69.433.2, 7 January 1958; BCA 30.1.0.0.69.433.3, 10 January 1958; BCA 30.1.0.0.69.433.5, 15 February 1958; BCA 30.1.0.0.69.433.8, 8 March 1958; BCA 30.1.0.0.69.433.12, 12 April 1958; BCA 30.1.0.0.69.434.5, 9 May 1958, BCA 30.1.0.0.69.434.8, 7 June 1958; BCA 30.1.0.0.69.434.13, 12 July 1958; BCA 30.1.0.0.69.434.16, 8 August 1958; BCA 30.1.0.0.69.435.2, 13 September 1958; BCA 30.1.0.0.69.435.15, 10 December 1958; BCA 30.1.0.0.69.435.15, 10 December 1958; BCA 30.1.0.0.69.436.2, 7 February 1959; BCA 30.1.0.0.69.436.6, 13 March 1959; BCA 30.1.0.0.69.437.2, 6 May 1959; BCA 30.1.0.0.69.437.6, 9 June 1959.

[56] BCA 30.0.001.000.000.39.235.4, 21 August 1965.

[57] American Embassy Ankara to Department of State, 23 July 1968, no file number, Subject Numeric Files, 1967–69; RG 59, NAB.

[58] American Consul General to Department of State, "Narcotics and Opium Report," 23 January 1953, 882.53/1-253, Central Decimal Files, 1950–54, RG 59, NAB.

[59] Riwyn Chase to Harry Anslinger, 17 February 1959, Turkey, 1957–59; FBN Files, 1916–70; DEA Records; RG 170, NAB.

[60] Memorandum: District #17, 24 November 1955, Turkey, 1955–56; FBN Files, 1916–70; DEA Records; RG 170, NAB.

[61] U.S. Senate 881.

[62] Lauren Goin to Charles Siragusa, 3 June 1958, Turkey, 1957–59; FBN Files, 1916–70; DEA Records; RG 170, NAB. According to a representative of the State Department's International Cooperation Administration (ICA), the number of hectares of opium cultivation did decline between

A series of compelling incentives confronted peasants who cultivated poppies throughout Turkey. Peasants were obliged to report to local authorities the projected amount of opium they would harvest in a given season. The physical isolation of many villages, coupled with the lack of traversable roads, often made regular oversight of harvesting activities by the Land Production Office difficult. Regional traffickers, who either worked independently or in conjunction with major wholesalers in Istanbul or Izmir, readily paid slightly higher prices for excess opium. In 1959, smugglers purportedly paid farmers between 200 and 300 lira for a kilo of raw opium, far exceeding the government price of 50 lira per kilogram at the time. Moreover, the fine for opium diversion (30 lira per kilo) did little to deter provincial producers from hoarding and selling contraband opium.[63]

American officials particularly noticed (or were made aware of) more generalized peasant suspicions and distrust of state authority. As one FBN progress report put it:

> The important Turkish gangsters from the cities—from whom a foreign trafficker would purchase—seem to follow a general policy of obliging such customers to take delivery of narcotics in the rural areas where these gangsters have their depots and are adequately protected by large groups of peasants with whom they have worked for years. In some cases it seems, an entire village will be associated, at least through friendship or perhaps through clannish ties, with the gangsters. The gangster is aided in his "public relations" in rural areas by the chief characteristics of all peasants: suspicion of and dislike for any authority (especially police), and admiration for the "big shot" law-breaker.

In the estimation of the FBN, peasant xenophobia towards foreigners in general, and Arabs in particular, strengthened the ties between local growers and smuggling syndicates.[64]

Statistics reported internally by the Turkish Interior Ministry demonstrate that only modest amounts of "narcotics material (*uyuşturucu maddesi*)" were interdicted in the years between 1954 and 1959:

1956 and 1958 (from 17,370 hectares, to 10,700 hectares). However, the representative Lauren Goin, warned Siragusa that:

> . . . the yield figures [attributed to the number of hectares of cultivation] seem to be pretty strange and do not seem to coincide with what the government would estimate the yields to be. I, also, do not have a great deal of confidence concerning the accuracy of the figures, but they're included for whatever information they might hold for you.

[63] Garland Williams to Harry Anslinger, 30 January 1958, Turkey, 1957–59; FBN Files, 1916–70; DEA Records; RG 170, NAB.

[64] Memorandum: District #17, 24 November 1955, Turkey, 1955–56; FBN Files, 1916–70; DEA Records; RG 170, NAB.

NARCOTICS MATERIAL INTERDICTED IN TURKEY, 1954–1959 (TURKISH SOURCES)[65]

	1954	1955	1956	1957	1958	1959	Totals (Kilos)
January	–	9	0	12.675	719.6	4.3	745.575
February	–	0	291.022	578.97	6.4	–	876.392
March	–	0	0	0	213	60.51	273.51
April	–	0	0.004	0	110	75.2	185.204
May	–	0	72.5	0	1.25	–	73.75
June	–	0	24.69	0	14.5	–	39.19
July	–	65.625	13.5	0	1340.388	–	1419.513
August	–	84.4	0	307.5	166.1	–	558
September	–	179	71	–	–		250
October	–	49	239	2.05	10.04	–	300.09
November	3	0	0	10	88.35		101.35
December	0	0	253.6	–	12.8	–	266.4
Totals (Kilos)	3	387.025	894.316	982.195	2682.428	140.01	5088.974

Yet in 1963, Turkish officials revealed a completely different set of statistics to their American counterparts:

NARCOTICS MATERIAL INTERDICTED IN TURKEY, 1952–1962 (AMERICAN SOURCES)[66]

Year	Opium (Kilos)	Morphine Base (Kilos)	Heroin (Kilos)	Totals (Kilos)
1952	38.5	14	28	80.5
1953	5	5.7	7.8	18.5
1954	488	35.5	4	527.5
1955	753	105	19	877
1956	97	40.5	25	162.5
1957	70	58	7	135
1958	147	28	3.3	178.3
1959	46	22.8	2	70.8
1960	1167	32.1	107.2	1306.3
1961	1137	32.2	5	1174.2
1962	2016	71	9.2	2096.2
Totals (Kilos)	5964.5	444.8	217.5	6626.8

[65] BCA 30.1.0.0.67.423.7, 4 July 1955; BCA 30.1.0.0.58.428.4, 1 February 1957; BCA 30.1.0.0.68.428.2, 18 January 1957; BCA 30.1.0.0.68.432.10, 1957; BCA 30.1.0.0.69.433.2, 7 January 1958; BCA 30.1.0.0.69.433.3, 10 January 1958; BCA 30.1.0.0.69.433.5, 15 February 1958; BCA 30.1.0.0.69.433.8, 8 March 1958; BCA 30.1.0.0.69.433.12, 12 April 1958; BCA 30.1.0.0.69.434.5, 9 May 1958, BCA 30.1.0.0.69.434.8, 7 June 1958; BCA 30.1.0.0.69.434.13, 12 July 1958; BCA 30.1.0.0.69.434.16, 8 August 1958; BCA 30.1.0.0.69.435.2, 13 September 1958; BCA 30.1.0.0.69.435.15, 10 December 1958; BCA 30.1.0.0.69.435.15, 10 December 1958; BCA 30.1.0.0.69.436.2, 7 February 1959; BCA 30.1.0.0.69.436.6, 13 March 1959; BCA 30.1.0.0.69.437.2, 6 May 1959; BCA 30.1.0.0.69.437.6, 9 June 1959.

[66] BCA 30.1.0.0.67.423.7, 4 July 1955; BCA 30.1.0.0.58.428.4, 1 February 1957; BCA 30.1.0.0.68.428.2, 18 January 1957; BCA 30.1.0.0.68.432.10, 1957; BCA 30.1.0.0.69.433.2, 7 January 1958; BCA 30.1.0.0.69.433.3, 10 January 1958; BCA 30.1.0.0.69.433.5, 15 February 1958; BCA 30.1.0.0.69.433.8, 8 March 1958; BCA 30.1.0.0.69.433.12, 12 April 1958; BCA 30.1.0.0.69.434.5, 9 May 1958, BCA 30.1.0.0.69.434.8, 7 June 1958; BCA 30.1.0.0.69.434.13, 12 July 1958; BCA 30.1.0.0.69.434.16, 8 August 1958; BCA 30.1.0.0.69.435.2, 13 September 1958; BCA 30.1.0.0.69.435.15, 10 December 1958; BCA 30.1.0.0.69.435.15, 10 December 1958; BCA 30.1.0.0.69.436.2, 7 February 1959; BCA 30.1.0.0.69.436.6, 13 March 1959; BCA 30.1.0.0.69.437.2, 6 May 1959; BCA 30.1.0.0.69.437.6, 9 June 1959.

It is difficult to interpret the differences between these two reported sets of statistics. Nor is it easy to discern patterns or flows of narcotics over this period of time. At the very least, they do seem to support the supposition that the amount of opiates trafficked out of Turkey grew in the years following the Second World War.

The actual production and smuggling of Turkish opiates, exclusive of the dealings and negotiations of major and minor brokers in Istanbul, was almost exclusively a rural enterprise. The FBN's first insights into how provincial cultivators and traffickers organized this trade stem from a string of cases made over a twelve-month period between December 1954 and 1955. The first case, which was successfully organized under the personal direction of Charles Siragusa, apprehended Ahmet Özsayar and twenty-six other traffickers outside of Adana with over 400 kilos of raw opium, morphine, and heroin.[67] The Özsayar case was a part of a broader operation conducted by police in Turkey, Greece, Syria, and Lebanon and was seen later as a benchmark effort for the FBN in Turkey. The second case, which like the first featured a successful cooperative effort between Turkish and American law enforcement officials, apprehended Mehmet Özyürek and seven other individuals outside of Uşak (located to the east of Izmir) in possession of over seventy-five kilos of morphine base and close to 700 kilos of unprepared opium. The cache from the Özyürek case also included multiple firearms (including those used in a gun battle with Turkish police) and the seizure of two laboratories used for processing raw opium into morphine base. According to the McClellan Committee's survey of the investigation, the case represented the largest postwar seizure of narcotics in either Turkey or in Europe.[68] A third case made in the region of Merzifon in eastern Anatolia from December 1955 netted American and Turkish authorities 150 kilos of opium and a similarly large cache of weapons (including swords and daggers).[69]

For reasons that remain unclear, the FBN only preserved the internal report from this latter case (no official report can be found in the 1954–55 folder for either the Özsayar and Özyurek cases). James Attie, the arresting officer in the case, personally played a role in assisting Turkish gendarmes in apprehending the seven individuals seized at the scene. The supposed ringleader of this "gang" was Nadir Alpten, a twenty-six-year-old resident of Merzifon who had previously made his reputation as a bandit (and "bully boy" in Attie's words) in the region. The other men taken into custody were similarly young in age (mostly between the ages of seventeen to twenty-eight). Most of these individuals appeared to have worked as drivers or helpers in Alpten's operation. One of the suspects, İsmet Karakavak, was noted as "a Kurd outcast" whose reputation as Alpten's "killer" was augmented by a longer history of kidnapping, murder, and rape in the region of Merzifon. Attie gives no indication that the band was associated with any major trafficker. Rather, it seems

[67] U.S. Senate 799; Siragusa and Wiedrich, *Trail of the Poppy*, 3–32.

[68] U.S. Senate 799.

[69] Memorandum: District #17, 25 December 1955, Turkey, 1955–56; FBN Files, 1916–70; DEA Records; RG 170, NAB; *Traffic in Opium and Other Dangerous Drugs for the Year Ended December 31, 1955* (Washington DC: U.S. Treasury Department, Bureau of Narcotics, 1956), 21.

that Alpten acted as a supplier of raw opium for purchasers and smugglers based in Gaziantep, located south and west of Merzifon.[70] Turkish authorities purportedly became aware of Alpten's operations after his partner, Fazlı Beden, approached a police informant, telling him that his Merzifon syndicate was looking for willing buyers in Istanbul.[71] After the arrest, it was discovered that Alpten and Beden had long invested the proceeds from their narcotics dealings locally in the town of Merzifon (with the two owning a bathhouse and grocery store, respectively).[72]

While both Istanbul and Izmir did serve as venues for arranging purchase and shipment of raw opium, morphine base, and heroin for major traffickers in Turkey, the Anatolian towns of Gaziantep, Iskenderun, and Kilis were the primary centers for the actual exchange of money and the exporting of illicit opiates out of Turkey in the postwar era.[73] After the money and drugs were exchanged in Gaziantep and Iskenderun, smugglers then transported their wares south towards the Turkish/Syrian frontier.[74] The small border town of Kilis, located fifty kilometers south of Gaziantep, was often the last point of departure for Turkish opiates bound for foreign markets. Kilis, according to one official from the US embassy who visited the town in 1968, was a grand open-air market for smuggled goods. The immense volume of cheap, and often poorly made, imported consumer goods that flooded into Kilis appeared to have overshadowed the steady flow of opiates that exited the town via the busy border crossing just south of the town or across the mountain paths that lay further outside the city. Considering the industriousness and relative prosperity gleaned from the illicit goods that surged through the town, the reporting American official noted, with no subtle irony, one of the signs posted on the main road entering Kilis. Adorning the sign was an exhortation from none other than Atatürk himself, declaring, "Turk! Be proud, work hard and take pride! (*Türk, oğun, çalış, güven!*)."[75]

[70] Memorandum: District #17, 25 December 1955, Turkey, 1955–56; FBN Files, 1916–70; DEA Records; RG 170, NAB.

[71] Memorandum: District #17, 13 December 1955, Turkey, 1955–56; FBN Files, 1916–70; DEA Records; RG 170, NAB; Charles Wighton, *Dope International* (London: Frederick Muller Limited, 1960), 55–59.

[72] Memorandum: District #17, 25 December 1955, Turkey, 1955–56; FBN Files, 1916–70; DEA Records; RG 170, NAB.

[73] FBN documents provide only some insight into the significance of Izmir as a center of narcotics trafficking in Turkey. Most references to Izmir found in FBN case files from the 1950s suggest İhsan Sekban played a key (if not dominant) role in monopolizing the exporting of opiates from this Aegean port city. In 1955, e.g., two Izmir-based traffickers revealed to FBN arresting agents that they had once sold over 200 kilograms of raw opium to Sekban a week before being apprehended with 100 kilos of opium. No report in either the records of the FBN or the Turkish press suggests that Sekban was ever accused or arrested on the basis of these accusations. See *Traffic in Opium and Other Dangerous Drugs for the Year Ended December 31, 1955* (Washington DC: U.S. Treasury Department, Bureau of Narcotics, 1956), 21.

[74] Memorandum: District #17, 24 November 1955; Turkey, 1955–56; FBN Files, 1916–70; DEA Records; RG 170, NAB; Memorandum Report, 6 January 1957, Iran Miscellaneous File; FBN Files, 1916–70; DEA Records; RG 170, NAB; Memorandum Report, 22 October 1958; Turkey, 1957–59; FBN Files, 1916–70; DEA Records; RG 170, NAB.

[75] American Embassy Ankara to Department of State, "Smuggling at Kilis, Turkish-Syrian Border," 23 July 1968, no file number, Subject Numeric Files, 1967–69; RG 59, NAB.

HEROIN'S MIDDLE PASSAGE: SYRIA, LEBANON, AND THE TURKISH OPIUM TRADE

Turkey's southern border with Syria is an artifact of the First World War. In December 1920, the Ottoman government agreed to the terms of the Treaty of Sevres, which formally separated the British and French mandate states of Syria and Iraq from the imperial core of Anatolia. The border separating Anatolia from the so-called "Arab lands" to the south however represented a revision of previous British and French territorial aims first articulated in the midst of the Great War. According to the secret Sykes-Picot Agreement of 1916, much of what is today southern Turkey (including territories as far north as Sivas and Malatya as well more immediate present-day border towns such as Iskenderun, Urfa, and Gaziantep) was to be awarded to France following the end of hostilities. The redrawing of the Ottoman imperial map, as well as the subsequent formation of the modern states of Turkey, Iraq, and Syria, did more than finalize the demise of the empire or truncate the future territorial claims of the Republic of Turkey. The imposition of these new borders, as well as the customs and migratory laws that accompanied their demarcation, radically transformed the social and economic dimensions of peoples straddling the frontier. The incorporation of the old Ottoman province of Mosul into the state of Iraq, for example, severed or severely hampered the region's once close economic, political, and social ties with the newly formed Turkish provinces of Diyarbakir and Van.[76] Turks in Gaziantep and Syrians in Aleppo found themselves in similarly constrained situations following the implementation of the international border between the two cities. The bisection of this integral region of trade and contact irrevocably altered the economic underpinnings of the region. The imposition of customs duties, official inspections, and import/export controls made much of what had been the free flow of goods and commodities an impossibility, laying the foundation for a lucrative and expansive black market.[77]

The production and sale of narcotics emanating from the *balad al-Sham* is a phenomenon that predated the foundation of the French mandates of Syria and Lebanon. Hashish use, as well as the production of hemp, was commonplace in prewar Syria as well as other regions in the Levantine world.[78] In the early days of the interwar period, the famed Sir Thomas Russell (more commonly known as Russell Pasha), the head of the Anglo-Egyptian Central Narcotics Intelligence Bureau, was among the first to crusade against hashish use in the region.[79] French authorities in Lebanon and Syria similarly, but unsuccessfully, also attempted to curtail the production of hemp in such regions as the Bekaa Valley and the Jebal

[76] For a treatment of transport and trade in the Levant and Mesopotamia, see Inalcik and Quataert 818–820.

[77] Schayegh, "The Many Worlds of 'Abud Yasin; or, What Narcotics Trafficking in the Interwar Middle East Can Tell Us about Territorialization".

[78] Schayegh, "The Many Worlds of 'Abud Yasin; or, What Narcotics Trafficking in the Interwar Middle East Can Tell Us about Territorialization," 296.

[79] Thomas Russell, *Egyptian Service 1902–1946* (London: John Murray, 1949), 229–230.

Druze.[80] Anti-hemp and opium efforts continued in the region with the achievement of Lebanese and Syrian independence in the postwar era. While local authorities were often quick to declare success in their campaigns against local hemp farmers, Garland Williams, one of the first FBN representatives to visit the Levant, reported to Harry Anslinger that internal security personnel in Lebanon were careful not to harm the fields belonging to politicians. Local producers, mindful of the fact that hemp plantations belonging to prominent politicians were exempt from government crackdowns, actively resisted hashish suppression efforts.[81]

Opium was also found in abundant amounts in interwar Lebanon and Syria. Some regions, such as the Jabal Druze, did produce opium for the local and transnational marketplace. However, cultivators had to contend with Turkish, as well as Iranian, sources in plying their trade. As one FBN agent later explained, Turkish opium held distinct advantages over the Syrian and Iranian varieties since it tended to possess the highest amount of morphine. Moreover, bringing opium across the Turkish-Syrian frontier posed few difficulties and was a shorter distance from Beirut than either Iran or the Jabal Druze.[82]

FBN interest and engagement in Lebanese and Syrian narcotics trafficking derived from the bureau's first efforts in Turkey. Charles Siragusa first visited Lebanon and Syria in September 1950, a trip that followed shortly after his initial foray into Turkey that summer. His detailed reports from that summer, as well as subsequent reports from other FBN agents from the 1950s, vividly portray the pervasiveness of narcotics trafficking in both countries. While the outbreak of civil war in Lebanon and the establishment of a united Syrian-Egyptian Arab Republic in 1958 did serve to interrupt the FBN's activities in Beirut, Damascus, and Aleppo, the archival record available to us gives us more than an adequate picture of how Turkish opium pervaded the inner workings of the drug trafficking networks that spanned the region.

Once opium crossed the Turkish-Syrian border, its first destination was usually Aleppo. While some Turkish opium did proceed across the border and towards Beirut in its unadulterated form, significant amounts of this raw product found their way into processing laboratories in Aleppo. Typifing the influence of the Aleppo connection to the eastern Mediterranean drug trade was the case of Gamal al-Masri. FBN efforts to apprehend al-Masri (who was born in Egypt or was of Egyptian parentage) dated back to 1954. After a four-year investigation, American agents accused Gamal and his brothers of being the single largest suppliers of opium and morphine to buyers and wholesalers in the city of Beirut.[83]

80 Subject: Hashish Campaign, Lebanon and Syria, 1944, 1 May 1945; Lebanon Files, 1945–53; FBN Files, 1916–70; DEA Records; RG 170, NAB.

81 Garland Williams to Harry Anslinger, 14 February 1949; Lebanon Files, 1945–53; FBN Files, 1916–70; DEA Records; RG 170, NAB.

82 Charles Siragusa to Harry Anslinger, 13 September 1950; Syria Files, 1948–67; FBN Files, 1916–70; DEA Records; RG 170, NAB.

83 George Abraham to Charles Siragusa, 13 October 1954; Syria: Gamal al Masri File; FBN Files, 1916–70; DEA Records; RG 170, NAB; Memorandum: District #17, 22 October 1955; Syria: Gamal al Masri File; FBN Files, 1916–70; DEA Records; RG 170, NAB.

Like most chemists and manufacturers, the processing of opium into heroin and morphine was a family affair for Gamal and his brothers (with their principal lab located inside the family home in Aleppo).[84] Unfortunately, FBN documents do not explore the personal, professional, or perhaps filial ties that bound al-Masri's operations to exporters based in Beirut. Nevertheless, after the four-year investigation (which incorporated the direct assistance of the Syrian national police), it is clear that Gamal al-Masri worked directly with some of the most powerful Beiruti traffickers in the eastern Mediterranean.

Al-Masri's arrest in 1958 did little to hinder the outflow of Turkish opium through Syria. Nor did his apprehension minimize the importance of Aleppo as a major distribution of refined and unrefined opiates. Yearly progress reports filed by FBN agents from the late 1950s and early 1960s make it clear that Syria remained vital to the trade in narcotics emanating from Turkey.[85] FBN agents, dating back to their first experiences in-country in the early 1950s, repeatedly underscored the congeniality of their Syrian counterparts in undertaking joint investigations. Nevertheless, by 1966, it seems that the friendliness and earnestness of the FBN's Syrian interlocutors was only skin-deep. In addressing Anslinger's successor, Henry Giordano, Agent Michael Picini sensed that recent failures in attaining arrests in Syria were marked by an air of official protection of local traffickers. Investigations appeared deliberately bungled once Syrian authorities arrived at various crime scenes. Since FBN agents could not act without their direct supervision, it was difficult to control the direction and prosecution of FBN investigations. "At any rate," Picini lamented, "whatever the problem in Syria is, it is difficult to get the true feelings of the Syrians."[86]

American agents operating in the eastern Mediterranean understood that, despite the cooperation or resistance of the Syrian police, the traffickers of Aleppo were of relatively minimal importance. The central clearinghouse for narcotics in the Levant, particularly for Turkish opiates, was the city of Beirut. Charles Siragusa's first visit to Turkey and Lebanon etched this conclusion firmly within the FBN's approach towards drug trafficking in the region.[87] To stop the flow of heroin into the United States, FBN agents reasoned that a firm stand had to be made in Lebanon.

The FBN's investigation into Gamal al-Masri's operations derived in part from how the Beirut marketplace functioned. Like Istanbul, Beirut was a city dominated

[84] Memorandum Report District 17, Gamil el Masri et al., 27 February 1958; Syria: Gamal al Masri File; FBN Files, 1916–70; DEA Records; RG 170, NAB.

[85] Memorandum: District #17, 24 November 1955; Turkey, 1955–56; FBN Files, 1916–70; DEA Records; RG 170, NAB; Memorandum, 10 March 1959; Turkey, 1957–59; FBN Files, 1916–70; DEA Records; RG 170, NAB; "Turkey," 24 March 1959, Turkey, 1957–59; FBN Files, 1916–70; DEA Records; RG 170, NAB; "Turkey," 16 March 1960; Turkey, 1960–61, FBN Files, 1916–70; DEA Records; RG 170, NAB; "Arrests in Turkey. . . Escape of Narcotic Traffickers," 14 April 1963; Turkey, 1961–63; FBN Files, 1916–70; DEA Records; RG 170, NAB.

[86] Michael Picini to Henry Giordano, 10 November 1966; Syria, 1956–66; FBN Files, 1916–70; DEA Records; RG 170, NAB.

[87] Charles Siragusa to Harry Anslinger, 20 September 1950; Lebanon Files, 1945–53; FBN Files, 1916–70; DEA Records; RG 170, NAB.

by a select number of major traffickers with connections to suppliers and wholesalers abroad. Among al-Masri's chief partners was a man by the name of Omar Makkouk. Like Gamal, Makkouk was a chemist based in the city of Beirut. Born in 1911, he had established himself by the 1950s as a chief manufacturer and distributor of refined opiates with ties to smugglers in Syria, Lebanon, and Iran.[88] Makkouk's dealings in the Mediterranean heroin trade, however, appear to have been largely in support of a wider network operated by Sami al-Khoury, arguably the most powerful and notorious drug traffickers in Lebanon's young history. Born in the predominantly Catholic town of Zahle, located in the hemp-rich district of the Bekaa Valley, al-Khoury was a young man when he began his career in smuggling.[89] At the age of twenty, Sami was imprisoned in Egypt in 1947 for smuggling hashish into the country on behalf of his family's holdings back in Lebanon. His three-year incarceration in Egypt did little to deter him from pursuing a career in the drug trade. By the early 1950s, al-Khoury was reputedly the largest wholesaler in opiates in Beirut and was a principal supplier, alongside Omar Makkouk, to Corsican syndicates based in Marseille.[90] His personal influence also extended into Istanbul. According to FBN sources, Hüseyin Eminoğlu and Ali Osman Tüter often dealt directly with Sami al-Khoury through intermediaries, arranging for large shipments of unrefined opium.[91]

Like in Syria, corruption at various levels of the Lebanese government and security service bedeviled FBN investigations into drug trafficking in Beirut. While Makkouk and al-Khoury were subject to prosecution in the 1950s, both men saw little jail time and continued to run their operations during their short stints in prison.[92] As Jonathan Marshall illustrates in his study of the Lebanese drug trade, FBN agents regularly lamented the official protection proffered to major narcotics dealers in the city of Beirut. Since many of Lebanon's most powerful politicians were prominent landowners (especially within the Bekaa Valley), and officers at various ranks within the state police service could be easily bribed, the threat of prosecution (which usually entailed only a few years' imprisonment) did little to deter traffickers. After two decades of escalating FBN interest and political pressure, combating the flow of Turkish opiates out of Beirut proved to be a hopeless task for even the most determined American officers.[93]

88 U.S. Senate 948–949.

89 Like in the case of Turkish organized crime syndicates, relationships based upon local connections buttressed the organizational structure of many of the Lebanese syndicates American agents encountered during the early postwar period. In particular, the city of Zahle served as a major point of origin for several prominent smugglers and traffickers. For example, Sami al-Khoury's longtime bodyguard, Antoine Harkouk, similarly hailed from Zahle. See Schaylegh, "The Many Worlds of 'Abud Yasin; or, What Narcotics Trafficking in the Interwar Middle East Can Tell Us about Territorialization"; U.S. Senate 947.

90 Wighton, *Dope International*, 63–65.

91 Elmore Gross to Charles Siragusa, 11 March 1955; Turkey Files, 1955–56; FBN Files, 1916–70; DEA Records; RG 170, NAB.

92 U.S. Senate 797, 798, 948.

93 Jonathan Marshall, *The Lebanese Connection* (Palo Alto, CA: Stanford University Press, 2012), 33–48.

BEIRUT, MARSEILLE, MONTREAL, NEW YORK: TURKISH HEROIN, THE CORSICAN MAFIA, AND THE BLOSSOMING OF THE NORTH AMERICAN UNDERWORLD

Opium, morphine, or heroin bought and sold in Beirut usually (although not exclusively) found its way upon ships bound for the French port of Marseille. As a city developed in large measure by French capital (a pattern further solidified during the interwar period), trade and traffic out of Beirut was regular, predictable, and seemingly lucrative.[94] Anecdotal accounts from the immediate postwar era suggest that many of those who were tasked with negotiating and securing narcotics in Beirut for the French market were Turkish or Ottoman born Armenians. This relationship, it seems, was rooted in the violent events surrounding the end of the Ottoman Empire and the makings of the modern Armenian diaspora. With the execution of the Armenian Genocide in 1915, tens of thousands of Armenians came to settle within the environs of northern Syria and coastal Lebanon. Still many more Armenian refugees took flight to France, with many permanently relocating to the city of Marseille.[95] As native Turkish speakers, many Armenians also possessed various degrees of fluency in Arabic, French, and other languages (including English). Men such as Hagop Kevorkian (born in Mardin in 1914) and Antranik Paroutian (born in Gardonne in 1925) were vital players in maintaining the stream of opiates out of Beirut and Istanbul and into the markets of Marseille, New York, and Montreal. Kevorkian, for example, was one of the principal buyers of opiates imported and refined by Omar Makkouk.[96] Paroutian's networks embraced an even wider network of buyers and distributers. According to the McClellan report, Antranik regularly frequented New York, Miami, Havana, and Montreal and was personally tied to each of the major underworld figures of Marseille.[97] According to Alvin Moscow's account from the early 1960s, the enmity born out of the deportation and massacres of the First World War did not interfere with the business relations formed between Armenian and Turkish traffickers. Ahmet Soysal, according to Moscow's reporting, openly and warmly embraced and entertained one Armenian trafficker (presumably either Kevorkian or

[94] For further discussion on the modern origins of Beirut as a metropole for trade and Mediterranean culture, see Jens Hanssen, *Fin de Siecle Beirut: The Making of an Ottoman Provincial Capital* (Oxford: Oxford University Press, 2005).

[95] In the early 1930s, e.g., over 20,000 Armenian migrants called Marseille home. For greater discussion of Armenian life in the diaspora in France, see Mary Lewis, *The Boundaries of the Republic* (Palo Alto, CA: Stanford University Press, 2007), 102; Maud S. Mandel, *In the Aftermath of Genocide: Armenians and Jews in Twentieth-Century France* (Durham, NC: Duke University Press, 2003).

[96] U.S. Senate 948.

[97] U.S. Senate 783, 883–4.

Paroutian) during a visit to Istanbul (an evening that resulted in the purchasing of large amounts of opium).[98]

The Armenians who helped purchase Turkish opiates represented only one element of a much larger network of gangs and criminal syndicates operating out of Marseille. With its origins in the interwar period, or perhaps earlier, the Marseille underworld comprised a unique collection of thugs, hustlers, and smugglers. As a seaport linked to markets and colonial entrepôts spanning the Mediterranean and the wider world, contemporaries often describe the criminal underground of the city as divided into discrete ethnic groups and divisions of labor. The lion's share of police attention, both domestically and internationally, remained fixed upon Corsican migrants who populated the networks of Marseille and whose interests extended well into the inner workings of the Paris underworld. Most notorious for their control over the production and transshipment of heroin and morphine, Corsican gangs were also noted for their control of prostitution and gambling rackets as well as armed robbery. Yet Corsican gangsters did not monopolize all elements of the city's drug and vice trades. Chinese and Vietnamese merchants and smugglers also controlled a portion of the sale and transfer of raw opium (ostensibly, it seems, in the interest of supplying addicts and wholesalers found in southeast Asia and among the city's Asian migrants). Hashish trafficking (which, like the city's supply of opiates, also stemmed from sources in the Levant) largely fell into the hands of Marseille's Arab diaspora, most of whom, it is assumed, derived originally from French colonial territories in North Africa.[99] Relations between these various interests, it should be said, did not always pass harmoniously. Sal Vizzini, one of the most active FBN agents in the greater Mediterranean theater during the 1950s and 1960s, recollects in his memoirs that there was twelve-month period in Marseille when twenty-eight people had either been shot, strangled, or stabbed to death as a result of infighting between Algerian and Corsican gangsters over control of the city's prostitution rackets.[100]

While FBN agents demonstrated some initial interests in the dealings of Chinese and Vietnamese traffickers operating around the city's port, American (and to some degree French) efforts remained fixed upon the various Corsican clans that dominated Marseille's heroin trade. Indeed, American and European agents had been tracking the activities of Corsican gangsters since the interwar period. A League of Nations report from 1937 found within the files of the FBN, for example, emphasizes the conclusion that Marseille was the undisputed center

[98] Moscow, *Merchants of Heroin*, 3–13. In his exposé of heroin trafficking, Moscow alters the names of the individuals he came into contact with while conducting his trade. However, the background he gives on a Turkish trafficker named Ahmet Baykal strongly suggests that he was Ahmet Soysal (e.g. saying that he was born in Kilis in 1928).

[99] Charles Siragusa to Harry Anslinger, 3 May 1951; France Files, 1951–59; FBN Files, 1916–70; DEA Records; RG 170, NAB; Charles Siragusa to Barrett McGurn, 3 March 1953; France Files, 1951–59; FBN Files, 1916–70; DEA Records; RG 170, NAB; George White to Harry Anslinger, 10 June 1948; George H. White Papers, Box 1, Folder 7, Special Collections Department, Stanford University.

[100] Vizzini, Vizzini: The Secret Lives of America's Most Successful Undercover Agent, 119.

of illicit heroin production in France. The report specifically references the dealings of Paul Carbone (a confederate of Louis Lyon), who was involved in the purchasing of opium from Leon Taranto's trading firm.[101] The outbreak of war and the Nazi occupation, however, clearly devastated the network Carbone and other Corsican gangsters helped to develop. In the absence of a lucrative drug trade, Carbone, François Spirito, and other prominent underworld figures resorted to profiteering from the black market produced by the war. French authorities, once the war ended, accused several noted Marseille gangsters of collaboration with the German occupation (Carbone would die in a bomb attack carried out by French Resistance forces).

Renewed opportunities to engage in the transatlantic drug trade brought about a reordering of the gangs of postwar Marseille. The ability of gangsters to adapt to the postwar drug trade was predicated on a number of factors. The war forced many seasoned gangsters to leave wartime France and continue their criminal trades abroad. A key example of this phenomenon is found in the case of Antoine D'Agostino, arguably one of the most powerful drug traffickers of postwar Marseille. Born in Algeria (but of Corsican extraction), D'Agostino had established himself first in Paris as the owner of a popular nightclub in the Pigalle section of the city. While it is not entirely clear how he attained his prominence within both the Paris and Marseille underworlds, his status as a black marketeer in occupied Paris marked him for death. With the capital charge of treason levied against him by the Gaullist provisional government, D'Agostino left liberated Paris for Canada. His stay in Montreal prompted other noted thugs to follow him, including two of his brothers as well as Joseph Orsini and François Spirito. In Montreal, these luminaries of the Marseille rackets forged or renewed ties with gangsters and syndicates with controlling interests over the clandestine trafficking of narcotics in North America. In addition to regularly shuttling back and forth between meetings in Montreal and New York, D'Agostino also established ties with traffickers in Winnipeg and Toronto. After falling out with elements of the Genovese crime family in New York, he shifted his operations to Mexico City alongside his brother Albert.[102]

Similar patterns of expatriate life and trading relations with local racketeers and smugglers can be found elsewhere among Corsican gangsters living in South America and the Caribbean during this time.[103] While D'Agostino's smuggling

[101] "League of Nations: Note on the Illicit Traffick in Dangerous Drugs in France during the Period from May 1st, 1937 to April 30th, 1938," 19 May 1938; France Files, 1927–39; FBN Files, 1916–70; DEA Records; RG 170, NAB.

[102] U.S. Senate 887, 955–956; Wighton, *Dope International*, 213–215.

[103] Galante and Sapin, *The Marseilles Mafia: The Truth Behind the World of Drug Trafficking*, 97–102. In their treatment of Auguste Ricord, Galante and Sapin discuss in detail the building of a complex network of smugglers and traffickers based in South America. Under the leadership of Ricord (but with the assistance of Alberto Guerini, brother of the two prominent Marseille bosses, Antoine and Meme), this network organized the trade in heroin to the United States through a string of Latin American countries including Argentina, Chile, Uruguay, Colombia, and Mexico.

network did eventually come to an end in a dramatic fashion following his arrest in Mexico in 1955, other French Corsican gangsters succeeded in establishing more permanent routes and operations across the Atlantic Ocean. Like the syndicates of Istanbul or Beirut, no single man or gang presided over the Corsican networks fashioned in the years immediately succeeding the Second World War. The McClellan Commission, for example, claimed that four groups were responsible for the overwhelming share of the heroin exported by the "French Connection." Eddie Egan's famous 1962 case in New York (which popularized the term "French Connection" for years to come) featured tangential associates of François Spirito's syndicate, a group the McClellan Commission would proclaim the largest and most powerful Corsican gang spanning the Atlantic.[104]

Further amplifying the influence and pervasiveness of Corsican gangs in North America was the relationship many gangsters from Marseille established with mafia *cosce* from western Sicily. Law enforcement and journalists were quick to explain ties between Corsicans and Sicilians as an expression of the cultural affinity between the two island peoples ("the two people call themselves cousins in their correspondence," as one FBN agent put it).[105] For whatever cultural affinities Corsican and Sicilian mobsters may or may not have shared, it is clear that the rapport established between elements of the Sicilian and Marseille underworlds was the result of discrete choices and efforts. A prime example of the interlocking and highly personal nature of the Corsican networks is found in the career of Joseph Orsini, who became a critical figure within Joseph Spirito's smuggling syndicate. A 1951 FBN investigation uncovered that Orsini, who was living illegally in the United States, dealt directly with gangsters such as Eugenio Giannini, who consorted with such notorious chieftains as Lucky Luciano, Vito Genovese, and other New York traffickers with ties to clans back in Sicily.[106] Anslinger and other members of the FBN remained convinced (or at least professed to be so certain) that Luciano was the central ringleader of the transatlantic heroin trade for much of the 1950s and 1960s. In addition to castigating him in the press and before the Senate, FBN agents in Italy and elsewhere relentlessly tracked Luciano's movements and interactions during the postwar years. The FBN's investment in bringing "Charlie Lucky" to justice did not result in any formal charges being levied against the former New York gangster (who, since 1946, had been living in exile in Italy). FBN assertions regarding Luciano's importance and involvement in the postwar heroin trade has come under increasing criticism in the last several decades. Kathryn

[104] Moore, *The French Connection*; U.S. Senate 722, 789.

[105] The notion that Sicilians and Corsicans called each other "cousins" appears in multiple sources related to FBN investigations. See Charles Siragusa to Barrett McGurn, 3 March 1953; France Files, 1951–59; FBN Files, 1916–70; DEA Records; RG 170, NAB; U.S. Senate 873; Wighton, *Dope International*, 33.

[106] Harry Anslinger to L. Ducloux, undated, France Files, 1951–59; FBN Files, 1916–70; DEA Records; RG 170, NAB; Charles Siragusa to Barrett McGurn, 3 March 1953; France Files, 1951–59; FBN Files, 1916–70; DEA Records; RG 170, NAB; *Traffic in Opium and Other Dangerous Drugs for the Year Ended December 31, 1951* (Washington DC: U.S. Treasury Department, Bureau of Narcotics, 1952), 22–23.

Meyer and Terry Parssinen's study of the opium politics in the twentieth century makes a convincing case for Luciano's irrelevance in the development of the postwar heroin trade, arguing instead that Harry Anslinger utilized Luciano's notoriety in order to elevate his own struggle against narcotics.[107] A similar argument can be found in Tim Newark's study, which employs further documentation from British and American archival sources.[108]

A final element that served to solidify the influence of Corsican gangs over the heroin trade, as well as their dominant position specifically with in the Marseille underworld, was indebted to the role many traffickers would play in postwar French politics. Alfred McCoy was among the first scholars to associate the rise of the Corsican mafia with the role many Marseille gangsters played in suppressing leftist strikes in the years following the end of the Second World War.[109] Like Sicily's Cosa Nostra, the inherent conservatism of the Corsican syndicates made them willing and loyal enablers of the Parisian security establishment (as well as the CIA) who sought to stem the spread of communism within France.[110] Such alliances, however, would arguably not have been possible without the complicity of the Marseille's political elite. Gangsters like Paul Carbone and François Spirito had enjoyed the political protection of the notoriously corrupt mayor Simon Siabiani (who governed the city during the late 1930s).[111] Marseille's reputation as the "Chicago of France" continued into the postwar period under the long tenure of city mayor Gaston Defferre. As mayor of Marseille from 1953 till his death in 1986, Defferre relied heavily upon the political support and personal muscle of a gangster named Louis Rossi.[112]

The seriousness with which Charles Siragusa perceived the threat of the Corsican mob, as well as their political allies in Marseille, compelled him to seek the assistance of a friend in the New York press. In March 1953, Siragusa penned an official letter to Barrett McGurn, a correspondent based in Paris for the *New York Herald Tribune*. Siragusa's correspondence with McGurn is interesting and unique considering the nature of the FBN records found today in the National Archive of the United States. Whereas most documents catalogued in this collection comprise field reports, internal notes, and correspondence or reproductions of official studies from external agencies, Siragusa's letter represents one of the few occasions when an agent consciously attempted to distill and reflect upon casework in a seemingly forthcoming and broad manner. Even fewer FBN documents feature a personal

[107] Meyer and Parssinen, *Web of Smoke: Smugglers, Warlords, Spies and the History of the International Drug Trade*, 281–286.

[108] Newark, *Lucky Luciano: The Real and the Fake Gangster*, 217–220.

[109] McCoy, *Politics of Heroin*, 53–63.

[110] Minayo Nasiali, "Native Republic: Negotiating Citizenship and Social Welfare in Marseille 'Immigrant' Neighborhoods Since 1945," (Ph.D. Dissertation: University of Michigan, 2010), 134–136.

[111] Simon Kitson, "Police and Politics in Marseille, 1936–8," *European History Quarterly* 37:81 (2007), 86–88.

[112] Nasiali, "Native Republic: Negotiating Citizenship and Social Welfare in Marseille 'Immigrant' Neighborhoods Since 1945," 129–131.

plea for support from the press. In this case, Siragusa sought out McGurn's confidence in the hopes he would write a story based upon his revelations.

Charles Siragusa's 1953 letter is a damning, but not necessarily unique, indictment of both the Corsican mafia and the French national police. Ethnic Corsicans controlled all levels of the Marseille heroin trade, Siragusa argued, including the chemical processing and transshipment to the United States. Their strength within Marseille was further amplified by their controlling interests in cigarette smuggling from North Africa, a steady yet still highly lucrative industry.[113] Above all, the ability of Corsican syndicates to strive and overcome the challenge of American and French law enforcement rested upon the multiple levels of corruption found within the city's judicial system. As Siragusa put it:

> All Corsicans act as though they were each other's cousins, crook and legitimate man alike. A Corsican policeman arrests a Corsican narcotics smuggler. The defendant is questioned by a Corsican district attorney. The latter recommends a stupid 3 month sentence. The Corsican judge goes along with the recommendation or considers it "too harsh" and reduces it further yet.

Siragusa's frustration with the city's law enforcement establishment (which, like many of Marseille's departments, was controlled by Corsicans) was exceeded by his overall dismay towards the penalties and statuates levied against heroin smugglers. Narcotics offenses, as Sıragusa saw it, were taken no more seriously than a disorderly conduct charge and often resulted in jail time ranging in months rather than years. For this reason Siragusa hoped that McGurn would write a story using the confidential information he reveals in the letter (although Siragusa pointedly stated that everything revealed in this piece of correspondence should be presented as unsourced and as the product of McGurn's own research).[114]

Charles Siragusa's intervention into the New York press spoke to the urgency with which the FBN saw the threat of the Corsican-controlled heroin trade. While Harry Anslinger and Henry Giodarno publicly denounced Communist China into the early 1960s as the chief source of the heroin consumed by American addicts, FBN agents, both privately and in yearly reports to Congress, openly alluded to the seemingly greater flows of Turkish heroin smuggled out of the port of Marseille.[115] As early as 1947, for example, the official FBN year end report submitted to Congress explicitly declared that Turkish opiates was the primary base for heroin and opium usage along the eastern seaboard, a trend that fell into line with prewar drug smuggling patterns.[116]

Much has been written about the evolution of the mafia in postwar America and how various crime families across the United States grew in power and influence

[113] Jerome Pierrat, *Une Histoire du Milieu* (Paris: Denoel, 2003), 279–295.

[114] Charles Siragusa to Barrett McGurn, 3 March 1953; France Files, 1951–59; FBN Files, 1916–70; DEA Records; RG 170, NAB.

[115] U.S. Senate 684.

[116] *Traffic in Opium and Other Dangerous Drugs for the Year Ended December 31, 1947* (Washington DC: U.S. Treasury Department, Bureau of Narcotics, 1948), 14.

through the heroin trade. In truth, no uniform policy was ever fully established among organized crime groups in the years immediately preceding the Second World War; while some families and bosses forbade the sale of narcotics, others, particularly lower level foot soldiers and associates, freely engaged in the trade with and without the knowledge or approval of their superiors or confederates.[117] Clearly the greatest beneficiaries of this postwar heroin trade in North America were found among the crime syndicates that dominated the New York and Montreal underworlds.[118] Via the "five families" of New York (most notably the Lucchese and Genovese clans) and the Vincent Cotroni family of Montreal, heroin was sold wholesale to smaller networks of distributors and racketeers.[119] This subdivision of labor is best exemplified by the intimate relationship the Genovese and Lucchese Families had with the "Bumpy" Johnson and Leroy Nicky Barnes syndicates, two of the principal retailers of heroin in Harlem between the 1950s and 1970s.[120]

Corsicans ultimately did not always have complete control over the circuitous route that Turkish heroin took into the United States. A less used, but still critical, route employed by smugglers of Turkish heroin passed through Mexico and across the southern border of the United States. In March 1951, FBN agents arrested Harold "Happy" Meltzer along with twenty-three other suspects in a grand conspiracy case charging the men with importing six million dollars' worth of narcotics a year into the United States. Happy Meltzer's roots in organized crime were first established in Los Angeles as a narcotics expert and gunman for Mickey Cohen, the famed LA mob boss of the postwar era. By the 1940s, Meltzer invested much of his energies in securing a stable source of heroin through Mexico for export into the California market. According to the FBN, Meltzer also sought to use Mexico City as a base of refinement for opium imported directly from Turkey. For this purpose he reached out to Michael Kalogrides, the same Istanbul trafficker and chemist who had trained and mentored Ali Osman Tüter. Kalogrides, it was planned, would establish the laboratories in Mexico while two merchant seamen, Ivan Dodig and Andelmo Kassini, would

[117] Joseph Bonanno, head of the Bonanno crime family for over thirty years, insisted that true "men of honor" did not associate themselves with narcotics trafficking. Nonetheless, despite internal consultations among various mafia factions in the United States, he did admit "the lure of high profits... tempted some underlings to freelance in the narcotics trade." See Joseph Bonanno with Sergio Lalli, *Man of Honor: The Autobiography of Joseph Bonanno* (New York: Simon and Schuster, 1983), 209–210.

[118] The role of Corsican gangsters in the makings of the drug trade in the United States appears to be portrayed minimally in several prominent studies of the American mafia. Selwyn Rabb, in his study of the New York families, emphasizes that it was mob connections with Sicilian clans that provided the bulk of heroin (Corsicans, according to Raab, were prominent initially but gave way to much stronger Sicilian influence). In discussing the pivotal Apalachain meeting of 1957, one of Raab's informants suggests that this conclave of gangsters (who were drawn from throughout the United States) agreed that new harsh federal penalties on drug trafficking required that mafia soldiers dealing in narcotics work alone in the hopes of insulating their bosses from prosecution. See Raab, *Five Families: The Rise, Decline and Resurgence of America's Most Powerful Mafia Empires*, 108–124.

[119] Lee Lamothe and Adrian Humphreys, *The Sixth Family: The Collapse of the New York Mafia and the Rise of Vito Rizzuto* (Mississauga, Ontario: Wiley, 2008), 9–13.

[120] Rufus Schatzberg and Robert Kelly, *African American Organized Crime* (New Brunswick, NJ: Rutgers University Press, 1997), 105, 124–125.

transport the raw opium across the Atlantic.[121] Meltzer did see significant jail time after pleading guilty on the charge (five years) but he attempted to resume his organized crime activities in California after his release. Although the FBN suspected him of continued engagement in the Mexican drug trade, it is not clear if his ties to the Turkish underworld were ever revived.[122]

"A COMMON HABIT OF AN EASTERN PEOPLE": THE IRAN–TURKEY CONNECTION

In March 1956, Michael Kalogrides' wife, Kalyopi, was arrested along with four Iranian nationals in Tehran. The five were seized inside a heroin-processing laboratory, supposedly the first one ever seized by Iranian national police. Like those of her husband, Kalyopi's activities were common knowledge among FBN agents in Turkey. Her arrest in 1956, however, typifies a largely forgotten chapter in the history of America's nascent war on drugs.[123]

American engagement with the state of Iran with regards to the flow and consumption of narcotics coincided with the FBN's initial efforts to track and interdict opium flows into the United States in the years preceding the conclusion of the Second World War. In 1942, for example, the FBN estimated that three-quarters of the opium seized in the United States was of Iranian origin.[124] Virtually all of these seizures entailed the capture of Chinese merchants and sailors found in possession of small quantities of opium (seemingly with the intent to market the drug in San Francisco's Chinatown).[125]

The steady flow of Iranian opium into the United States surged in the immediate aftermath of the Second World War, prompting Anslinger to treat Iranian (as well as Turkish) opiates with greater care and seriousness.[126] Between 1948 and 1949, he assigned two of his most trusted agents, George H. White and Garland

[121] "21 Indicted in a Wide Plot to Smuggle Opium to US," *New York Times* 6 March 1951. Charles Siragusa to Harry Anslinger, 27 July 1950, Turkey, 1950; FBN Files, 1916–70; DEA Records; RG 170, NAB; Martin Pera to Charles Siragusa, 30 April 1951, Turkey: Martin Pera File; FBN Files, 1916–70; DEA Records; RG 170, NAB. Ivan Dodig had been a person of FBN interest as early as 1950 when it was discovered that he had worked with Vasil Arcan's smuggling network.

[122] Memorandum Report District #17, 2 November 1955, Turkey Files: 1955–56; FBN Files, 1916–70; DEA Records; RG 170, NAB; U.S. Senate 781.

[123] Charles Siragusa to Harry Anslinger, 27 July 1950, Turkey, 1950; FBN Files, 1916–70; DEA Records; RG 170, NAB; U.S. Senate 798. In 1955, both Michael and Kalyopi Kalogrides were deported to Greece where they re-established a laboratory for processing heroin. See Elmore Gross to Charles Siragusa, 12 February 1955, Turkey Files: 1955–56; FBN Files, 1916–70; DEA Records; RG 170, NAB.

[124] *Traffic in Opium and Other Dangerous Drugs for the Year Ended December 31, 1942* (Washington DC: U.S. Treasury Department, Bureau of Narcotics, 1943), 16.

[125] *Traffic in Opium and Other Dangerous Drugs for the Year Ended December 31, 1944* (Washington DC: U.S. Treasury Department, Bureau of Narcotics, 1945), 26–28.

[126] By 1947, opium derived from Turkish sources began to overtake the trade in Iranian opium. See *Traffic in Opium and Other Dangerous Drugs for the Year Ended December 31, 1947* (Washington DC: U.S. Treasury Department, Bureau of Narcotics, 1948), 14.

Williams, to undertake official tours of Iran in order to assess the severity of illicit trafficking out of Iran itself. Both men, each a seasoned veteran of narcotics work within the United States, presented a bleak picture of affairs from the capital city of Tehran. Addiction was rampant, with as many as 10 percent of the capital's population hooked on opium.[127] Men and women of all ages and of various social stations smoked opium. There was little official oversight in terms of the drug's production or export (both men documented large shipments across Iran's western border with Turkey as well as out of the Persian Gulf).[128] Most ominously, Iran's most prominent families, including the shah's own kin, profited from the trade.[129]

The nature of the Iranian opium trade in the first decade after the war was in keeping with trends seen over the previous century in Iran. Opiate use in Qajar Iran, like the Ottoman Empire, was a common feature in Iranian popular society long before the advent of the modern era. As in the Ottoman Empire, the development of the Chinese opium market following the Opium Wars prompted Iranian cultivators to expand domestic production in order to capitalize on the lucrative export in East Asia. Within the context of the greater Middle East, anecdotal evidence drawn from the mid-twentieth century suggests, for example, that addiction in Iran appeared particularly acute in comparison with imperial and post-Ottoman Turkey.[130]

In the aftermath of the Constitutional Revolution of 1905, domestic reformers in Iran increasingly saw opium as an unnecessary burden upon a society weakened by Western imperialism. Unlike their Ottoman or Turkish counterparts, representatives from Tehran joined their European and American counterparts in the passing of the International Opium Convention in 1912.[131] The collapse of Qajar rule and the rise of the Pahlavi dynasty under Reza Shah in 1925 did not dull Iran's commitment to upholding the Hague consensus. Between 1925 and 1941,

[127] For Commissioner of Narcotics Anslinger from White #3, 11 May 1948, George H. White Papers, Box 1, Folder 7, Special Collections Department, Stanford University; Letters from Garland M. Williams to H. J. Anslinger, Commissioner of Narcotics Regarding the Narcotics Situation in the Near East, 1 February 1949, George H. White Papers, Box 1, Folder 7, Special Collections Department, Stanford University.

[128] For Commissioner of Narcotics Anslinger from White #1, 1 May 1948, George H. White Papers, Box 1, Folder 7, Special Collections Department, Stanford University.

[129] Letters from Garland M. Williams to H. J. Anslinger, Commissioner of Narcotics Regarding the Narcotics Situation in the Near East, 9 February 1949, George H. White Papers, Box 1, Folder 7, Special Collections Department, Stanford University. Among the families that profited from the opium trade Williams lists are the Pahlavi, Vahabzadeh, Ebtehajh, Namazee, and Ardalan families.

[130] One UN observer noted, e.g., that ethnically Turkish Azeris tended not to be drug addicts (as opposed to Persian-speaking Iranians) due to their "racial origins." See "Field Notes of United Nations Advisor to the Narcotics Control Administration of Iran on a Tour of Control Offices and Agencies in Azerbaijan from 27th of October to 7th November 1962," Iran File, 1961–63; Subject Files of the Bureau of Narcotics and Dangerous Drugs, 1916–70; Records of the Drug Enforcement Administration; Record Group 170; National Archives Building II, Silver Spring, MD; Garland Williams to Harry Anslinger, 30 January 1958, Turkey File, 1957–59; FBN Files, 1916–70; DEA Records; RG 170, NAB; MacDonald 143–145.

[131] Hansen, "Learning to Tax: The Political Economy of the Opium Trade in Iran, 1921–1941," 97–99; "The Opium Situation in Iran," 7 July 1971, CIA/ORR Job[?] SOTO 1315A, Box 24, Folder S-3686-S3716, CIA Records Search Tool (CREST), NARA.

Reza Shah labored to enforce a statewide monopoly on opium production as well as to attempt to curtail domestic consumption. By 1936, the number of officially sanctioned opium producing provinces was greatly curtailed. Pahlavi efforts to limit production continued into the postwar years until the petroleum crisis of the Mossadegh era.[132]

Iran's recalcitrance towards opium trafficking and production (which came in part as a result of declining petroleum revenues during the nationalization crisis) prompted intense diplomatic efforts from both Washington and the United Nations.[133] In the wake of Mohammed Mossadegh's overthrow, which resulted in a substantial rise in state royalties on petroleum sales, Tehran switched tack again and re-imposed a total ban upon poppy cultivation.[134] Iran's decision to ban poppy cultivation in 1955 was refreshing news for policymakers in Washington. Unlike Iran, Turkey's Democratic government refused to accept that locally produced opiates were the cause of America's budding heroin epidemic (since, in the words of Interior Minister Namık Gedik, Turkish opium was "tightly regulated" by Ankara).[135] Tehran's decision to cooperate more openly with Washington's nascent "war on drugs" therefore provided a needed and essential model for future agreements should America's global campaign against narcotics proceed successfully.

After 1958, Garland Williams would assume full-time duties as the official narcotics advisor to the Iranian government (serving under the State Department's Office of Public Safety in the United States Official Mission to Iran). As a member of the American military mission to Iran, Williams' appointment to this post spoke to both his professional and political standing within American national security circles as well as to the political sensitivity with which Washington and Tehran approached the opium issue. As one of Anslinger's earliest recruits into the FBN, Garland Williams was awarded the Exceptional Civilian Service Award for investigative work. Like other high-ranking members of the FBN, Williams was also an early member of the Office of Strategic Service, where he was trained as a counterintelligence officer.[136] Williams' tasks, in his own words, were framed against the larger struggle against Soviet hegemony. Iran's participation in Washington's anti-narcotics efforts would provide, Garland Williams argued, a first step in bringing other opium-producing states to heel. According to his own version of the "domino theory," Iran's acquiescence would pressure other troublesome states like Turkey, India, Pakistan, Afghanistan, Thailand, Vietnam, Singapore, and Hong Kong to follow suit, leaving Red China as the isolated source

[132] Hansen, "Learning to Tax: The Political Economy of the Opium Trade in Iran, 1921–1941," 107–109.

[133] "Narcotics Agency Scores Iran Anew," *The New York Times* 3 January 1950; "China and Iran Cited as Opium Offenders," *The New York Times* 21 August 1952.

[134] Hanson, "Learning to Tax: The Political Economy of the Opium Trade in Iran, 1921–1941," 109.

[135] See e.g. A. Gilmore Flues to Harry Anslinger, 23 January 1959, Iran File, 1958–60; FBN Files, 1916–70; DEA Records; RG 170, NAB; Garland Williams to Harry Anslinger, 13 May 1958, Iran File, 1958–60; FBN Files, 1916–70; DEA Records; RG 170, NAB.

[136] Valentine, *The Strength of the Wolf*, 105.

of the heroin plaguing the United States. If opium production and trafficking was allowed to grow and thrive unchecked, an ever growing population of unwitting addicts could eventually lead to greater Communist subversion both at home and abroad.[137]

The onset of a total prohibition in Iran in 1955 did appear to lead to deep cuts in opium usage and addiction. Although reports vary (since the Iranian government generally did not issue statistics on use and addiction), Harry Anslinger suggested before a US Senate committee that opium use had dropped from two million users to around fifty thousand.[138] Addiction, however, persisted. Continued opium use among so many Iranians was the subject of a great deal of American conjecture. As one reporting CIA officer put it, opium use was a "common habit of the eastern people, who seek in opium the best consolation in life."[139] Several reports provide lurid accounts of the pervasiveness of drug use in Iran (such as "heroin" parties in upper-class sections of Tehran).[140]

In light of such seeming moral intransigence, policing methods in Iran concomitantly became a regular topic in many of the briefs Williams and others submitted to Washington. Although at times portrayed in flattering terms, provincial policemen and gendarmes were alternatively described as a venal, corrupt, illiterate, and lazy.[141] Williams himself posited that there was little need for the US to supply helicopters to Iran for drug interdiction purposes since they would be used simply as "toys" by local operators.[142] Nevertheless, the support the United States did offer to Iran was helping to "move Iran into the twentieth century."[143]

Tehran's turn towards prohibiting cultivation prompted opium traffickers to look beyond the country's borders for sources of supply. Particularly worrisome for the United States and Iran was the flow of Afghan opium into illicit markets.[144] Trade and traffic in opium between Afghanistan and Iran was generally fluid before

137 Garland Williams to Harry Anslinger, 10 April 1960, Iran File, 1958–60; FBN Files, 1916–70; DEA Records; RG 170, NAB.

138 From Tehran to Department of State, 8 April 1958, Iran File, 1958–60; FBN Files, 1916–70; DEA Records; RG 170, NAB. U.S. Senate 702.

139 "Opium Traffic," 22 June 1955, CIA-RDP 73B00296R000300070022-8, CIA Records Search Tool (CREST), NARA.

140 Manfred Mandrot to Mr. O'Carroll, 9 December 1961, Iranian File, 1961–63; FBN Files, 1916–70; DEA Records; RG 170, NAB.

141 Manfred Mandrot to Chief of Mission, Imperial Iranian Gendarmerie, 7 August 1962, Iranian File, 1961–63; FBN Files, 1916–70; DEA Records; RG 170, NAB; Garland Williams to Harry Anslinger, 30 September 1958, Iran File, 1958–60; FBN Files, 1916–70; DEA Records; RG 170, NAB.

142 Garland Williams to Harry Anslinger, 10 April 1960, Iran File, 1958–60; FBN Files, 1916–70; DEA Records; RG 170, NAB.

143 A. Gilmore Flues to Garland Williams, 3 December 1958, Iran File, 1958–60; FBN Files, 1916–70; DEA Records; RG 170, NAB.

144 Generally speaking, the files found in the Iran section of the FBN's records suggest that Pakistani-grown opium also posed an issue for the anti-narcotics regime in Iran. However, it seemed to Garland Williams, e.g., that Pakistan served more as a transit point of Afghani opium than as site of origin. See Garland Williams to Harry Anslinger, 10 April 1960, Iran File, 1958–60; FBN Files, 1916–70; DEA Records; RG 170, NAB; "Summary of Proceedings of Conference of Mutual Assistance for the Prevention of the Smuggling of Narcotic Drugs on the Iran-Pakistan Border (14-16 July 1962)," Iran File, 1961–63; FBN Files, 1916–70; DEA Records; RG 170, NAB.

1955, with smugglers supplying the drug to areas facing shortages in either state.[145] After 1955, however, the polarity of the trade permanently shifted in favor of traders in Afghan opium. While opium production and sales could be found in various corners of Afghanistan (with Kandahar being among the main centers of distribution and sale), the region of Badakhshan, in the far north of the country, provided the bulk of illicit opium production.[146] A variety of routes across the Iranian border lay open to smugglers seeking to bring their wares to Iran. In addition to routes through Pakistan, it was reported that unguarded portions of the Soviet frontier proved accessible to narcotics traffickers.[147]

Opium smugglers on the immediate sides of the Iranian/Afghan frontier tended to be members of specific tribal communities.[148] The tribal aspect of the Iranian/Afghan trade in opium particularly bedeviled political and security officials in Tehran. Since its conception in the 1920s, the Pahlavi regime had fiercely sought to subdue or extend greater centralized control over the various tribal confederations occupying large swaths of the Iranian countryside.[149] While Tehran's anti-tribal campaigns had achieved a great many successes by mid-century, tribal units still continued to maintain considerable amounts of autonomy in more remote portions of the Iran.[150] American agents who toured Iran's eastern frontier tell of near constant firefights between state security forces (who were often poorly trained, supplied, or led) and heavily armed bands of smugglers.[151] From the vantage point

[145] Letters from Garland M. Williams to H. J. Anslinger, Commissioner of Narcotics Regarding the Narcotics Situation in the Near East, 26 January 1949, George H. White Papers, Box 1, Folder 7, Special Collections Department, Stanford University.

[146] "End of Tour Report for Garland Williams, 24 June 1959 to 23 June 1961," Iran File, 1961–63; FBN Files, 1916–70; DEA Records; RG 170, NAB; Garland Williams to Harry Anslinger, 27 February 1960, Iran File, 1958–60; FBN Files, 1916–70; DEA Records; RG 170, NAB; Garland Williams to Harry Anslinger, 10 April 1960, Iran File, 1958–60; FBN Files, 1916–70; DEA Records; RG 170, NAB.

[147] Garland Williams to Harry Anslinger, 26 May 1960, Iran File, 1958–60; FBN Files, 1916–70; DEA Records; RG 170, NAB.

[148] Directorate of Intelligence, "The French-Turkish Connection: The Movement of Opium and Morphine Base from Turkey to France (December 1971)," CIA-RDP 73B00296R000300070022-8, CIA Records Search Tool (CREST), NARA; "Information on a Case of Illicit Traffic in Narcotics or on a Seizure," 13 August 1962, Iran File, 1961–63; FBN Files, 1916–70; DEA Records; RG 170, NAB. Specific tribes involved in drug trafficking cited in the FBN files are the (Baluchi) Noori and (Pashtun) Alizai tribes. For later examples of Pashtun resistance to anti-opium efforts, see Jonathan Randal, "Afghanistan's Promised War on Opium," *The Washington Post* 2 November 1978.

[149] Kaveh Bayat, "Riza Shah and the Tribes: An Overview," in Patricia Cronin (ed.), *The Making of Modern Iran: State and Society under Riza Shah, 1921–1941* (London: Routledge, 2003), 213–219.

[150] Letters from Garland M. Williams to H. J. Anslinger, Commissioner of Narcotics Regarding the Narcotics Situation in the Near East, 26 January 1949, George H. White Papers, Box 1, Folder 7, Special Collections Department, Stanford University. In reporting on a nationwide opium suppression campaign waged by the gendarmerie in 1965, the American agent, Manfred Mandrot, surmised that there would be some resistance from various tribes but the gendarmerie believed it had "sufficient firepower this year to overcome them." Manfred Mandrot to Michael Picini, 23 February 1965, Iranian File, 1964–67; FBN Files, 1916–70; DEA Records; RG 170, NAB.

[151] Directorate of Intelligence, "The French-Turkish Connection: The Movement of Opium and Morphine Base from Turkey to France (December 1971)," CIA-RDP 73B00296R000300070022-8, CIA Records Search Tool (CREST), NARA; Garland Williams to Harry Anslinger, 10 April 1960, Iran File, 1958–60; FBN Files, 1916–70; DEA Records; RG 170, NAB; "Information on a Case of

of the smugglers, the reward for engaging in such a risky trade went beyond the immediacy of monetary compensation. Traffickers in Afghan opium also tended to trade in Iranian gold, a prized commodity often used as wedding presents in Afghanistan, Pakistan, and India.[152]

After the institution of prohibition, Turkish opium also flooded across the frontiers of Iranian Azerbaijan and Kurdistan.[153] Of the twenty-five tons of opium seized by Iranian authorities in 1961, 65 percent of it was purportedly of Turkish origin.[154] Bilateral cooperation on border related issues (particularly illicit trafficking) between Ankara and Tehran was slow to develop due to the Turkish government's insistence that no smuggling problem existed on the Turkish/Iranian frontier. The signing of a cooperative agreement in 1959 ultimately proved cosmetic since trafficking networks could just as easily transport contraband across Iran's largely unprotected border with Iraq.[155]

Well into the 1970s, American sources typically described the smuggling of Turkish opiates into Iran as a uniquely "Kurdish" issue.[156] Tehran's rigorous efforts at suppressing nationalist sentiments and political recalcitrance among Iranian Kurds, as well as other "tribal" peoples, only exacerbated the severity of smuggling along the Turkish frontier. As in the case of the Iranian/Afghan border, regular firefights broke out between state security forces and Turkish-Kurdish smugglers.[157] Conversely, Iranian, Turkish, and American authorities were little concerned with the roles played by Turkish and Iranian Azeris in the trade since Turks generally speaking (according to one observer) "have no history of heavy addiction, possibly due to their racial origin."[158]

Illicit Traffic in Narcotics or on a Seizure," 13 August 1962, Iran File, 1961–63; FBN Files, 1916–70; DEA Records; RG 170, NAB; "Opium Fight Kills 18 in Iran," *The New York Times* 17 June 1957.

152 Garland Williams to Harry Anslinger, 7 August 1960, Iran File, 1958–60; FBN Files, 1916–70; DEA Records; RG 170, NAB; R.S. Turnbull to Commissioner of Police, New Scotland Yard, 25 January 1963, Iran File, 1961–63; FBN Files, 1916–70; DEA Records; RG 170, NAB.

153 Charles Siragusa to Paul Knight, 19 November 1956, Iran Miscellaneous File; FBN Files, 1916–70; DEA Records; RG 170, NAB; "Field Notes of United Nations Advisor to the Narcotics Control Administration of Iran on a Tour of Control Offices and Agencies in Azerbaijan from 27th of October to 7th November 1962," Iran File, 1961–63; FBN Files, 1916–70; DEA Records; RG 170, NAB; Garland Williams to Harry Anslinger, 23 January 1960, Iran File, 1958–60; FBN Files, 1916–70; DEA Records; RG 170, NAB.

154 John Cusack to Harry Anslinger, 2 March 1962, Iran File, 1961–63; FBN Files, 1916–70; DEA Records; RG 170, NAB.

155 Directorate of Intelligence, "The French-Turkish Connection: The Movement of Opium and Morphine Base from Turkey to France (December 1971)," CIA-RDP 73B00296R000300070022-8, CIA Records Search Tool (CREST), NARA; Garland Williams to Harry Anslinger, 27 February 1960, Iran File, 1958–60; FBN Files, 1916–70; DEA Records; RG 170, NAB.

156 Philip Heymann to Benjamin Civiletti, 14 January 1980, Southwest Asian Heroin File; FBN Files, 1916–70; DEA Records; RG 170, NAB; Garland Williams to Harry Anslinger, 27 February 1960, Iran File, 1958–60; FBN Files, 1916–70; DEA Records; RG 170, NAB.

157 "CENTO Conference on Narcotics Control, Tehran—June 12, 1961," Turkey Files: 1960–61; FBN Files, 1916–70; DEA Records; RG 170, NAB.

158 "Narcotics Control Administration, Iran, Fifth Progress Report of U.N. Advisor Covering Last Quarter 1962," 11 April 1963; Iran File, 1961–63; FBN Files, 1916–70; DEA Records; RG 170, NAB.

For all of the efforts expended by Garland Williams and his successors based in Iran, FBN records seem to suggest that agents in Turkey took little interest in the activities of smugglers operating on the Turkish/Iranian border. There is no documentary evidence that suggests that FBN agents, for example, sought to probe or hinder the sale of opiates eastward. In 1952, one State Department official did recognize the ease and regularity with which Kurds in Hakkari traversed the Turkish-Iranian border. However, in his estimation, such activities were only relevant if they led to the spread of Communist propaganda into Turkey.[159] However, speaking in 1962, agent John Cusack posed that since Iran did not "concern us directly," there was no need for the FBN to establish an office in Tehran (a condition that would change only if Iranian heroin was found in greater quantities in the United States).[160] Moreover, FBN files from officers based in Turkey in the 1950s and 1960s make little reference to the power or impact Kurds had over the Turkish narcotics trade. Save a few individuals arrested in the Anatolian interior (such as Nadir Alpten's confederates), American agents appear to have been oblivious of the construction of Kurdish smuggling syndicates in the far east of Turkey. According to Charles Wighton's 1960 exposé of the global narcotics trade, Turkish authorities in Ankara were hesitant in their treatment of "their rowdy Kurdish minority." Moreover, Turkish police officers, according to Wighton, were "reluctant to penetrate into the 'little Chicago' of Gaziantep,'" a town that was dominated by notorious opium traffickers "wanted—but not arrested—for every crime, including murder."[161] As late as 1979, a DEA report would only state that "family and ethnic ties" eased Kurdish smuggling across the Turkish/Iranian border.[162] Turkish sources appear similarly vague as to the early history of Kurdish smuggling in Eastern Anatolia. Behçet Cantürk's "memoir," for example, only references the fact that his hometown of Lice was long a center of illicit trafficking and trade (a trade that for years formed the livelihood of his relatives).[163]

Despite the questions that surround the formation and evolution of trafficking networks in the region, it is clear that the pervasiveness of Turkish and Afghan smuggling ultimately doomed Tehran's commitment to opium prohibition. After more than fourteen years of money, time, and effort spent, Mohammad Reza Shah announced in March 1969 that the Iranian government would permit the resumption of opium cultivation. A controlled renewal of opium farming, the shah explained, would be the best method to "cure existing addicts and then clamp down with greater vigor on the expansion of opium smoking." An equally important factor in reversing Tehran's policies was the potential revenue to be garnered from the legal trade in anesthetics (since Iranian opium possessed a higher

159 American Embassy to Department of State, "A Report on the Kurds in Southeastern Turkey," 8 December 1952, 882.41/12-852, Central Decimal Files, 1950–54, RG 59, NAB.

160 John Cusack to Harry Anslinger, 2 March 1962; Iran File, 1961–63; FBN Files, 1916–70; DEA Records; RG 170, NAB.

161 Wighton, *Dope International*, 38–39.

162 Philip Heymann to Benjamin Civiletti, 14 January 1980, Southwest Asian Heroin File; FBN Files, 1916–70; DEA Records; RG 170, NAB.

163 Soner Yalçın, *Behçet Cantürk'ün Anıları* (Istanbul: Doğan Kitap, 2007), 18–19.

degree of morphine than opium produced in southeast Asia).[164] According to FBN sources, discontent with prohibition could be found among various members of the Iranian elite long before the Shah's policy reversal in 1969. Prominent landowners particularly complained to Garland Williams that Iranian smugglers and dealers in opium enriched themselves as a result of the illicit trade in the drug. Meanwhile, landowners in Turkey, Pakistan, and Afghanistan profited from the laxness with which their respective governments approached opium cultivation.[165] Ironically, this turn was predicted by FBN agents years in advance. According to one internal survey of the state of narcotics trafficking in Turkey in 1960, it was supposed that continued opium trafficking between Turkey and Iran would convince the Iranian government to "get the financial benefit of renewed opium production as see a loss of their money to other producers and illicit traffickers."[166]

HEROIN, COCAINE, AND THE EARLY COLD WAR YEARS: TURKEY WITHIN A GLOBAL CONTEXT

The FBN's strategy and approach towards narcotics smuggling in and out of Iran alludes to a broader range of dilemmas facing the United States and its allies in terms of the scope and complexity of narcotics trafficking in the two decades following the Second World War. The fact that Turkish opium traffickers were not alone in circumventing Iran's prohibitions of the trade, production, and use of narcotics reflects the harsh reality that opium and heroin, along with other drugs, were commodities cultivated, manufactured, and transported by individuals and in states spanning much of the globe. In thinking about Turkey within the wider context of the global narcotics trade during the early stages of the Cold War, one can only speculate as to Turkey's relative importance within the world's narcotics market. Statistics and narrative reports on the market shares of drugs of various origins, as seen in this and in later chapters, were highly politicized and hypothetical. Moreover, the prevalence and significance of American reports and investigations tend to emphasize (at the expense of other countries and markets) the preeminence of the United States as the principal destination for drugs produced and sold worldwide.

Nevertheless, despite these limitations, various studies of the Cold War era do provide some comparative base of understanding and interpreting the evolution of the Turkish narcotics trade during this pivotal period. Scholars of organized crime and the international drug trade remain indebted to Alfred McCoy's seminal study of "the politics of heroin," a work first published in 1972. Through extensive field research and interviews (which led him literally to poppy fields in remote corners

164 Eric Clark, "Iran Revises Opium Policy," *The Washington Post* 18 March 1969.

165 Garland Williams to Harry Anslinger, 20 April 1961, Iran File, 1958–61; FBN Files, 1916–70; DEA Records; RG 170, NAB.

166 "Opium Production," 16 March 1960, Turkey File, 1960–61; FBN Files, 1916–70; DEA Records; RG 170, NAB.

of southeast Asia), McCoy constructs an intricate picture of the individuals, networks, and supply routes that dominated the international drug trade during the second half of the twentieth century. The bulk of his research focuses upon southeast Asia, which, in McCoy's estimation, became the beating heart of the world's heroin trade from the 1960s onward.[167] Like the trade in Turkish heroin discussed earlier, he introduces the reader to a rich tapestry of actors critical to the construction of this trade. At the core of his study is the impact Cold War clandestine operations had upon both stimulating the growth of southeast Asia's heroin industry as well as its role in laying the foundations for the groups that transported and sold heroin in North America and elsewhere.

McCoy vigorously contends that opium cultivation and heroin manufacturing reached a critical juncture in the years after 1945. While the opium fields and drug syndicates of China had long been a focal point of the Asian narcotics trade, Mao Tse-tung's victory over Chiang Kai-shek's Kuomintang prompted a sudden change in the nature of both the consumption and production of opiates in the region. Mao's heavy-handed suppression of opium use, as well as the eradication of poppy fields in southern portions of China, not only eliminated the historical epicenter of global opium consumption but also destroyed a vital source of opium on the global export market.[168] Nevertheless, concurrent to the Chinese Communist Party's anti-narcotics crusade following the closure of the Chinese Civil War in 1949, new centers of opium harvesting and procurement began suddenly to emerge to the south in Burma, Laos, Thailand, and Vietnam. Market forces stemming from supply and demand, in McCoy's estimation, did not incite this seemingly abrupt shift. Rather, as he painstakingly demonstrates, a broad coalition of Cold Warriors and local allies (including elements of French intelligence, the CIA, the Corsican underworld, the Kuomintang, Thai, and Vietnamese officials, and Hmong tribesmen) set out to appropriate the region's opium heroin trade in order to finance and mobilize anti-Communist operations in Asia. In the face of budgetary constraints, as well as the need to mobilize men and communities tied to opium production, American, French, and local agents and officials colluded in helping to form new pipelines of heroin and opium out of southeast Asia. Wholesalers, chemists, and smugglers in Hong Kong, McCoy explains, played a similar role to the traffickers in Turkish opium operating out of Beirut and Marseille during this same period of time. With the decline and collapse of the Green Gang (whose members migrated in part to Hong Kong after the Second World War), a similarly criminal secret society known as the Chiu Chau assumed control of laboratories and distribution routes ranging from southeast Asia, Australia, and the United States. Precisely how the Chiu Chau constructed this empire, let alone where and to whom this syndicate sold their wares, remains largely unexplored. Unlike the French Connection,

[167] McCoy, *Politics of Heroin*, 158.

[168] Zhou Yongming, "Nationalism, Identity and State-Building: The Antidrug Crusade in the People's Republic, 1949-1952," in Timothy Brook and Bob Tadashi Wakabayashi (eds.), *Opium Regimes: China, Britain and Japan, 1839–1952* (Berkeley: University of California Press, 2000), 380–403.

a network that was investigated and delineated on both sides of the Atlantic, the men and means of exchange that defined heroin trafficking out of Asia has yet to be revealed to the public.[169]

Recent scholarship has produced a far more complete picture of how Latin American drug trafficking networks emerged during the postwar era. Using the extensive holdings of both the American and Mexican archives, Luis Astorga, in particular, provides a fairly vivid rendering of the evolution of Mexican narcotics trafficking syndicates following the Second War. On a state-by-state basis, particularly focusing upon networks based in the state of Mexico, Baja California, Chihuahua, Sonora, Sinaloa, and Tamaulipas, Astorga offers intimate details of many of the key individuals and networks who exported heroin, marijuana, and cocaine north of the border. In each case, he pays close attention to the role of politicians linked to the Institutional Revolutionary Party in patronizing and abetting the activities of local farmers and smugglers. The cases Astorga cites in his portrayal of the various men and women who comprised Mexico's expansive underworld conform to no single stereotype or pedigree. Pablo Macias Valenzuela, a major trafficker of opium from Sinaloa, had served as Mexico's Secretary of Defense during the Second World War and held multiple positions within the country's regional military command structure.[170] Jorge Asaf y Bala, the reputed "Al Capone of Mexico," was the scion of a prominent Lebanese-Mexican family with extensive connections to the heroin and cocaine trade in the country.[171] Conversely, Maria Dolores Estevez Zuleta, otherwise known as Lola la Chata, grew up in poverty in the La Merced district of Mexico City before reigning over one of the largest prewar heroin distribution networks in Mexico.[172] In surveying the country's significance within the international drug trade during the Cold War, Astorga's research underscores the fact that Mexico continued to be an important source for heroin imports into the American southwest. However, while some of the heroin exported from the United States to Mexico originated from Mexico's Pacific states, it also clear that Mexico City and other entrepôts were weigh stations for both heroin and cocaine manufactured abroad. Prominent members of the Marseille milieu, including Antoine D'Agostino, maintained personal ties with traffickers in Mexico City (D'Agostino was in fact arrested in the capital in 1955 and deported to Canada for trial).[173]

Cuba under the Prio Socarras and Batista regimes similarly served as a critical point of transit within the international drug trade. According to Eduardo Saenz Rovner, the monopoly enjoyed by French and American gangsters over the trade of heroin in and out of Havana was undergirded by diasporas with strong ties to

[169] McCoy, *Politics of Heroin*, 270–282.
[170] Astorga, *Drogas sin Frontieras*, 133.
[171] Astorga, *Drogas sin Frontieras*, 300–302; Valentine, *Strength of the Wolf*, 201.
[172] Elaine Carey, "'Selling is more of a Habit than Using': Narcotraficante Lola la Chata and Her Threat to Civilization," *Journal of Women's History* 21.2 (2009), 62–89.
[173] Astorga, *Drogas sin Frontieras*, 299, 321; U.S. Senate 804.

individuals within the police, military, and bureaucracy.[174] Native and expatriate Cubans, meanwhile, developed their own inroads into the Pan-American cocaine trade. Havana's centrality within cross-Caribbean trade, coupled with the closely intertwined trade relations between Cuba and the United States, appeared to have lent Cuban sailors, smugglers, and government officials a critical edge in forming a wide-ranging distribution network between North and South America. Castro's seizure of power further amplified the strength of the Cuban diaspora trade in cocaine as larger, and politically connected, communities took root across the Americas after 1959.[175]

As Paul Gootenberg's *Andean Cocaine* makes clear, no single country or syndicate monopolized production and smuggling of cocaine out of South America during the "pre-Colombian era." Small groups of Chileans and Peruvians, followed by tightly wound cooperatives of Argentinians and Brazilians, smuggled modest amounts of cocaine out of Bolivia and other parts of the Andean region. Gootenberg is careful to point out, however, that unlike the French Connection and other heroin networks, cocaine smuggling before the 1970s was not a trade defined by highly integrated and hierarchical criminal outfits. Rather, Pablo Escobar's antecedents comprised "a loose, diverse and independent diaspora of Latin American ethnic traders, elite gadflies, political refugees, and petty criminals."[176] While Gootenberg does not go as far as McCoy in suggesting that the rise of the cocaine trade in the postwar era was the byproduct of Cold War intrigues, he does suggest that aggressive American anti-narcotics policies had a countervailing effect upon South America, often compelling (rather than deterring) criminal entrepreneurs and recalcitrant farmers to seek out profits through the cocaine trade.

Each of the works discussed above affirms broader trends seen in the case of Turkey and its role within the opiate trade. Narcotics trafficking, as a commodities industry, grew steadily through the postwar era. There appears to be nothing monolithic about this trade in terms of personnel or routes that comprised the global drug trade during this era; criminal networks were often fluid and defined by loose connections defined by ethnic diaspora ties and shared economic interests. The growing complexity and vibrancy of the narcotics trade during this era cannot be divorced from the politics of the Cold War. More importantly, traffic and traders in narcotics, be it Mexico, Cuba, Vietnam, or Thailand, often played important roles or had strong ties with individuals tasked with the management of state affairs. Indeed, it was through such relationships that more successful criminal enterprises were established and thrived.

[174] Saenz Rovner, *The Cuban Connection: Drug Trafficking, Smuggling and Gambling in Cuba from the 1920s to the Revolution,* 103–112.

[175] Andres Lopez Restrepo and Alvaro Camacho Guizado, "From Smugglers to Warlords: Twentieth Century Colombian Drug Traffickers," *Canadian Journal of Latin American & Caribbean Studies* 28.55–56 (2003), 249–263.

[176] Gootenberg, *Andean Cocaine,* 287. Also see Paul Gootenberg, "The 'Pre-Colombian' Era of Drug Trafficking in the Americas: Cocaine, 1945–1965," *The Americas* 64.2 (October 2007), 133–176.

As one reflects further upon Turkey in light of the emergence of the various narcotics trafficking networks of the postwar era, several points of continuity appear between past trends in organized criminal behavior and this emerging period. The most glaring point of continuity between the late Ottoman/early Republican era is the ongoing association between organized criminal behavior and certain "minority" groups found within Turkey's evolving urban and rural landscape. On the one hand, we see the continued links between elements of Istanbul's non-Muslim mercantile class and the trade in narcotics. Orthodox Christians, and to a lesser degree Turkish Jews, remained key players within the Turkish underworld into the early 1950s. Even with the gradual disappearance of prominent Christian and Jewish traffickers (a phenomenon that may or may not have been encouraged by government authorities), former Ottoman Armenian subjects continued to occupy pivotal positions in the organization and transshipment of narcotics across the Mediterranean. While it is certainly the case that Armenian merchants were often notable middlemen in global trade before the outbreak of the First World War, the importance of Armenian traffickers within the postwar heroin trade does not appear to be directly linked to the prominence of past families or networks that operated under the aegis of Ottoman rule. The dealings of Hagop Kevorkian or Antranik Paroutian instead appear to have been the direct result of the demographic and economic shifts following the Armenian deportations of 1915. The documents and testimony available to us seem to suggest that men like Kevorkian, Paroutian, and others utilized their linguistic and cultural backgrounds (skills that perhaps amplified their personal ties to Corsican and Lebanese smugglers) to ingratiate themselves into networks that predated the end of the Second World War.

On the other hand, with the decline of Turkey's non-Muslim networks, we see the ascendency of several Muslim syndicates that possess certain similarities to the gangs that existed towards the end of the Ottoman Empire. Like the *çetes* of the First World War and the Turkish War of Independence, American and Turkish sources emphasize that two key ethnic groups, Laz and Kurds, tended to populate or even dominate the activities of these trafficking groups. While this emphasis upon the distinct ethnic "minority" character of prominent smuggling operations may in part be influenced by the longstanding inclination of Turkish officials to see criminal behavior as an inherently "minority" trait, the nature of the heroin and opium trade, coupled with ongoing demographic trends within Turkey, suggest that the ethnic or regional bonds shared by narcotics traffickers did influence the formation and management of certain specific groups. In looking at Turkish and American analyses of the procurement and smuggling of opium in central and eastern Anatolia, the roots of Kurdish involvement in the drug trade appear obvious; the proximity of Kurdish communities to opium growing regions and the border gave local Kurdish smugglers an advantage in conducting cross-border trade. The rise of Istanbul's Laz syndicates, by contrast, appears to be directly associated with past patterns of migration and settlement. If one extrapolates further from the biographies of İhsan Sekban and Hüseyin Eminoğlu, it may be said that these kingpins of the postwar heroin trade had simply followed in the footsteps of other wayward migrants from Turkey's northeastern Black Sea coast. Yet unlike past waves of Laz migration (which often resulted in voluntary or forced settlement in villages or small town quarters in Yalova, Bolu, or Kartal), the city of Istanbul, which promised greater amounts of economic opportunity, exclusively drew seasoned and potential criminals like Sekban and Eminoğlu. In Istanbul, it appears that Laz traffickers, and non-traffickers alike, continued to find a stable and vibrant community of kinsmen and former neighbors willing and able to sustain and promote their new lives in town (all despite past state efforts to forbid Laz settlement in the city).

Interestingly, in the early stages of the postwar period, one sees little to no mention of Albanians and North Caucasians involved in the Turkish drug trade.[177] Aside from the one person of Albanian descent identified as being a member of İhsan Sekban's inner circle, the FBN's records offer only vague insights into the possible role played by Turkish Albanians in the postwar Istanbul drug trade (a topic that will be discussed in Chapter 5). Considering the historical continuities in the perceptions of these two groups, within official accounts at least, why did Albanian and Circassian criminals not figure in the emerging order of powerful smuggling syndicates in Turkey immediately after 1945? On the basis of the information available to us, one can only speculate as to the answer to this question. It may be the case, for example, that the prominence of Laz migrants in certain key professions along the Istanbul seaport (such as lightermen and sailors) offered more contemporary Laz settlers an advantage in engaging in the contemporary smuggling trade.

Another possibility, one that is still not well understood in the case of Republican Turkey, is perhaps rooted in the changing nature of migration and economic upward mobility among the country's very large immigrant communities. Mass migration into Turkey largely gradually waned during the interwar period (particularly after the population exchanges with Greece in 1923 and 1924). The onset of Soviet rule in the Caucasus, for example, does not appear to have prompted a mass exodus of North Caucasian groups on a par with refugee crises of the nineteenth century.[178] The numbers of Balkan migrants seeking refuge in Turkey also steadily declined between the interwar and early postwar periods. While the establishment of closer relations between Belgrade and Ankara in 1953 did instigate a sudden exodus of Albanians from Yugoslavia, the socio-economic character of this wave of newcomers differed dramatically from past surges in migration. Unlike the refugee

177 A general survey of American documents has yielded only one case where Circassians were found to have played a role in smuggling or manufacturing narcotics. In 1935, a Turkish official reported to the League of Nations the arrest of a gang in Istanbul comprising "four Circassians of Turkish nationality" involved in manufacturing heroin in the village of Yeni Bosna outside of Istanbul. While the gang operated the factory (with the aid of an Italian citizen named Moiz), a foreign national by the name of Armando was the main distributor of the gang's heroin production. See "Discovery of a Clandestine Drug Factory at Istanbul on June 13th to 14th, 1935," 19 July 1935; Turkey Files, 1935–50; FBN Files, 1916–70; DEA Records; RG 170, NAB.

178 Mitat Çelikpala, "From Immigrants to Diaspora: Influence of the North Caucasian Diaspora in Turkey," *Middle East Studies* 42.3 (2006), 426. According to Çelikpala, most of those who fled the Soviet takeover were members of the elite and intellectual classes of the Caucasus.

crisis spawned by the Balkan Wars, most of the 180,000 Yugoslav nationals who settled in Turkey between 1946 and 1970 did not come in great haste or with no possessions in tow.[179] Virtually all migrants during this period arrived at the Turkish border with preapproved visas issued by Turkish consular officials. Many settled in Turkey in close proximity to friends and family members and integrated rapidly into the local economy and culture of their newly adopted towns or cities. The Turkish government of the postwar era, unlike the CUP or Kemalist regimes before them, was far warmer in their treatment of migrants, allowing for the establishment of local and national diaspora associations after 1950.[180]

In looking at these new patterns of migration, the changing nature of migration into Turkey may have been accompanied by changes in the lives of second- and third-generation migrant groups historically associated with banditry or other forms of criminal behavior. While there is a general lack of detailed analysis of how migrant groups assimilated in Turkey, studies from the United States provide some possibile points of reference on this topic. Jenna Weissman Joselit, in her study of Jewish gangsters and organized crime in the United States between 1900 and 1940, suggests that population shifts from older impoverished areas to newer, more gentrified districts in New York City helped to ameliorate issues of crime and recidivism among the city's Jewish diaspora. Moreover, she suggests that immigration limits placed upon European migrants may also have allowed second-and third-generation American Jews greater freedom to integrate into middle-class neighborhoods and professions (as well as restricting the number of first-generation poor migrants susceptible to partaking in organized criminal activity).[181] Whether these trends hold true for groups like Albanians and Circassians in Turkey remains to be seen.[182]

Still another possibility is that criminals of various backgrounds, including Albanians, participated in other organized criminal behavior exclusive of the drug trade. While the economic growth of the young state rose modestly over the decades following independence, it seems clear that a generalized pattern of mass urbanization did lead to changes in the ways migrants and natives experienced work and crime. In 1927 there were a total of five cities in Turkey with populations of more than 50,000. By 1950, that number had grown to eleven. A decade later, twenty-seven cities in Turkey had populations of over 50,000.[183] With this rise in

179 Nurcan Özgür-Baklacıoğlu, "Devletlerin Dış Politikaları Açısından Göç Olgusu: Balkanlar'dan Türkiye'ye Arnavut Göçleri (1920-1990)," (Ph.D. Dissertation: Istanbul University, 2003), 480.

180 Alexandre Toumarkine, "Kafkas ve Balkan Göçmen Dernekleri: Sivil Toplum ve Milliyetçilik," in Stefanos Yerasimos et al. (eds.), *Türkiye'de Sivil Toplum ve Milliyetçilik*, (Istanbul: İletişm Yayınları, 2001), 425–450.

181 Jenna Weissman Joselit, *Our Gang: Jewish Crime and the New York Jewish Community, 1900–1940* (Bloomington: Indiana University Press, 1983), 157–172.

182 Söner Çagaptay's study clearly demonstrates the various degrees to which certain migrant groups were restricted from entry into Turkey following independence as well as the severity with which Ankara attempted to integrate and Turkify these populations. However, wider study is needed to understand the degree to which these policies were successful. See Soner Çağaptay, *Islam, Secularism and Nationalism in Modern Turkey: Who is a Turk?* (Abingdon: Routledge, 2006).

183 John Kolars, "The Integration of the Villager into the National Life of Turkey," in Kemal Karpat et al. (eds.), *Social Change and Politics in Turkey: A Structural-Historical Analysis* (Leiden: E.J. Brill, 1973), 191.

the urban population in Turkey, crime in urban centers, like Istanbul, appeared to have skyrocketed. According to the *New York Times*, court cases in the former Ottoman capital had jumped from 9,636 in 1938 to over 300,000 in 1947.[184] Crime in major urban centers continued to increase after the multi-party elections in 1950. According to one State Department study in 1962, public prosecutors in Istanbul were stretched to capacity in keeping up with rising caseloads (despite the opening of new judicial courts).[185] Police in Izmir were similarly hampered by budgetary and manpower constraints.[186] The growing number of rural migrants, as well as declining economic conditions beginning in the late 1950s, were among the causes associated with perceptions of Turkey's urban crime problem.[187]

The Istanbul press in this era continued to document the activities of *kabadayı* figures in the city. One figure who appeared with relative frequency within the pages of the local and national press was *Arnavut* Cafer (Cafer the Albanian), a noted *kabadayı* who was arrested and placed on trial for a series of violent crimes. Cafer appeared to have frequented select neighborhoods known for their nightlife and seediness (particularly Beyoğlu, Tepebaşı, and Taksim). Cafer did not appear to belong to a gang although his dealings (which included the murder of a hotel owner, Necati Mutlacan) did appear to include others of Albanian descent. Beyond the immediate details of Cafer's various violent exploits, which included shootings, poisonings, and fist fights over money and other personal matters, press accounts of his activities offer virtually no other insights into his background or his personal or financial pursuits. Instead, coverage of *Arnavut* Cafer, like press accounts of other well-known criminals from the era, offers little beyond the immediate details of a bloody event or a noteworthy trial.[188]

Other articles offer only hints as to ethnic make up, formation, or inner workings of Istanbul's criminal underworld beyond the narcotics trade. In the summer of 1953 for example, *Milliyet* reported the outbreak of gang warfare between two groups calling themselves "The Laz (*Lazlar*)" and "The Bridge Boys (*Köprü Hamallar*)." According to the account, the two youth gangs engaged in a running street battle in the district of Galata after insults were traded (a fight which left one

[184] "Turkey Troubled by Crime Increase," *New York Times* 7 December 1947.

[185] Betty Carp to Department of State, 4 September 1962, 782.31/9-462, Central Decimal Files, 1960–63, RG 59, NAB.

[186] Donald B. Eddy to Department of State, 12 February 1959, 882.52/2-159, Central Decimal Files, 1955–59, RG 59, NAB.

[187] Betty Carp to Department of State, 4 September 1962, 782.31/9-462, Central Decimal Files, 1960–63, RG 59, NAB; Betty Carp to Department of State, 19 November 1963, Subject Numberic Files, 1963, RG 59, NAB.

[188] "Dolapdereyi Birbirine Katan Sabıkalılar," *Milliyet* 30 September 1950; "Tarlabaşında Vukua Gelen Arbede," *Milliyet* 11 November 1950; "Beyoğlunda bir Kumarhane daha Basıldı," *Milliyet* 6 November 1951; "Cafer bir Genci Vurdu," 16 October 1952; "Tepebaşı Cinayeti bir Tertip Eseri Mi," *Milliyet* 27 July 1956; "Cinayet içinde bir Cinayet" *Milliyet* 29 July 1956; "Arnavut Cafer ile Arkadaşı Yeni bir Suçtan Adliyeye Veriliyor," *Milliyet* 3 February 1957; "Polisin Yardımını İsteyen Kabadayı," 1 July 1957; "Arnavut Cafer Boğazdaki bir Otelde Haadise Çıkardı," *Milliyet* 12 March 1958; "Arnavut Cafer Muş'a Sürgün Gönderilecek," *Milliyet* 18 May 1958; "Arnavut Cafer Nezaret Altında," *Milliyet* 12 June 1963; "Sürdünden kaçan Arnavut Cafer Adliyede Tutuldu," *Milliyet* 23 May 1968.

boy dead).[189] What roles these street gangs, or even individual *kabadayı*, played within the Istanbul drug trade is generally unclear. Archival documents from the United States and Turkey make no mention of either youth gangs or *kabadayı* as factors in the construction of drug trafficking networks in the two decades following the Second World War. As we will see in the last chapter, it is only later, during the 1970s and 1980s, that individuals claiming the mantel of the *kabadayı* tradition asserted themselves as prominent figures within the Turkish drug trade.[190]

There is a last point of comparison one can make between the emerging order of narcotics traffickers (and *kabadayı* as well) and the imperial legacies of Anatolia's *çetes* and *kabadayıs*. As seen in the later stages of Ottoman history, there are several instances witnessed in the postwar era where organized crime (particularly drug trafficking) and politics overlap. Bribery, as one might expect, certainly was at the foundation of many of the relationships formed between politicians, security officials, and narcotics traffickers. Other factors, however, also undergirded collusion and cooperation between gangsters and government agents. In looking specifically at American records between the years 1948 and 1960, we see numerous cases where prominent underworld figures aided both American and Turkish law enforcement officials in their efforts to stem the flow of opium and heroin out of the country. In exchange for information on rival or petty narcotics traffickers, American and Turkish officers granted noted gangsters protection from prosecution (leverage that clearly allowed many of the most powerful narcotics dealers in Istanbul to flourish during this period of time). Other pieces of evidence gleaned from the FBN records also suggest that the anti-narcotics operations in Istanbul and the Anatolian interior provided American and Turkish officials political and legal cover to conduct clandestine activities exclusive of their duties. While it is not clear whether or not elements of Istanbul's underworld aided Turkish and FBN agents in these activities, sources from this period strongly suggest that American and Turkish counter-narcotics investigations abetted espionage operations, killings, and other dubious activities.

Understanding how narcotics trafficking and politics intersected in the years between 1948 and 1960 requires a deeper understanding of the establishment and conduct of joint American-Turkish operations during this period of time. The next chapter will delve more closely into how American and Turkish officials and agents perceived and approached narcotics and organized crime in Turkey. As we shall see, American and Turkish comprehension of opium and heroin trafficking relates directly to the evolution of this working relationship as well as the degree to which narcotics traffickers and gangsters influenced and impacted the politics and management of the Turkish state.

189 "Kan Gütme Yüzünden Bir Cinayet Daha İşlendi," *Milliyet* 26 June 1953.

190 One of the few exceptions of *kabadayı* involvement in heroin trafficking before the 1970s can be found in the case of *Arnavut Küçük* Cafer (or Little Cafer the Albanian). Evidently of no relation to the more famous *kabadayı* of the same name, *Arnavut Küçük* Cafer, or Cafer Şunay, was arrested in 1952 for selling heroin in a hamam within the old city of Istanbul. In the spring of 1961, Cafer was shot dead over a gambling dispute. See "Hamamda bir Tevkif," *Milliyet* 11 March 1952; "Arnavut Cafer Yedi Kurşunla Öldürüldü," *Miliyet* 6 March 1961.

4

Police Work: Counter-Narcotics Operations and Intelligence Gathering in the Early Cold War

One evening in early June 1948, George White slowly made his way into the Eriko, a watering hole of the lowest sort in the Tepebaşı section of Istanbul. Upon approaching the bar, he attracted the attention of a woman who introduced herself as Melina. With rough and broken English, Melina promptly took the stranger for a potential "john" looking for a woman for the evening. White declined the offer. He pointedly declared that he was in search of heroin, not to use but to buy and sell in large quantities. Melina initially resisted but soon gave way and offered to introduce him to someone who could help him with his request. After a few minutes she returned with a man who introduced himself as Vasil Arcan. Vasil, with the assistance of the barmaid's translation, questioned White further. After convincing Vasil that he was a merchant seaman with contacts in New York, White agreed with the Turk that he would purchase five kilos of heroin from him.

Two days later White met with another man identified as "Bob," who led him to a private home in Tepebaşı. In the company of "Bob" (later identified as İradodos Terapyamos) and the owner of the home, "Joe" (Yasef Kariyon), White was furnished with 250 grams of brown heroin. After testing and approving the sample, he consented to purchasing a total of three kilograms of heroin. The three agreed upon a price of $2,000, which White promised to return with in a few hours. Upon re-entering the house that afternoon, White presented Joe with his fee (which was paid in both Turkish lira and dollars). Once the deal was done, White pulled out both a badge and gun. Joe initially panicked but was soon convinced that if he resisted, the American would kill him. With the two suspects subdued, he then broke a small window in order to signal to the large cohort of Turkish police lurking outside to come and assist him. Minutes passed but no one entered the building. Frustrated, White hurled a chair through another window, hoping that this act would attract the attention of the officers waiting outside.[1] After "Joe" and "Bob" were placed under arrest, Turkish officers then descended upon a home

[1] The account given here is based upon the following two sources: Commissioner of Narcotics Anslinger from White #10, 10 June 1948, George H. White Papers, Box 1, Folder 7, Special Collections Department, Stanford University; James Phelan, "The Calculating Colonel and the Turkish Trap," *True: The Men's Magazine* (January 1960), 71–78. While the latter account appeared in the popular press, the account largely corresponds to White's 1948 internal report and contemporary local press reporting.

across the Bosphorus in Üsküdar, seizing another sixteen kilos of heroin.[2] Vasil Arcan, who was apparently oblivious of the raids, was later apprehended outside the American consulate. Arcan, White later explained, had hoped to apply for a visa to the United States and would have eluded capture had White not bumped into him leaving the building.[3]

White's investigation was the subject of a brief wave of news coverage in both the American and Turkish press. A short account from the Associated Press appeared in the *New York Times* on the day of the bust, declaring that a million dollars in narcotics had been seized (White internally suggested that the street value of the drug was closer to $36,000).[4] The Istanbul daily, *Akşam*, covered the story for several days further, recounting through interviews and court testimony the events that led to the arrest of the four individuals charged with heroin trafficking.[5] The tone of the Associated Press piece, it appears however, ruffled some feathers among elements of the local press and government in Istanbul. A month after the incident, US Consul General, C. E. Macy, personally wrote to the governor of Istanbul in appreciation of the assistance the head of the local narcotics division (Namık Karayel) afforded to White during the operation. Macy's note to the governor, he later explained, was meant to offset American coverage that "gave too much space to the achievements of Mr. White and not enough to the ground work laid by the Turkish Police."[6]

As one looks beyond the immediate press coverage of White's exploits that summer, there are elements to this story that are more intriguing or suspicious than simply the arrest of a handful of Istanbul drug traffickers. The bust, as White made clear privately to his superiors, was not purely the product of his own investigative abilities. The entire investigation was the result of Namık Karayel's intervention, who personally identified Vasil Arcan as a potential target.[7] After his arrest and arraignment, Arcan was allowed to leave prison and was most probably never tried for his role in arranging the sale of heroin. Moreover, the public prosecutor, before an open court, declared that Arcan was most probably trying to sell White carpets

[2] "Heroin Kaçakçıları," *Akşam* 5 June 1948.

[3] Commissioner of Narcotics Anslinger from White #10, 10 June 1948, George H. White Papers, Box 1, Folder 7, Special Collections Department, Stanford University.

[4] Commissioner of Narcotics Anslinger from White #9, 4 June 1948, George H. White Papers, Box 1, Folder 7, Special Collections Department, Stanford University; "US Traps 4 in Istanbul," *New York Times* 4 June 1948.

[5] "Heroin Kaçakçıları," *Akşam* 5 June 1948; "Amerikaya Eroin Kaçıran Şebeke Nasıl Yakalandı," *Akşam* 6 June 1948; "Eroin Kaçakçıları," *Akşam*, 8 June 1948; "Eroinçilerin Muhakemesine Dün Başlandı," *Akşam* 9 June 1948.

[6] C. E. Macy to Secretary of State, 13 July 1948, Turkey 1943–48; FBN Files, 1916–70; DEA Records; RG 170, NAB.

[7] One important difference emerges between White's account of the investigation and the testimony given in the first criminal proceedings that followed the arrest of Vasil Arcan, Yusef Kariyon, and İradodos Terapyamos. According to Melina, who was interrogated in open court, White specifically asked to speak with Vasil Arcan. On approaching her, it appears he did not mention to Melina that he was interested in purchasing heroin. See "Eroinçilerin Muhakemesine Dün Başlandı," *Akşam* 9 June 1948.

and not heroin.[8] It would later be revealed that Arcan, like several other major traffickers in Istanbul, was a police informant.[9]

Other aspects of George White's visit to Istanbul were never disclosed to the press. While he had never traveled through Turkey before his 1948 stay, White knew and called upon a series of acquaintances and former comrades while he was in the city. Many of these individuals were current employees of the newly established Central Intelligence Agency. Others were former agents or informers from the Office of Strategic Services. By his own admission, it was with the assistance of these men that he quickly grasped the nature of narcotics trafficking in Turkey.

The 1948 raid in Tepebaşı was the first of many investigations to be carried out by the Federal Bureau of Narcotics in Turkey. Very few of these investigations received the sort of press coverage that George White and his Turkish compatriots enjoyed in June 1948. In surveying the files found in the National Archives in College Park, Maryland, it appears that the overwhelming majority of the cases opened by the FBN in the next two decades were far less successful. Most leads, and many enquiries, went nowhere and were abandoned. Without the aid of Turkish archival sources (which are thought to be housed in the Ministry of the Interior), it is not clear what the rate of success or failure was for the Directorate of Public Security (*Genel Emniyet Müdürlüğü*, or DPS) during this period of time. Local press reporting, as well as internal American surveys, largely suggest that most successes came at the expense of petty users, dealers, and traffickers in drugs. When Turkish authorities did bring major narcotics violators to justice during this era, it was rare that an American agent or agency took any credit.

This chapter largely represents an attempt to explore the nature and significance of Turkish and American cooperative counter-narcotic efforts in the years between 1948 and 1967. The purpose of this survey is three-fold. Building upon the last chapter, this section attempts to understand how and why American and Turkish officials came to understand and collectively approach organized crime in Istanbul. Secondly, it sheds light on the degree to which opiate traders and smugglers influenced and interacted with individuals and institutions within the local administration of Istanbul as well as the national government in Ankara. Thirdly, this chapter attempts to highlight the degree to which American and Turkish clandestine operations overlapped with the policing (and to some degree the construction) of the Turkish drug trade.

In order to adequately broach all three of these themes, one must address a broader array of issues and trends that provide the backdrop to this first era of direct American and Turkish cooperation on narcotics issues. How we comprehend and perceive the making of the Turkish opium and heroin trade during the postwar era is the direct result of the expansion and operational development of Turkish and American law enforcement institutions at this point in history.

[8] Rızı Çandır to Frank White, 30 June 1948, Turkey 1943–48; FBN Files, 1916–70; DEA Records; RG 170, NAB.

[9] Charles Siragusa to H. J. Anslinger, 14 August 1950; Turkey, 1950; FBN Files, 1916–70; DEA Records; RG 170, NAB.

FBN agents sent to Turkey generally arrived with a strong knowledge of, and even stronger opinions on, the world of organized crime back in the United States. For this select group of individuals, the fight against drug traffickers in Istanbul and the Anatolian interior was one and the same as the struggle against gangsters and mafia families back in New York or Chicago. If the accounts of American agents are to be believed, the threat of organized crime and the heroin trade did instill in the Turkish officers employed by the Directorate of Public Security a comparable sense of urgency or dread. While the representatives of these two states did amiably agree and cooperate on a variety of issues and tasks, it seems clear that Turks were apprehensive, or at worst hostile, towards the influence and demands of their American counterparts during the course of the two decades following the Second World War.

American interest in policing and interdicting narcotics emanating from Turkey also occurred at a time when key internal and foreign security institutions in both the United States and Turkey were subjected to an unprecedented pattern of reform and expansion. With the close of the Second World War, the FBN grew rapidly in size. With a larger budget in hand, Washington afforded Harry Anslinger and his men greater leverage in pursuing drug traffickers both at home and abroad. As narcotics increasingly came to be seen as a fundamental threat to the domestic security of the United States, the FBN sought to establish a firm physical presence in key trafficking cities and regions around the world. The internationalization of the FBN's crusade against drugs mirrored a much larger and equally concerted effort undertaken by other elements of the United States' military and intelligence establishment to solidify American support abroad and integrate important allied states into a collective security framework. Within the context of the Cold War, this posturing and engagement with foreign allies led the FBN, like other arms of the American government, to proselytize and construct new approaches and institutions in various localities abroad (including Turkey).

Documents, memoirs, and studies exclusive of those found in the National Archives further suggest that the FBN's activities in Turkey and elsewhere particularly augmented the work of the CIA. The working relationship formed between these two bodies was born during the Second World War but gained greater strength and complexity as the United States entered the Cold War. The evidence presently available to the public suggests that the FBN helped to further shroud CIA clandestine activities at home and abroad while at the same time amplifying the reach of its intelligence gathering and paramilitary operations. In the case of Turkey, it is also clear that the CIA helped to provide American narcotics agents with information on the Turkish underworld as well as governmental contacts within Ankara.

The onset of the Cold War prompted a similar expansion in the size, capacity, and scope of the state security services in Turkey. The threat of a Soviet invasion to the east, coupled with ever greater apprehensions towards leftist or seditious movements in the country, led to increased attention and diligence in monitoring and policing in the republic during the first two decades after the Second World War. In the case of counter-narcotics activities, reform of Turkey's Directorate of Public Security was initially the responsibility of one man, Kemal Aygün. Under Aygün's leadership, the DPS devoted more time, energy, and emphasis to drug interdiction than at any time before his tenure as head of the department. While Aygün was a vocal proponent of "Americanizing" the policing of narcotics in the country, FBN agents grew increasingly frustrated with his tenure as chief of the DPS. By 1960, this relationship would come to a crashing end with the overthrow of the civilian government. When the dust finally settled from the coup of 1960, Anslinger and other agents in the FBN came to realize that their closest ally in Turkey had abetted and protected many of the most prominent traffickers in the country.

The story of Kemal Aygün's rise and fall, as well as the more generalized evolution of Turkey's approach towards organized crime and drug trafficking, was symptomatic of the more profound changes that took place in the republic during the middle decade of the twentieth century. Aygün's ascendency to the heights of power in Ankara in 1950 came upon the coattails of the election of Adnan Menderes' Democratic Party in the country's first ever genuinely multi-party election. The Democratic victory radically changed the complexion of Turkey's national and local leadership, introducing new personalities and prerogatives into the country's body politic. Nevertheless, even with this dramatic infusion of new blood into Turkish politics, it is clear that Democratic Party officials, as well as local bureaucrats and law enforcement officers, were forced to contend with the gathering financial clout and political influence of major drug traffickers in Istanbul, Izmir, and elsewhere. The charges of corruption and complicity that were eventually levied against Aygün were equally (but often not publicly) applied to other figures of lesser or equal political weight. In some sense, the story of narcotics and policing in the Menderes era points to the fact that drug traffickers did exercise some degree of political authority. The charges of corruption and complicity levied against Aygün and many others provide some basis to suggest that major figures within Turkey's underworld were becoming more normalized and integrated within the function of Turkish governance and politics. At same time, it is also clear that elements of the Turkish state were critical players in expanding and developing the strength of Turkey's illicit narcotics economy.

In surveying both the documentary evidence and the testimony and news reporting from this era, there is one aspect of counter-narcotics politics and policing in the Menderes era that remains somewhat elusive. According to contemporary sources, drug interdiction efforts undertaken by Aygün and the DPS may have similarly provided a vehicle for a more generalized pattern of domestic and foreign intelligence gathering. Moreover, particularly in the wake of his indictment by the military regime in 1960, there is some evidence that suggests that Kemal Aygün and the Democratic Party may have tapped the Turkish underworld to fill the ranks of privately armed gangs or paramilitary squads. While it is difficult to completely validate these latter claims, such a direct alliance formed between the

Democratic Party and the urban thugs would have been in keeping with early trends from the late Ottoman and early Republican periods.

AGENTS, BUDGETS, AND METHODS: CRITICAL FACTORS IN THE MAKING OF THE FBN'S CRUSADE IN TURKEY, 1945–67

Crime and Communism were, in the words of J. Edgar Hoover, the "twin enemies" of freedom in postwar America.[10] Yet, for much of his reign after the Second World War, Hoover publicly refused to accept the existence, let alone singular impact, of the so-called "American mafia" upon the United States. Harry Anslinger, by contrast, vigorously and vociferously denounced the threat of organized crime. First before the Kefauver Committee in 1950, and then later before the John McClellan's Senate hearings in 1963, Anslinger was vocal in his insistence that the American mafia was a coordinated, yet decentralized, conspiracy that dominated all major criminal activities within the United States. Adding further credence to this thesis was the aid and testimony offered by Charles Siragusa and George White (who both served as investigators on the behalf of the Kefauver Committee). The publicity Anslinger gleaned from the Kefauver hearings also allowed him to advance a related, but separate, thesis connected to an issue with which had long occupied his professional career. Heroin, he argued, was increasingly becoming a weapon at the disposal of communists abroad. Before the Kefauver Committee, and then later in front of the McClellan Committee, Anslinger would claim that China was the chief exporter of narcotics into the United States, an act that allowed the Chinese Communist Party to infiltrate and influence the United States.[11] "There is every possibility," Anslinger declared in his autobiography, "that some of the Commies and fellow travelers may join hands with the world-wide syndicate—for profits and subversive politics combined. There is every possibility that they may try to make narcotics a new 'sixth' column to weaken and destroy selected targets in the drive for world domination."[12]

Statistics reported by the FBN itself however seem to belie the severity or extent to which narcotics posed a mortal danger to American society at the close of the Second World War. In 1947, for example, the FBN reported over 2,340 "violations" concerning narcotics (a quarter of which stemmed from arrests in New York State alone).[13] That number rose to over 2,500 in 1952 and then dipped to over 2,000 in 1955.[14] Between 1953 and 1956, the FBN estimated that 35,835 people (out of

[10] Bernstein, *Greatest Menace*, 48.
[11] See McWilliams, *Protectors*, 152–153.
[12] Anslinger and Oursler, *The Murderers: The Story of the Narcotics Gang*, 295.
[13] *Traffic in Opium and Other Dangerous Drugs for the Year Ended December 31, 1947* (Washington DC: U.S. Treasury Department, Bureau of Narcotics, 1948), 29.
[14] *Traffic in Opium and Other Dangerous Drugs for the Year Ended December 31, 1952* (Washington DC: U.S. Treasury Department, Bureau of Narcotics, 1953), 26; *Traffic in Opium and Other Dangerous*

a population of over 150 million people) had been treated for addiction to drugs.[15] The FBN did report a significant rise in the number of individuals hospitalized for drug addiction ten years later, but still this number remained fairly small (59,720) compared to the size of the overall population of the United States.[16]

There were challenges to Anslinger's position on the importance (let alone existence) of the Chinese heroin conspiracy as well. The Soviet Union, as well as other states, rejected Anslinger's Communist heroin conspiracy out of hand.[17] British authorities in Hong Kong, for example, declared the notion of a clandestine heroin industry in the PRC "ridiculous and unfounded," declaring instead that there had not been a major seizure of opiates from the PRC since 1949.[18] Opposition to the American stance towards China was relatively minor compared to other difficulties Anslinger encountered during his interactions with the United Nations during the 1950s. For much of the decade, Anslinger worked diligently to steer the international community toward a newer, stronger convention governing the global narcotics trade. As the 1950s progressed, more representatives within the United Nations dissented from American demands that tight international restrictions be placed upon narcotics production. Anslinger's work ultimately came to naught in 1961 with the passage of the UN Single Convention on Narcotics. In addition to imposing less than satisfactory international mandates over drug producing states, as well as the lack of an endorsement for incarcerating drug users (termed "civil commitment" at the time), he rightly feared that the convention would no longer justify the existence of the FBN. In the absence of specific language mandating states to create of a "special administration" to supervise narcotics enforcement at a national level (which was contained in a 1931 League of Nations convention), Anslinger lost the political and diplomatic cover that helped cement the authority and autonomy enjoyed by the FBN since its establishment.[19]

Nevertheless, despite these challenges, Anslinger's bureau enjoyed an extraordinary wave of fiscal and political support in Washington in the two decades following the Second World War. In 1945, the United States Congress appropriated

Drugs for the Year Ended December 31, 1955 (Washington DC: U.S. Treasury Department, Bureau of Narcotics, 1956), 38.

15 *Traffic in Opium and Other Dangerous Drugs for the Year Ended December 31, 1956* (Washington DC: U.S. Treasury Department, Bureau of Narcotics, 1957), 36. According to Charles Siragusa, the figures on "drug addicts" reflect the number of regular opiate users in the United States. These figures, according to his autobiography, were accumulated through health officials and police officers. He states that while some had estimated that there were a half a million addicts in the United States in the early 1960s, he argues that such a speculative figure conflates those who smoke marijuana infrequently or use other drugs (such as barbiturates, tranquilizers, or hallucinogens) with those who are regular heroin users. See Siragusa and Wiedrich 204–205.

16 *Traffic in Opium and Other Dangerous Drugs for the Year Ended December 31, 1966* (Washington DC: U.S. Treasury Department, Bureau of Narcotics, 1967), 51.

17 Anslinger and Oursler, *The Murderers: The Story of the Narcotics Gang*, 229; McWilliams, *Protectors*, 151.

18 McWilliams, *Protectors*, 152–153. With Anslinger's retirement in 1967 and the breakup of the FBN, Washington finally repudiated the FBN's former accusations towards China and recognized Beijing's successful campaign against opium production. See McCoy, *Politics of Heroin*, 124.

19 McAllister, *Drug Diplomacy in the Twentieth Century*, 98, 190–192, 221–222.

a little over $1.3 million in funding for the FBN. By 1962, the year Anslinger would retire from federal service, Congress allotted $4.4 million to the bureau.[20] While the FBN remained largely underfunded in the postwar era, this significant expansion in federal support for the FBN resonated in the general growth of law enforcement institutions throughout the United States during this period time. In 1940, Hoover's FBI comprised of over 2,400 agents. By 1960, the FBI employed close to 15,000 agents.[21] Indeed the expansion of US federal law enforcement agencies was in keeping with the tone and political sensitivities of the early Cold War era. While administratively separate from the military, the maturation and augmentation of the FBN resonates strongly within the overall construction of America's postwar "national security state." Increased defense spending during the Truman era, for example, complemented major innovations within the field of American civil-military relations, such as the creation of the CIA and the National Security Council. Grave ideological and geo-strategic concerns and apprehensions during this era gave way to Washington's open-ended commitment to fund and further expand any and all agencies or departments that could be utilized to uphold American national and international interests.[22] Even the Peace Corps, an agency that seemed to embody sincere and altruistic values, was viewed within national security circles as having a defined role to play in maintaining American security interests abroad.[23]

Turkey featured prominently within the emerging Cold War framework of American security policy. In a conversation with then Ambassador George McGhee, Adnan Menderes was adamant that Turkey was "the bulwark" of Middle Eastern defense against the Soviet Union.[24] Between 1948 and 1971, Turkey received close to $4.4 billion in military aid from Washington (as well as another $185 million in loans for military and security purposes).[25] Millions of dollars of direct military aid from Washington led to the construction of large military bases (such as İncirlik in southern Turkey) and the modernization of, and supply of provisions to, various elements of Turkey's armed forces.[26] American military aid (which also came in the form of expertise as well as direct funding) was further augmented by direct economic assistance coming from Washington. Under the auspices of the Marshall Plan, Turkey received $183 million in economic support

[20] Kinder, "Shutting Out Evil," 131.

[21] Todd Masse and William Krouse, "The FBI: Past, Present and Future," Congressional Research Service (<http://www.fas.org/irp/crs/RL32095.pdf>), accessed 28 September 2012.

[22] See Douglas Steward, *Creating the National Security State* (Princeton, New Jersey: Princeton University Press, 2008).

[23] Elizabeth Cobbs Hoffman, "Decolonization, The Cold War, and the Foreign Policy of the Peace Corps," in Peter Hahn and Mary Ann Heiss (eds.), *Empire and Revolution: the United States and the Third World Since 1945* (Columbus: Ohio State University, 2001), 123–153.

[24] Memorandum of Conversation, by the Ambassador in Turkey (McGhee), 10 February 1952, *Foreign Relations of the United States, 1952–1954, Vol. VIII: Eastern Europe; Soviet Union; Eastern Mediterranean* (Washington DC: Government Printing Office, 1988), 877.

[25] Jim Zanotti, "Turkey-U.S. Defense Cooperation: Prospects and Challenges," Congressional Research Services, 8 April 2008, 4.

[26] George S. Harris, "Turkey and United States," in Kemal Karpat (ed.), *Turkey's Foreign Policy in Transition, 1950–1974* (Leiden: E.J. Brill, 1975), 56–57.

from the United States.[27] In the hopes of boosting Turkey's agricultural sector, Washington provided American-made capital goods, such as tractors, to Turkish farmers and financed the construction of dams and roads.[28] The enthusiasm with which Turkey greeted, and needed, American financial assistance also prompted the Soviet Union to extend offers of additional aid.[29]

While it is difficult to determine the nature of his initial grand strategy, Anslinger appeared to have viewed Turkey, and the Middle Eastern theater at large, as central to the American struggle against the global illicit trade in narcotics.[30] Anslinger's gambit towards the PRC aside, internal correspondence within the FBN make it abundantly clear that suppression of Turkish opium at its source was crucial to stamping out the threat of addiction in the United States.

Over the course of twenty years encompassing the FBN's direct involvement in counter-narcotics operations in Turkey, three critical factors within the control of the bureau consistently inhibited or hindered the work of American agents. The first, and arguably the least discussed, of these factors was the lack of training in Turkish language, politics, and culture. Virtually none of the agents sent to Turkey between 1948 and 1967 possessed any knowledge of Turkish (Sal Vizzini claimed to have picked up enough Turkish to speak with is colleagues after a few years in-country).[31] While some agents did speak a second language with some ability, all of the FBN's representatives often had to rely upon translators in order to interact with Turkish-speaking locals (be they criminals, informants, or officials).

A second constraining factor was money. While the FBN's budget certainly did rise throughout the 1950s and 1960s, monetary support for agents engaging in investigations in Turkey and elsewhere was often slim. Years later, reflecting back upon his career in the bureau, Joe Arpaio stated that the FBN "was so starved for funds and, subsequently ran such a bare-bones organization," that he was initially deprived of money for a plane ticket to fly his wife out to accompany him during his long tour in Turkey.[32] Neither Arpaio, nor any other member of the FBN, ever made such feelings known in their official correspondence with Anslinger or any other superior officer. Anslinger, in his memoirs, instead made a point of the fact that life as an agent was indeed a solitary challenge. Agents, he explained, were not paid by the hour and had to endure long periods of time undercover with little outside support (to the point of having to suffer arrest, prosecution, and imprisonment in order maintain their cover). Both big and small cases were made through individual initiative and ingenuity. A genuinely fine and committed

[27] William Hale, *Turkish Foreign Policy, 1774–2000* (London: Routledge, 2012), 83.

[28] Zürcher, *Turkey*, 234–236.

[29] Current Intelligence Bulletin, 13 April 1956,CIA-RDP79T00975A002500170001-5, CIA Records Search Tool (CREST); National Archives Building II, College Park, MD.

[30] "Amerikaya Eroin Kaçıran Şebeke Nasıl Yakalandı," *Akşam* 6 June 1948.

[31] In the file folder for the year 1951–52, someone transcribed a list of words and phrases related to opium trafficking (such as *afyon*/opium, *afyonkeş*/opium smoker, *esrar çekmek*/to smoke hashish, *esrar tekkesi*/hashish den, *uyuşturucu*/narcotics, and so forth). Aside from this, there is no evidence in the FBN files that agents received any official training in the Turkish language. See also Memorandum Report, 26 January 1960, Turkey, 1960–61, FBN Files, 1916–70; DEA Records; RG 170, NAB.

[32] Joe Arpaio and Len Sherman, *Joe's Law* (New York: Amacon, 2008), 153–154.

agent, in Anslinger's estimation, was "imbued with the purpose—a crusader. He lives this war against the narcotics hoods."[33]

A third, and more complicated, challenge that plagued the work of the FBN was the availability of reliable, independent sources of intelligence. There were two prospective sources of information that could aid an agent undertaking investigations abroad. The first was the International Criminal Police Organization or Interpol. Interpol did supply the FBN and other national and local law enforcement bodies with general files detailing the basic biographical information and arrest record of suspects. However, beyond interacting and coordinating with multiple policing agencies, Interpol possessed no means to verify independently the information they gathered.[34] A second possible source of information and support for an agent working abroad was the CIA. As mentioned in the last chapter, the CIA did possess a detailed file on major Istanbul traffickers as early as 1948 (which suggests that much of this information was grandfathered into the agency from the OSS). While the files in the possession of the National Archives make no other specific reference to information specifically gleaned from the CIA, the memoirs of Sal Vizzini, who served in Turkey during the 1950s, make it clear that the FBN actively shared information with their CIA counterparts. In Vizzini's case, his CIA contact in the US consulate in Istanbul, whom he dubs "Napoleon," was capable of supplying him with a number of valuable items and services at a moments notice: fake IDs, reliable translators, guns, and secure lines of communication.[35] In exchange for this support, Vizzini subcontracted his services to the agency and personally undertook clandestine operations on their behalf.

In spite of the shreds of information FBN agents in Turkey began with upon their arrival to Istanbul in 1948, Anslinger's men were able to construct a fairly complex picture of the Turkish narcotics trade with the help of the DPS and through their own devises. George White, for example, received a photo array sheet complete with names, addresses, and recent arrest records of notorious drug trafficking offenders in the summer of 1948.[36] Later in the fall of 1951, the "second section" (or narcotics bureau) of the local DPS office in Istanbul provided Agent Frank Sojat with an updated list of "first hand" and "second hand" drug traffickers active in the city.[37]

Most of the information gleaned by American and Turkish operatives was clearly obtained through interactions with paid informants. The use of paid informants was an investigative tool much favored by the FBN. Getting evidence to convict traffickers with deep ties to local communities (particularly among police

[33] Anslinger and Oursler, *The Murderers: The Story of the Narcotics Gang*, 132–134.

[34] For more on the history of Interpol, see Fenton Bresler, *Interpol* (New York: Penguin Books, 1993).

[35] Vizzini, *Vizzini: The Secret Lives of America's Most Successful Undercover Agent*, 108.

[36] Untitled photo array sheet (Turkish version), 1948, Turkey, 1943–48; Subject Files of the Bureau of Narcotics and Dangerous Drugs, 1916–70; Records of the Drug Enforcement Administration, Record Group 170; National Archives Building II, Silver Spring, MD.

[37] Frank Sojat to Harry Anslinger, 1 October 1951, Turkey, 1951–52; FBN Files, 1916–70; DEA Records; RG 170, NAB.

departments, majors, judges, and district attorneys) was, in Anslinger's own words, "one of the most challenging assignments in law enforcement." Nevertheless, as he suggests in his memoirs, a variety of personal reasons often did lead some within the underworld to talk: "profit, for special consideration in their own cases, help for a wife or mother who may be ill or dying, for revenge or merely for conscience."[38] While he emphasized that the bureau did its best to "protect these men to the fullest measure" out of fear of retribution, what Anslinger leaves unmentioned in his explanation of the FBN's approach towards policing was the degree to which these "special employees" (as the FBN termed them) remained active within the underworld both before and after the completion of an investigation. As we shall see, many prized informants assisting both American and Turkish efforts in Istanbul continued to thrive as narcotics dealers for years under the guise of their "special employee" status.

These challenges, as well as other mitigating factors, often did deter the FBN's endeavors in Turkey. Yet, as one looks at the full circumference of the bureau's activities during the immediate postwar era, it is clear that the FBN enjoyed a considerable amount of success in investigating, arresting, and prosecuting a great many major traffickers in both the United States and abroad. In 1945, FBN officers helped to coordinate the arrest of well over a hundred individuals in the United States and Mexico linked to a heroin trafficking syndicated known as the "107th Street Mob" in New York City.[39] In 1951, a New York district attorney, with FBN assistance, finally secured an indictment and a long prison sentence for Irving Wexler (better known as Waxey Gordon) on narcotics charges, ending the reign of one of the most powerful drug traffickers of the interwar era.[40] As the 1950s progressed, the FBN would rein in other major trafficking networks headed by such notorious gangsters as Antoine D'Agostino,[41] Joseph Orsini,[42] Vito Genovese,[43] Giuseppe Pici (reputed aid to Lucky Luciano),[44] Jorge Asaf y Bala,[45] and Giusippe Controni.[46] These high-profile arrests, coupled with the bureau's participation in both the Kefauver and McClellan committees, affirmed a critical thesis central to

[38] Anslinger and Oursler, *The Murderers: The Story of the Narcotics Gang*, 4–5.

[39] *Traffic in Opium and Other Dangerous Drugs for the Year Ended December 31, 1945* (Washington DC: U.S. Treasury Department, Bureau of Narcotics, 1946), 22–24; *Traffic in Opium and Other Dangerous Drugs for the Year Ended December 31, 1946* (Washington DC: U.S. Treasury Department, Bureau of Narcotics, 1947), 19–20.

[40] *Traffic in Opium and Other Dangerous Drugs for the Year Ended December 31, 1951* (Washington DC: U.S. Treasury Department, Bureau of Narcotics, 1952), 16.

[41] *Traffic in Opium and Other Dangerous Drugs for the Year Ended December 31, 1955* (Washington DC: U.S. Treasury Department, Bureau of Narcotics, 1956), 9.

[42] *Traffic in Opium and Other Dangerous Drugs for the Year Ended December 31, 1951* (Washington DC: U.S. Treasury Department, Bureau of Narcotics, 1952), 22.

[43] *Traffic in Opium and Other Dangerous Drugs for the Year Ended December 31, 1958* (Washington DC: U.S. Treasury Department, Bureau of Narcotics, 1959), 24.

[44] *Traffic in Opium and Other Dangerous Drugs for the Year Ended December 31, 1959* (Washington DC: U.S. Treasury Department, Bureau of Narcotics, 1960), 20.

[45] *Traffic in Opium and Other Dangerous Drugs for the Year Ended December 31, 1959* (Washington DC: U.S. Treasury Department, Bureau of Narcotics, 1960), 20.

[46] *Traffic in Opium and Other Dangerous Drugs for the Year Ended December 31, 1959* (Washington DC: U.S. Treasury Department, Bureau of Narcotics, 1960), 21.

the FBN's *modus vivendi*. The American mafia was part of a single global conspiracy bent on undermining the very foundation of the United States. While the mafia in the United States was a nearly exclusively Italian syndicate that coordinated, with totalitarian precision, much of the organized criminal activity in the country, it possessed strong allies analogously constructed along ethnic or regional lines (such as the Corsicans of Marseille or the Laz of Istanbul). Like the Communist Party, narcotics trafficking, complete with all of its international dimensions, represented something ideologically and culturally (in some sense even racially) foreign or "alien" to mainstream American society.[47]

The revelations of Joseph Valachi added greater texture to the FBN analysis of the threat of organized crime in the United States and elsewhere. Valachi, a self-proclaimed foot soldier in the Genovese crime family of New York and the star witness of the McClellan hearings of 1963, provided unparalleled insight into the workings of organized crime in America. He detailed the configuration, personalities, and culture that made up the American mafia (a cosmology that was often illustrated with the aid of schematic charts featuring pictures and rankings of various mafia figures from around the United States). He affirmed that the American mafia evolved out of a seminal gang war between Sicilian and American-born Italian factions during the 1930s. Since the Castellammarese War ended in 1931, an integral governing body known as the National Commission presided over both national and international operations conducted by "La Cosa Nostra."[48]

To this day, Joseph Valachi's revelations inform or sustain many popular perceptions of organized crime in the United States and have provided grist for both film and television adaptations of mafia life.[49] Cumulatively, since the 1960s, the American definition of organized crime, which emphasizes the centrality of coherent, conspiratorial "ethnic" syndicates that dominate a coterie of illicit trades, has been adopted by foreign governments and international agencies as a model approach in investigating and describing "mafias" worldwide.[50] Arguably specific historical trends have undergirded the Americanization, or more broadly homogenization, of law enforcement approaches towards organized crime around the world. As Peter Andreas and Ethan Nadelmann point out, the establishment of regimes of international law enforcement is a phenomenon born out of the growth and solidification of European empires beginning in the eighteenth century. Beginning with the struggles against international piracy and slave-trading, states like Great Britain and France provided both the framework and the mechanisms (principally large powerful navies) to enforce standardized notions and institutions of law enforcement on a global scale. Local and international law enforcement

[47] Woodiwiss, *Organized Crime and American Power*, 243–248.

[48] For a critical reading of the Castellammarese War and its impact upon organized crime in the United States, see Block, *East Side West Side*, 3–9. For discussion of the Commission's construction, see Bonanno with Lalli, *Man of Honor: The Autobiography of Joseph Bonanno*, 159–165.

[49] See, e.g., Peter Maas, *The Valachi Papers* (New York: Harper Paperback, 2003); Woodiwiss, *Organized Crime and American Power*, 260–261.

[50] Woodiwiss, *Organized Crime and American Power*, 362–389.

standards have grown even more homogenized through the ascendency of the United States as a hegemonic power during the twentieth century.[51]

The degree to which Washington has pursued the fight against organized crime simultaneously at home and abroad is symptomatic of a broader pattern of Cold War era thinking and strategizing. The threat of the "international communist conspiracy," coupled with Washington's new founded position as a global hegemon, allowed American policymakers an unparalleled opportunity to engage and influence foreign policing and intelligence services in the hopes of securing and maintaining a robust defense of the United States and its foreign interests. Counter-narcotics operations particularly allowed Cold War policymakers with an effective and agreeable medium to affect bureaucratic and administrative reform and achieve consensus among its allies. Jonathan Marshall's study of American counterinsurgency strategy further emphasizes that the fight against drugs has provided a means to equip and support various foreign governments engaged in combating domestic dissidents and guerrillas.[52] As one assumes a wider view of American approaches towards organized crime, and the specific ties various syndicates had with the heroin trade, it is clear that the activities of the FBN, which included both pursuing criminals as well as defining the nature of the crimes and criminals involved, served to amplify the growing hegemonic influence and reach of the United States during the Cold War.

Yet even as the FBN attempted to make the case that Turkish opium and heroin traffickers formed a monolithic syndicate operating in conjunction with similarly unitary or coherent crime groups in Lebanon, France, and the United States, reports and statements released by the FBN often undermine the degree to which Anslinger and others publically portrayed the integral nature of organized crime both domestically and abroad. Virtually none of the major cases investigated by the FBN in the mid-1950s, such as the Özsayar and Özyürek cases, point to the existence of singularly defined or discrete narcotics networks or organizations in Turkey (comparable to such notorious groups as the Cali or Medellin cartels). More importantly, despite the presentation of schematic charts and maps linking major heroin wholesalers in Istanbul with smugglers and distributers in Beirut or Marseille, internal FBN records contain very few documents that describe or depict Turkish trafficking networks as coherent "gangs" or "mafias."[53] Perhaps of greater importance, the end of year reports issued by the FBN contain a multitude of cases of individuals and networks seemingly unconnected to the men and syndicates that formed the "French Connection." Ongoing seizures of merchant seamen possessing small quantities of opium and heroin on ships at various ports suggest

[51] See Peter Andreas and Ethan Nadelmann, *Policing the Globe: Criminalization and Crime Control in International Relations* (Oxford: Oxford University Press, 2006).

[52] Jonathan Marshall, *Drug Wars: Corruption, Counterinsurgency and Covert Operations in the Third World* (Forestville, CA: Cohen & Cohen Press, 1991), 11–28.

[53] Maps, detailing the connections between major Turkish traffickers (such as Hüseyin Eminoğlu, Ali Osman Tüter, İhsan Sekban, and others) and their counterparts in Lebanon (such as Sami al-Khoury and Antranik Paroutian) and France (such as Jean-Baptiste Croc, Dominiques Ventura, and Dominique Albertini), can be found appended to the final report of the McClellan Commission.

that the trafficking of opiates into the United States continued to be a trade plied by small-time entrepreneurs and smugglers as well as large, well-organized criminal outfits (a trend rooted in the interwar period).[54] It was not until the late 1960s that the FBN offered estimates of the percentage of narcotics (particularly opiates) controlled by the groups and individuals connected to the Istanbul-Beirut-Marseille trade (a topic to be discussed in the next chapter). Nevertheless, if the FBN's own reporting is to be believed, one may surmise that there were many "connections" dealing in opiates produced in Turkey (as well as elsewhere) that escaped the FBN's direct attention and publicity.

The FBN's need to emphasize the threat of large, coherent criminal networks (at the expense of smaller informal ones), as well as the bureau's prime emphasis placed upon exclusively ethnic, foreign, or "alien" groups involved in activities like drug trafficking, has received much in the way of contemporary criticism. In looking back on this moment in the development of American approaches towards the transnational nature of organized crime, present-day scholars have posited that even such prominent syndicates such as New York's five families are less coherent or highly-integrated than they often are portrayed. Jay Albanese, for example, points to Joe Valachi's testimony as evidence of the loose nature of organized crime in New York City. The one-time Genovese foot soldier agreed with Senator Jacob Javitz's characterization that every member of the family "operates by himself" and forms criminal partnerships with associates at their own discretion.[55] Moreover, Albanese argues that contemporary law enforcement bodies, like the FBN decades earlier, often fall into an "ethnicity trap" when analyzing the organization and motivational nature of organized crime. Rather than broach the problem of narcotics trafficking as an industry or broadly-based trade, organized criminal activities continued to be labeled as ethnic or regional operations, affirming (deliberately or by association) the notion that certain ethnicities are prone to certain types of criminal behavior.[56]

While such characterizations may indeed be rooted in historically rooted bigotries towards certain ethnic groups, the postwar context and the institutional prerogatives that impacted the FBN's first efforts in Turkey, as well as the broader fight against heroin trafficking in the Mediterranean, played an equally important role in shaping American perceptions of the Turkish underworld. Agents like

[54] In their year-to-year reporting, the FBN took careful note of the names of those in possession of opiates and the quantities of opiates seized. It is also interesting to note that many of those seamen (as well as local contacts) arrested possessed names of apparent Asian (presumably Chinese), Latino (often presumably Mexican), or Italian origin. One thing that does not come through clearly from the FBN's end of year reporting is consistent attention to the origins of heroin and other opiates seized. Considering the complexity of the heroin trade during the postwar era, the ethnicity of a suspect or the location of an arrest does not necessarily offer definitive clues as to the origins of the drugs discovered during the FBN's operations. A Mexican national seized at the US-Mexican border in California may be found in the possession of heroin, e.g. from either Mexico, Turkey, or Southeast Asia (since Mexico acted as conduit for opiates from all three of these locations).

[55] Jay Albanese, *Transnational Crime and the 21st Century* (Oxford: Oxford University Press, 2011), 6–7.

[56] Albanese, *Transnational Crime*, 5–6. See also Abadinsky, Organized Crime, 41–49.

George White and Charles Siragusa arrived in Istanbul in search of a local mafia to defeat. Past and present investigations in the United States clearly informed such an endeavor. In seeking out Turkey's "Lucky Luciano" (a title Sal Vizzini bestowed upon Hüseyin Eminoğlu), American agents readily applied to their Turkish investigations many of the constructs that suited their approach towards America's mafia underworld (such as the exclusivity of certain ethnic groups involved in the trade and the highly organized nature of criminal syndicates).[57] Turkish officials in Istanbul, who often seemed equally disposed to emphasize the exclusively ethnic character of narcotics trafficking (not to mention other crimes), seemingly obliged the FBN with assessments detailing the activities of Laz, Greek, or Jewish smugglers and wholesalers.

Considering the timeframe and context, one finds many interesting parallels between the conclusions of the Kefauver Committee Report on Organized Crime (released in May 1951) and the FBN's understanding of organized crime in Turkey. The Kefauver Committee posited, for example, that while crime was organized on "a syndicated basis to a substantial extent in many cities" in the United States, gangs in two particular cities, New York and Chicago, dominated a variety of criminal trades throughout the country. Two specific gangs, namely the "Accardo-Guzik-Fischetti syndicate" of Chicago and the "Costello-Adonis-Lansky" syndicate of New York, are mentioned as the main arbiters of organized criminal activity in the early 1950s.[58] As we shall see, the FBN made similar claims about the internal power structure within Turkey's underworld, suggesting that gangs in two cities, Gaziantep-Kilis and Istanbul, were at the core of the country's drug trade. While FBN agents did not conclude, like the Kefauver Commission, that a predominant clandestine culture in the mold of the Italian-American mafia defined the behavior in Istanbul or other parts of Anatolia, investigators in Turkey did often draw comparisons between Sicilians, Corsicans, and Istanbul's "Laz" gangsters.[59] The FBN, like the Kefauver Commission, typically emphasized the impact of large, coherent organized crime groups at the expense of explaining or highlighting the roles played by small, independent or loosely organized syndicates. Like the syndicates of New York and Chicago the Kefauver Commission details in its reports, the FBN consistently, but subtly, underscored the notion that drug

[57] Vizzini, *Vizzini: The Secret Lives of America's Most Successful Undercover Agent*, 99.

[58] U.S. Senate, *The Kefauver Committee Report on Organized Crime, Volume 5* (Washington DC: United States Congress, 1951), 1–2.

[59] U.S. Senate, *The Kefauver Committee Report on Organized Crime, Volume 5* (Washington DC: United States Congress, 1951), 147–50. Authors of the Kefauver Commission Report repeatedly refer to the mafia as a "binding" agent among various criminal syndicates, one that particularly served the interests of groups like the "Costello-Adonis-Lansky syndicate." The commission specifically stated that "the Mafia today is not confined to persons of Sicilian origin." "It would be most unfortunate," the commission continued, "if any inferences were erroneously drawn in any way derogatory to the vast majority of fine law-abiding [American] citizens of Sicilian and Italian extraction." Nevertheless its jaundiced treatment of the history of the mafia in both Italy and the United States, a history that emphasizes almost exclusively the role of Italian-Americans, leave little doubt that the culture of organized crime in the United States in the 1950s possessed a strong Sicilian component.

trafficking and black market smuggling inside of Turkey betrayed a "business-like" approach to crime that was "modern" in its origins.[60]

Interestingly, the voices and opinions of Turkish officers found within the bureau's case files seem to affirm the FBN's general impression of the nature of organized crime in Turkey during the 1950s and beyond. One finds no document, report, or extract suggesting that the DPS rejected or critiqued the way in which the FBN perceived the criminal underworld of Istanbul or the Anatolian interior. If anything, the information supplied by Turkish officers regularly affirmed the FBN's conception of the Istanbul narcotics underworld as constituting a largely uniform, highly organized, and hegemonic *milieu* that dominated the country's drug trade. Despite the significance it would hold during the 1970s and after, neither Turkish nor American sources mention Istanbul's *kabadayı* culture as a source or nexus of drug trafficking or organized crime in the city.

Turkish law enforcement experienced its own renaissance in terms of its organization, focus, and methods. Like the case of the FBN, the politics of the Cold War, and the evolving nature of the Turkish state, informed many of these changes. However, a unique set of conditions influenced Ankara's Directorate of Public Safety. As we shall see, a somewhat different array of security concerns often sublimated or mitigated how the DPS approached narcotics and organized crime. Moreover, in an era that featured the establishment of a new political elite, emerging personal and institutional relationships between politicians and prominent criminals often tempered the way in which the DPS approached narcotics trafficking and traffickers.

NARCOTICS AND NATIONAL SECURITY IN POSTWAR TURKEY

> As an issue that corroded the inner workings of society (*cemiyetin iç bünyesini*) it will be remembered well that at one time this issue [narcotics trafficking] took on a very serious form. However, with regards to the prevention of narcotics production, trade and use by citizens, this danger is now being fundamentally resisted (*önlenmiş*) after years of merciless struggle.[61]
>
> Adnan Menderes, 1955

Three weeks after George White aided local police in the arrest of Vasil Arcan and his accomplices, Istanbul police effected a raid on an opium den in Tahtakale, located close to the heart of the city's historic core. During the course of the raid police arrested the owner of the establishment, *Kürt* Ziya (Ziya the Kurd), along with three unnamed addicts found *in flagrante delicto*. Two days later, on 27 June, the press reported the arrest of two men dealing drugs openly to addicts in Ankara. The two men, Cemal Cosak and Mehmet Yılmaz, supposedly confessed upon their

[60] U.S. Senate, *The Kefauver Committee Report on Organized Crime, Volume 5* (Washington DC: United States Congress, 1951), 145.

[61] BCA 30.01.00.000.15.82.4, 6 March 1955.

apprehension that they had sold two kilograms of heroin over the course of the previous month.[62]

For close to forty years, the US State Department accumulated stories like these from the Istanbul press. On either a monthly or quarterly basis, a consular official provided Washington with itemized digests of all incidents in the city and beyond related to narcotics, including major arrests (such as the prosecution of İhsan Sekban in July 1950) as well as more minor infractions (such as persons found smoking or injecting drugs in hamams or on public streets). In keeping with the nature of contemporary Turkish press reporting, no information on the arrestee, in terms of their personal history or significance, is provided within these compiled news abstracts (often, nothing more than the person's first name is listed). Nothing within the files of the FBN or the State Department offers any insight into why these records were amassed for such a long period of time. The existence of these regular reports does not appear directly connected to the bureau's investigations (since they do not appear regularly within the FBN's files currently on record in the National Archives in College Park, Maryland). Nevertheless, they do offer a contemporary observer some perspective upon the day-to-day operations and activities of narcotics police in Istanbul.

It is difficult to establish a statistical or correlative analysis of the State Department's summaries of narcotics arrests in the postwar era.[63] Given the fact that much of this information was gleaned from the press, it is difficult to establish with certainty whether or not the incidents truly represent the extent of drug-related activity in the city. Be that as it may, in the years between 1950 and 1963, most of the incidents reported concerned individuals nominally unattached to major traffickers mentioned within the files of the FBN (the most notable individuals mentioned in State Department surveys of the press are the Soysal brothers,[64] İhsan Sekban,[65] Topaç Osman,[66] Sefer Bezal,[67] and,

[62] "Subject: Narcotics Offenses," 23 July 1948, Turkey, 1943–48, Subject Files of the Bureau of Narcotics and Dangerous Drugs, 1916–70; Records of the Drug Enforcement Administration; Record Group 170; National Archives Building II, College Park, MD.

[63] For example, the FBN's files do not contain State Department reporting from the years 1957–59. There is some reporting between 1960 and 1963, however this attention to the press also fades between 1964 and 1967.

[64] "Narcotics Offenses in the Municipality of Istanbul," 20 October 1950, Turkey, 1950 Subject Files of the Bureau of Narcotics and Dangerous Drugs, 1916–70; Records of the Drug Enforcement Administration; Record Group 170; National Archives Building II, College Park, MD. On the Soysal brothers, see "Narcotics Offenses in the Municipality of Istanbul," 13 February 1963, Turkey, 1961–64, Subject Files of the Bureau of Narcotics and Dangerous Drugs, 1916–70; Records of the Drug Enforcement Administration; Record Group 170; National Archives Building II, College Park, MD.

[65] "Narcotics Offenses in the Municipality of Istanbul," 22 January 1951, Turkey, 1961–64, Subject Files of the Bureau of Narcotics and Dangerous Drugs, 1916–70; Records of the Drug Enforcement Administration; Record Group 170; National Archives Building II, College Park, MD.

[66] "Illicit Traffic in Narcotics—Municipal District of Istanbul," 10 November 1953, Turkey, 1953–54, Subject Files of the Bureau of Narcotics and Dangerous Drugs, 1916–70; "Narcotics Offenses in the National District of Istanbul," 13 February 1958, Turkey, 1957–59, Subject Files of the Bureau of Narcotics and Dangerous Drugs, 1916–70.

[67] "Narcotics Offenses in the National District of Istanbul," 13 February 1958, Turkey, 1957–59, Subject Files of the Bureau of Narcotics and Dangerous Drugs, 1916–70; "Narcotics Offenses in the

perhaps, Vasil Arcan).[68] The vast majority of the accounts reprinted in the short synopses supplied by the vice-consuls in Istanbul deal with more pedantic or less serious violations of Turkey's narcotics laws: the arrest of petty dealers, overdose deaths, sentencing hearings for smugglers or the discovery of small heroin factories inside family homes or apartments. Most of those arrested were Muslim men (a few with ethnic epithets like Arab or Kurd), although accounts do mention the incarceration of women and non-Muslims at various points during the 1950s.

Taken as a whole, the State Department's reading of the Istanbul press gives the impression that the policing of narcotics in the 1950s and early 1960s was a local matter. Targeting addicts and other public demonstrations of drug use and addiction (especially street dealing) appears to have been a priority by the mid-1950s. Speaking in June 1952, Istanbul governor Fahrettin Gökay boasted that increased policed surveillance in the Tahtakale section of the city prevented the district's "heroin maniacs" from getting a fix from local dealers.[69]

FBN files give few details as to the background or the circumstances that defined the typical narcotics user in postwar Turkey. Like the United States, most official surveys of drug use in Istanbul came from local hospitals. In 1950, an asylum in Bakırköy (located just west of the city) revealed to the press that it was treating 1,534 persons for narcotics addiction. The overwhelming majority of these patients (1,442) were men who used heroin (only 12 percent of cases in the hospital used either opium, hashish, or morphine). A survey of the occupations of these addicts suggests that most were of low class standing. Of the professions found among patients, the top three forms of employment were "artisans and idle persons" (52 percent), "workmen" (18 percent), and technical workmen (11 percent). Of the ninety-two women housed in the hospital, 5 percent were prostitutes while 3.5 percent were "family mothers."[70]

Internal correspondence between the FBN and the Turkish Interior Ministry gives the impression that most of those picked up on narcotics charges were treated as petty offenders. Of the 2,384 people arrested between 1953 and 1959 in cases involving heroin, morphine, cocaine, or hashish, only thirty received sentences of ten years or more (one individual had received a death sentence, but as of 1959, the case was still awaiting a verdict upon appeal). Interestingly, over a third of those charged on drug-related offenses (850 persons) were acquitted of all charges during this same period of time. This high rate of acquittal, in Garland Williams' estimation, most probably related to poor investigational procedures or flaws within the prosecution strategy. But considering that the vast majority of persons (over 60 percent) received sentences of ten years or less, using, selling, or producing narcotics

National District of Istanbul," 13 February 1963, Turkey, 1961–64, Subject Files of the Bureau of Narcotics and Dangerous Drugs, 1916–70.

68 "Illicit Traffic in Narcotics in the Municipal District of Istanbul," 22 January 1951, Turkey, 1951–52, Subject Files of the Bureau of Narcotics and Dangerous Drugs, 1916–70.

69 "Illicit Traffic in Narcotics in the Municipal District of Istanbul," 19 May 1956, Turkey, 1955–56, Subject Files of the Bureau of Narcotics and Dangerous Drugs, 1916–70.

70 "Illicit Traffic in Narcotics in the Municipal District of Istanbul," 22 January 1951, Turkey, 1951–52, Subject Files of the Bureau of Narcotics and Dangerous Drugs, 1916–70.

appears to have been a crime of no great consequence in postwar Turkey.[71] The laxness of Turkish courts in sentencing both major and minor traffickers particularly galled American agents. In November 1950 for example, İhsan Sekban was sentenced to a one-year-nine month term in prison plus an additional two years of exile in the city of Diyarbakir.[72]

An intensified program of policing drug use and drug selling in Turkey was only one component of the reforms undertaken by the country's security services in the postwar era. As one looks at the broader evolution of governance in the republic after the Second World War, officials in Ankara, Istanbul, and elsewhere devoted only some of their attention to the Turkish narcotics industry. In order to understand how Turkish agents approached drug (particularly heroin) related crime after 1945, one must give equal attention to the structural make up of the state security services under the DPS as well as the individuals and political conditions that helped shape the priorities that defined the era.

As a dependant of the Ministry of the Interior, the DPS managed a broad array of policing concerns exclusive of pedestrian crimes. Administratively, the DPS formed a separate body from the country's gendarmerie service, which, as of 1951, formed a 13,000-man body tasked with maintaining law and order in rural districts around the country.[73] Local urban constabulary units possessed discrete sections with assigned tasks and prerogatives. The second section of the Istanbul police department, for example, undertook all investigations related to narcotics violations.

A significant portion of the directorate's interests, which included maintenance of urban police forces throughout Turkey, was of a political nature. A general survey of the functions of the DPS (provided to the FBN in 1951) lists a number of internal bureaus tasked with combating and monitoring subversive activities. In addition to maintaining surveillance of more contemporary potential threats, such as Communists, revolutionaries, foreigners, and minorities (including, but not limited to, Kurds), the DPS appeared to maintain active interest in more antiquated would-be dissidents and traitors (such as Armenian propagandists, supporters of the banished Ottoman monarchy, and individuals charged with treason and stripped of Turkish citizenship following the Turkish War of Independence). The directorate's jurisdiction supposedly did not extend to activities abroad, but one specific branch of the department did collect information from Turkish businessmen, merchants, and tourists venturing out of the country.[74]

[71] Garland Williams to Harry Anslinger, 20 January 1958, Turkey, 1957–59, Subject Files of the Bureau of Narcotics and Dangerous Drugs, 1916–70.

[72] "Illicit Traffic in Narcotics in the Municipal District of Istanbul," 22 January 1951, Turkey, 1951–52, Subject Files of the Bureau of Narcotics and Dangerous Drugs, 1916–70.

[73] "Survey of the General Directorate of Public Safety," undated, Turkey, 1951–52; Subject Files of the Bureau of Narcotics and Dangerous Drugs, 1916–70; Records of the Drug Enforcement Administration; Record Group 170; National Archives Building II, College Park, MD.

[74] "Survey of the General Directorate of Public Safety," undated, Turkey, 1951–52; Subject Files of the Bureau of Narcotics and Dangerous Drugs, 1916–70; Records of the Drug Enforcement Administration; Record Group 170; National Archives Building II, College Park, MD.

While Ankara may have had some reason to fear pro-monarchists and Kurdish dissidents during the interwar period, the fact that supposed traitors from the late Ottoman period remained a concern for the state's internal security services underscores the degree to which imperial apprehensions remained an institutionalized feature of republican politics.[75] Like CUP and Kemalist officials before them, governors, bureaucrats, and law enforcement agents during the 1950s and 1960s also continued to struggle with the problem of rural violence and lawlessness. While the archival record remains incomplete, a sampling of security reports (*asayiş raporları*) from the years between 1963 and 1969 offers greater clarity as to the degree to which violent crime and upheaval in the countryside continued to weigh upon the minds of officials in Ankara.[76] In addition to crimes such as murder, rape, and kidnapping, gendarmes (and police to a limited degree) kept track of animal rustling (*büyükbaş hayvan hırsızlıkğı*) and violence between villages and tribes (*köyler ve aşiretler arasında silahli olay*).[77] Most reports from this era, unlike those from the 1920s or 1930s, do not make mention of particularly problematic regions of Turkey. Nevertheless, appended maps on some reports do give the sense that violent rural crime was endemic to every corner of the country.

TURKISH GENDARMERIE STATISTICS: VIOLENT CRIME AND PROPERTY THEFT[78]

	Jan.	Feb.	Mar.	Apr.	May	Jun.	Jul.	Aug.	Sept.	Oct.	Nov.	Dec.
1964												
Theft	9		8									17
Murders	91		142									147
Battles with Official Detachments	6		2									2
Shots Fired at Official Detachments	2		4									3
Animal Thefts	24		31									32

(*Continued*)

[75] Söner Çagaptay, in his analysis of migration and identity politics during the interwar period, speaks at great length on Ankara's fears of minority dissidents and anti-Kemalist activists. Until the 1930s, e.g., the Turkish Interior Ministry gathered intelligence on such exiled anti-Kemalist dissidents as Çerkes Ethem and Eşref Kuşçubaşı, who supposedly remained committed to undermining the young Turkish Republic. See Çagaptay, "Crafting the Turkish Nation," 217–218.

[76] In addition to the fact that the record is thoroughly incomplete, security reports during much of the 1950s are very vague in classifying acts of violence. Rather than making distinctions between types or causes of theft and violence, statistical records from the Democratic era list criminal acts under such general titles as skirmishes (*müsademe*), border attacks (*hudut tecavüzü*), and thefts (*gasp ve soygun*) as a result of hold ups (*yol kesmek*) or house break-ins (*ev basmak*). See BCA 30.1.0.0.66.410.9, May 1948; BCA 30.1.0.0.67.418.1, 7 June 1952; BCA 30.1.0.0.67.423.7, 4 July 1955.

[77] During the late 1950s, it appears that the Interior Ministry also kept statistics on murders based on revenge (*intikam*), blood feuds (*kan gütme*), and personal disputes (*ihtilaflar*). These categories are discontinued in the reporting from the 1960s. BCA 30.1.0.0.68.428.4, 1 February 1957.

[78] BCA 30.1.00.00.72.457.2, 11 March 1966; BCA 30.1.00.00.72.457.6, 20 May 1966; BCA 30.1.00.00.72.458.2, 7 February 1967; BCA 30.1.00.00.72.458.3, 4 March 1967; BCA 30.1.00.00.72.458.5, 4 April 1967; BCA 30.1.00.00.72.458.7, 7 June 1967; BCA 30.1.00.00.72.458.13,

(Continued)

	Jan.	Feb.	Mar.	Apr.	May	Jun.	Jul.	Aug.	Sept.	Oct.	Nov.	Dec.
Violence between Villages or Tribes	4		7									2
1965												
Theft	22		27	27	36	26	24	48	52	35	31	35
Murders	117		159	159	189	204	227	226	235	180	152	130
Battles with Official Detachments	4		5	5	4	6	5	9	9	6	5	4
Shots Fired at Official Detachments	9		10	10	13	15	18	9	14	16	16	8
Animal Thefts	9		17	17	52	49	42	62	45	26	29	20
Violence between Villages or Tribes	1		3	3	1	1	2	1	4	3	0	0
1966												
Theft	18		30	24	24	30	38	31	34	52	32	12
Murders	178		186	207	207	217	263	258	258	247	197	150
Battles with Official Detachments	6		5	10	6	6	12	8	9	52	4	2
Shots Fired at Official Detachments	9		19	16	14	20	19	10	15	5	10	7
Animal Thefts	24		30	21	40	55	51	42	64	29	36	16
Violence between Villages or Tribes	0		3	1	7	7	4	1	2	4	1	1
1967												
Theft	14	5	5	15	21	16	20	27	30	33	17	
Murders	165	118	196	213	222	264	254	286	251	237	183	
Battles with Official Detachments	3	1	5	5	4	8	6	7	9	9	3	
Shots Fired at Official Detachments	7	4	4	11	3	11	14	13	5	2	11	
Animal Thefts	7	12	16	18	38	38	49	40	40	34	26	

(Continued)

17 July 1967; BCA 30.1.00.00.72.458.14, 7 August 1967; BCA 30.1.00.00.72.458.15, 9 September 1967; BCA 30.1.00.00.72.458.16, 16 October 1967; BCA 30.1.00.00.72.458.17, 10 November 1967; BCA 30.1.00.00.72.458.18, 6 December 1967; BCA 30.1.00.00.72.458.20, 9 January 1968; BCA 30.1.00.00.72.459.3, 7 December 1968; BCA 30.1.00.00.72.460.1, 8 February 1969; BCA 30.1.00.00.72.460.2, 11 March 1969; BCA 30.1.00.00.72.460.3, 8 April 1969; BCA 30.1.00.00.72.460.4, 5 June 1969; BCA 30.1.00.00.72.460.6, 3 July 1969; BCA 30.1.00.00.72.460.9, 5 September 1969; BCA 30.1.00.00.72.460.10, 3 October 1969; BCA 30.1.00.00.72.460.11, 8 November 1969.

(Continued)

	Jan.	Feb.	Mar.	Apr.	May	Jun.	Jul.	Aug.	Sept.	Oct.	Nov.	Dec.
Violence between Villages or Tribes	0	1	0	4	0	1	3	3	2	1	1	
1968												
Theft	19	6	9	23	23	23	24	39	30	34		17
Murders	231	183	189	237	235	296	286	274	270	183		175
Battles with Official Detachments	5	6	6	6	6	17	5	7	9	15		5
Shots Fired at Official Detachments	8	3	7	7	7	15	18	14	8	12		2
Animal Thefts	19	5	14	23	40	33	37	49	36	38		11
Violence between Villages or Tribes	2	1	1	1	2	1	2	2	1	4		0
1969												
Theft		5		10	20?		26	42	35			8
Murders		183		225	241		281	316	279			181
Battles with Official Detachments		2		4	4		21	18	11			3
Shots Fired at Official Detachments		5		10	14		17	12	16			17
Animal Thefts		9		26	27		19	21	44			9
Violence between Villages or Tribes		0		1	3		2	1	0			2

TURKISH NATIONAL POLICE STATISTICS: VIOLENT CRIME AND PROPERTY THEFT[79]

	Jan.	Feb.	Mar.	Apr.	May	Jun.	Jul.	Aug.	Sept.	Oct.	Nov.	Dec.
1964												
Theft	3		14									12
Murders	21		30									30
Home Invasion	0		0									0
Animal Thefts	5		5									7

(Continued)

[79] BCA 30.1.00.00.72.457.2, 11 March 1966; BCA 30.1.00.00.72.457.6, 20 May 1966; BCA 30.1.00.00.72.458.2, 7 February 1967; BCA 30.1.00.00.72.458.3, 4 March 1967; BCA 30.1.00.00.72.458.5, 4 April 1967; BCA 30.1.00.00.72.458.7, 7 June 1967; BCA 30.1.00.00.72.458.13, 17 July 1967; BCA 30.1.00.00.72.458.14, 7 August 1967; BCA 30.1.00.00.72.458.15, 9 September

(Continued)

	Jan.	Feb.	Mar.	Apr.	May	Jun.	Jul.	Aug.	Sept.	Oct.	Nov.	Dec.
1965												
Theft	4		12	10	9	14	21	15	13	11	7	17
Murders	21		36	45	38	29	43	50	38	38	50	29
Home Invasion	2		1	0	2	1	2	1	2	6	2	2
Animal Thefts	2		7	11	10	6	2	13	5	24	9	4
1966												
Theft	7	12	12	14	22	22	14	15	21	19	18	10
Murders	26	43	42	32	42	45	61	45	57	47	38	38
Home Invasion	1	2	3	1	3	1	2	0	0	1	1	3
Animal Thefts	8	3	6	3	6	7	5	3	5	8	14	1
1967												
Theft	2	5	6	7	10	12	23	4	9	6	8	
Murders	31	29	35	51	61	51	51	60	47	53	36	
Home Invasion	2	0	2	5	1	1	1	0	0	1	0	
Animal Thefts	1	1	1	72	5	6	7	6	3	1	1	
1968												
Theft		8	8	7	11	5	7	12	7	5		
Murders		47	57	64	57	61	69	76	58	56		
Home Invasion	2	2	0	0	1	1	1	6	1			
Animal Thefts	3	2	1	2	1	6	0	1	0			
1969												
Theft				3	7		9	16	11			
Murders				56	74		66	79	74			
Home Invasion			3	3		1	4	8				
Animal Thefts			2	2		4	5	14				

The onset of the Cold War and the emergence of a more assertive Soviet Union amplified Turkish paranoia regarding the country's internal security. Turkish participation in the Korean War helped to heighten the potential threat of Soviet aggression.[80] Despite their diminutive size as an official party, Turkish Communists

1967; BCA 30.1.00.00.72.458.16, 16 October 1967; BCA 30.1.00.00.72.458.17, 10 November 1967; BCA 30.1.00.00.72.458.18, 6 December 1967; BCA 30.1.00.00.72.458.20, 9 January 1968; BCA 30.1.00.00.72.459.3, 7 December 1968; BCA 30.1.00.00.72.460.1, 8 February 1969; BCA 30.1.00.00.72.460.2, 11 March 1969; BCA 30.1.00.00.72.460.3, 8 April 1969; BCA 30.1.00.00.72.460.4, 5 June 1969; BCA 30.1.00.00.72.460.6, 3 July 1969; BCA 30.1.00.00.72.460.9, 5 September 1969; BCA 30.1.00.00.72.460.10, 3 October 1969; BCA 30.1.00.00.72.460.11, 8 November 1969.

80 There is comparatively little on the social history of Turkey during the course of the Cold War. See John Vander Lippe, "Forgotten Brigade of the Forgotten War: Turkey's Participation in the Korean War," *Middle East Studies* 36.1 (January 2000), 92–102.

gleaned much attention in the Turkish press.[81] With the arrival of tens of thousands of Turkish immigrants forced out of Bulgaria between 1950 and 1953, it appears that local law enforcement officials in Istanbul, and elsewhere, gave greater credence to the native (and largely overblown) threat of Communist subversion.[82]

While anxiety over the threat of the Soviet Union and the spread of Communism did reinforce long-standing and deeply embedded apprehensions found within the Turkish state, the onset of the postwar era brought on new political and social trends that fundamentally changed the nature of governance in the country. After over a quarter of a century in power, the Republican People's Party conceded control over the Turkish National Assembly to Adnan Menderes and the Democratic Party (DP) in May 1950. A number of historical precedents, some dating as far back as the First World War, were shattered as a result of this dramatic change in leadership. The ascendency of the DP ushered in a decidedly younger generation of reformers, statesmen, and technocrats into positions of power in both Ankara and the provinces. While many of the principal DP members did serve in the Turkish War of Independence (including Adnan Menderes, Celal Bayar, and Refik Koraltan), the party lacked the sort of strong ties the RPP shared with the military. Unlike many of the individuals who comprised the core ranks of the RPP (as well as the Committee of Union and Progress), a significant number of notable members of the DP were men born and raised in Anatolia (as opposed to the former Ottoman territories of the Balkans). Taken as a whole, the rule of the DP is often seen as an era that featured a loosening of some of the more intense and penetrating reforms undertaken during the Kemalist period (especially with respect to the state's strident commitment to secularism). It may be said that the rise of the DP itself was deeply indebted to vocal American support. American backing for the DP in the election of 1950 certainly helped to lay the groundwork for the close political, military, and economic ties the United States and Turkey would share over the next few decades.

Among those who helped to steer the emerging postwar order in Turkey was a career bureaucrat by the name of Kemal Aygün. His path to power, as well as his precipitous fall from grace, is illustrative of his times and critical to the specific history of Turkish-American anti-narcotics cooperation. Although little is known about his parents, it is evident that Kemal benefited greatly from the fame and exploits of his uncle, Refik Koraltan, a hero of the Turkish War of Independence and seminal

[81] Nazım Hikmet, a nationalist poet and longtime Communist activist, received particular popular attention in 1950 after he undertook a hunger strike in protest of his false imprisonment. See Saime Göksu and Edward Timms, *Romantic Communist: The Life and Work of Nazım Hikmet* (New York: Palgrave Macmillan, 1999), 212–253. For the evolution of the Turkish Communist Party during the early stages of the Cold War, see Jacob Landau, *Radical Politics in Turkey* (Leiden: Brill, 1974), 101–105.

[82] Huey Louis Kostanick, "Turkish Resettlement of Bulgarian Refugees, 1950–1953," *Middle East Journal* 9.1 (1955), 41–52; Geoffrey Lewis, "Political Change in Turkey Since 1960," in William Hale (ed.), *Aspects of Modern Turkey* (London: Bowker, 1976), 18; Martin Pera to Charles Siragusa, 9 March 1951, Turkey, 1951–52, FBN Files, 1916–70; DEA Records; RG 170, NAB.

member of the early republican government.[83] Like his uncle, Aygün also chose the budding Turkish bureaucracy as his avenue into politics. After a brief stint working as a district administrator, Aygün entered the Directorate of Public Safety. Aygün's big promotion occurred in June of 1950 when he was elevated to head the Istanbul branch of the Directorate of Public Safety.[84] It is not a coincidence that such a rise in the ranks of the department occurred within a month of the critical election of May 1950. The Democratic victory concomitantly benefited Kemal Aygün's uncle, Refik Koraltan, who helped to establish the DP in 1946, and, as a result, became president of the Turkish Grand National Assembly for the next ten years.[85]

Within two years of assuming leadership over the Istanbul branch, Kemal Aygün would again be promoted, this time to head the entire Directorate of Public Safety. His tenure within the DPS made him a fixture of Istanbul's political landscape, a status that would result in his election as mayor of the city in 1958. Together with the Prime Minister of Turkey, Adnan Menderes, Aygün helped to oversee one of the most dramatic "urban renewal" projects the city of Istanbul had ever experienced.[86] The capriciousness with which Istanbul was "modernized" mirrored the DP's grander ambition to solidify its power over the country. Despite coming to power after decades of autocratic rule under the RPP, Menderes and the Democratic establishment resorted to many of the dictatorial practices favored by their predecessors (such as rigging elections and curtailing freedom of the press). Such designs earned the Menderes regime bitter enemies among the Turkish military and elements of the former Republican regime.[87]

Kemal Aygün is an important figure in Turkey's unfolding relationship with the FBN and the evolution of Turkey's initial approaches towards narcotics in the first two decades of the Cold War. His personal connection to individuals within the inner circle of the DP, a status affirmed by the pivotal offices he would hold during the 1950s, made him an invaluable interlocutor between Washington and Ankara. It was through his interventions as head of the DPS that American and Turkish cooperative efforts rapidly took effect. Aygün's personal sponsorship of FBN/DPS enterprises in Turkey clearly afforded joint narcotics operations an air of official legitimacy and urgency, an aspect that often greatly impressed his American counterparts. Without his cooperation, or the cooperation of his closely linked subordinates, American agents possessed no basis for their activities in the country.

[83] After the establishment of Atatürk's republican government in 1923, Koraltan went on to serve for twenty years in the assembly and at various levels of the provincial government. Most of Refik Koraltan's memoirs, however, are devoted to his contributions to the independence struggle. See Refik Koraltan, *Bir Politkacının Anıları* (Ankara: Hacettepe-Taş Yayınevi, 1999).

[84] "Yeni İdari Değişiklikler," *Milliyet* 26 June 1950.

[85] Frank Sojat to Harry Anslinger, 5 February 1952, Turkey, 1951–52, FBN Files, 1916–70; DEA Records; RG 170, NAB.

[86] Murat Gül, *The Emergence of Modern Istanbul* (London: I.B. Tauris Publishers, 2009), 140–171.

[87] For further background on the significance of the Democratic period and the origins and ramifications of the 1960 coup, see Kemal Karpat, "The Military and Politics in Turkey, 1960–64: A Socio-Cultural Analysis of a Revolution," *American Historical Review* 75.6 (October 1970), 1654–1683.

BUILDING CASES: THE FIRST YEARS OF FBN/DPS COLLABORATION

On 20 July 1950, Charles Siragusa boarded a KLM flight bound for Istanbul. The trip had been officially cleared through the State Department in concert with the consent of the Turkish government. According to this formal agreement, Siragusa was coming to Istanbul in order "to cooperate with Turkish police in exposing narcotics traffic between the United States and Turkey."[88] In his memoirs, Siragusa is vague as to the specific goals of his first trip to Turkey in July 1950.[89] Even without a grand strategy guiding his initial tour of Turkey, Siragusa's activities and appointments clearly followed the operational approach undertaken by George White in 1948. Between 24 July and 25 August, Siragusa would send twenty-two detailed "progress reports" directly to Harry Anslinger, each detailing, in fluid and descriptive language, his experiences and impressions incurred while in-country.[90] The general tone of his summaries, coupled with the accounts of the individuals he met and the information he learned, leave little doubt as to the specific purpose of his trip: to uncover the top heroin smugglers in Turkey and, if possible, to make an arrest.

His trip coincided with a momentous period in the development of the FBN. During the course of 1950, the FBN would open a permanent office in Rome, the first of many such offices established on foreign soil. Over time, Siragusa transformed the city into a central outpost in undertaking future investigations in Europe and the Middle East.[91] Siragusa's first visit to Istanbul, coupled with his immediate relocation to Italy, consummated the FBN's transformation into a police force with a genuinely global reach (a process that clearly began with Anslinger's active engagement of foreign governments during the interwar period). The eventual opening of an FBN field office in Istanbul in 1960 occurred as the bureau planted firm roots in such cities as Beirut (opened in 1954), Paris (1959), Marseille (1961), Hong Kong (1963), Mexico City (1963), and Bangkok (1963). The list of international offices now under the management of the Drug Enforcement Administration is now far more expansive, numbering eighty-five locations in sixty-six countries worldwide.

His first act upon arriving in Istanbul was to contact the American Consulate and to make appointments with multiple members of the consular staff. Among the first men he met was G. Joseph Zogby, the CIA officer who supplied him with

[88] Department of State to General Directorate for Security, undated, Turkey, 1950, FBN Files, 1916–70; DEA Records; RG 170, NAB.

[89] Siragusa and Wiedrich , The Trail of the Poppy, 5. He makes mention of the fact that Anslinger had assigned him to go abroad in order to address the dire state of narcotics use among young people in the United States.

[90] Siragusa's personal correspondence with Harry Anslinger continued well after he departed from Istanbul in late October. From Beirut and Marseille, Siragusa continued to write highly detailed and personal accounts of his experiences abroad (which lasted at least until the middle of 1951). The relatively brusque and unedited tone of Siragusa's writings makes this set of documents among the more unique pieces of evidence found in the files available in the FBN's records in the National Archive.

[91] Valentine, *Strength of the Wolf*, 105–106.

his first intelligence file on the principal smugglers and producers of heroin in the country.[92] While he mentions in his memoirs that he spent much of the winter and spring of 1950 poring over the FBN's internal files from Europe and the Middle East in anticipation of his trip that summer, the information Zogby provided to Siragusa appears to have contained many new revelations.[93]

In the days immediately following his meetings at the consulate, Siragusa sought to meet with several individuals who had helped to lay the groundwork for George White's 1948 investigation in Turkey. The first local contact he made a point of meeting was Rıza Çandır, a journalist who worked as a foreign correspondent for the Turkish News Agency (*Türk Haberler Ajansi*).[94] Together with Çandır, Siragusa had lunch with Lieutenant Colonel Charles W. Edwards, an assistant foreign attaché attached to the U.S. Air Force. In addition to being close friends of George White, both men shared a similar history. During the Second World War, Edwards (whom White knew from his time in Cairo) served as an OSS point of contact in Istanbul. Çandır, it appears, was an important source for OSS intelligence during the war as well (due in part to his prestige as a journalist and his fluency in six languages). With the war over, both men continued to remain active in intelligence circles. While Edwards maintained connections with the CIA, Çandır continued to operate (in White's estimation) on behalf of the "Turkish secret political police."[95]

Of the two, Rıza Çandır appeared to be the most knowledgeable about the state of narcotics trafficking in Turkey. Back in 1948, White met with Çandır nine times over the course of his stay in Istanbul. In addition to discussing the state of organized crime in Marseille and the processing of raw opium, Çandır introduced White to sailors (including a sea captain) from the Black Sea (leaving one to assume that the "Laz" nature of the Istanbul underworld may have been discussed).[96] However, judging from letters the two men would exchange into the 1950s, it appears that White's relationship with Çandır continued to generate intelligence for the FBN.[97]

[92] Charles Siragusa to Harry Anslinger, 24 July 1950, Turkey, 1950; FBN Files, 1916–70; DEA Records; RG 170, NAB.

[93] Siragusa and Wiedrich, The Trail of the Poppy, 85. According to Siragusa, Garland Williams had recently compiled a list of major violators, a list which included İhsan Sekban (who was the principal focus of the CIA's report).

[94] "Gazeteci Rıza Çandır Öldü," *Milliyet* 28 September 1979.

[95] Commissioner of Narcotics Anslinger from White #10, 10 June 1948, George H. White Papers, Box 1, Folder 7, Special Collections Department, Stanford University. It is not clear what White means by Turkey's "secret political police." Assuming he is correct, one could assume that Çandır worked for either the Directorate of Public Safety (in the political section) or on behalf of the National Security Service (*Milli Emniyet Hizmeti*). As for Edwards' role in intelligence gathering and narcotics activity, he did prove willing to introduce Siragusa to a local contact, another former OSS operative by the name of Teodor Anastasio, who provided further details on İhsan Sekban and his activities. See Charles Siragusa to H. J. Anslinger, 24 July 1950, Turkey, 1950; FBN Files, 1916–70; DEA Records; RG 170, NAB.

[96] George White Diary, Entries 21 May 1950–9 June 1950, George H. White Papers, Carton 7, Book 1950, Special Collections Department, Stanford University.

[97] According to a letter sent in 1951, Çandır suggested to White that Charles Siragusa was out of his depth during his month-long stay in Istanbul. In addition to employing a rather "shady character" as a translator (a future FBN informant by the name of Charles Diamond), Siragusa often came close to subjecting himself to physical danger (which the Istanbul police "had a hell of a time" preventing). In terms of his investigative approach, Siragusa's "lone wolf" posturing during his stay led him

Charles Siragusa's meetings with Edwards and Çandır were soon followed by an official appointment with Kemal Aygün, who had only recently become the chief of the Istanbul police department.[98] Their first encounter, much to Siragusa's disappointment, did not go well. Although he found the Istanbul chief cordial, his hopes of quickly establishing a cooperative relationship regarding anti-narcotics operations were dashed. Though hesitant to admit it, Siragusa went so far as to confess to Anslinger that his Turkish counterpart perhaps had set him up before he had even arrived in the city. Reports of an impending secret American anti-narcotics mission to Istanbul were circulating in local papers on the very day Siragusa landed.[99] Two days before his meeting with Aygün, local police arrested İhsan Sekban, referred to by newspapers as one of the most notorious traffickers in the city.[100] However, when Siragusa broached Sekban's apprehension with Aygün, he was flatly told that Sekban would probably never see trial. İhsan Sekban had the best lawyers in the city and friends in high places. In other words, in Siragusa's estimation, the Istanbul police not only betrayed his presence to the press, but also placed the city's most notorious trafficker under arrest as a way to save face.[101]

Relations between Aygün and Siragusa continued to ebb and flow over the next two years. After Aygün's appointment as head of the DPS, however, his manner and approach towards his American counterparts changed. Correspondence and meetings between FBN agents and Aygün's office warmed considerably and appear to have led to more fruitful displays of cooperation.[102] Aygün appeared far more thankful for the support he received from the FBN and repeatedly expressed interest in adopting more "Americanized" methods of policing. As head of the DPS, he attempted to centralize the directorate's power and increase intelligence sharing among its various branches.[103] He, along with other leading officials in Ankara, voiced support for reforming Turkey's penal laws with respect to narcotics

to attempt to do too much with few resources. At the time, Çandır claimed he was too busy to help and lacked personal contacts in either the underworld or among "cloak and dagger gents." See Riza Chandir to George White, 7 March 1951; Turkey, 1951–52; FBN Files, 1916–70; DEA Records; RG 170, NAB.

98 One of the last, and among the more intriguing, intelligence sources Siragusa met with was Abdullah F. L. Ma. Ma served in the Chinese consulate for ten years until the end of the Chinese Civil War in 1949. In 1948, White had met with him (alongside Riza Çandır) and during their meeting, Ma claimed to have intelligence upon the location of heroin factories in the city, information he would share in exchange for a visa to the United States. Siragusa, dubious about Ma's sincerity, declined the offer. See Charles Siragusa to H. J. Anslinger, 24 July 1950, Turkey, 1950; FBN Files, 1916–70; DEA Records; RG 170, NAB.

99 "Beyaz Zehir Kaçakçıları," *Akşam* 24 July 1950.

100 "Milyonar Eroinci Yakalandı," *Cumhuriyet* 25 July 1950.

101 Charles Siragusa to H. J. Anslinger, 26 July 1950, Turkey, 1950; FBN Files, 1916–70; DEA Records; RG 170, NAB.

102 According to Valentine's interview with Martin Pera, Kemal Aygün did not receive American requests for cooperation well because of the poor press coverage the DPS had received as a result of George White's investigation in 1948. See Valentine, *Strength of the Wolf*, 161.

103 Frank Sojat to H. J. Anslinger, 5 January 1952; Turkey, 1951–52; FBN Files, 1916–70; DEA Records; RG 170, NAB; "Opium Production," 16 March 1960; Turkey, 1960–61; FBN Files, 1916–70; DEA Records; RG 170, NAB.

violations.[104] In return, Charles Siragusa personally invited several of Aygün's men to be trained in American counter-narcotics methods at an FBN facility in Italy.[105] Alongside specific changes to the narcotics bureau attached to the DPS, a more general wave of reforms swept over Turkey's policing infrastructure. Under the direction of an American civilian advisor, the organization, labor codes, and equipment of the DPS was upgraded and regularized.[106]

As the 1950s progressed, FBN agents found Aygün more and more elusive in terms of his time, contact, and attention (particularly after he simultaneously assumed control over the DPS and the governorship of Ankara in 1955). In his absence, three DPS officers managed day-to-day contact and collaboration with American agents. After Aygün became head of the DPS in 1952, the Department of the Interior appointed another veteran officer, Alaattin Eriş, to take his place as head of the Istanbul branch of the DPS. Until 1955, Eriş entrusted two junior officers, Ali Eren and Galip Labernas, to coordinate with their American counterparts on individual investigations.

Following Siragusa's departure from Turkey in August 1950, a series of seasoned FBN agents assumed responsibility for initiating cases and conducting investigations in Turkey. Between 1951 and 1967, the bureau sent a number of officers to Turkey for short stints of service: Paul Knight, Martin Pera, John Cusack, Elmore Gross, Sal Vizzini, James Attie, Joe Arpaio, and Michael Picini.[107] While there is no single official directive found within the contents of the FBN's Turkey files detailing the responsibilities and regulations of American operations while in-country, it is clear that Ankara and Washington did agree upon a series of ground rules for FBN operations. For example, Ankara eventually stipulated that American agents could not venture into the Anatolian countryside without the presence of either Ali Eren and Galip Labernas.[108] FBN agents actively updated their Turkish counterparts in Istanbul about their movements and interactions with criminal informants and potential suspects. According to Joe Arpaio, American agents were forbidden from carrying firearms (a directive that was apparently ignored with some regularity).[109] Perhaps of greatest importance, the FBN's files make it clear that the testimony of American officers was not required when suspects were brought to trial.

[104] American Consulate General, Istanbul to Secretary of State, "Narcotics Report—Turkey," 17 September 1952, 882.53/9-1752, Central Decimal Files, 1950–54, RG 59, NAB.

[105] Garland Williams to Harry Anslinger, 20 April 1958, Iran File, 1958–60; FBN Files, 1916–70; DEA Records; RG 170, NAB.

[106] Ali Dikici, "Demokrat Parti Döneminde İç Güvenlik ve Türk Polis Teşkilatı, *Akademik Bakış* 3.5 (Winter 2009), 68–70.

[107] According to a 1960 report, agents came irregularly to Turkey between 1956 and 1960. Before that period, the reports of Elmore Gross suggest that the FBN had a much more sustained presence in Turkey between 1951 and 1956. See unlabeled report, 16 March 1960, Turkey, 1960–61, FBN Files, 1916–70; DEA Records; RG 170, NAB.

[108] Memorandum: District #17, 24 November 1955; Turkey, 1955–56; FBN Files, 1916–70; DEA Records; RG 170, NAB.

[109] Arpaio and Sherman, *Joe's Law*, 153, 164. On one arrest, Arpaio claimed to have held thirty smugglers at gunpoint even though he had no legal authority to arrest them.

Of the hundreds of pages of reports that are found in the FBN's records, relatively few of them offer intimate details of their investigations. The most detailed accounts of FBN arrests made in the 1950s can be found instead in the memoirs of Sal Vizzini and Charles Siragusa. Siragusa, for example, reveals much about the Ahmet Özsayar investigation in Adana in 1954 (a case that was made through the intervention of FBN Agent Paul Knight, the Beirut chief of police, Amir Farid Chehab, and a Greek informant) but, as previously mentioned, there is no archival record available which corroborates his rendering of the case.

Sal Vizzini provides even more striking, and peculiar, anecdotes regarding his own time in Turkey during the late 1950s. Vizzini opens his recollections of his experiences in Turkey with his efforts to apprehend both Ali Osman Tüter and Hüseyin Eminoğlu, who he identifies as chief narcotics traffickers and smugglers in Istanbul. Miraculously, he was able to personally acquaint himself with Tüter through an informant in Italy, who was compelled by police in Rome to write a letter to the Istanbul trafficker on Vizzini's behalf. With the help of a locally based American pilot named Dan Klein as an interpreter, Vizzini visited Tüter at his home and agreed to the purchase of cheap American cigarettes that Vizzini had acquired through a store reserved for American military personnel. This initial deal, according to Vizzini, afforded him "a reference" that he used in interacting with other dealers based in Istanbul. With this newfound credibility among local dealers, Vizzini claims to have arrested a half dozen "small fry traffickers" inside of a month.[110]

Vizzini asserts that he was also able to arrange a meeting with Hüseyin Eminoğlu at an Istanbul restaurant soon after his encounter with Ali Osman Tüter. Posing as a crooked airline pilot, Vizzini used a Turkish police informant as a reference to approach Eminoğlu with an offer to buy morphine base (claiming that he had connections in Sicily that could process the drug into heroin). After Eminoğlu appeared disinterested in the deal, he then offered to furnish the smuggler with $2,000-worth of American cigarettes. The proposition peaked Eminoğlu's interest, who in turn proposed that Vizzini meet with him after a ship carrying "miscellaneous cargo" docked in Istanbul's harbor. With this scrap of information in hand, Vizzini and his Turkish counterparts, Ali Eren and Galip Labernas, hatched a plan to apprehend Eminoğlu once the ship reached port. The plan apparently worked. Some time later (the memoirs give no indication of the timeframe or dates), Turkish police seized Eminoğlu at the docks alongside a ship named the *Adana*, which was found to have illicitly carried twenty-five tons of coffee and ten tons of English nylon in its holdings.[111]

Despite the significance with which both Eminoğlu and Tüter were viewed by the FBN, none of these cases are referenced in the bureau's case files. Hüseyin Eminoğlu was arrested (alongside Fahrettin Soysal and Ali Bezal) in August 1959 for the crime Vizzini describes above.[112] While Vizzini states that Eminoğlu

[110] Vizzini, *Vizzini: The Secret Lives of America's Most Successful Undercover Agent,* 102–106.

[111] Vizzini, *Vizzini: The Secret Lives of America's Most Successful Undercover Agent,* 109–112.

[112] "Büyük Kahve Kaçakçılığı Elebaşıları Yakalanmadı," *Akşam* 9 August 1959; "Kahve Kaçakçılığının 13. Sanığı Tevkif Edildi," *Akşam* 14 August 1959; "Kahve Kaçakcılığı Tahkikatı İlerliyor," *Cumhuriyet* 4 August 1959; "30 Ton Kahve Kaçakçılığının Duruşması," *Cumhuriyet* 4 September 1959; "Üç Kahve Kaçakçısı Tevkif Edildi," *Milliyet* 9 August 1959; "Kahve Kaçakçılığı

received ten years in prison for the crime, later press reporting gives the impression that he was set free and remained active in illicit trafficking (since Eminoğlu was later placed under arrested in 1960, 1964, and 1969 on smuggling charges).[113] Further complicating the accuracy of Vizzini's story is the name of the boat that was associated with Eminoğlu's apprehension. While press reports cite no specific ship associated with it in 1959, a search of the newspaper *Milliyet* reveals that a ship called the *Adana* was implicated in no less than eight smuggling seizures between 1958 and 1961.[114] While it is certainly possible that there was more than one ship called *Adana* that regularly travelled in and out of the port of Istanbul, the regularity with which a ship by this name was mentioned in the press raises the suspicion that it was perhaps habitually searched for illicit goods.

As frustratingly silent as the FBN archival record is on the makings of individual cases (particularly successful ones), intelligence reports submitted by agents from the 1950s are fairly rich in detail. Beginning with Charles Siragusa's first excursion to Turkey, FBN agents regularly updated lists of major and minor traffickers active in the city of Istanbul. The manner with which these lists were maintained and revised between 1950 and 1960 reflected both the acquisition of new information and the evolving perceptions of the conspiratorial and organizational nature of the networks FBN agents encountered. American and Turkish agents regularly followed, photographed, or tracked the whereabouts of potential targets (often with the help of criminal informants).

Most of the individuals mentioned within these updated lists did not attract regular or sustained FBN interest. Those individuals who tended to be of greater interest (such as İhsan Sekban, Hüseyin Eminoğlu, Ali Osman Tüter, Ali Bezal, and Sefer Bezal) are often referred to as associates of specific "mobs" or gangs.[115] Between 1950 and 1960, the make up, and preeminence, of specific "mobs" identified by the FBN did change with some regularity. In 1950, for example, Agent Frank Sojat references three specific groups headed by İhsan Sekban, Ahmet Soysal, and Hüseyin Eminoğlu as occupying dominant positions within Istanbul's heroin market. In addition to these three bands (possessing nine, eight, and five members, respectively), Sojat lists another twenty-two individuals, some working in cooperatives of two to four, who made some mark upon the city's drug

Duruşması Başladı," *Milliyet* 4 September 1959; "Milyonluk Kahve Kaçakcılığı Sanıkları Tahliye Edildi," *Milliyet* 20 January 1960.

[113] "150 Ton Tütün Motorla Triyeste'ye Kaçırıldı," *Milliyet* 20 June 1960; "Mahkeme Salonunda Bir Sanık Muayene Edildi," *Milliyet* 12 March 1964; "Telefonlar Dinlenerek Kaçakçılar Yakalandı," *Milliyet* 27 June 1969.

[114] "Adana Vapurunda Yine Kaçak Eşya Bulundu," *Milliyet* 7 August 1958; "Üç Gemide Kaçak Eşya Bulundu," *Milliyet* 1 November 1958; "Adana Vapurunda Yine Kaçak Mermi Bulundu," *Milliyet* 24 April 1959; "Adana Vapurunda Yine Kaçak Eşya Bulundu," *Milliyet* 7 November 1959; "'Adana'da Kaçak Saat ve Bilezik Ele Geçti," *Milliyet* 6 Feburary 1960; "Dışarıyıya 1.5 Kilo Esrar Kaçıran 5 Tayfa Getirildi," *Milliyet* 18 March 1960; "Döviz Kaçakçısı bir Müzisyen Yakalandı," *Milliyet* 4 March 1961; "Adana Vapurunda Kaçak Eşya Bulundu," *Milliyet* 29 March 1961.

[115] Paul Knight to Charles Siragusa, 61 January 1955, Turkey, 1955–56, FBN Files, 1916–70; DEA Records; RG 170, NAB.

trade that year.[116] In 1955, Agent Elmore Gross categorically listed three specific "organizations," in descending order, as responsible for sending "large quantities of morphine base and heroin" from Turkey: the "Mavromatis-Paskalides-Foti organization," the "Hüseyin-Osman-Kalkavan organization," and the "Denizkurdu-Kirazli-Sarafin organization."[117] Gross's 1955 summation of the major trafficking networks differs from Sojat's earlier appraisal in two interesting regards. While both men mention discernibly key individuals, such as Eminoğlu and Tüter, the inclusion of the Mahmut Denizkurdu gang (which is mentioned in only a few documents) in the 1955 list comes at the expense of other individuals and supposed syndicates of long-standing weight and significance (particularly that of the Soysal brothers). Moreover, Gross clearly forsakes Sojat's approach of mentioning prominent individuals who handled smaller portions of the trade, thus giving the impression that the Istanbul underworld was the exclusive domain of three powerful gangs.

Neither the FBN nor the DPS premised their respective opinions or impressions purely on the basis of outside observations. FBN agents habitually assumed the identities of a variety of shady characters in order to infiltrate smuggling rings and apprehend potential suspects (with both Siragusa and Vizzini at times posing as Italian mobsters). At times, Turkish officers like Labernas or Eren did act as undercover operatives in order to fabricate an arrest.[118] Subversion of prospective narcotics networks by undercover agents ultimately provided limited amounts of actionable intelligence throughout the 1950s and 1960s. Instead, throughout this era, both the FBN and DPS replied heavily, at times almost exclusively, upon the information and insights provided to them by paid criminal informants. Many informants, according to Vizzini, were killed after smugglers discovered their acts of collusion with the police.[119]

As noted earlier, building a network of reliable informants based in Istanbul was among Charles Siragusa's first tasks during his stay in the city in the summer of 1950. His meetings with Rıza Çandır and Charles W. Edwards did provide him with some early leads as well as a few connections to individuals familiar with the current state of drug trafficking in Istanbul. However, subsequent agents assigned to Turkey would eventually discard or no longer maintain ties with these early contacts (including Çandır and Edwards).

Three weeks into his initial stay in Turkey, Siragusa acquired the bureau's most prominent and long-standing Turkish "special employee." On the morning of 30

[116] "List of Important Narcotics Violators (Heroin Manufacturers) in Istanbul," 25 October 1951, Turkey, 1951–52, FBN Files, 1916–70; DEA Records; RG 170, NAB.

[117] Elmore Gross to Charles Siragusa, 27 March 1955, Turkey, 1955–56, FBN Files, 1916–70; DEA Records; RG 170, NAB.

[118] In one case, Ali Eren went undercover as an "import-export" officer alongside Sal Vizzini (who played an Italian sea captain) in the arrest of Asım Bintepe. Memorandum Report, 26 January 1960, Turkey, 1960–61, FBN Files, 1916–70; DEA Records; RG 170, NAB.

[119] According to Vizzini, he once paid $12,000 to an informant for arranging an arrest. Of the thirty informants he recruited, eight were murdered. See Vizzini, *Vizzini: The Secret Lives of America's Most Successful Undercover Agent*, 101.

July 1950, a Greek sailor by the name of Yovakim Kiriyako arranged for a meeting between Siragusa and Hüsnü Soysal. A report from 1948 detailing Soysal's identity and status as a chemist was in Siragusa's possession before their meeting, allowing the agent some pretext with which to approach this potential informant. Kiriyako, who knew the chemist's nephew, Ali Tocksan, had arranged the appointment with Soysal with the offer that an Italian (Siragusa) was seeking to buy heroin. When the two finally met on the thirtieth, Soysal surprised his American suitor, claiming that he knew that Siragusa was a policeman sent from the United States and that he wanted to help him regardless. After Siragusa adamantly denied the charge (and threatened to "beat his brains in"), the two parted.[120] Siragusa was left bewildered by the encounter and confided in Anslinger that he believed that Kemal Aygün again had blown his cover (leading him to declare that he would no longer share information with the DPS). Siragusa relented eleven days later and communicated with Soysal that they should meet to discuss his potiential service as an informant. Soysal happily agreed to the second meeting and offered him information on an individual named Vasil Karamanli, who he claimed was "the most important violator in all of Turkey."[121] Over the following week, Soysal promised to set Karamanli up by arranging for the purchase of morphine. Karamanli, after several meetings, refused point blank to make the deal after having been warned by the police (specifically Ali Eren) that American agents were seeking to arrest him.[122]

Hüsnü Soysal's failure to deliver Vasil Karamanli into the hands of the authorities did not deter Siragusa from utilizing him as a source of information or as potential "cutout figure" to draw suspected drug traffickers into a bust. In 1955, Siragusa put Agent Elmore Gross in contact with Soysal in the hopes of setting up several prominent traffickers in staged narcotics sales. That winter, the FBN hoped to approach Sefer Bezal (also known as Parlak Sefer), who, like the mysterious Vasil Karamanli before him, Soysal labeled "the largest trafficker in Istanbul." Soysal agreed to try to negotiate with him on the sale of a small quantity of heroin yet claimed that their past dealings had ended badly (Sefer, it seems, refused to pay him due to the poor quantity of heroin previously delivered).[123] Later in April,

[120] Charles Siragusa to Harry Anslinger, 31 July 1950, Turkey, 1950, FBN Files, 1916–70; DEA Records; RG 170, NAB.

[121] Charles Siragusa to Harry Anslinger, 10 August 1950, Turkey, 1950, Turkey, 1950, FBN Files, 1916–70; DEA Records; RG 170, NAB.

[122] Charles Siragusa to Harry Anslinger, 20 August 1950, Turkey, 1950, Turkey, 1950, FBN Files, 1916–70; DEA Records; RG 170, NAB; Charles Siragusa to Harry Anslinger, 14 August 1950, Turkey, 1950, Turkey, 1950, FBN Files, 1916–70; DEA Records; RG 170, NAB.

[123] Elmore Gross to Charles Siragusa, 19 February 1955, Turkey, 1955–56, FBN Files, 1916–70; DEA Records; RG 170, NAB; Elmore Gross to Charles Siragusa, 23 February 1955, Turkey, 1955–56, FBN Files, 1916–70; DEA Records; RG 170, NAB. Sefer Bezal was arrested in 1958 during a search carried out by Ali Eren. According to Eren's own account, he had encountered Bezal after propositioning Osman Topaç, a drug trafficker with connections to heroin refiners in Naples, to act as an informant. When Eren discovered Topaç was attempting to dodge his commitment as an informant, and sell small amounts of morphine, he forced Osman to open the door to his apartment, where Eren discovered Bezal and a kilo of morphine base. See Memorandum Report, 26 Februrary 1958, Turkey, 1957–59, FBN Files, 1916–70; DEA Records; RG 170, NAB.

Soysal succeeded in arranging the purchase of 250 kilos of heroin from a smuggler named Foti, a Greek trafficker associated with İhsan Sekban and Nickli Eftimyadis (more commonly known by his nickname, Mavromatis). When the time came to exchange the drugs and money, Foti demurred, stating that he would only sell him fifteen kilos at a time (apparently on the basis that Turkish courts typically sentenced individuals caught with less than twenty kilos to only three months in prison). Soysal allegedly demanded the full amount of heroin and broke off negotiations.[124] Despite promises to complete the sale of heroin in the near future, subsequent FBN reports contain no reference to the transaction or to Foti's arrest.

Recent screenings conducted by the National Archives have resulted in the "blacking out" of many of the names of the FBN's other informants (under the auspices of protections afforded by the Freedom of Information Act to anonymous law enforcement informants). Nevertheless, from what can be gathered from various files in the FBN collection, special employees other than Hüsnü Soysal did prove equally willing in luring suspects out in the open. Obtaining an arrest, let alone a successful prosecution, often appears to have been more difficult. In 1958, two small-time drug traffickers, Ahmet and Mehmet Dişkaya, were compelled to inform upon a number of illicit opium producers and traffickers in the region of Afyon after Mehmet was arrested in possession of ten grams of heroin and an automatic pistol.[125] Like the Foti case, there is no indication in the available FBN records that the Dişkaya brothers were successful in contriving an arrest (although another special employee did aid in the arrest of Gazi Yücel, one of the suspects identified by the brothers).[126] Two years later, Ali Eren introduced Sal Vizzini to another potential informant named Vedat Kantarcı. Kantarcı professed to be a close friend of Cemal Özüdoğru, a "major" producer of morphine in the town of Samsun, located along Turkey's central Black Sea coast. He volunteered to visit Özüdoğru in Samsun and return to Istanbul in the hopes of arranging a meeting between the two policemen and the potential suspect. After several months passed, Kantarcı reported that no deal was imminent. Özüdoğru, he declared, was shutting down his operations in the wake of the military coup against the Menderes government that May. For some unexplained reason (Vizzini notes that his informant did not elaborate), the coup, as well as some "difficult times just prior to the change in government," compelled the chemist to postpone any future illicit business dealings.[127]

[124] Elmore Gross to Charles Siragusa, 19 April 1955, Turkey, 1955–56, FBN Files, 1916–70; DEA Records; RG 170, NAB.

[125] Memorandum Report, 21 October, 1958, Turkey, 1957–59, FBN Files, 1916–70; DEA Records; RG 170, NAB; Memorandum Report, 31 October, 1958, Turkey, 1957–59, FBN Files, 1916–70; DEA Records; RG 170, NAB; Charles Siragusa to M. Sicot, 8 February 1957, Turkey, 1957–59, FBN Files, 1916–70; DEA Records; RG 170, NAB.

[126] Memorandum Report, 26 July 1959, Turkey, 1957–59, FBN Files, 1916–70; DEA Records; RG 170, NAB.

[127] Memorandum Report, 23 February 1960, Turkey, 1960–61, FBN Files, 1916–70; DEA Records; RG 170, NAB; Memorandum Report, 26 January 1960, Turkey, 1960–61, FBN Files, 1916–70; DEA Records; RG 170, NAB; Memorandum Report, 19 August 1960, Turkey, 1960–61, FBN Files, 1916–70; DEA Records; RG 170, NAB.

In October of 1958, Agent Paul Knight wrote a pointed critique of the FBN's strategy of using criminal informants in his investigation. After conferring with his Turkish colleagues, he came to the following conclusions:

> In Turkey there is a group of men who specialize either in converting opium to base or in gathering opium and base for sale to an exporter. . . Examples of such people, also known to us, would be: Husnu Soysal, Osman Ozdemir, Nur Oven, Ahmed Diskaya. It will be noted that all these men have worked for us and/or the Turkish police. What happens, is this: when one of these men, all traffickers themselves, wants to make a little extra money, or is pressed by the police, he accepts a proposition from someone who wants him to convert opium for him, or goes to the country and orders opium or base—then he gives this case to the police. According to the Turkish police, such action has become more common now that the penalties for trafficking in base or operating a lab are so severe in Turkey. Almost always these men carry on their own traffic while or after giving a case to the police...

Knight emphasized that such cases are often deemed successful "since they result in seizures and arrests." However, experience had shown that the use of such special employees would never halt or interfere with the activities of such major traffickers as Ali Osman Tüter or Hüseyin Eminoğlu. Individuals like Hüsnü Soysal in particular would never aid the police to apprehend major violators for fear of harming their own illicit affairs.[128]

There were other concerns with the employment of criminal informants that weighed heavily upon the minds of FBN agents. Turkish police officers regularly harassed or intimidated the FBN's special employees even after their relationship with American agents was made known to the DPS. This trend began with Siragusa's first experiences in Istanbul in 1950, when Ali Eren warned Vasil Karamanli that American agents were investigating him. Agent James Attie was particularly blunt about his discomfort with Eren's unethical treatment of local informants. In addition to preempting one meeting with a potential special employee (claiming that the man was in hospital with pneumonia), Eren had confronted another informant and furiously demanded part of the man's reward for a successful arrest.[129] Sal Vizzini met with similar experiences when dealing with Turkish police and criminal informants. Ongoing police pressure on special employees to reveal information strictly to the DPS, coupled with regular informant shakedowns for money, compelled Vizzini ultimately to keep his coterie of snitches a secret from his Turkish colleagues.[130]

Nevertheless, FBN agents, both in their regular reporting as well as in their memoirs, often commended or praised the Turkish officers who assisted them in their operations in Istanbul and inner Anatolia. Charles Siragusa, despite his earlier

[128] Memorandum Report, 22 October 1958; Turkey, 1957–59; FBN Files, 1916–70; DEA Records; RG 170, NAB.

[129] Memorandum Report, 10 February 1956, Turkey, 1955–56, FBN Files, 1916–70; DEA Records; RG 170, NAB.

[130] Vizzini, *Vizzini: The Secret Lives of America's Most Successful Undercover Agent*, 101–102.

trepidations, once referred to Kemal Aygün as a "personal friend."[131] Ali Eren once told Sal Vizzini that he swore "on the name of the Prophet" that he would never lie to him, a pledge Vizzini claims Eren kept during his stay in Turkey.[132] Indeed, agents from the FBN and the DPS did spend much time together, at times forming friendships, and they did successfully bring several traffickers, both big and small, to justice.

However, the full body of the FBN's internal correspondence reveals a very different pattern of disconcerting impressions of their colleagues in the DPS. Time and again, Kemal Aygün, Ali Eren, and Galip Labernas behaved in ways that left the bureau questioning their professionalism and loyalties. By the time the rule of the DP came to an end, the relationship between the FBN and the DPS left much to be desired.

CORRUPTION AND ESPIONAGE

Charles Siragusa left Turkey in the late summer of 1950 with doubts regarding the future of FBN operations in Turkey. Beyond the lack of successfully prosecuted cases during his initial visit, his interactions with Kemal Aygün and members of the Turkish police troubled him. His replacement in Turkey, Martin Pera, voiced many of the same concerns his boss had expressed months earlier; in addition to Aygün's unwillingness to share needed intelligence, local policemen hindered his every step initiating his investigations in Istanbul.[133] Tensions further escalated in the spring of 1951 when Aygün suggested that a Turkish undercover agent should clandestinely smuggle heroin into the United States and attempt to set up an American suspect purchasing the drug. Siragusa responded furiously to the plan, declaring the plot, which was a clear case of entrapment, was "proof positive" of Aygün's "shameful tactics and insincerity for international narcotic law enforcement cooperation."[134]

In March 1951, Harry Anslinger wrote to Siragusa directly, reassuring him of the future of the FBN's mission in Turkey. Siragusa did excellent work while abroad, Anslinger assured him, and indeed he too was "very, very disappointed in the indications of sabotage by the Istanbul police." As a matter of recourse, the head of the FBN suggested that the American ambassador in Ankara could intervene and take him to see "top-flight Turkish authorities" so that he could

[131] Elmore Gross to Charles Siragusa, 18 June 1955; Turkey, 1955–56; FBN Files, 1916–70; DEA Records; RG 170, NAB.

[132] Vizzini, *Vizzini: The Secret Lives of America's Most Successful Undercover Agent*, 108.

[133] Martin Pera to Charles Siragusa, 9 March 1951, Turkey, 1951–52, FBN Files, 1916–70; DEA Records; RG 170, NAB. During his interactions with Aygün, Pera repeatedly requested but did not receive a list of suspects he had been promised. In summarizing his feelings in 1951, Pera stated that, "I have yet to be convinced that the police here have done anything but frustrate my attempts to make a case here." Nevertheless, he also admitted that he had "to do Aygun justice" and highlighted the fact that "Istanbul is fast becoming a center of Turkey's political problems."

[134] Charles Siragusa to Harry Anslinger, 13 March 1951, Turkey, 1951–52, FBN Files, 1916–70; DEA Records; RG 170, NAB.

"diplomatically lay the cards on the table." Anslinger's instructions to Siragusa for this meeting were blunt:

> Let these people know that we realize that an attempt is being made to hoodwink us; that we assume the Ankara government is entirely out of sympathy with such face-saving and venal activities by the Istanbul police; that we assume the Turkish government has enough interest in the welfare of its own people and in stopping the flood of heroin into this country, etc., etc., etc., to wish this bi-country campaign against Turkish heroin to continue."

Siragusa complied with his superior's suggestions and arranged to meet with the DPS head, Survet Sürenkök, with a detailed list of complaints and observations.[135] Before the meeting, George White privately suggested to Anslinger that Siragusa change his approach towards the police. Turkish police, he explained, were "fiercely nationalistic" and could not be "kicked around" like their "conquered" Italian counterparts.[136]

On the morning of 30 March, Siragusa and Pera appeared before Gerald Keith, counselor to Ambassador George Wadsworth. Keith assured the two agents that the ambassador was aware of their troubles and was seeking to remedy the situation. While the counselor did not provide details, and emphasized the matter was considered "top secret," he made it clear to Siragusa that "in the near future certain actions will take place which will have a very beneficial effect upon law enforcement in general in all of Turkey." For this reason, and that fact that "the current political situation in Turkey was of such a nature," it was not going to be possible for the two men to meet personally with Sürenkök at that time.[137] Siragusa later surmised that major police reforms were imminent, reforms that would lead to a shake-up within the upper ranks of the DPS.[138]

Whatever occurred thereafter, Kemal Aygün's approach towards the FBN softened. In January 1952, shortly before his appointment to head of the DPS, Aygün met with Agent Frank Sojat, who had recently arrived in Istanbul. The meeting was congenial as the two discussed his recent participation in an official visit to Washington and New York in the company of the DPS chiefs from Izmir and Ankara.[139] Evidence of improving relations with the DPS were further displayed in successive meetings in September and November 1952 between Aygün and American Consul General Frederick Merrill. On both occasions, Aygün reiterated pledges he made to Frank Sojat that the DPS understood the severity of narcotics

[135] Charles Siragusa to Harry Anslinger, 30 March 1951, Turkey, 1951–52, FBN Files, 1916–70; DEA Records; RG 170, NAB.

[136] George White to Harry Anslinger, 14 March 1951, Turkey, 1951–52, FBN Files, 1916–70; DEA Records; RG 170, NAB.

[137] Charles Siragusa to Harry Anslinger, 30 March 1951, Turkey, 1951–52, FBN Files, 1916–70; DEA Records; RG 170, NAB.

[138] Charles Siragusa to Harry Anslinger, 31 March 1951, Turkey, 1951–52, FBN Files, 1916–70; DEA Records; RG 170, NAB.

[139] Frank Sojat to Harry Anslinger, 5 January 1952, Turkey, 1951–52, FBN Files, 1916–70; DEA Records; RG 170, NAB.

trafficking in Turkey, going so far as to invite Harry Anslinger to visit Turkey in order to further relations between the DPS and the FBN.[140]

As Aygün grew more distracted with his personal affairs as head of both the DPS and governor of Ankara, FBN agents increasingly relied upon Alaattin Eriş, the DPS chief in Istanbul, as their main point of contact in organizing their operations in Turkey. While Aygün increasingly struck a more conciliatory tone with the FBN after 1952 (for example, advocating the creation of an American-style "central narcotics bureau" in the country),[141] Eriş's exchanges with the bureau's agents grew increasingly more antagonistic and noncompliant as time passed. Elmore Gross at first reported to Siragusa in March 1955 that the Istanbul police chief had placed all of "his facilities at our disposal" and had "shown an honest and sincere desire to assist us in every way." "It is my intention," Gross qualified however, "to keep our relations as such."[142] Within two weeks of these statements, his impressions of Eriş began to change. At a meeting with his chief assistants, Eriş made his feelings clear in no uncertain terms that he despised all special employees and compelled Gross to write Siragusa that their criminal informants were intentionally misleading their investigations.[143]

In mid-April 1955, an unnamed man boasting police credentials accosted an FBN informant, code named GM, who was seated with a suspect at a restaurant in Izmir. The man placed GM under arrest, slapping him, and kicking him in the groin several times. Days after the assault on GM, Ali Eren met with Agent Gross and related a series of surprising developments. When Eren met with Eriş soon after the Izmir incident, a member of Istanbul's city council (and former chair of the Democratic Party) named Naki Hıncal inexplicably arrived to attend the meeting. At the meeting, Hıncal confessed to being the man who had posed as the officer and explained he was attempting to shake down GM for money in connivance with the suspect seated at the table. Ali Eren, weeping uncontrollably before Gross for several minutes, then claimed that the Istanbul DPS chief had sworn him to secrecy, fearing that revelations regarding Hıncal's involvement with a potential narcotics suspect would harm the DP's forthcoming election chances. Alaattin Eriş, Eren went on to explain, was politically indebted to Hıncal after the politician had helped him to elude corruption charges. Now, as head of the DPS office in Istanbul, Eriş was politically indebted to the Minister of the Interiror, Namık Gedik, whose son attended Bosphorus University with the officer's financial support.[144]

140 American Consular General (AmConGen) to Department of State, 14 November 1952, Turkey, 1951–52, FBN Files, 1916–70; DEA Records; RG 170, NAB; American Consular General (AmConGen) to Department of State, 17 September 1952, Turkey, 1951–52, FBN Files, 1916–70; DEA Records; RG 170, NAB.

141 Frank Sojat to Harry Anslinger, 1 October 1951, Turkey, 1951–52, FBN Files, 1916–70; DEA Records; RG 170, NAB.

142 Elmore Gross to Charles Siragusa, 17 March 1955, Turkey, 1955–56; FBN Files, 1916–70; DEA Records; RG 170, NAB.

143 Elmore Gross to Charles Siragusa, 1 April 1955, Turkey, 1955–56; FBN Files, 1916–70; DEA Records; RG 170, NAB.

144 Elmore Gross to Charles Siragusa, 1 May 1955; Turkey, 1955–56; FBN Files, 1916–70; DEA Records; RG 170, NAB.

Charles Siragusa greeted Gross's disclosures with caution and concern. In his immediate correspondence with Anslinger, he confessed that the allegations greatly jeopardized FBN operations in Turkey and preferred to let Eriş's transgressions pass (reasoning that he had been ordered to cover the incident up upon Ankara's orders).[145] Matters grew more complicated into the early summer of 1955. In a secret telegram delivered to Gross, Aygün revealed that he "possessed definitive evidence" that the Istanbul DPS chief was associated with İhsan Sekban and other top traffickers. According to Gross, Aygün made the following statement:

> I found that Sekban had purchased the Ada Plazi Beach House on the outskirts of Istanbul, and was using this place to load narcotics on boats to send out of Turkey. I told Eris to do something about this. I know for a fact that Eris gave orders that this place was not to be touched.
>
> Sekban owns interests in most of the gambling houses and bordellos in Istanbul. I have checked the records and know that these places have never been raided. These orders were given by Eris. I have this documented. All of the smaller places, not belonging to Sekban only last a short time. I know for certain, and, if necessary, can offer proof, that Eris is in partnership with Sekban in the operation of these places. I also know that Eris is protecting Sekban from arrest for dope peddling.

Ali Eren, who met with Gross alongside Aygün, also stated that the he had placed Sekban under surveillance and had personally seen Sekban playing cards with Alaattin Eriş.[146]

In late June, Siragusa flew out to Ankara to meet with Aygün and Namık Gedik to discuss Eriş in greater detail. At the meeting, Aygün forced Siragusa (as he later described it) to reveal all the of details of Hıncal's attack (which were confirmed by GM, who accompanied Siragusa to the meeting). Upon leaving Ankara, Siragusa again confided in Anslinger that there was something more to this incident than met the eye. Aygün, it appeared, hated Eriş and was seeking to destroy him.[147]

Alaatin Eriş would suffer a near-fatal political crisis later that summer. When the smoke cleared from the anti-Christian pogroms of 6–7 September 1955, an official government inquiry would hold the head of Istanbul's DPS office responsible for much of the violence.[148] Aygün, in meeting with Elmore Gross a month after the riots, could not be more elated. The violence had prompted a complete

[145] Charles Siragusa to Harry Anslinger, 9 Mary 1955, Turkey, 1955–56; FBN Files, 1916–70; DEA Records; RG 170, NAB.

[146] Memorandum Report, 24 June 1955, Turkey, 1955–56; FBN Files, 1916–70; DEA Records; RG 170, NAB; Elmore Gross to Charles Siragusa, 18 June 1955, Turkey, 1955–56; FBN Files, 1916–70; DEA Records; RG 170, NAB.

[147] Charles Siragusa to Harry Anslinger, 27 June 1955, Turkey, 1955–56; FBN Files, 1916–70; DEA Records; RG 170, NAB.

[148] "Anti-Menders Group Among DP Deputies in the Grand National Assembly; Anti-Greek Riots in Turkey," 23 November, 1955, Central Intelligence Agency Declassified Files, Released 7 December 2011. According to this assesement, "the riots were obviously well-planned and organized from their inception." Moreover, the report states that "Word was passed to Police officials in cities that on such and such a night certain demonstrations were to be held and the Police should look the other way."

shake-up of the Interior Ministry. Gedik, who was seen as Eriş's political patron, resigned. Following the appointment of a new interior minister and head of Istanbul's DPS office, Ankara assigned Aygün to the head of the DPS (which he had previously only occupied on a temporary basis). Confident of his opponent's demise, he explained to Gross that Eriş's association with Sekban had helped to seal his fate (in fact, changes in the Interior Ministry had been contemplated even before the anti-Christian attacks that summer).[149] Meanwhile, around the same time Gross met with the vengeful Kemal Aygün, Alaatin Eriş sought an audience with Charles Siragusa. At the meeting, the disgraced officer offered his services to the FBN as an informant, explaining that he possessed important contacts in the Istanbul underworld with information on major traffickers involved in the opium trade between Turkey and Syria. Siragusa appeared to have considered the offer (but it is unclear if their relationship went any further than their meeting in October).[150] Fortunately for Eriş, the events of 1955 did not completely end his career. He would remain as a civil servant into the 1960s, eventually becoming governor of the province of Sakarya.

Istanbul was not the only town that featured corruption at high levels. In October 1952, Agent Frank Sojat met with Necat Lufti Örküş, who had previously served as head of the DPS office in Izmir. A few months earlier, Örküş was reassigned to the main DPS office in Ankara. The transfer, in his opinion, was punishment for his investigations into the activities of İhsan Sekban.[151] Sekban, Sojat reported, held considerable sway over the mayor of Izmir, Rauf Onursal, who was a frequent guest at the notorious smuggler's house.[152] With his transfer out of the Izmir office, Örküş made it clear that Sekban's general political connections in the city made it impossibile to undertake an investigation, let alone exact an arrest or seizure, in the city.[153]

In the months leading up to events surrounding the September 1955 pogroms, one detects a significant change in strategy in terms of the focus of joint FBN/DPS operations. During his meetings in Ankara with Aygün and Gedik, Charles Siragusa was advised that more significant progress could be made if further investigations were undertaken in the Anatolian countryside. Rather than target Istanbul-based middlemen, Aygün specifically recommended that focusing on peasants and smugglers diverting opium in key rural areas, such as Afyon, would

149 Memorandum Report, 15 September 1955, Turkey, 1955–56; FBN Files, 1916–70; DEA Records; RG 170, NAB: Memorandum Report, 27 October 1955, Turkey, 1955–56; FBN Files, 1916–70; DEA Records; RG 170, NAB.

150 Memorandum Report, 27 October 1955; Turkey, 1955–56; FBN Files, 1916–70; DEA Records; RG 170, NAB.

151 Frank Sojat to Harry Anslinger, 8 October 1952, Turkey, 1951–52; FBN Files, 1916–70; DEA Records; RG 170, NAB; Frank Sojat to Harry Anslinger, 1 October 1951, Turkey, 1951–52; FBN Files, 1916–70; DEA Records; RG 170, NAB.

152 Frank Sojat to Harry Anslinger, 5 February 1952, Turkey, 1951–52; FBN Files, 1916–70; DEA Records; RG 170, NAB.

153 Frank Sojat to Harry Anslinger, 8 October 1952, Turkey, 1951–52; FBN Files, 191–70; DEA Records; RG 170, NAB.

prove more fruitful.[154] This was not the first occasion that Aygün had made such a recommendation. As early as March 1951, Martin Pera, upon Aygün's recommendation, made a tour of the opium producing regions of Afyon and Kütahya. In Pera's opinion at that time, a shift towards the countryside did seem warranted; local oversight over the harvesting of opium was poor to non-existent.[155] Siragusa, writing to Anslinger in July 1955, agreed to this new approach. Few investigations in Istanbul between 1952 and 1955 had produced any fruit.[156]

Major arrests made between 1954 and 1955 seem to have affirmed the validity of the conclusions reached early by Aygün and Pera. However, decreased emphasis on halting the Turkish opiate trade in Istanbul resulted in increasing FBN dependence upon Ali Eren and Galip Labernas as interlocutors and supervisors over the nature and intensity of joint operations overall. Even with the conclusion of the Özsayar, Alpten, and Özyürek cases, Agent James Attie, ever trenchant in his criticisms, was displeased with the behavior of these two DPS officers. "Without making any useless accusations," Attie reported in November 1955, it was often the case that "investigations have come to a rather abrupt and unexplained end through leakage of information." The only reason why the Özyürek case was successful, in his estimation, was that both Eren and Labernas were unaware of the details of the investigation until the very last minute. Both men, however, were held in high regard by Kemal Aygün and were "entrenched in the narcotics enforcement not only in Istanbul but thoughout the nation."[157] Attie found Eren an especially problematic officer, often demurring from investigations altogether (either because of the lack of money, the dangers of working in remote areas, or sheer ambivalence).[158]

The intransigence demonstrated by Eren and Labernas in undertaking investigations in the Anatolian interior compounded other elements of distrust between the FBN and these two DPS agents. Suspects were habitually beaten while in Istanbul police custody, a fact that often led sympathetic juries to acquit suspects caught red-handed.[159] Ali Eren's habitual intimidation of criminal informants, which often resulted in demands for money, further emphasized FBN fears that the poor salaries paid by the DPS only fueled such acts of corruption.[160] American Consul

[154] Charles Siragusa to Harry Anslinger, 27 June 1955, Turkey, 1955–56; FBN Files, 1916–70; DEA Records; RG 170, NAB.

[155] Martin Pera to Charles Siragusa, 21 March 1951, Turkey; 1951–52, FBN Files, 1916–70; DEA Records; RG 170, NAB.

[156] Charles Siragusa to Harry Anslinger, 5 July 1955, Turkey, 1955–56; FBN Files, 1916–70; DEA Records; RG 170, NAB.

[157] Memorandum Report, 24 November 1955, Turkey, 1955–56; FBN Files, 1916–70; DEA Records; RG 170, NAB.

[158] Memorandum Report, 15 December 1955, Turkey, 1955–56; FBN Files, 1916–70; DEA Records; RG 170, NAB; Memorandum Report, 10 February 1956, Turkey, 1955–56, FBN Files, 1916–70; DEA Records; RG 170, NAB; Memorandum Report, 13 December 1955, Turkey, 1955–56; FBN Files, 1916–70; DEA Records; RG 170, NAB.

[159] Elmore Gross to Charles Siragusa, 23 February 1955; Turkey, 1955–56; FBN Files, 1916–70; DEA Records; RG 170, NAB.

[160] "Survey of the General Directorate of Public Safety," undated, Turkey, 1951–52; Subject Files of the Bureau of Narcotics and Dangerous Drugs, 1916–70; Records of the Drug Enforcement Administration; Record Group 170; National Archives Building II, College Park, MD.

General Fredrick Merrill specifically warned Siragusa and the FBN in 1951 against dealing with Kemal Aygün, claiming, "I am not sure I trust *any* Turkish chief of police, particularly when salaries are so low!"[161]

Despite the few successes scored in Turkey during the 1950s, the overall weight of FBN reports from this era paints a very troubling picture of the bureau's operations. Considering how poor relations between the FBN and the DPS often were during this seminal period, what incentive did Anslinger and his men possess to stay on in Istanbul? Surely, regardless of the frequent points of conflict that emerged between the two agencies, Turkey's centrality within the international heroin trade left the FBN with little choice but to remain active and endure the repeated acts of duplicity and corruption witnessed among the officers of the DPS. There is another reason for the FBN's commitment to its Turkish operations, one that is never mentioned within the bureau's case files. If the available testimony is to be believed, it would appear that the FBN's presence in Istanbul allowed for the execution of clandestine operations undertaken by the CIA.

Sal Vizzini's memoirs stand as the sole source that speaks to CIA/FBN clandestine operations during this stage of the Cold War. Over the course of his career, Vizzini's fieldwork for the bureau would take him all over the world as an undercover operative.[162] While based in Turkey, Vizzini regularly collaborated with Harold Fiedler, a CIA operator attached to the Turkish security service who also possessed an office in the US consulate (Fielder may be the man Vizzini refers to as Napoleon at different points in his memoirs). In 1960, while touring the Turkish/Soviet border under Fiedler's instructions, Vizzini shot and killed two men. Vizzini, in a later interview, stated the shootings were covered up by the FBN and were reported as a "junk deal gone bad."[163] Yet no report referencing the incident can be found with the FBN's files.

Sal Vizzini's off-the-books collaboration with the CIA was not unique or isolated to Turkey. In his autobiography, Vizzini reveals instances during a tour of Lebanon where he personally undertook clandestine operations at the CIA's behest.[164] Interviews conducted by Douglas Valentine further affirm the often-blurred relationship between the CIA and the FBN. In surveying the history of the FBN, Valentine makes clear that narcotics agents were useful in providing a veneer of legitimacy for gathering intelligence both abroad, and, more controversially, at home. His status as an FBN agent, as Vizzini later explained, provided him a "cover within a cover" that allowed him further immunity from local or foreign surveillance.[165]

161 Fredrick Merrill to H. J. Anslinger, 23 October 1951; Turkey; 1951–52, FBN Files, 1916–70; DEA Records; RG 170, NAB.

162 Valentine, *Strength of the Wolf*, xvi.

163 Valentine, *Strength of the Wolf*, 278.

164 Vizzini, *Vizzini: The Secret Lives of America's Most Successful Undercover Agent*, 175–193.

165 Vizzini, *Vizzini: The Secret Lives of America's Most Successful Undercover Agent*, 175. For more thorough discussion of the CIA's use of narcotics enforcement as cover for clandestine action, see Marshall, *Drug Wars*, 35–62.

The trade and production of narcotics, as it would turn out, was an element found in a variety of strategically important battlegrounds of the Cold War. As far back as the prewar period, the need to form alliances with pro-American forces abroad often trumped the FBN's anti-narcotics operations. In China, Anslinger personally ignored reports detailing drug dealings among Chiang Kai-shek's Nationalist forces.[166] With the outbreak of the Cold War, the FBN either ignored or provided political cover for CIA-backed allies in southeast Asia and Latin America.[167] Closer to home, both George White and Charles Siragusa provided critical support for the CIA's "truth drug" experiments with marijuana and LSD in New York and San Francisco.[168] Recently declassified documents suggest that the CIA's collaboration with (and often appropriation of) narcotics operations continued well into the 1970s (a phenomenon that at times embroiled drug enforcement officers).[169]

Outside the case of Turkey in the 1950s and 1960s, there is evidence that suggests the CIA coveted the gangsters and smugglers used by the FBN as informants in order to conduct more dubious operations. In 1960, William K. Harvey, a chief in the CIA's intelligence branch, approached Charles Siragusa to help run the QJ/WIN program, an effort to form a unit of gangsters from around the world to be deployed for executive assassination missions. Although Siragusa later testified that he refused the assignment "on moral grounds," Harvey's role in contracting the services of prominent American gangsters in order to kill Fidel Castro suggests that such a plan was not a one-time affair.[170]

Over the course of the 1950s, the FBN realized that Kemal Aygün and his loyalists in the DPS also operated under a dual pretense. In late April 1955, FBN agents learned that Aygün was "engaged in covert and political intelligence" while he was simultaneously governor of Ankara and head of the DPS.[171] Over time, it became clear that both Eren and Labernas were a part of Aygün's small network of spies (the two men allegedly operated out of the Şark Hotel in Istanbul).[172] It was generally surmised that local Communist activities in Istanbul were the primary focus of the three men. However, Charles Siragusa speculated that joint operations with the FBN may have provided cover for Aygün's agents abroad. In 1956, the FBN invited Captain Galip Labernas to train with the bureau in Italy. Charles Siragusa suspected that in addition to receiving this training, Labernas was also gathering

166 Walker, *Opium and Foreign Policy*, 69.

167 Vizzini, *Vizzini: The Secret Lives of America's Most Successful Undercover Agent.*

168 Valentine, *Strength of the Wolf*, 134–147.

169 See inserted documents in Douglas Valentine, *The Strength of the Pack* (Walterville, OR: Trine Day, 2009), 431–440.

170 Alan Block, *Perspectives on Organized Crime* (Dordrecht: Kluwer Academic Publishers, 1990), 214–216; Howard Jones, *The Bay of Pigs* (Oxford: Oxford University Press, 2008), 91; Valentine, *Strength of the Wolf*, 227.

171 Charles Siragusa to Kemal Aygün, 13 April 1955; Turkey, 1955–56; FBN Files, 1916–70; DEA Records; RG 170, NAB; Elmore Gross to Charles Siragusa, 18 June 1955; Turkey, 1955–56; FBN Files, 1916–70; DEA Records; RG 170, NAB.

172 Charles Siragusa to H. J. Anslinger, 5 December 1956; Turkey, 1955–56; FBN Files, 1916–70; DEA Records; RG 170, NAB; Memorandum, 10 March 1959; Turkey, 1957–59; FBN Files, 1916–70; DEA Records; RG 170, NAB.

"political intelligence" on Aygün's behalf. In conversations with Labernas, Siragusa emphasized that he would "strenuously object" to any Turkish intelligence operations while he was in Italy.[173]

Aside from Labernas's stay in Italy, FBN files give very little indication of American policy towards Turkish clandestine operations in Istanbul or elsewhere. Circumstantial evidence does suggest however that there was some degree of coordination (or at least contact) between Kemal Aygün and the CIA. In 1951, during his visit to New York and Washington, Aygün, along with the Izmir and Ankara DPS chiefs, met with George White for two straight days in the company of a man White refers to as "CIA Fallon" in his diaries.[174] White's dairies give no indication of the topics discussed during this meeting. A Freedom of Information Act request submitted to the CIA has also yielded no leads as to the nature of the relationship, if any, between Kemal Aygün and Langley.[175]

It is even more difficult to contextualize Aygün's activities within the broader history of the Turkish secret service.[176] Most studies of Turkish clandestine operations are rather vague as to the organizational structure and personnel that comprised the three successive spying agencies that have existed in Turkey since 1923.[177] While some evidence suggests that Kemal Aygün was aware of official domestic clandestine operations conducted in Istanbul while he was mayor, nothing in the FBN files (or any other public source for that matter) suggests he was a regular agent of the National Security Service (the predecessor to Turkey's contemporary clandestine service, the National Intelligence Organization).[178]

In the absence of any clues as to the nature or purpose of his activities, it is reasonable to surmise that Aygün's circle of agents formed a personal contingent of spies. As seen in Chapter 1, the existence and use of private or unofficial intelligence and paramilitary units is a historical phenomenon dating back to the late Ottoman and early Republican eras. Other pieces of evidence, aside from the accusations levied against Kemal Aygün, suggest that this phenomenon continued into the early Cold War years. According to statements made during his trial in 1960, Menderes was formally accused of forming a "militia formation (*milis teşkilatı*)" of 600 men in advance of the anti-Greek pogroms of September 1955.

173 Martin Pera to Charles Siragusa 5 March 1951; Turkey, 1951–52; FBN Files, 1916–70; DEA Records; RG 170, NAB.

174 George White Diary, Entries 7 November–8 November 1951, George H. White Papers, Box 7, Special Collections Department, Stanford University.

175 In reponse to my request for files on Kemal Aygün, the CIA stated on 30 September 2010 that it can "neither confirm nor deny the existence" of records on Aygün and that any information that did exist was to remain classified (in part pursuant to the CIA Act of 1949).

176 See İlhan Bahar, *Teşkilat-ı Mahsusa, MİT ve İstihbarat Örgütleri* (Istanbul: Kum Saati Yayıncılık, 2009); Gültekin Ural, *Teşkilat-ı Mahsusa'dan MİT'e: Abdullah Çatlı ve Susurluk Olayı* (Istanbul: Kamer Yayınları, 1997).

177 Tuncay Özkan, *MİT'in Gizli Tarihi* (Istanbul: Afla, 2003).

178 Soner Yalçın, *Efendi: Beyaz Türklerin Büyük Sırrı* (Istanbul: Doğan Kitapçilik, 2004), 510. According to Yalçın's interlocutors, Aygün was a witness to the torturing of prisoners conducted by members of the Turkish National Security Service (*Milli Emniyet Hizmeti*).

Many of these individuals drawn into this militia were local Istanbul *kabadayıs* and were paid 25 lira each to rough up anti-Democratic opponents.[179]

The significance of this blending of tasks and interests on the part of American and Turkish narcotics officers and spies exceeds the operational value such alliances may offer. One could reasonably speculate that the utility of employing narcotics officers in an intelligence or clandestine capacity at the very least made up for the failures of anti-drug regimes. One could go still further, as other scholars and commentators have suggested, and contend that policing the drug trade is often nothing more than a façade that only partially shields more dubious operations conducted by elements of the state.[180]

A POINT OF RECKONING: THE 1960 COUP AND THE FALL OF KEMAL AYGÜN

Turkey's first decade of multiparty democracy took a violent turn on 27 May 1960. With tanks and soldiers in the streets of cities and towns throughout the country, a collective of military officers seized power in Ankara that morning. Tensions in Turkey had risen dramatically in the lead-up to the military's intervention. In April, the DP governor of Kayseri, with troops in support, had prevented RPP leader İsmet İnönü from speaking in the province. Later that month, the Menderes government formed a commission tasked with investigating supposedly unlawful activities carried out by the RPP. Ahead of the finding of the commission, Ankara mandated a complete cessation of political activity in the country (including a strict regime of newspaper censorship). The ban, coupled with the attempted arrest of several professors, prompted student protests on the campus of Istanbul University, leading to an army crackdown and the death of one student.

The May coup, its leaders declared, was not intended to put an end to democracy but to liberate it from the gross mismanagement and dictatorial tendencies of Prime Minister Adnan Menderes' Democratic Party. It soon became clear to the citizens of Turkey that the regime's leaders and many of its subordinates were to pay a penalty for their supposed crimes. Menderes was placed under arrest alongside the rest of the DP's top men. The military's retribution extended deep into Turkish society. Scores, perhaps hundreds, of bureaucrats and state officials were rounded up.[181] For most of the DP's erstwhile leaders, the small island of Yassıada,

[179] "DP'nin Milis Teşkilatı Kurduğu Açıklandı," *Milliyet* 25 June 1960; "Aziz Ozan '6–7 Eylül,' Hadiseleri Tertiptır,' Diyor," *Milliyet* 24 October 1960.

[180] In surveying US clandestine support for narcotics-dealing allies in Burma and Thailand in the aftermath of the Second World War, William Walker poses that US policymakers "abetted corruption" and the drug trade in the hopes of maintaining anti-Communist efforts in Asia. See Walker, *Opium and Foreign Policy*, 220. This thesis is perhaps most thoroughly developed in Alfred McCoy's *The Politics of Heroin*.

[181] American Embassy, Ankara to Secretary of State, 7 June 1960; Central Dispatch Files, 1960–63; General Records of the Department of State; RG 59, NAB.

located just off the coast of the city of Istanbul, served as both their place of imprisonment and the setting for their future trials.

Among the higher-profile prisoners taken to Yassıada was Kemal Aygün. A month after the coup, the American consulate in Istanbul caught wind of a story regarding Aygün from a trusted informant. A military physician sent to examine Kemal Aygün found that the prisoner had "lost control" and was weeping incessantly. He confessed that he had committed many crimes. Once tried, Aygün was certain he would be rightfully put to death.[182]

The trials on Yassıada placed Kemal Aygün as a conspirator within a series of crimes, including organizing a plot to kill former Prime Minister İsmet İnönü, launching an attack on student protesters outside Istanbul University, falsely expropriating property in Istanbul, and managing a Democratic slush fund.[183] In some of these cases, such as the so-called Topkapi plot against İsmet İnönü, it appears that Aygün's guilt was based upon association with other accused figures.[184] Other trials, particularly several held outside of Yassıada, painted Aygün as a more direct actor. One such case featured Kemal Aygün as the main organizer of a bribery and extortion scandal involving brothels throughout the city of Istanbul. He and Ferit Avni Sözen, then mayor and police chief were charged with extracting thousands of lira in payments from pimps and gamblers. Ironically, among those asked to testify against Sözen was Vasil Arcan, the same narcotics trafficker and police informant captured by George White back in 1948.[185]

By the time of his arrest, the FBN had little day-to-day contact with Kemal Aygün. His prosecution, however, did lead to a shake-up within the ranks of Istanbul's narcotics bureau. As early as June 1960, US Army intelligence reported a general purge of officers, particularly "hatchet men," within the national police force.[186] The coup government's cleansing of the ranks included Aygün's long time retainers in the DPS, Ali Eren and Galip Labernas, who were respectively forced into retirement and transferred out of the office.[187] Their replacements within the Istanbul branch did make several interesting disclosures regarding Kemal Aygün's tenure and legacy within the Istanbul section of the Directorate of Public Safety. According to Hüseyin Cağlar, the post-coup head of the Istanbul branch's criminal

182 American Consulate General, Istanbul to Secretary of State, 22 June 1960, 782.00/6-2260, Box 2040, Central Decimal Files, 1960–63; RG 59, NAB.

183 American Consulate General, Istanbul to Secretary of State, 2 December 1960, 782.00/12-260, Box 2040, Central Decimal Files, 1960–63; RG 59, NAB.

184 American Consulate General, Istanbul to Secretary of State, 12 December 1960, 782.00/12-1260, Central Decimal Files, 1960–63; RG 59, NAB; American Consulate General, Istanbul to Secretary State, 20 March 1961, 782.00/3-2061, Central Decimal Files, 1960–63; RG 59, NAB.

185 "Rüşvet Davasında Şahitler Dinlendi," *Milliyet* 9 March 1961; "Randevuculardan Haraç Toplayan 2 Kişi Tevkif Edildi," *Milliyet* 5 October 1960. It was also noted in the press that he received multiple salaries for his duties as mayor, which added up to close to 30,000 lira a month. See "Aygün Belediyeden Her Ay 27.333 Lira Almış," *Milliyet* 5 April 1961.

186 USARMA, Ankara to Secretary of State, 6 June 1960, 782.00/6-660, Central Decimal Files, 1960–63; RG 59, NAB.

187 John Cusack to H. J. Anslinger, 23 June 1960; Turkey, 1960–61; FBN Files, 1916–70; DEA Records; RG 170, NAB; Vizzini, *Vizzini: The Secret Lives of America's Most Successful Undercover Agent,* 198.

section, Kemal Aygün was completely corrupt. He, along with his "lackey," Ali Eren, had long protected the city's top traffickers. Under Aygün's direction, Eren had shielded the worst violators by focusing the bureau's investigative powers on small-time traffickers.[188]

Revelations that the FBN's principal partners in Turkey had long been participants in the Turkish underworld appear to have had no official impact upon Washington's approach towards the Turkish drug trade. When Aygün was sentenced to life in prison in the fall of 1961, Siragusa posted only a brief report to his boss, Harry Anslinger. Aygün, Siragusa declared, was not only "a sincere and effective collaborator," but also "very pro-American and a great admirer of our Bureau."[189]

THE LOST DECADE: FBN/DPS INVESTIGATIONS IN THE 1960S

Kemal Aygün escaped the death penalty despite multiple convictions during the Yassıada trials and other investigations. In 1963, along with convicted President Celal Bayar, he was allowed to leave prison for health reasons.[190] One year later, Cemal Gürsel, acting prime minister and leader of the May 1960 coup, issued an official pardon to the disgraced Istanbul mayor.[191] Perhaps because of the speciousness of many of the charges levied against Menderes and his government, Aygün quietly remained a prominent citizen. Before he died in 1979, he served as chairman of Turkish Airlines.[192] A number of noted mourners attended his funeral, including the former prime minister and founder of the Justice Party, Süleyman Demirel.[193]

Despite being subject to similar accusations that compelled Ali Eren to retire, Galip Labernas remained within the DPS. After an extended deployment to eastern Anatolia, Labernas returned to duty as a narcotics officer in 1961. In 1962, he was appointed to head the newly minted Central Narcotics Bureau (CNB) in Ankara. Despite the fact that the FBN had long advocated the creation of such an office, Labernas's tenure as head of the bureau was highly reminiscent of the obstinacy and friction that marked the FBN's early relationship with the DPS. American attempts to collaborate with officers within the Turkish gendarmerie were repeatedly thwarted by Labernas and his allies in the CNB, arguing the FBN

[188] John Cusack to H. J. Anslinger, 22 September 1960; Turkey, 1960–61; FBN Files, 1916–70; DEA Records; RG 170, NAB. The phrase appears as commentary posed by Anslinger along the margins of the reports.

[189] Charles Siragusa to H. J. Anslinger, 16 September 1961; Turkey, 1960–61; FBN Files, 1916–70; DEA Records; RG 170, NAB.

[190] "Tahliye Edilenlerin Durumları İncelenecek," *Milliyet* 31 March 1963.

[191] "Gürsel Aygün'ü Affetti," *Milliyet* 24 September 1964.

[192] "Kemal Aygün; THY İdare Meclisi Başkanlığına Seçildi," *Milliyet* 15 April 1972.

[193] "Aygün ve Taşkıran'ın Cenazeleri Dün Toprağa Verildi," *Milliyet* 7 May 1979.

would only be permitted to carry out investigations in the countryside if they possessed definitive evidence that a crime committed in the interior would result in illegal opiate shipments to the United States.[194] In 1967, he personally contacted one of the FBN's criminal informants with an offer to pay him a higher monthly reward for information in exchange for ending the informant's relationship with American agents.[195] Labernas, in the FBN's estimation, "was not interested in narcotics enforcement," a claim bolstered by the fact that the CNB remained woefully underfunded and understaffed (Labernas and another agent were reportedly the bureau's only assigned officers). Shortly before the FBN's dissolution in 1967, Agent Michael Picini concluded that the CNB had not made one case since its inception.[196]

Despite the profound level of mistrust that existed between Labernas and the FBN, American agents were encouraged to "cultivate" his favors and forge strong relations with other ranking officers. Agents did find some common ground with Officer Abdullah Pektaş, who was assigned to the Istanbul narcotics section after the coup. Pektaş admittedly "hated" Labernas, whom he viewed as a "political" officer (which Joe Arpaio interpreted as a reference to his former duties as an intelligence agent under Kemal Aygün).[197] Pektaş, unlike his predecessors in the 1950s, did not attempt to obstruct FBN investigations in the interior (which Joe Arpaio attests to in his memoirs). Nevertheless, Arpaio and others did find cause to criticize some of his approaches towards his police work (particularly his lack of enthusiasm and his distrust of modern surveillance methods).[198] All in all, John Cusack, when counseling Arpaio on relations with the DPS, insisted that the FBN had to remember its place within Turkey. "We assist the police," Cusack asserted, "they do not assist us."[199]

Friction between the FBN and Labernas ultimately did not dampen more positive changes in the relationship between Ankara and American agents during the 1960s. For much of the decade, the FBN enjoyed regular and supportive contact with three new additions to the Turkish Interior Ministry: İhsan Araş, head of the DPS in 1963, subsequent DPS head Ahmet Demir (1963–67), and Halit Elver,

[194] John Cusack to Ihsan Aras, 29 November 1962, Turkey, 1961–64; FBN Files, 1916–70; DEA Records; RG 170, NAB; "Meeting with General Director of Turkish National Police Ahet Demir, at Ankara, on August 14, 1963," 24 August 1963, Turkey, 1961–64; FBN Files, 1916–70; DEA Records; RG 170, NAB; "Re-organization of Istanbul 8th Section (Treasury) Police, by Chief Rafet Kaplangi," 28 Feburary 1966, Turkey, 1965–67; FBN Files, 1916–70; DEA Records; RG 170, NAB.

[195] "Halit Elver and the Central Narcotics Bureau of the Turkish National Police-Ankara," 27 March 1967, Turkey, 1965–67; FBN Files, 1916–70; DEA Records; RG 170, NAB.

[196] "Halit Elver and the Central Narcotics Bureau of the Turkish National Police-Ankara," 27 March 1967, Turkey, 1965–67; FBN Files, 1916–70; DEA Records; RG 170, NAB.

[197] Joseph Arpaio to John Cusack, 24 September 1962, Turkey, 1961–64; FBN Files, 1916–70; DEA Records; RG 170, NAB.

[198] Memorandum Report, 14 February 1963, Turkey, 1961–64; FBN Files, 1916–70; DEA Records; RG 170, NAB; "Re-organization of Istanbul 8th Section (Treasury) Police, by Chief Rafet Kaplangi," 28 Feburary 1966, Turkey, 1965–67; FBN Files, 1916–70; DEA Records; RG 170, NAB.

[199] "Police Cooperation," 13 December 1962, Turkey, 1961–64; FBN Files, 1916–70; DEA Records; RG 170, NAB.

Turkish liaison to Interpol. Araş was instrumental, for example, in preempting orders issued by Galip Labernas forbidding American agents from cooperating with the gendarmerie and operating in the interior.[200] In 1963, he opened the country's most modern police station in Istanbul, following this four years later with the opening of a new police academy in the city.[201] In 1964, J. Edgar Hoover received Halit Elver and Ahmet Demir in Washington, giving them a commemorative plaque and a Turkish translation of Hoover's *A Study of Communism*.[202]

The sincerity of the FBN's approval of Demir and Elver was put to the test in spring of 1964 when Joe Arpaio received a letter from the local commander of the US Air Force's Office of Special Investigations (OSI). According to the letter (which is not appended to the FBN's files), a former DPS officer by the name of Kemal Özköy accused Ahmet Demir and Halit Elver of an unknown set of corruption charges. Joe Arpaio dismissed the accusations out of hand and suspected that Galip Labernas had a hand in spreading these rumors. Halit Elver affirmed these suspicions, suggesting that the charges were an election ploy to undermine the ruling Justice Party that had replaced the post-coup military regime.[203] Özköy's charges, however, did not go unheeded by either the press or the courts. One year later, the Istanbul daily, *Akşam*, ran a series of articles on Ahmet Demir and Haydar Özkin, DPS chief in Istanbul, accusing them of "permitting gambling, prostitution and narcotics smuggling to flourish in Istanbul, primarily for the huge pay-offs they receive from the criminal element behind these crimes." Articles further claimed the FBN had fabricated investigations in order to distribute monetary rewards to high-ranking police officers in the country.[204] In January 1967, an Istanbul court opened an official bribery investigation into Ahmet Demir's tenure as head of the DPS (an office he had left some time previously).[205] Neither the available FBN reports nor local news coverage refer to an official outcome to this investigation. Since Demir had left the DPS by 1967, it is not clear if the FBN continued to doubt the accusations levied against their former ally or what effect, if any, the charges had upon the final investigations undertaken by the bureau.

[200] "Police Cooperation," 13 December 1962, Turkey, 1961–64; FBN Files, 1916–70; DEA Records; RG 170, NAB; Memorandum Report, 15 January, 1962, Turkey, 1961–64; FBN Files, 1916–70; DEA Records; RG 170, NAB.

[201] "Türkiye'nin En Modern Polis Karakol Açıldı," *Milliyet* 15 January 1963; "Yeni Poli Okulu Dün Törenle Açıldı," *Milliyet* 14 May 1967.

[202] "Türk Polisinden F.B.I. Başkanına," *Milliyet* 11 April 1964.

[203] Joseph Arpaio to Michael Picini, 21 March 1964, Turkey, 1964–65; FBN Files, 1916–70; DEA Records; RG 170, NAB. According to FBN Agent Richard Salmi, Elver was unpopular with his colleagues because he was on the CIA payroll. See Valentine, *Strength of the Wolf*, 404.

[204] "Articles appearing in Istanbul newspaper 'Aksam' concerning General Director Ahmet Demir, and Istanbul Chief of Poliec Hydar Ozkin," 5 April 1965; FBN Files, 1916–70; DEA Records; RG 170, NAB.

[205] "Ahmet Demir Hakkında İdari Soruşturma Açıldı," *Milliyet* 18 January 1967; "Ahmet Demir'in Dosyası Sorgu Yargıçlığında," *Milliyet* 15 February 1967.

Between the periods of support and obstructions experienced by officers in the field, the FBN did continue to make cases alongside the DPS between 1960 and 1967. During this period of time, regular FBN reports to the US Congress made note of four cases made in 1960,[206] six in 1961,[207] seven in 1962,[208] ten in 1963,[209] five in 1964,[210] two in 1965,[211] two in 1966,[212] and a final two cases completed in 1967.[213] Virtually all of these cases were made outside of Istanbul. In 1963, for example, Agent Joe Arpaio, while in the company of Galip Labernas or Abduallah Pektaş, arrested a string of illicit traffickers and opium farmers in the towns of Afyon,[214] Balıkesir,[215] Kayseri,[216] Denizli,[217] and Konya.[218] In a one-week period, Arpaio and Labernas seized a ton of opium and eleven kilos of morphine in a series of lightning raids through Denizli, Çal, Istanbul, Izmir, Konya, Beyşehir, and Kayseri.[219]

Perhaps the most famous case brought to court during this era occurred in 1964, a case in which the FBN appear to have played no active role. In January of that year, Ahmet and Fahrettin Soysal, as well as Hüseyin Eminoğlu and Sefer Bezal, were taken into custody for attempting to smuggle ninety kilos of morphine on board a Marseille bound ship. In addition to these well-known smugglers, Mehmet Refik Can, member of the Üsküdar city council, was indicted as an accomplice to

206 *Traffic in Opium and Other Dangerous Drugs for the Year Ended December 31, 1960* (Washington DC: U.S. Treasury Department, Bureau of Narcotics, 1961), 37.

207 *Traffic in Opium and Other Dangerous Drugs for the Year Ended December 31, 1961* (Washington DC: U.S. Treasury Department, Bureau of Narcotics, 1962), 135–136.

208 *Traffic in Opium and Other Dangerous Drugs for the Year Ended December 31, 1962* (Washington DC: U.S. Treasury Department, Bureau of Narcotics, 1963), 32–33.

209 *Traffic in Opium and Other Dangerous Drugs for the Year Ended December 31, 1963* (Washington DC: U.S. Treasury Department, Bureau of Narcotics, 1964), 44–46.

210 *Traffic in Opium and Other Dangerous Drugs for the Year Ended December 31, 1964* (Washington DC: U.S. Treasury Department, Bureau of Narcotics, 1965), 46–48.

211 *Traffic in Opium and Other Dangerous Drugs for the Year Ended December 31, 1965* (Washington DC: U.S. Treasury Department, Bureau of Narcotics, 1966), 24–25.

212 *Traffic in Opium and Other Dangerous Drugs for the Year Ended December 31, 1966* (Washington DC: U.S. Treasury Department, Bureau of Narcotics, 1967), 21–22.

213 *Traffic in Opium and Other Dangerous Drugs for the Year Ended December 31, 1967* (Washington DC: U.S. Treasury Department, Bureau of Narcotics, 1968), 11–12.

214 American Embassy Rome to Secretary of State Washington DC, 8 April 1963, Rome 2099, Subject Numeric Files, 1963, RG 59, NAB; American Embassy Rome to Secretary of State Washington DC, 27 July 1963, no file number, Subject Numeric Files, 1963, RG 59, NAB; American Embassy Rome to Secretary of State Washington DC, 21 October 1963, Rome 1102, Subject Numeric Files, 1963, RG 59, NAB.

215 American Embassy Rome to Secretary of State Washington DC, 11 September 1963, Rome 701, Subject Numeric Files, 1963, RG 59, NAB.

216 American Embassy Rome to Secretary of State Washington DC, 3 April 1963, Rome 2505, Subject Numeric Files, 1963, RG 59, NAB.

217 American Embassy Rome to Secretary of State Washington DC, 27 March 1963, Rome 1983, Subject Numeric Files, 1963, RG 59, NAB.

218 American Embassy Rome to Secretary of State Washington DC, 1 April 1963, Rome 2035, Subject Numeric Files, 1963, RG 59, NAB.

219 "Cooperation obtained from Central Narcotics Agency, Ankara, Turkey," 4 April 1963, Turkey, 1961–63; FBN Files, 1916–70; DEA Records; RG 170, NAB; John Cusack to Ihsan Aras, 9 April 1963, Turkey, 1961–63; FBN Files, 1916–70; DEA Records; RG 170, NAB.

the crime.[220] While Refik Can had never been placed under arrest before for narcotics trafficking, internal correspondence from 1955 suggests that the FBN was familiar with his name and activities well before the 1964 trial. In May of that year, James Attie, Ali Eren, and another Turkish officer attempted to arrange a meeting with Can in order to purchase a quantity of prepared morphine. Attie described Can as a "fearful person" and was confident that, if taken into custody, the trafficker would work for the FBN as a criminal informant. Successive reports from 1955 make no mention of whether or not the arrest occurred. Be that as it may, Attie claimed that Can was indeed a major player in the Istanbul narcotics underworld with direct connections to Sami al-Khoury's smuggling ring in Beirut.[221] The DPS maintained a biographical file on Can (who, like other major "Laz" traffickers, was born in Rize) alongside the likes of Nazim Kalkavan.[222]

As the 1960s progressed, one notices a stark shift in the nature of the FBN's reporting of its activities. Unlike earlier correspondence penned by Charles Siragusa, James Attie, and others active in Turkey during the 1950s, reports submitted by agents in the 1960s are markedly short and lack much detail. Few documents found in this era possess the candidness and loquaciousness of the correspondence of the previous decade. More strikingly, up until the bureau's dissolution in 1967, the FBN's internal records make scant mention of investigations into the major Istanbul traffickers that attracted so much attention during the 1950s. While Agent Joe Arpaio makes reference to his participation in the arrest of Ahmet Soysal in 1962, there is no follow-up report submitted in the wake of his prosecution.[223] At no point following the 1960 coup do the names İhsan Sekban or Hüseyin Eminoğlu appear within the pages of the FBN's final investigative reports of the era.[224]

In 1970, the American Embassy in Ankara convened a formal "working group" tasked with updating and collating data on Turkey's "opium situation and illicit trade." Representatives from several departments made up the group, including participants from the Departments of State, USAID and other agencies. The Bureau of Narcotics and Dangerous Drugs (BNDD), which had been formed out of the skeleton of the FBN in 1967, also sent a representative and provided key intelligence for the meeting. The working group discussed a number of issues pertaining

[220] "Baz Morfin Kaçıran Bir Şabeke Yakalandı," *Milliyet* 31 January 1964; Newsday, *The Heroin Trail*, 35.

[221] James Attie to Charles Siragusa, 9 May 1955, Turkey, 1955–56; FBN Files, 1916–70; DEA Records; RG 170, NAB.

[222] Arai Yumak to Charles Siragusa, 12 November 1955, Turkey, 1955–56; FBN Files, 1916–70; DEA Records; RG 170, NAB.

[223] John Cusack to Ihsan Aras, 29 November 1962, Turkey, 1961–64; FBN Files, 1916–70; DEA Records; RG 170, NAB.

[224] It appears that Ali Osman Tüter and Sefer Bezal were under FBN investigation in 1966. However, it appears these cases did not result in prosecutions. See "Re-organization of Istanbul 8th Section (Treasury) Police, by Chief Rafet Kaplangi," 28 Feburary 1966, Turkey, 1965–67; FBN Files, 1916–70; DEA Records; RG 170, NAB.

to opiates in Turkey, particularly the possibility of abolishing opium production in the country altogether. When it came to the topic of smuggling, the group composed two respective lists of individuals responsible for "morphine base shipments of 100 to 600 KGS." In their estimation, two major groups which "resided or had representatives in Istanbul" were active in Turkey in 1970. The two groups, according to the working groups, comprised the following individuals:

Group One: The Laz from the former Province of Lazistan

1) Hüseyin Eminoğlu
2) Refik Can
3) Ali Kambur
4) Mehmet Ali Işık
5) Hüseyin Nar
6) İhsan Sekban (alias İhsan Seymenoğlu)
7) Sefer Bezal and brother Ali Bezal
8) Nuri Bostan (alias Nuri Bostancı)
9) Ali Pandur

Group Two: From the Gaziantep/Kilis Area

1) Mustafa Sevcan
2) Hüseyin Çil Family Organization
3) Mehmet Külekçi and son-in-law Hayrettin Yağcı
4) İbrahim Yanartaş
5) Mehmet Döğme
6) Mehemt Akman (alias Hagi Akman)
7) Birratin [Fahrettin?] Soysal and his brother Ahmet Sosyal
8) Mustafa Şahin.[225]

Taken at face value, the 1970 Ankara working group's report reveals how little had changed over the course of the two decades in which the United States had been investing directly into understanding and policing narcotics trafficking in Turkey. On the one hand, despite a series of trials and incarcerations, many of the men who were long thought to be the principal architects of the Istanbul opiate trade, Ahmet Soysal, Hüseyin Eminoğlu, and İhsan Sekban in particular, remained at large and continued to be active in cultivating Turkey's opium market. The threat of prison, and in some cases actual convictions by Turkish courts, appear not to have deterred this generation of influential traffickers and smugglers.

[225] American Embassy Ankara to Secretary of State, 18 November 1971, Ankara 7893, Subject Numeric Files, 1963, RG 59, NAB.

On the other hand, the group's understanding of the internal dynamics of the Turkish opiate trade stands as a testament to the enduring vision of the FBN's generalized comprehension of powerful organized crime groups. In singling out the individuals listed earlier, the BNDD, as well as other American agencies, evidently continued to perceive a core set of exclusive syndicates as central pivots of Turkish heroin trafficking. The group's conception of a singular "Laz syndicate" based in Istanbul, coupled with its assertion that groups based in Antep and Kilis formed one discrete conspiracy, clearly harks back to earlier projections of the ascendency of major "gangs" at the heart of the Turkish opiate trade. Moreover, an argument can be made that such assertions generally reflect how in American officials perceived organized crime groups at home (such as those cited by the Kefauver Commission in 1950). In other words, one gets the sense that for the sake of consistency, simplicity, and legibility, it behooved the BNDD, like the FBN before it, to dispense with any suggestion that heroin trafficking in Turkey was an industry that was multi-dimensional, polymorphic, or fluid. By focusing upon major traffickers, and coupling them together into two uniform groups, the Ankara working group clearly renders heroin trafficking in Turkey as a coherent and monolithic conspiracy.

ACCEPTABLE LOSSES: TURKEY, COUNTER-NARCOTICS, AND THE COLD WAR

Sal Vizzini, reflecting back upon his career, later recalled Istanbul to be a "city of unending intrigue, half-Asian and half-European, an ancient metropolis where corruption had been a way of life for a thousand years."[226] Hyperbole aside, the DPS appears to have given a shard of credence to American perceptions of Turkish crime and corruption. The FBN's arrest record in Turkey between 1948 and 1967, however impressive depending upon the years one takes into account, cannot conceal the impression that little was achieved during this period of time. All of the major figures of the era, Sekban, Eminoğlu, Bezal, and the Soysals, remained active and seemingly undeterred by the threat of prosecution or prison. The flow of opiates out of Turkey continued unabated throughout the 1950s and 1960s. Rising rates of addiction and street crime in the United States (as well as France) attested to the fact that heroin derived from Turkish opium was found in greater quantities than at any point previously. From the perspective of American officials, cooperation offered by members of the DPS was often negated by acts of corruption, resistance, and duplicity. While Turkish policing methods had improved and grown more expansive over the course of the 1950s and 1960s, instability often racked the upper ranks of the narcotics section of the DPS. Charges of corruption against Kemal Aygün, Ali Eren, Galip Labarnas, Abdullah Pektaş, Halit Elver, and Ahmet Demir not only resulted in public scandals and trials, but also in strained

[226] Vizzini, *Vizzini: The Secret Lives of America's Most Successful Undercover Agent*, 99.

relations and mistrust between the FBN and DPS. With the dissolution of the FBN in 1967, there was every reason to believe that Anslinger's self-proclaimed crusade in Turkey, dating back to 1930, had largely failed.

While it is hard to escape the profundity and seriousness of these conclusions, it must, however, be said that the story of the heroin trafficking, organized crime, and political corruption in Turkey during this period remains a one-sided narrative. Further revelations from the archives of the Directorate of Public Safety will hopefully add greater clarity to the impressions and experiences of Turkish officers and officials discussed in this chapter. With the testimony of Turkish observers from this period, scholars will hopefully develop a narrative that will complicate and challenge the biases found in the still largely incomplete records left by the FBN.

Through the reports and correspondence found in the National Archives, we can confidently draw four important conclusions regarding the evolution of opiate trafficking in Turkey during this pivotal period. The records of the FBN strongly suggest that American approaches and priorities greatly influenced how counter-narcotics operations were conducted in Turkey. FBN agents, as partners with DPS officers and as instructors and sponsors, contributed to the professionalization and standardization of policing practices in Turkey. Even though many agents lacked fundamental training in Turkish language, culture, and politics, as well as suffering from a chronic lack of money and institutional support, American officers provided a new framework and inspired greater urgency among their Turkish counterparts in dealing with drug trafficking and organized crime. As a result of these efforts, both the FBN and the DPS helped to shed greater light upon the dramatic rise in opiate smuggling in Turkey.

Secondly, it seems relatively clear that American agents helped to define and expose the make-up and activities of both major and minor drug trafficking syndicates based in Turkey. In comparing and contrasting American reports from Turkey with the overall progression of anti-organized crime operations within the United States, it is reasonable to suggest that the experiences and observations of American agents in the United States greatly influenced how the FBN perceived the Turkish traffickers agents hoped to bring to justice. Recent scholarship and criticism of American approaches towards organized crime imply that many of the conclusions drawn by the FBN during this era may have oversimplified or misconstrued the real nature of the various smuggling syndicates that operated in Turkey during this period of time. Like the case of the American mafia, heavy emphasis was placed upon the exclusively ethnic character of the so-called "Laz gangs" of Istanbul (even though Laz gangsters often cooperated with individuals of different regional or ethnic backgrounds). FBN agents equally tended to highlight the activities of large-scale or major trafficking syndicates at the expense of smaller independent outfits and networks (even though most of the individuals apprehended during this period of time were members of far smaller and less notorious groups).

Thirdly, the records of the FBN underscore the fact that narcotics traffickers, as well as the narcotics trafficking trade as a whole, had begun to influence both politics and policing in Turkey. Corruption helped to forge close relationships between politicians, police officers, and drug traffickers in the Menderes era. The cases of

Refik Can and Naki Hıncal provide evidence of the fact that political leaders did actively contribute to the growth and development of the Turkish drug trade. The protection offered by other Turkish officials, such as Alaattin Eriş and Kemal Aygün, equally contributed to the success of key figures within the Turkish underworld (namely, İhsan Sekban). More broadly, the need to contract criminal informants for the purpose of gathering intelligence and making arrests allowed pivotal players within Istanbul's *milieu* to remain active in the drug trade under the umbrella of official protection from prosecution. In this regard, one may say that elements of the FBN, the DPS, and the Democratic and Justice Parties were key contributors to the growth and development of organized crime in Cold War Turkey.

Lastly, it is clear that counter-narcotics operations in Turkey provided a means for both American and Turkish intelligence networks to operate clandestinely during this era. FBN reports, as well as Sal Vizzini's memoir, admittedly offer only brief glimpses into this world. Nevertheless, on the basis of this scant evidence, one may say with some certitude that Istanbul became a cockpit for clandestine intrigues during the Cold War. Combating the drug trade in Turkey, in the words of Sal Vizzini, provided an essential "cover within a cover" for both American and Turkish officers tasked with executing covert operations in the service of Western interests.

One finds an undeniable current of frustration through many of the reports submitted by FBN agents during this era. Without saying so explicitly, it appears that many American officers (despite many declarations to the contrary) held their Turkish colleagues in low regard. How, despite the years invested, could Turkish officials abide by the corruption and indifference seen within their ranks? Did the DPS, city officials, and national leaders not realize that Turkey was at the heart of a lingering and growing epidemic of drug addiction in the United States and elsewhere? Was their cooperation, in the words of Charles Siragusa, simply an act "to save face" and deflect blame?

When interpreting the FBN's dour impressions of corruption within the DPS and the civil government of the Republic of Turkey, it is essential also to consider the tortuous history of organized crime in the United States during these very same years. Corruption within the ranks of local, state, and even federal law enforcement bodies, as well as the support supplied by politicians of various stature, provided similar levels of protection for organized crime groups and activities in the United States for generations. Herbert Asbury's seminal works on New York, Chicago, and New Orleans offer numerous examples of collaboration between gangsters, smugglers, policemen, and politicians dating back to the mid-nineteenth century. In looking more closely at a city like New York, it is clear that powerful racketeers, such as Frank Costello, were essential cogs utilized by the Democratic Party to maintain Tammany Hall's control over the city for generations.[227] Mark Haller,

[227] Daniel Czitrom, "Underworlds and Underdogs: Big Tim Sullivan and Metropolitan Politics in New York, 1889–1913," *The Journal of American History* 78.2 (September 1991), 536–558; Raab, *Five Families: The Rise, Decline and Resurgence of America's Most Powerful Mafia Empires*, 62–65.

among others, similarly argues that the economic livelihoods based upon organized criminal activities supplemented the incomes of peoples from various walks of life in Chicago during the twentieth century, thus creating a co-dependency system based upon protection and personal enrichment between lawbreakers and otherwise law abiding citizens alike.[228] Investigations into the assassination of John F. Kennedy have contributed to our understanding of how organized crime impacted the functioning of government at both local and national levels. Jack Ruby's role in murdering Lee Harvey Oswald has helped shed light upon the influence of Joseph Civello over the politics of Dallas and Texas at a large.[229] The Kennedy assassination gave further imputus for the US disclosure of the collaborative efforts of the CIA and major organized crime figures towards overthrowing Fidel Castro.

Charges of corruption and collaboration, ironically, helped bring an end to the FBN's reign as the premier counter-narcotics body in the United States. Even before Harry Anslinger took the reigns of the FBN, Roland Nutt, son of Anslinger's predecessor in the Bureau of Narcotics, was accused of doctoring the income taxes of Arnold Rothstein, one of the most notorious bootleggers and drug smugglers of the interwar period.[230] Improper procedures, theft, and bribe-taking dogged the FBN into the postwar era, particularly in the New York field office.[231] In 1967, the Department of Treasury created a task force to investigate a wide range of corruption charges emanating from the FBN's New York office. By the end of the year, a slew of active and former agents were arrested for their roles in selling and distributing marijuana, cocaine, and heroin. According to Andrew Tartaglino, who headed the investigation, 140 people were suspected of similar acts of corruption during the inquiry (although many never saw trial or prison for their roles in the scandal). Decades later, several individuals, such as George Gaffney, claimed that Tartaglino's campaign against wrongdoing within the ranks of the FBN was largely a witchhunt based upon faulty information and personal squabbles.[232]

With the integrity of the FBN called into question, the Johnson administration took dramatic steps that redefined Washington's role in undertaking its long-held position in enforcing and maintaining counter-narcotics policy in the United States and abroad. In February 1968, the administration decreed that the FBN would be integrated into a new agency entitled the Bureau of Narcotics and Dangerous Drugs. Alongside agents employed by a younger, more modest agency named the Bureau of Drug Addiction Control, FBN officers would henceforth be placed under the authority of the Department of Justice. Although nominally meant to streamline and rationalize control over the nation's drug policies, the Johnson administration's decision to close down Anslinger's old bureau had a

228 Mark Haller, "Organized Crime in Urban Society: Chicago in the Twentieth Century," *Journal of Social History* 5.2 (Winter 1971–72), 210–234.

229 Peter Dale Scott, *Deep Politics and the Death of JFK* (Berkeley: University of California Press, 1996), 129–131.

230 Valentine, *Strength of the Wolf*, 15.

231 Valentine, *Strength of the Wolf*, 209–221.

232 Valentine, *Strength of the Wolf*, 440–454.

dramatic effect upon the political and procedural culture the FBN had developed since its inception. The creation of the BNDD signaled an end to the operational autonomy many agents had previously enjoyed in the field. The FBN's independent, free-wheeling approach towards counter-narcotics operations gave way to a new political hierarchy that did not value the field experiences or seniority of its agents. Symbolic of this change was the appointment of John Ingersoll to head the BNDD, a California-born bureaucrat who had never made a field arrest nor personally conducted a criminal investigation. Henry Giordono, who had succeeded Anslinger and had served in the FBN for almost thirty years, was passed over for promotion and retired from service in 1969.[233]

The closure of the FBN seems to mark an important turning point in our understanding of narcotics trafficking, organized crime, and politics in Turkey as well. While the BNDD's files remain classified or uncatalogued at present, internal correspondence within the State Department from the 1970s seems to suggest that the narcotics agents ceased to play a defining role in American-Turkish relations with respect to narcotics trafficking and opium production. In the absence of this voice within the historical record, we are left with few resources privy to the investigations that revealed the names and methods of the most notorious drug traffickers of the following decade. Nevertheless, as the next chapter demonstrates, it is clear that historic changes were underway in Turkey during the 1970s that would change the nature of the narcotics trade between the eastern Mediterranean, Europe, and North America. More importantly, the sources that are available point to an historic shift in the symbiotic relationship between drug traffickers and legitimate power brokers active during the decade.

[233] Douglas Valentine, *The Strength of the Pack* (Walterville, OR: Trine Day, 2009), 1–10.

5

The Great Turn: The Transformation of Heroin and Organized Crime in the 1970s

On the morning of 1 February 1973, the *New York Times* published two stories that were emblematic of the city's growing narcotics crisis. On the front page of the paper, local correspondent David Burnham reported that nearly one-fifth of all the cocaine and heroin seized by the New York Police Department (NYPD) between 1961 and 1972 had been stolen from evidence lockers in police headquarters. Police Commissioner Patrick Murphy announced that the estimated value of the missing drugs totaled $73 million. Much of the heroin that had mysteriously vanished from police custody had been seized in the famous "French Connection" case of 1969.[1] The investigation into the missing drugs continued into the next year, eventually leading to the indictment of Vincent Papa, a gangster associated with the Lucchese crime family, and Frank King, a former member of NYPD's Narcotics Squad.[2] King's acquittal, Papa's death in prison, as well as the mysterious deaths of other potential suspects, ultimately prevented local and federal prosecutors from ever resolving this scandal.[3]

On that same February morning, the *Times* printed a second story linked to the city's drug crisis. Buried in the middle of the paper was an account of a federal indictment of a convicted heroin dealer named Vincent Pacelli. Pacelli, who was already in prison on narcotics charges, stood accused of murdering a twenty-eight-year-old model and mother named Patsy Parks. US Attorney Whitney North Seymour Jr. told reporters that Pacelli had stabbed the young woman to death and set her body on fire after she had been compelled to testify in a narcotics case against him. Pacelli's father, the *Times* noted, was also in prison serving a long sentence from a separate narcotics case from 1965 and had been implicated in the disappearance of an actress who was also scheduled to testify against him.[4]

Across town on Long Island, reporters at *Newsday* also presented readers with stories tied to New York's ever-growing heroin epidemic. However, the scope and ambitions of *Newsday*'s coverage that day differed dramatically from the stories attended to that morning by the *New York Times*. On 1 February 1973, Nassau County's daily paper announced that it would begin to publish a series of articles

[1] David Burnham, "Police Drug Loss Now $73 Million," *New York Times* 1 February 1973.

[2] Paul Montgomery, "Ex-Officer Cited by Nadjari Jury," *New York Times* 11 May 1974.

[3] Ralph Blumenthal, "Mobster Makes Offer on French Connection Case," *New York Times* 21 February 2009.

[4] Arnold Lubasch, "Heroin Dealer Indicted in Killing of Model, Witness at His Trial," *New York Times* 1 February 1973.

on the impact heroin had upon this corner of suburban New York. Over the next month, a team of fourteen journalists recounted the experiences and discoveries they had amassed over a year-long investigation. A core question buttressed each of the pieces printed in the paper over the course of the ensuing month: exactly how did heroin find its way to the streets and neighborhoods of Nassau County, Long Island? To answer this question, reporters first travelled to Turkey to understand suburban New York's heroin crisis at its source.

State Department officials in Ankara first caught wind of the *Newsday* series soon after the paper began publishing the articles in early February. The Istanbul daily, *Tercuman*, eventually reprinted translations and synopses of seven of the articles dealing with affairs in Turkey. The Turkish Foreign Ministry had also cabled abstracts of *Newsday*'s findings to their mission in New York City. Whether in English or in Turkish, *Newday*'s portrayal of the heroin trade in Turkey was damning. Illicit opiate harvesting was continuing despite a new policy of prohibition on the drug's cultivation. A series of prominent smugglers, called *patrons* (or bosses), monopolized heroin trafficking out of Istanbul and southern Turkey. Government officials were complicit in the trade, a charge evidenced by the appearance of a government minister at the funeral of a known underworld figure.

While official and public reaction to the series was characterized as relatively "muted," some of the revelations appear to have caused some discomfort among US government representatives. Charges of corruption and smuggling at various levels of the Turkish government apparently worried the US embassy, since such claims only fueled the suspicion that Washington was "mistrustful and unappreciative" of the assistance Turkey had rendered to the United States on opium-related issues in the past.[5] Moreover, *Newsday*'s assertion that the government of Bulgaria actively collaborated in the Turkish drug trade was officially greeted with surprise and circumspection (even though such claims had been made privately within American circles years previously).[6] Perhaps worst of all, *Newsday*'s coverage seemed to suggest that a change in government in Ankara would lead to an annulment of the prohibition on opium production in Turkey, an act that would have undone years of negotiations and compromise.[7]

The articles profiled above were emblematic of the tense political climate of this era. Heroin assumed an ever-larger place within American perceptions of crime, corruption, and urban decay in the United States. As the social and political upheaval of the 1960s began to take its toll upon the American state and civil society, many came to interpret narcotics abuse, and heroin addiction in particular, both as a symptom and the source of America's declining fortunes both at home and abroad. Turkish perceptions of the impact of heroin on domestic civil and

[5] American Embassy Ankara to Department of State, 15 February 1973, Ankara 1154, Subject Numeric Files, 1970–73, RG 59, NAB.

[6] "Bulgaria Implicated by 'Newsday' in Narcotics Smuggling," 9 February 1973, 24915, Subject Numeric Files, 1970–73, RG 59, NAB.

[7] "Newsday Article on Heroin," 6 February 1973, 22468, Subject Numeric Files, 1970–73, RG 59, NAB.

political affairs may be characterized as somewhat more subdued in comparison to the United States. Nonetheless, as the 1970s progressed, drug trafficking, as well as the apparent political influence of those involved in the trade, did appear to play an important role in instigating and perpetuating an atmosphere of increasing violence and uncertainty in the Turkish Republic. By the end of the decade, a series of scandals left few doubts as to the power and influence the Turkish narcotics underworld wielded over the country.

The early 1970s also witnessed a series of profound shifts in American and Turkish policy towards the opium trade. While Washington had played an indelible role in influencing Ankara's approach towards opiate production since the interwar period, the election of Richard Nixon in 1968, coupled with the military coup of 1971, prompted a radical reassessment in the two countries' treatment of the trade. For the first time in the history of their relationship, heroin trafficking assumed a position of primary importance in formal relations between the United States and the Republic of Turkey. After much debate, and even greater amounts of political pressure, Washington succeeded in compelling Ankara to implement a complete ban on opium production in the country. The victory the Nixon administration claimed after this announcement, however, proved to be short-lived. Despite the challenges posed by this ban, which lasted from 1971 to 1974, opiate smugglers in Turkey demonstrated a suppleness and flexibility that allowed the country's narcotics underworld to survive and even flourish. By 1980, it is clear that older and newer trafficking syndicates had begun to adapt to larger trends occurring in the global narcotics trade, a trend that laid the foundation for Turkey's contemporary status as a leading wholesale purveyor, as opposed to producer, of opiates and other narcotics in Europe, North America, and beyond.

The lack of Turkish and American archival materials for this period adds significant obstacles to the writing of this chapter. Documents drawn from the National Archives in Maryland (largely composed of State Department correspondence), the Nixon Library, and the Central Intelligence Agency are among the few primary sources that offer an American perspective upon the events and trends that dominated the 1970s. There is virtually no archival base in Turkey available to researchers that may help shed light upon the evolution of narcotics trafficking and organized crime during this period. Journalistic accounts, and a smattering of interviews and investigative stories do, however, add some interesting insights upon this era. Through these Turkish sources, we do obtain a far clearer and more detailed rendering of the inner workings of the Turkish underworld, a picture that is admittedly far closer to the actual events and individuals that defined this era than at any point during the first half of the twentieth century.

THE WAR ON DRUGS BEGINS: NIXON, TURKEY, AND THE OPIUM CRISIS OF THE EARLY 1970s

Richard Nixon entered the White House in January 1969 with a pledge to end the Vietnam War and to bring "peace and honor" to Southeast Asia. His domestic agenda, in no uncertain terms, was explicitly far more bellicose. During the campaign of 1968, Nixon railed against the rise in crime and the culture of drugs that plagued American cities and college campuses. In his address to the Republic National Convention, he promised to "launch a war against organized crime" and avowed that "a new front" would be opened against "narcotics peddlers" corrupting the "lives of the children of this country."[8] Nixon's staunch position on crime and drugs did indeed reflect his own personal hatred for the cultural and political iniquities he associated with the American left.[9] But his stance constituted more than just a personal vendetta or a cunning effort to court a "silent majority" that demurred from or was dismayed by the popular movements of the 1960s. Drug use, especially heroin consumption, undeniably did rise throughout the tumultuous 1960s. Violence and crime, on the part of addicts and drug dealing gangs and syndicates, concomitantly soared in its wake.[10] New York City, more than any other city or region of the country, experienced the worst of the twin crises of drug use and crime. The statistics of the era portray a seemingly cold reality that crime and narcotics had begun to grossly impact the lives of New Yorkers, particularly those living towards the bottom of the socio-economic ladder.[11] Between 1960 and 1976, the number of murders in New York climbed from 390 a year to over 1,600. Robbery rose by over 1,200 percent during this period. In an era beset by conflict and reaction as a result of the civil rights movement, the rise in crime and addiction further amplified racial tensions in the city. For much of the 1970s, New York City, as it appeared to many, was a city on the verge of collapse and failure.[12]

It was against this backdrop in 1969 that President Nixon, in a direct appeal to the US Congress, called for a new comprehensive national policy on narcotics and crime. In his 14 July message to the legislative branch of the government, Nixon outlined a ten-point agenda on drugs, an agenda that entailed appeals for greater funding for law enforcement and treatment efforts, the passage of new surveillance and procedural laws meant to aid in the policing of the narcotics trade and further investment into education and other public outreach programs. Added to these ten provisions was a call for greater coordination and engagement with foreign governments in states where narcotics were produced.[13] Nixon, of course, was not the first

[8] <http://www.presidency.ucsb.edu/ws/index.php?pid=25968> (accessed 7 November 2012).

[9] Richard Davenport-Hines, *The Pursuit of Oblivion: A Global History of Narcotics* (New York: W. W. Norton Company, 2004), 420–421.

[10] For discussion of Baltimore, one particularly hard hit city, see Jonnes, *Hep-cats, Narcs and Pipe Dreams: A History of America's Romance with Illegal Drugs*, 250–254.

[11] The research of Edward Jay Epstein offers some critique of the statistical data on crime and drug use in New York from this period. According to Epstein, the statistics purporting a relationship between addiction and crime were intentionally skewed by Nelson Rockefeller in order to secure election and pass more stringent policing laws. See Edward Jay Epstein, *Agency of Fear: Opiates and Political Power in America* (New York: G. P. Putnam's Sons, 1977), 38–45.

[12] Eric Schneider, *Smack: Heroin and the American City* (Philadelphia: University of Pennsylvania Press, 2008), 117–122.

[13] Roy Reeds, "President Urges a National Drive on Narcotics Use," *The New York Times*, 15 July 1969; "Text of Nixon's Message to Congress Proposing 10 Steps in Fighting Narcotics," *The New York Times*, 15 July 1969.

American president to foreground the threat of drugs as a national priority. Each president dating back to Harry Truman had labeled the struggle against narcotics abuse and trafficking a national priority to some degree.[14] In hindsight, however, Nixon's 1969 message to Congress has assumed critical significance in the history of the drug trade. Given the ever escalating nature of US interest and engagement in counter-narcotics efforts post-1969, the president's pronouncement that summer has since been labeled the opening salvo of the modern-day "war on drugs."[15]

Nixon's crusade against drugs was formally set in motion two months later, in September 1969, on the Mexican/American border. In a campaign dubbed Operation Intercept, 2,000 American Customs and BNDD officers were deployed to various crossing points, aggressively searching cars and trucks for contraband narcotics. In addition to holding up traffic and aggravating motorists, Mexican officials greeted the operation with indignation. The diplomatic row spawned a wave of embarrassing disclosures for the Nixon White House, which had hoped the action would signal the administration's earnestness and resolve on the threat of narcotics trafficking. Meanwhile, back in Washington, a number of cabinet members, as well as several high-profile congressional members, lobbied the White House for more direct and decisive action. Daniel Patrick Moynihan, then a member of the White House staff, specifically advocated that narcotics control be elevated to a national security issue (as opposed to a concern restricted to American law enforcement officials). That summer, Henry Kissinger, Nixon's national security advisor, convened a working group of principal policymakers, dubbed the Ad Hoc Cabinet Committee on Narcotics, tasked with forming a more coherent long-term strategy for the administration's policies on narcotics.[16]

On 20 October 1969, Attorney General John Mitchell and Acting Undersecretary of State Elliot Richardson submitted to Henry Kissinger a comprehensive report detailing their analysis and recommendations on the "heroin problem" facing the United States. The gravity of the crisis, in their estimation, was huge. There were over 100,000 heroin addicts then residing in the United States. Each year, 3,000 kilograms of heroin entered the country. Of this, 80 percent of the heroin consumed in the United States was processed in France. The principal source of French heroin, in the estimation of the report's authors, was the Republic of Turkey. Mexican heroin comprised the lion's share of the remaining heroin consumed in the United States (an estimated 15 percent), while opiates from Burma, Laos, Thailand, and southern China made up the remaining 5 percent.[17]

14 Jonnes, *Hep-cats, Narcs and Pipe Dreams: A History of America's Romance with Illegal Drugs*, 262–263.

15 For an account of the early days of Nixon's war on drugs, see Dan Baum, *Smoke and Mirrors: The War on Drugs and the Politics of Failure* (New York: Little, Brown and Company, 1997).

16 Epstein, *Agency of Fear: Opiates and Political Power in America*, 81–85.

17 Memorandum for the President, 20 October 1969; Box 30; White House Special Files, Staff Member and Office Files: Egil Krogh, 1969–73; Richard Nixon Presidential Library and Museum, Yorba Linda, California.

As the principal source of illicit heroin consumption within the US, France and Turkey had to be approached with greater purpose and urgency. French and Turkish officials, the report advised, were well aware of American desires to halt the trafficking of narcotics through their respective territories. In the case of France, Mitchell and Richardson advocated that Washington press Georges Pompidou's government to undertake a more rigorous campaign to suppress existing heroin factories in the country. It was further suggested that greater pressure be brought to bear on Paris in the hopes of increasing the number of American narcotics officers stationed in-country (as well as accepting greater amounts of American technical assistance). Unfortunately, neither Richardson nor Mitchell had much faith in American abilities to hold France accountable should they not comply with Washington's demands. An "Operation Intercept" effort conducted against French commerce and tourism would only spark retaliation rather than cooperation.[18]

The report made similarly bold recommendations regarding potential diplomatic approaches to Turkey. The United States, in the view of the report's two authors, should put pressure on Turkey to halt opium production entirely by the end of 1971.[19] Various levels of the recently re-elected Turkish government were to be made aware that American officials would broach the topic of opium eradication over the remainder of 1969 (beginning with an official meeting between the White House and Prime Minister Süleyman Demirel in December). The United States, as a way of speeding the transition and softening the blow of the policy, would offer financial aid through USAID. If Ankara did not comply with Washington's demands, a number of mechanisms could be employed to compel Turkey to undertake eradication more swiftly. Mitchell and Richardson suggested that military and domestic aid could be cut to the tune of some $140 million. Even though the Turks had previously warmed to the idea of opium eradication, the report warned that pressing Ankara too hard would have adverse effects upon relations with Turkey. It was feared that American access to bases in Turkey (including electronic listening posts close to the Soviet Union) could be jeopardized. Worse still, Turkey's membership of NATO could be adversely affected if Ankara and Washington came to an impasse on narcotics suppression.[20]

Mitchell and Richardson's report makes it clear that the proposed policies in dealing with Turkish opium were not altogether new. Three years before the convening of the Ad Hoc Cabinet Committee on Narcotics, Süleyman Demirel, whose Justice Party had been elected by a strong majority to the Turkish Grand National Assembly in October 1965, had floated the idea of ending opium cultivation to a committee within the government.[21] The American Embassy in

[18] Memorandum for the President, 20 October 1969.

[19] Memorandum for the President, 20 October 1969.

[20] Memorandum for the President, 20 October 1969.

[21] American Embassy Ankara to Department of State, 17 December 1966, Ankara 2931, Subject Numeric Files, 1964–66, RG 59, NAB.

Ankara had discussed the issue of opium eradication with Foreign Minister İhsan Çağlayangil. According to embassy dispatches, Ambassador Park T. Hart made it clear to his Turkish counterpart that President Lyndon Johnson was "deeply concerned about crime" in which Turkish-derived heroin played a "very important part." Çağlayangil assured Hart that the Demirel government was serious about the issue, but was concerned about how to compensate farmers when opium cultivation ceased.[22] The plan appeared to have floundered after these first diplomatic discussions between the United States and Turkey due in part to opposition from the RPP's contingent within the assembly.[23] While an absolute ban was not forthcoming, Ankara did cut the number of opium producing provinces in the country from twenty-one to twelve in 1967.[24]

As the Nixon administration sought to resume negotiations on Demirel's opium eradication plan, the claim that Turkish sources accounted for 80 percent of the heroin consumed in the United States assumed greater and greater significance. As a figure representing the profundity of Turkey's impact upon America's heroin crisis, government reports and journalists repeatedly employed the 80 percent figure without debate or qualification. Internal correspondence within US circles, however, cast some doubt upon the validity of this claim. FBN reports from the 1950s make no projections as to a percentage of Turkish opiates found within the American marketplace. In 1966, the Johnson administration maintained that Turkish opium accounted for only 8 percent of the heroin consumed in the United States.[25] A CIA report from 1970 muddies the water further, suggesting that Turkish opium in 1968 and 1969 accounted for 80 percent of the heroin consumed in *both* the United States and Western Europe (an amended map in the report denotes that 30 percent of the heroin used in the United States arrived from France).[26] Even French officials, speaking to American diplomats as late as 1970, disputed the notion that clandestine labs in Marseille refined such large quantities of Turkish opium.[27]

The sudden rise in this estimate, according to journalist Edward Jay Epstein, came as a result of two decisions made in the early stages of the Nixon administration. Administration officials assumed, first, that one-quarter of all opium

[22] American Embassy Ankara to Department of State, 22 October 1966, Ankara 2060, Subject Numeric Files, 1964–66, RG 59, NAB.

[23] American Embassy Ankara to Department of State, 20 July 1970, Ankara 4592, Subject Numeric Files, 1970–73, RG 59, NAB; American Embassy Ankara to Department of State, 15 July 1970, Ankara 4426, Subject Numeric Files, 1970–73, RG 59, NAB.

[24] Directorate of Intelligence, "The French-Turkish Connection: The Movement of Opium and Morphine Base from Turkey to France (December 1971)," CIA-RDP 73B00296R000300070022-8, CIA Records Search Tool (CREST), National Archives and Records Administration, College Park, MD.

[25] American Embassy Ankara to Department of State, 22 October 1966, Ankara 2060, Subject Numeric Files, 1964–66, RG 59, NAB.

[26] "The World Opium Situation," October 1970, CIA-RDP73B00296R000300060031-9, CIA Records Search Tool (CREST); National Archives Building II, College Park, MD.

[27] "French Ambassador's Meeting July 7 with Acting Secretary: Part III—Narcotics Control," 7 July 1970, 108918, Subject Numeric Files, 1970–74, RG 59, NAB.

produced in Turkey was diverted along illicit lines. It was then supposed that virtually all the illicit opium arrived in the United States as heroin. These two suppositions, Epstein argues, discounted the possibility that illicit opium may have remained within Turkey or was exported to countries aside from the United States (particularly Iran).[28]

Through his interviews with governmental officials in the mid-1970s, Epstein argues that ulterior political motives moved the Nixon administration to name Turkey as a primary source of heroin abuse in the United States. Kissinger's ad hoc committee, as seen earlier, acknowledged that Turkey's dependence upon American aid allowed Washington greater leverage in attempting to force a change in Ankara's policy towards opium cultivation. Admittedly, the United States possessed little to no influence over other countries where opium production was prevalent (particularly such states as Laos, Burma, or India). Turkey's susceptibility to American pressure, therefore, seemed to provide a more politically attractive opportunity to score an early victory in Nixon's war on drugs. One member of the ad hoc committee, speaking to Epstein years later, admitted that "Turkey was the only country where we could expect dramatic results, and that was what the president wanted."[29]

Two meetings, on 24 October and 3 November, sealed the course of US policy on Turkish opium. Kissinger, in chairing the first session comprising of the ad hoc committee's members, again emphasized the president's commitment to confronting heroin trafficking into the United States, making the issue a centerpiece of American foreign policy (a turn which, in Daniel Patrick Moynihan's estimation, was a "historic" event in the history of the country's foreign relations).[30] On 3 November, the committee affirmed its recommendation of following a two-pronged approach towards France and Turkey. The State Department would make clear to Georges Pompidou "in the strongest and most explicit way" that a crackdown on heroin processing needed to occur within continental France. Both President Nixon and the State Department would approach Prime Minister Süleyman Demirel with a similar sense of urgency, although the committee was fairly confident that Turkey would agree to interdicting the 1970 opium harvest. Moynihan provided the only voice of dissent at the meeting, stating that calling for an end to opium production in Turkey was "just more fucking around."[31] His distrust of Turkish responsiveness towards US demands was again reiterated that December in a conversation with American Ambassador William

[28] Epstein, *Agency of Fear: Opiates and Political Power in America*, 89. According to CIA estimates, 60% of the 100 million tons of opium diverted to the illicit marketplace came to the United States. The remaining 40 million tons of illicitly produced opium was exported to Iran. See "The World Opium Situation," October 1970, CIA-RDP73B00296R000300060031-9, CIA Records Search Tool (CREST); National Archives Building II, College Park, MD.

[29] Epstein, *Agency of Fear: Opiates and Political Power in America*, 87.

[30] "Heroin Traffic: Meeting of October 24," 24 October 1969; Box 30; White House Special Files, Staff Member and Office Files: Egil Krogh, 1969–73; Richard Nixon Presidential Library and Museum, Yorba Linda, California.

[31] Memorandum for Mr. Bud Krogh from J. F. Lehman, 3 November 1969; Box 30; White House Special Files, Staff Member and Office Files: Egil Krogh, 1969–73; Richard Nixon Presidential Library and Museum, Yorba Linda, California.

Handley. Considering the history of Ankara's resistance to American concerns regarding heroin trafficking, the future senator of New York suggested that the United States bomb Istanbul's iconic Blue Mosque in retaliation. In a memorandum submitted to the Assistant Secretary of State for Near Eastern and South Asian Affairs, Handley allegedly suggested that Moynihan's comment was not a joke.[32]

Washington's diplomatic offensive against France began in earnest in the first half of 1970.[33] After personal interventions by President Nixon and BNDD head John Ingersoll (who met with Georges Pompidou and other members of his government through the year), French officials promptly escalated efforts to suppress the Marseille underworld.[34] In the summer of 1970, the number of narcotics officers operating in Marseille rose from nine to forty-seven.[35] By 1972, the French *Sureté* placed hundreds of underworld figures under arrest and seized over half a dozen conversion labs.[36] Meanwhile, violence broke out between rival gangs in Marseille, further thinning the ranks of the city's multiple syndicates.[37] State Department officials, in turn, greeted France's overtures as a sign that the Marseille mafia had met its match. The new measures enacted by Paris, State Department officials hoped, had resulted in both the easing of America's heroin epidemic as well as the "destruction of organized crime groups throughout Europe."[38] American confidence in the seriousness of the French government's actions was further bolstered by a growing recognition in Paris of a parallel heroin crisis present within France. According to statistics gathered by the French Ministry of Interior, the total number of individuals arrested for narcotics

[32] Memorandum from the Director of the Office of Turkish Affairs (Cash) to the Assistant Secretary of State for Near Eastern And South Asian Affairs (Cisco), 18 June 1970, *Foreign Relations of the United States, 1969–1976, Vol. XXIX: Eastern Europe; Eastern Mediterranean, 1969–1972* (Washington DC: Government Printing Office, 2007), 1065–1066.

[33] For a copy of the letter Nixon sent to Pompidou, see "State Department: Suggested Message," undated; Box 30; White House Special Files, Staff Member and Office Files: Egil Krogh, 1969–73; Richard Nixon Presidential Library and Museum, Yorba Linda, California. Pompidou, for his part, disputed Nixon's claim that 80% of heroin destined for the United State passed through France. See Georges Pompidou to Richard Nixon, 21 November 1969; Box 30; White House Special Files, Staff Member and Office Files: Ergil Krogh, 1969–73; Richard Nixon Presidential Library and Museum, Yorba Linda, California.

[34] American Embassy Paris to Secretary of State, 14 May 1970, Paris 6080, Subject Numeric Files, 1970–74, RG 59, NAB. Before the summer of 1970, there were still some lower level French officials who denied American assertions that Marseille was a central processing center for heroin in the country. As for May 1970, pressure from Paris clearly overcame the bureaucratic resistance found in the south of France.

[35] Department of State Telegram, 5 December 1970, 198616, Subject Numeric Files, 1970–74, RG 59, NAB. Many new officers arriving in the south of France came from outside of the region, apparently breaking with the practice of employing older officers with historic ties to the Marseille *milieu*.

[36] American Embassy Paris to Secretary of State, 12 December 1971, Paris 21176, Subject Numeric Files, 1970–74, RG 59, NAB.

[37] American Embassy Paris to Secretary of State, 30 December 1971, Paris 21162, Subject Numeric Files, 1970–74, RG 59, NAB.

[38] American Embassy Paris to Secretary of State, 16 February 1973, Paris 3974, Subject Numeric Files, 1970–74, RG 59, NAB.

use had jumped from over 200 in 1969 to 30,000 in 1972. Of the 30,000 alleged narcotics users in France, heroin addicts comprised a total of between three and five thousand people.[39]

Newsday's research team, which spent three months in France in 1971, discovered very different attitudes held by American and French officials on the question of heroin trafficking. Political protection for many of Marseille's leading narcotics traffickers continued to foil any attempt to bring the heads of the city's underworld to justice.[40] In terms of the laboratories seized by 1972, *Newsday* reporters claimed that only one operational lab had been uncovered. Most of the arrests made during the early 1970s comprised midlevel or petty traffickers and drug pushers.[41] *Newsday* also cast doubt on the seriousness with which Paris and Washington had invested greater manpower into policing heroin trafficking in the south of France. The number of French customs agents working in southern France, *Newsday* discovered, was lower in 1971 than it was twenty years earlier. Even the BNDD had reduced its number of officers in the country from twelve to ten between 1969 and 1972.[42]

In surveying the repercussions of *Newsday's* coverage of French-American efforts against narcotics trafficking, the American Embassy in Paris reported in December 1972 that the managing reporter for the paper's team, Robert Greene, actually seemed "impressed with current Franco-American cooperation and successes."[43] Nevertheless, as a group "well financed, equipped with bugging devices" and with "plenty of time," American Ambassador James Watson criticized Greene and his reporters as having a "propensity for scandal" and an "absence of inhibiting scruples."[44] The degree to which *Newsday's* team was equipped with surveillance and recording devices raised suspicion within French government circles as well, with some officials declaring to the American Embassy that it was "hard to believe" that Robert Greene was "actually a journalist." Nevertheless, internal State Department correspondence gives no indication as to their perceptions of the veracity of their reporting, stating only that the embassy was prepared to issue statements affirming their "satisfaction with Franco-American cooperation on narcotics suppression."[45]

[39] American Embassy Paris to Secretary of State, 28 December 1973, no document number, Subject Numeric Files, 1970–74, RG 59, NAB. Also see Larry Collins and Dominique Lapierre, "The French Connection—In Real Life," *The New York Times* 6 February 1972.

[40] Newsday, *The Heroin Trail*, 78.

[41] Newsday, *The Heroin Trail*, 88. It should be noted that there were some doubts within American circles as to the impact French seizures of illicit laboratories had upon the drug trade. According to one report, it was recognized that still many more labs remained operational in France in 1972 and that even with the arrests and seizures made, there were still "enough labs out there to prevent destroying the trade." See American Embassy Paris to Secretary of State, 16 February 1973, Paris 3974, Subject Numeric Files, 1970–74, RG 59, NAB.

[42] Newsday, *The Heroin Trail*, 90–91.

[43] American Embassy Paris to Secretary of State, 21 December 1972, Paris 24546, Subject Numeric Files, 1970–74, RG 59, NAB.

[44] American Embassy Paris to Secretary of State, 10 October 1972, Paris 24546, Subject Numeric Files, 1970–74, RG 59, NAB.

[45] American Embassy Paris to Secretary of State, 21 December 1972, Paris 24546, Subject Numeric Files, 1970–74, RG 59, NAB.

Washington's initial apprehensions towards France contrasted sharply with the optimism many policymakers professed in their appraisal of Turkish reactions in the fall of 1969. At the end of November the CIA and BNDD submitted a study outlining future plans and expectations in initiating counter-opium policies in Turkey. Opium suppression in Turkey, the two agencies cautioned, would not instantly fix America's heroin crisis. Instead, it constituted the first step in a longer struggle. The two agencies projected that a policy of eradication and crop substitution was, in the long run, politically and financially "manageable." American aid, both in terms of the direct transfer of funds and technical assistance, was crucial to the program's eventual success. Even though there were doubts that Ankara would not completely implement an absolute ban in 1970, both the BNDD and CIA expressed confidence that Demirel possessed enough authority and commanded enough respect to see the program through. The two groups did admit that "some elements of officialdom" did probably profit from illicit trafficking in Turkey but the Turkish bureaucracy remained "less corrupt than in most Middle Eastern countries."[46]

Negotiations on the opium question in Turkey appear to have opened formally in April 1970 in a meeting between Henry Kissinger and Melih Esenbel, Turkish Ambassador to Washington. The Secretary of State's message to his Turkish counterpart was urgent and abrupt: Turkey had to act quickly and decisively to end opium production. Opium, Kissinger explained, was the only problem inhibiting relations between the two allies. Worse still, Turkey's reputation was beginning to suffer in the eyes of Congress and the American public. Should Ankara move quickly to completely end the cultivation of poppies, the United States would "more than compensate" Turkish farmers for their losses. Speed, however, was essential. Ambassador Esenbel assured Kissinger that Demirel's position on the matter had not changed and that "a high-level decision" had been made to end poppy cultivation completely, but it was simply a question of time.[47]

The governing Justice Party's incremental approach towards eradication became increasingly clear to American officials as negotiations stretched into the summer. The Land Production Office in Ankara, which oversaw opium production, would allow farmers to plant poppies that year but seek to buy the entire crop itself. Foreign Ministry officials further pledged that Turkey would finally comply with the 1961 United Nations Single Convention on Narcotics and pass a comprehensive licensing law governing the production of opium.[48] Despite increasing public pressure and opposition in the National Assembly, the Demirel government

[46] BNDD to Jean Dours, Director General, Police Nationale, 13 September 1969; Box 30; White House Special Files, Staff Member and Office Files: Egil Krogh, 1969–73; Richard Nixon Presidential Library and Museum, Yorba Linda, California.

[47] Memorandum of Conversation, 1 April 1970, *Foreign Relations of the United States, 1969–1976, Vol. XXIX: Eastern Europe; Eastern Mediterranean, 1969–1972* (Washington DC: Government Printing Office, 2007), 1062.

[48] Telegram from the Embassy in Turkey to the Department of State, 18 July 1970, *Foreign Relations of the United States, 1969–1976, Vol. XXIX: Eastern Europe; Eastern Mediterranean, 1969–1972* (Washington DC: Government Printing Office, 2007), 1069–1071.

also unilaterally reduced the number of opium-producing provinces from twelve to seven.[49] Nixon, after personally meeting with Handley later in the summer of 1970, remained undeterred by the public backlash that was slowing the pace of the Turkish government's reforms. He again reiterated his serious interest in domestic drug abuse in the United States and pointedly told Handley to explain to the Turkish government that the opium issue was "terribly important to us."[50]

Mounting waves of violence and political upheaval in Turkey soon superseded talks between Ankara and Washington on the question of opium eradication. Despite his initial stature as the most prominent politician to succeed Menderes, Süleyman Demirel faced increased opposition in the National Assembly at the hands of a reinvigorated Republican Peoples' Party under Bülent Ecevit. An even more troubling political trend confronting the ruling Justice Party was the rise in leftist and rightist activism. A number of strikes and demonstrations, such as a trade union protest in the Istanbul district of Kadıköy in June 1970, resulted in violent police crackdowns and arbitrary arrests. From Ankara's perspective, the growing confidence and radicalism of Turkey's left had dangerous and destructive overtones. A string of bank robberies and kidnappings carried out by leftist students signaled to many in the capital that law and order was breaking down throughout the country.[51] The Turkish military, until the spring of 1971, remained cautiously supportive of Demirel's government despite growing concerns over the surge in violence on college campuses and in major Turkish cities. The abduction of four American soldiers by a radical student group in March 1971 prompted a final break between Demirel and the Turkish military's high command. At midday on 12 March 1971, radios throughout the country broadcast the news that the prime minister had resigned. In a move reminiscent of the overthrow of Adnan Menderes, the chief of Turkey's general staff, Memduh Tağmaç, had issued a memorandum demanding Demirel's removal after the government had led the country into "anarchy, fratricide and social and economic discord."[52]

The military's intervention into domestic affairs, as well as the appointment of a new prime minister, Nihat Erim, did not discourage the Nixon White House from pursuing the opium question to its ultimate conclusion. In late March 1971, the CIA completed a study of Turkey's policy towards opium in light of the recent coup. Admittedly, the chief task for the new prime minister was to address the climate of violence and disorder gripping the country. Passage of a new licensing law, in the CIA's estimation, would probably be held up as a result of the

[49] Çağrı Erhan, *Beyaz Savaş: Türk-Amerikan İlişkilerinde Afyon Sorunu* (Ankara: Bilgi Yayınevi, 1996), 104–105; Alfred Friendly, "Turkish Program Curbing Opium Poppy," *The New York Times* 11 June 1970.

[50] Memorandum of Conversation, 17 August 1970, *Foreign Relations of the United States, 1969–1976. Vol. XXIX: Eastern Europe; Eastern Mediterranean, 1969–1972* (Washington DC: Government Printing Office, 2007), 1073–1074.

[51] Istanbul Consulate to Secretary of State, 30 July 1971, Istanbul 888, Subject Numeric Files, 1970–73, RG 59, NAB.

[52] Ahmad, The Making of Modern Turkey (London: Routledge, 2002), 204–205; Öktem, *Angry Nation: Turkey Since 1989*, 49.

current political climate. Nevertheless, the Agency offered hope that the new military-backed government would look favorably upon continuing negotiations in the wake of the collapse of the RPP's political opposition to counter-opium efforts.[53] Interestingly, this is not the first official mention within American circles of seeking support from the Turkish military on the opium issue. In June 1970, James Watson, American Ambassador to France, suggested that the United States could enlist the support of the Turkish military to support Demirel's drive towards eradication. The military, he suggested, was likely to hold the opinion that politicians had "made [a] mess of opium control" in the past. Moreover, the military had "openly accused or strongly implied certain Menderes regime officials were involved [in] opium traffic as major violators."[54] The State Department, in a cable addressed to William Handley in April 1971, largely discounted the idea of including Turkish generals directly into the negotiations. While the embassy was given some clearance to make "discrete contacts" with military leaders in order "to make clear" American concerns, the State Department saw "no advantage" in including the Turkish brass in forthcoming negotiations.[55]

Fortunately for the Nixon White House and the State Department, Prime Minister Nihat Erim proved to be more a willing and active partner than his predecessor. In meetings with Ambassador Handley in April and May, Erim was explicit in his desires to proceed quickly towards eradication. Opium control had been a principle upheld by Atatürk; the issues to be resolved were not matters of principle but approach.[56] As a native of Kocaeli, located just east of Istanbul, he declared that peasants in his home province had grown opium but, as a result of government restriction, the trade had largely been abandoned. The only question remaining to be answered, in Erim's opinion, was what cash crop would substitute the cultivation of opium.[57] When Hadley returned home to Washington in June, the topic of substitution was specifically raised in a meeting with President Nixon and other high-ranking officials. Secretary of the Treasury John Connally proposed that onions, sugar beets, or perhaps textile factories could replace poppies as a source of income for Turkish farmers. Nixon, who presided over the meeting, appeared disinterested in the technicalities of the debate within opium. He was encouraged that Turkey had proposed a reduction of opium-producing provinces (numbering

[53] Memorandum from Harold Saunders of the National Security Council Staff to the President's Deputy Assistant for Domestic Affairs (Krogh), 25 March 1971, *Foreign Relations of the United States, 1969–1976. Vol. XXIX: Eastern Europe; Eastern Mediterranean, 1969–1972* (Washington DC: Government Printing Office, 2007), 1085.

[54] American Embassy Paris to American Embassy Ankara, 13 June 1970, Paris 7764, Subject Numeric Files, 1970–73, RG 59, NAB.

[55] Telegram from the Department of State to the Embassy in Turkey, 13 April 1971, *Foreign Relations of the United States, 1969–1976. Vol. XXIX: Eastern Europe; Eastern Mediterranean, 1969–1972* (Washington DC: Government Printing Office, 2007), 1088–1089.

[56] American Embassy Turkey to Secretary of State, 22 April 1971, no document number, Box 632; National Security Council (NSC) Files, Country Files—Middle East; Richard Nixon Presidential Library and Museum, Yorba Linda, California.

[57] Telegram from the Embassy in Turkey to the Department of State, 18 May 1971, *Foreign Relations of the United States, 1969–1976. Vol. XXIX: Eastern Europe; Eastern Mediterranean, 1969–1972* (Washington DC: Government Printing Office, 2007), 1092–1093.

four by 1972). The toughest problem, as Nixon perceived it, was that Ankara did not possess full control over its territory (a predicament that plagued opium-producing states such as Laos and Thailand). Handley suggested that it would probably cost $50 million of American aid, delivered over the course of three-to-four years, to "get Turkey out of the opium business." Nixon, who pointedly declared drug use in the United States a "national security issue," stated that he would pay $50 million "in one year if it would get the job done."[58]

On 26 June, four days before Ankara was contractually obligated to dictate its opium harvesting policy for the following year, American and Turkish officials achieved a final breakthrough in their negotiations. Contrary to expectations, Erim agreed to a policy of total opium eradication following the end of harvest in 1971. In exchange for this declaration, the United States would offer opium farmers $15 million to be donated over the next three-to-four years. Washington was also obligated to deliver an additional $10 million in aid in the fiscal years of 1972 and 1973. Erim further requested that Nixon issue a statement affirming America's friendship with Turkey and fully recognize Ankara's efforts on eradication. Furthermore, Erim requested that Nixon explicitly promise American help for affected areas and that US-Turkish military collaboration continue unimpeded. In explaining the sudden escalation in Ankara's plans to implement the eradication program, Erim told Handley that the United States had "a reliable ally in Turkey and that in the end it was not money but friendship that induced him to make the decision for eradication."[59]

On the eve of the declaration, Erim's Foreign Minister, Osman Olcay, convened one last meeting at his home with William Handley to discuss the final details of the opium agreement. Olcay, who had been in Iran during earlier discussions between Handley and Erim, claimed he was not fully privy to the parameters of the final negotiations that occurred. Two issues, in his reading of the agreement, remained outstanding. First, the $10 million dollars the United States had allocated to the Turkish government in aid did not seem sufficient. Secondly, he questioned whether the United States could uphold its promise to extend long-term aid to farmers forced to abandon opium cultivation. On both counts, Hadley was firm and forthright. The opium issue, Hadley contended, encompassed the "entire range" of US-Turkish relations. "$35 million," he added cryptically, "was not a small amount when you consider what else Turkey is getting." When it came to affirming the American promise of future aid, Hadley was even more blunt. Many in the US Congress, he warned Olcay, were considering cutting off aid to Turkey altogether because of the opium issue. In light of these veiled threats and

[58] Memorandum of Conversation, 14 June 1971, *Foreign Relations of the United States, 1969–1976. Vol. XXIX: Eastern Europe; Eastern Mediterranean, 1969–1972* (Washington DC: Government Printing Office, 2007), 1096–1098.

[59] Memorandum from Secretary of State Rogers to President Nixon, 28 June 1971, *Foreign Relations of the United States, 1969–1976. Vol. XXIX: Eastern Europe; Eastern Mediterranean, 1969–1972* (Washington DC: Government Printing Office, 2007), 1099–1100.

pronouncements, the Turkish foreign minister gave his final approval to the agreement with only minor American alterations.[60]

On 1 July, Erim issued the declaration banning the planting of opium poppies after 1972. In explaining his decision, the prime minister struck a compassionate and emotive tone. "The youth of the world," he declared, "has taken on an oppressive calamity." Members of the international community had taken notice of the disparities in the official collection and processing of opium in Turkey and were concerned with the problem of illicit diversion. A total ban on opium production would address this calamity plaguing young people and fulfill Turkey's commitments to international agreements on counter-trafficking.[61] Richard Nixon, who held a brief press conference that same day, lauded Erim's "courageous, statesmanlike action." The accord, the president declared, was "by far the most significant breakthrough that has been achieved in stopping the source of heroin in our worldwide offensive against dangerous drugs."[62]

With an agreement in hand, representatives in Washington and Ankara turned to the challenges of oversight and development in lieu of the cessation of opium production in Anatolia. The BNDD continued to assist both police and gendarmes in monitoring the end of the opium trade. As the ban began to take effect, BNDD agents accompanied Turkish officers in closing down illicitly produced morphine and opium in the province in Afyon.[63] BNDD agents also continued to provide technical assistance and training to both policemen and gendarmes (such as establishing English classes for young cadets).[64] In June of 1972, Turkey's Finance Ministry came to a final agreement with American officials on the transfer of $35.7 million in aid.[65] The Nixon administration, elated with its victory, formally invited Nihat Erim to the White House in May 1972, allowing the president to personally thank his Turkish counterpart for his efforts in bringing the Turkish opium question to an end.[66] Soon after Erim's departure from Washington, Nixon signed legislation endowing $1 billion in funds for the office of the country's first "drug czar" (more formally known as the Special Office for Drug Abuse Prevention). The audience assembled before the president

60 Telegram from the American Embassy in Turkey to the Department of State, 30 June 1971, *Foreign Relations of the United States, 1969–1976. Vol. XXIX: Eastern Europe; Eastern Mediterranean, 1969–1972* (Washington DC: Government Printing Office, 2007), 1101–1104. One of the few modifications Olcay suggested, that Handley readily agreed to, was language in the agreement that stipulated that the Turkish Grand National Assembly would pass legislation banning the planting of poppies. How, Olcay questioned, could a "democratic country" guarantee passage of any legislation? Handley agreed and altered the agreement to state that the assembly would "undertake to seek passage banning further opium poppy production."

61 Erhan, *Beyaz Savaş: Türk-Amerikan İlişkilerinde Afyon Sorunu*, 121–122.

62 John Herbers, "Nixon Says Turks Agree to Ban the Opium Poppy," *The New York Times* 30 June 1971.

63 Izmir to Ankara, 8 October 1972, Ankara 7082, Subject Numeric Files, 1970–73, RG 59, NAB.

64 American Ambassador Ankara to Secretary of State, 1 December 1972, Ankara 8534, Subject Numeric Files, 1970–73, RG 59, NAB.

65 Erhan, *Beyaz Savaş: Türk-Amerikan İlişkilerinde Afyon Sorunu*, 129.

66 Erhan, *Beyaz Savaş: Türk-Amerikan İlişkilerinde Afyon Sorunu*, 128.

cheered when mention was made of Ankara's ongoing commitment to maintaining the ban on opium production.[67]

Robert Greene and his team from *Newsday* did cast some doubt on the level of cooperation the United States actually received from Turkey in the months following the 1971 declaration. After visiting the village of Değirmendere in the province of Afyon, reporters took pictures of a hidden cache of poppy seeds farmers had saved in anticipation of the ban.[68] American officials, speaking off the record, cast doubt upon the figures presented to them by Turkish officials regarding the amount of opium harvested between 1970 and 1972.[69] More importantly, *Newsday* and other publications in the United States and Turkey echoed the dismay of provincial farmers threatened by the impending end of poppy harvesting. Peasants speaking to reporters in 1972 repeatedly voiced fears that poverty loomed for all those affected by the ban.[70]

The Nixon administration's policies towards Turkey received particularly damning coverage from Jack Anderson, the *Washington Post*'s famed political insider and muckraking reporter. In January 1973, Anderson reported that Ankara secretly requested an additional $400 million in aid in order to compensate the country's opium farmers. According to a secret report from the Government Accountability Office (GAO), Turkish generals also demanded greater American support for the sitting military-backed government. The survival of the current government was directly linked to the opium issue since, the report claimed, the military (which was not dependent upon popular support) had approved the ban. Once democracy returned to Turkey, it appeared doubtful that Nixon's agreement with Turkey would survive.[71]

Through his personal sources, Anderson also reported that he had received secret correspondence from within the BNDD. According to the documents in his possession, the BNDD did have confidence in Orhan Erbuğ, the head of the DPS. Even though the BNDD appeared satisfied with the progression of the ban, doubts continued to linger within the bureau regarding the accountability of officers within the DPS. According to one intelligence report, Abdullah Pektaş, who had begun his work with the DPS following the 1960 coup and had assisted the FBN in multiple investigations, was suspected of meeting with "a major narcotics trafficker." As a result of this meeting, Pektaş had reputedly ordered junior officers not to harrass the trafficker any further.[72]

Political developments in Turkey added further complications to the prospects of maintaining the ban. Internal strife within the government forced Nihat Erim to resign from his position as prime minister in December 1971. Although Turkish President Cevdet Sunay reappointed him to his post within days of his resignation,

[67] Dana Adams Schmidt, "Nixon Signs Law to Curb Drug Abuse," *New York Times* 22 March 1972.

[68] Newsday, *The Heroin Trail*, 5–8.

[69] Newsday, *The Heroin Trail*, 16.

[70] Juan de Onis, "Opium Poppy Gone, Turkish Farmers Ask Why Has U.S. Done This to Us?" *New York Times* 9 August 1973.

[71] Jack Anderson, "Turks Warn on Poppy-Growing," *Washington Post* 8 January 1973.

[72] Anderson, "Turks Warn on Poppy-Growing."

Erim, citing health reasons, then formally left politics in May 1972. Instability continued to hamper the succeeding government of Ferit Melen, who called for a general election in the spring of 1973. While not resulting in an immediate victory, the Republican Peoples' Party, headed by Bülent Ecevit, emerged in January 1974 as the dominant party within a coalition government with the recently founded National Salvation Party (NSP). Ecevit's ascendency to the position of prime minister concomitantly entailed the rise of the NSP's founder, Necmettin Erbakan, to the forefront of national politics. As an outspoken advocate of Islamist politics, Erbakan shared little in common ideologically with his senior partner. Nevertheless, both men agreed in principle to rescind the 1971 opium ban.[73]

Ecevit's government first broached a renegotiation of the opium agreement with the United States a month after attaining power. In early February 1974, Turkey's new prime minister met with William Macomber, who assumed the role of ambassador to Turkey following William Handley's departure in 1973. The meeting between the two men was cordial but strained. Ecevit informed Macomber that he had not fully made up his mind regarding Turkey's position on opium production but appeared to be leaning towards a resumption of poppy cultivation. The American ambassador asserted that an agreement had been reached between the two countries, a claim his Turkish counterpart vigorously disputed. "No self-respecting government," Ecevit contended, "would ever make such an agreement" and declared that the policy was the result of Ankara's unilateral action. In considering an abrogation of the ban, two principal issues concerned the prime minister. The ban had left many farmers unemployed and impoverished, a state of affairs that led directly to RPP's victory in a general election. Moreover, the world was facing a shortage of medical grade morphine, which other opium-producing states were unable to address. If opium production did resume, Macomber was assured that the drug would be cultivated on state run farms, thus limiting the possibility of illicit diversion into the black market.[74]

Harold Saunders of the National Security Council, in a subsequent memo to Henry Kissinger, admitted that it was not clear what Ecevit's true desires were with regards to a renegotiation of Turkey's opium policies. While it was expected that more money could be demanded from the United States to implement the ban, Saunders was conscious of the prime minister's public pledges to rescind the ban altogether. Reversing the ban certainly possessed significant risks (chief among them being the uncertain state of Ankara's controls over production in the future). Nevertheless, resumed opium cultivation did liberate the United States from "an endless chain of Turkish demands for financial compensation." He advocated that

[73] Ahmad, The Making of Modern Turkey, 303–319.

[74] American Embassy Ankara to Secretary of State, 7 February 1974, no document number, Box 632; National Security Council (NSC) Files, Country Files—Middle East; Richard Nixon Presidential Library and Museum, Yorba Linda, California.

American negotiators begin with a "tough stand" that could be softened as discussions progressed.[75]

In March 1974, the Turkish Foreign Ministry officially informed the State Department that the sowing of poppy seeds would begin anew on state-controlled farms in the province of Afyon. Turkish Agricultural Minister Korkut Özal declared that the new regime, which would formally commence in October of that year, would allow for greater control and oversight of opium production on newly created state-run farms.[76] This first sign of Turkey's reversal on opium cultivation had been expected within the White House. As early as 11 March, the National Security Council suggested that "sympathetic consideration be given to the option of US acquiescence in Turkish resumption of production." In addition to freeing the United States from further commitments of monetary aid, Harold Saunders and Henry Appelbaum of the NSC staff stated that "a completely hardline, negative stance" would hurt American-Turkish relations and result in unilateral production either with or without government controls put into place.[77]

Heated discussion between the State Department and the Turkish Foreign Ministry continued through the spring, resulting in a postponement of a final decision on the opium question until the summer of 1974. In the meantime, two Congressmen from the State of New York, Charles Rangel and Lester Wolff, visited Turkey in order to survey the prospects of Turkey's future opium policies. The hostile welcome they received from officials and farmers led the two New York representatives (who represented the heroin-plagued districts of Harlem and Nassau County, respectively) to put greater pressure upon the Nixon administration to maintain a hardline stance against Ankara. Both Congressmen questioned Turkey's strategic and military value as an American ally when considering Washington's options in dealing with a resumption of Turkish opium production. In an effort to placate his constituency in Harlem, Rangel openly contemplated severance of all military aid to Turkey. "The hell with them," he declared, "if they violate their agreement."[78]

Ecevit notified the US Embassy of the government's formal decision on opium production on 1 July 1974. According to new bylaws, poppy cultivation could continue in seven provinces that coming fall. William Maccomber, US ambassador to Turkey, reacted to this news with a stern warning to the prime minister. Odds on, Congress would cancel all military aid to Turkey, thus bringing US-Turkish relations to their lowest point since the Second World War. Ecevit, clearly confident in

[75] Memorandum for Secretary Kissinger, 15 Februrary 1974, no document number, Box 632; National Security Council (NSC) Files, Country Files—Middle East; Richard Nixon Presidential Library and Museum, Yorba Linda, California.

[76] "Turk is Bringing Opium Message," *New York Times* 13 March 1971.

[77] Memorandum for Secretary Kissinger, 11 March 1974, no document number, Box 632; National Security Council (NSC) Files, Country Files—Middle East; Richard Nixon Presidential Library and Museum, Yorba Linda, California.

[78] Memorandum of Conversation, 8 April 1974, no document number, Box 632; National Security Council (NSC) Files, Country Files—Middle East; Richard Nixon Presidential Library and Museum, Yorba Linda, California; Erhan, *Beyaz Savaş: Türk-Amerikan İlişkilerinde Afyon Sorunu*, 136–137.

the final ruling, replied that he "would have thought Turkish-American relations ran deeper" than the ambassador supposed. Besides, turning back, in his estimation, was now an impossibility. Retaining the ban "would result in no government, and no relationship with [the] US."[79]

While considering the dire consequence American policymakers envisioned following Ankara's change in political course, intervening events that summer served to smooth the way back to more peaceable relations between the United States and Turkey. On 20 July, Turkish troops stormed across the beaches outside of Girne in Northern Cyprus. The escalation of military tensions between Turkey and Greece in the early part of that year clearly weighed far more heavily upon the mind of Henry Kissinger, who met with Turkish Foreign Minister Turan Güneş three months before the reversal of the ban. During their half-hour conversation, the topic of Cyprus and Greco-Turkish relations occupied the bulk of their attention. Kissinger, at the close of discussions, only modestly reiterated the American position on opium cultivation, suggesting that the minister "consider American public opinion." Güneş assured Kissinger that Turkey "was not going to be poisoning anybody" and that plans for a strict oversight regime on opium production was forthcoming. Kissinger agreed that Turkey and the United States wanted the same thing and that he had "learned more" than he wanted "to know about opium" in recent weeks. "I may go into the business myself," Kissinger quipped as the meeting adjourned.[80]

Richard Nixon's political life came to a crashing end within weeks of Ankara's decision on opium. Two weeks after Nixon's resignation, Gerald Ford approved of Kissinger's suggestion to commence negotiations over American assistance for Turkish new opium control measures. In an effort to please Congress, Ford also agreed that Ankara be informed that American military and economic assistance could be severed should Turkey not take adequate steps to prevent narcotics smuggling in the United States (a procedure which was in keeping with the Foreign Assistance Act of 1961).[81]

Greco-Turkish hostilities on the island of Cyprus, as opposed to the question of opium, served to negate Ford's hopes of pacifying Congress. In February 1975, Congress passed an arms embargo against Turkey due to the illegal use of American weaponry during the Cyprus conflict. Ankara responded with the seizure of American military instillations and threats to reconsider its broader military alliance with the United States. Fearing a total collapse of Turkish-American relations, Ford, on an official visit to Helsinki in July, met with Süleyman Demirel (who

[79] Telegram from the American Embassy in Turkey to the Department of State, 2 July 1974, *Foreign Relations of the United States, 1969–1976. Vol. XXIX: Eastern Europe; Eastern Mediterranean, 1969–1972* (Washington DC: Government Printing Office, 2007), 669.

[80] Memorandum of Conversation, 15 April 1974, *Foreign Relations of the United States, 1969–1976. Vol. XXX: Greece; Cyprus; Turkey, 1973–1976* (Washington DC: Government Printing Office, 2007), 666.

[81] Memorandum from the President's Assistant for National Security Affairs (Kissinger) to President Ford, 21 August 1974, *Foreign Relations of the United States, 1969–1976. Vol. XXX: Greece; Cyprus; Turkey, 1973–1976* (Washington DC: Government Printing Office, 2007), 678–682.

succeeded Ecevit as prime minister after a general election in March). The meeting, according to official minutes, passed cordially. Ford reported to Demirel that efforts were being made in the Senate to lift the embargo. The only sticking point, according to the president, was the potential resistance of the "black congressman" Charlie Rangel, who continued to press for greater reforms on the opium issue in Turkey. After Demirel summarized a series of control measures enacted (such as limiting the acreage of land used for cultivation and the establishment of a new counter-narcotics unit), Ford appeared pleased and promised to meet with Rangel in order to assuage his fears. With that, the two heads of state returned to more pressing issues involving Cyprus.[82]

The question of Turkey's stand on opium cultivation largely faded from American public view after 1975. Despite some initial outrage from elements of the American press, attention in Washington during the Ford and Carter administrations turned instead towards southeast Asia as a front for the suppression of illicit narcotics trafficking. Given the seriousness with which the Nixon administration approached Ankara's policies towards opium, as well as the rapid changes in political tack that occurred during the early 1970s, one may well ask what effect this era had upon American-Turkish relations on the issue of heroin and narcotics trafficking. In historical hindsight, the Nixon era represented an abrupt sea change in both the approach and significance of drug politics in both countries. For the first time since the interwar period, law enforcement bodies on both sides of the Atlantic occupied a secondary role in negotiations between Turkey and the United States on issues related to drugs and smuggling. The force and urgency with which the White House and the State Department sought to engage both civilian and military leaders in Ankara did prompt, for a brief time at least, decisive and comprehensive changes to the ways in which the narcotics trade between the two countries was approached. While Ecevit's intervention in the negotiations in 1974 did lead to a complete reversal in the policies of the United States and Turkey, all available sources, as we shall see, suggest that Nixon's aggressive policies did succeed to some extent. The Republic of Turkey, by 1980, did cease to be a major producer of illicit opium on the world stage.

Yet, taking a broader look at the emerging patterns of the international narcotics trade during the 1970s, this brief episode in American-Turkish foreign relations appears only to have changed the nature of Turkey's role within the illicit transnational market. Well before Nixon formally announced his war on drugs, internal reports circulating within the US government pointed to the commencement of a new order in both Turkey and the global drug trade. More than anything, Turkey's brief experiment with opium prohibition only conditioned the pace and magnitude of these seismic shifts.

[82] Memorandum of Conversation, 31 July 1975, *Foreign Relations of the United States, 1969–1976. Vol. XXX: Greece; Cyprus; Turkey, 1973–1976* (Washington DC: Government Printing Office, 2007), 772–774.

DISSECTING THE HEROIN EPIDEMIC: TURKEY AND CHANGING PATTERNS OF THE INTERNATIONAL DRUG TRADE

Between 1970 and 1972, the CIA produced at least three general studies analyzing the evolving state of heroin trafficking from the Republic of Turkey. In the first report from October 1970, "The World Opium Situation," specific attention is given to Turkey's evolution as a center of opium production. CIA sources, in surveying patterns of trade up until the mid-1950s, affirmed many of the conclusions previously reached by the FBN and others. Virtually all illicit opium harvested in Turkey in the immediate postwar period was exported to its neighbors to the south and east. Only a portion of this trade flowed directly, as opium, to France and Italy for processing into morphine and heroin. During this era, which featured the end of Chinese production, Turkish opium faced stiff competition in the illegal global marketplace from Iranian and Indian sources.[83]

The CIA noticed a series of discernible shifts in the nature of Turkish smuggling activities after 1955. Tehran's decision to ban opium production in 1955 sparked a sudden rise in illicit smuggling in Turkey as well as in Afghanistan and Pakistan. Similar rises also occurred in the mid-1950s in Burma, Laos, and Thailand. In the wake of the Iranian ban, consumers and traffickers in Europe and North America turned to Turkish-derived opiates to satisfy demand. Increasingly, smugglers between Turkey, France, and Italy contrived new routes directly across Mediterranean shipping lanes as well as overland through eastern and central Europe. By 1970, morphine, instead of raw opium, was the primary form of illicit Turkish exports.[84]

In their assessment of affairs in October 1970, the CIA appeared hopeful that recent steps taken by Ankara would curb illicit production in Turkey. The total acreage of land used for poppy cultivation had reportedly dropped from 42,000 to 13,000 hectares between 1960 and 1969. The corresponding production of legally harvested opium dropped by more than half (from 365 to 127 tons). Greater enforcement measures undertaken in Turkey, Iran, France, and the United States also appeared to be hindering illicit smuggling out of Asia Minor. These progressive measures, however, came at a cost. CIA sources reported a rise in production and smuggling of opium out of Afghanistan. In 1969, the Agency also reported that heroin trafficking out of the "Far East" had increased "perhaps several fold." In the midst of this ballooning pattern of smuggling and cultivation in central and eastern Asia, crime groups in Marseille, which faced increasing pressure at the hands of French police, had begun to diversify and disperse their heroin refinement operation to other corners of Europe. Even in the United States, new trafficking syndicates, such as those comprising Cuban exiles, were beginning to emerge.[85]

83 "The World Opium Situation," October 1970, CIA-RDP73B00296R000300060031-9, CIA Records Search Tool (CREST); National Archives Building II, College Park, MD.

84 "The World Opium Situation," October 1970.

85 "The World Opium Situation," October 1970.

A far more refined and specific CIA study of Turkish drug trafficking was produced in December 1971. Entitled "French-Turkish Connection," this second study focused greater attention upon the mechanics of smuggling operations across the Mediterranean and Europe. While making no projections about the future of opium production in the aftermath of the 1971 ban, the CIA offers a damning assessment of law enforcement efforts over the previous decades. The price of illicit morphine, depending on the location of purchase, had declined or remained the same over the decade. Although greater international controls on narcotics trafficking did create "more problems for the traffickers," authorities had seized only a small portion of the opium and morphine smuggled out of Turkey. For all the efforts expended, the CIA observed "no critical shortages" in the materials needed for the production of heroin.[86] Even with Turkey's ban on opium, it was estimated that traffickers would turn to Yugoslav, Afghan, or southeast Asian sources, thus causing a "major realignment in the smuggling routes now serving French traffickers." In any event, French traffickers had begun to stockpile Turkish morphine as early as 1970 in anticipation of Turkey's prohibitionist policies.[87]

In addition to considering past events, the "French-Turkish Connection" report offered even more striking revelations regarding the state of the heroin trade in 1971. With Turkey's prohibition upon opium production looming, the CIA noticed a dramatic reorientation in smuggling patterns out of Turkey. The smuggling of raw opium between Turkey and Syria, once a major corridor of traffic, had begun to recede.[88] While Lebanese merchants continued to play a defined role in trade, smugglers out of Beirut were increasingly shipping refined Turkish morphine between Turkey and France (either directly or via Lebanon). These changes in trafficking patterns also entailed the emergence of two new weigh stations for the transshipment of Turkish morphine and heroin. By 1971 the Federal Republic of Germany, the CIA gathered, had begun to emerge as a central clearing house for heroin distribution activities in both Europe and further on in North America. Traffickers, in anticipation of the 1971 ban, had established depots throughout both West Germany and Turkey containing one- to two-ton deposits of morphine. While middlemen in West Germany were often compelled to pay between 50 percent and 300 percent more for morphine than their competitors in France, use of German storage facilities allowed added protection and security while transferring Turkish morphine to the refinement laboratories in Marseille and elsewhere.

The second, and more surprising, new nexus of Turkish drug trafficking identified by the CIA was Bulgaria. "The role of Bulgaria in the field of international

[86] Directorate of Intelligence, "The French-Turkish Connection: The Movement of Opium and Morphine Base from Turkey to France (December 1971)," CIA-RDP 73B00296R000300070022-8, CIA Records Search Tool (CREST), National Archives and Records Administration, College Park, MD.

[87] Directorate of Intelligence, "The French-Turkish Connection: The Movement of Opium and Morphine Base from Turkey to France (December 1971)."

[88] Directorate of Intelligence, "The French-Turkish Connection: The Movement of Opium and Morphine Base from Turkey to France (December 1971)." According to the CIA, this change was in part due to the fallout of the Six-Day War in 1967.

narcotics," according to the Agency, "has increased tremendously in the last several years." This Warsaw Pact state, it seemed, was more than just a transitory stop for smugglers carrying their wares from east to west. Instead, CIA sources suggested than an air of official collusion seemed to preside over the trade within Bulgaria's borders. Bulgarian trucks carrying Turkish cargo were rarely stopped for inspection. Narcotics smugglers, when caught, often received only a small fine and were compelled to repurchase the drugs for a certain percentage of their estimated value. Bulgaria, as a whole, had become a "safe haven" for Turkish drug smugglers who used Sofia as a center for both narcotics and arms sales.[89]

A third report, produced by the CIA's Critical Collection Problems Committee, was produced in October 1972. As a study of "intelligence activities against narcotics and dangerous drugs," the report adds few new details to the nature of Turkish drug trafficking activities during this era. With its focus upon current governmental capabilities to track and evaluate contemporary trends in the narcotics trade, the study reflects instead upon the gaps in the Agency's knowledge of the state of affairs in the world heroin market. In the case of Turkey, a variety of state agencies, including the Department of State, the Department of Agriculture, the BNDD, and the CIA did possess good intelligence on the nature and scale of opium production in Anatolia. What remained unclear, even with the aid of Turkish official sources, was the degree to which local growers, traffickers, and smugglers had cached stocks of opium (seemingly an especially acute problem with the ban now in full effect). The CIA also pleaded ignorance to the state of opium production in Afghanistan, and to some degree, Pakistan. One year after the drafting of the "French-Turkish Connection" report, the CIA remained uncertain as to how traffickers in France would replace Turkish morphine in its heroin production. Even the location of functioning heroin processing laboratories, in the wake of Paris's crackdown on traffickers in Marseille, generally remained a mystery.[90]

Unfortunately, the archival record in the United States offers no insights into how American government officials perceived the Turkish heroin trade in the years between 1972 and 1979. State Department, BNDD, and Drug Enforcement Administration (DEA) records remain classified or unreleased (with no indication if and when they will be made available to the public). Nevertheless, one study does shed further light upon the trends first documented by the CIA in the early 1970s. As the Carter administration came to a close, investigators under Attorney General Benjamin Civiletti initiated a study on the influx of heroin from southwest Asia into the United States. Peter Bensinger, head of the DEA, highlighted the problem to his counterparts in the Department of Justice in a letter addressed to Civilletti's deputy attorney general in December 1979. Recent seizures, according to Bensinger, had pointed to an increased availability and purity of heroin

[89] Directorate of Intelligence, "The French-Turkish Connection: The Movement of Opium and Morphine Base from Turkey to France (December 1971)."

[90] Critical Collection Problems Committee, "Intelligence Activities Against Narcotics and Dangerous Drugs," October 1972, CIA-RDP88B00365R000200050042-6, CIA Records Search Tool (CREST), National Archives and Records Administration, College Park, MD.

in the country. As an example, the DEA chief cited the August 1979 arrest in New York of two Turkish nationals, alongside two local Cuban associates, in possession of nine pounds of pure heroin. The origin of this heroin was the so-called "Golden Crescent" of Afghanistan, Pakistan, and Iran. This upsurge in heroin trafficking imperiled both the United States and countries in Europe. According to Bensinger, more than 600 people had died over the course of 1979 as a result of heroin overdoses. Considering the outbreak of revolution in Iran and the recent Soviet invasion of Afghanistan, there appeared to be little chance that effective controls could be placed upon the source of this new heroin epidemic.[91]

Turks, according to Justice Department sources, occupied the central hub of this trade. Opium sold at local bazaars was often purchased by Iranian or Turkish middlemen. Trafficking between Iran and Turkey, which was the main supply route during the initial stages of the trade, was in the hands of Turkish Kurds who processed the opium into heroin and morphine in clandestine labs close to the border. Turkish smugglers then exported the drugs to Europe via a number of different routes. Some smuggled heroin overland to depots or refinement centers in Sicily, northern Italy, southern France, or into Germany via the Balkans. A certain percentage passed through East Germany via flights on East German Airlines (since customs oversight at Schönenfeld Airport was notoriously lax). Within Europe, sources suspected Iranian and Turkish dealers of selling smaller amounts of heroin to importers bound for the United States. As seen in the New York case, some Turkish dealers were even venturing into the United States intent on distributing the heroin themselves.[92]

Clearly a revolution was afoot in the 1970s. Within the course of a decade, syndicates within Turkey had largely ceased to be the producers and purveyors of raw opium for manufacturers and smugglers based in Europe and North America. Turkish criminal groups, by 1980, instead came to define themselves as wholesalers and retailers of heroin, a status that afforded them both greater profits and greater influence within the trade. Signs pointing to this fundamental change in Turkish drug trafficking are visible, in fits and starts, as early as the 1950s. The confluence of factors that led to this change comprised both pressures from inside and outside of Turkey.

To understand this transformative era in history, one must first appreciate the dramatic supply and demand shifts within the world narcotics market that impacted Turkey's role within the heroin trade. Perhaps the first, and most significant, factor to influence Turkish opium producers and smugglers was the onset and sudden abrogation of the Iranian prohibition regime. Tehran's tough stand on opium production and addiction discernibly gave cause for a rise in opium production. Similar reactions were seen, as discussed earlier, in Afghanistan and Pakistan. The Shah's decision to reverse the ban in 1969 did not halt opium

[91] Peter Bensinger to Paul Michel, 31 December 1979, Subject Files of Attorney General Epstein, Southwest Asian Heroin, RG 60, NAB.

[92] Peter Bensinger to Paul Michel, 31 December 1979, Subject Files of Attorney General Epstein, Southwest Asian Heroin, RG 60, NAB.

imports into Iran. Turkey's own brief experiment with opium prohibition, it seems however, served to further stimulate opiate production in Afghanistan and Pakistan. According to the CIA's 1971 study on the issue, buyers and suppliers in Iran increasingly sought out trafficking networks in Pakistan and Afghanistan to fulfill local demand.[93] Some in the American press speculated as early as 1973 that Afghan opium was beginning to have an impact upon the American heroin market as well.[94] Afghanistan's ascendency as a center for raw opium production appeared to have influenced Turkish smuggling networks in the wake of the 1971 ban. While traffickers had prepared for the last poppy harvest by stockpiling caches of raw opium and morphine, American documents give no indication that Turkish smuggling rings expected a resumption of the pre-1971 status quo. Instead, the CIA and Justice Department studies suggest that Turkish traffickers counted upon Afghanistan to take up the slack left by Turkey's new governmental regime on opium production.

It appears that Turkish smugglers also benefited from similar fluctuations in other parts of the world heroin market during the 1970s. As the American war in Vietnam drew to a close, investigators and analysts documented a dramatic rise in consumption of southeast Asian heroin in the United States. The growing seizure rate of heroin from Thailand, Laos, and Burma prompted swift action from the Nixon administration in 1973, leading to an intense bilateral effort by the DEA to suppress opium production at their various sources. Washington initiated a similarly intense program of engagement with Mexican law enforcement in 1975 in the hopes of striking out against opium cultivation in the north and west of the country.[95] American endeavors in Thailand and Mexico did bear some fruit, leading to substantial drops in heroin consumption by the late 1970s.[96] Since no single competitor emerged to replace the pre-eminent position Turkish heroin once held in the American marketplace, conditions were right, according to the DEA, for Turkish smugglers to ply heroin from Afghanistan or Pakistan in the United States with greater ease and availability.[97]

93 "The French-Turkish Connection: The Movement of Opium and Morphine Base from Turkey to France (December 1971)," CIA-RDP 73B00296R000300070022-8, CIA Records Search Tool (CREST), NARA; "Opium Production in Iran," 7 July 1971, CIA/ORR Job[?] SOTO 1315A, Box 24, Folder S-3686-S3716.

94 Jack Anderson, "Corsicans Set Up 'Afghan Connection,'" *The Washington Post* 2 March 1973; Stanley Karnow, "U.S. Fears Increased Flow of Heroin from New Sources," *The Washington Post* 6 September 1972.

95 McCoy, "Stimulus of Prohibition," 48–49. The effect of these campaigns are, however, doubted by the writings of Jonathan Marshall and Bertil Lintner. See Bertil Lintner, "Heroin and Highland Insurgency in the Golden Triangle," in Alfred McCoy and Alan Block (eds.), *War on Drugs: Studies in the Failure of U.S. Narcotics Policy* (Boulder, Colorado: Westview Press, 1992), 296; Jonathan Marshall, "CIA Assets and the Rise of the Guadalajara Connection," in Alfred McCoy and Alan Block (eds.), *War on Drugs: Studies in the Failure of U.S. Narcotics Policy* (Boulder, CO: Westview Press, 1992), 202–203.

96 DEA, "Threat Assessment: Middle East Heroin," 6 December 1979, Subject Files of Attorney General Epstein, Southwest Asian Heroin, RG 60, NAB.

97 DEA, "Threat Assessment: Middle East Heroin."

Changes in patterns of demand also contributed to the ability of Turkish traffickers to navigate the oscillating nature of the world heroin market during the 1970s. While Washington's robust policies towards narcotics trafficking did appear to lead to substantial declines in heroin use in the United States, demand outside of North America exploded during the decade. At the expense of declining amounts of heroin from southeast Asia, "Middle East heroin" (smuggled by Turks and Iranians) enjoyed a preferred status among users in the Netherlands and Italy in the late 1970s. The impact was felt with even greater force in West Germany, which possessed an addict population of between 68,000 and 80,000 people by 1979.[98] Australia also witnessed increased rates of heroin addiction and drug seizures (although it appears many of the country's users relied upon southeast Asian heroin sources).[99]

These changes in international conditions do not completely explain the causes of Turkey's transformation during this period. While various fluctuations in production and demand of heroin allowed Turkey to remain relevant in the drug trade, such factors do not explain the ability of traffickers, and perhaps producers, of opiates to adapt to the evolving circumstances at home and abroad. In some sense, traffickers based in Turkey had long maintained a supple infrastructure that permitted opiate exports through multiple routes. While FBN agents did repeatedly emphasize the centrality of the smuggling route through Syria and Lebanon, officers reporting from the mid-1950s understood that major Istanbul wholesalers also relied upon direct sea traffic between Turkey and France as a means to bring morphine to refiners in Marseille. The establishment of a Balkan route, across Turkey's Greek and Bulgarian borders, also existed during this time as well (although traffickers tended to prefer routes via Lebanon or direct to Marseille).[100] The emergence of Bulgaria and Germany as important connections in Turkish heroin trafficking in the early 1970s appears to break, at face value, many of the precedents established in the immediate postwar era. Yet, as one peruses American reports from the 1950s and 1960s, it seems that the establishment of an overland Balkan and central European route was a process that gradually took hold.

A critical factor leading to the opening of Bulgaria as an important transit center for narcotics was the continued growth of the small arms trade during the middle of the twentieth century. Weapons, it seems, were an illicit commodity traded with some frequency in Turkey in the years immediately after the Second World War. As mentioned previously, İhsan Sekban, as well as others, traded in guns smuggled into Turkey as early as 1950.[101] It appears however that it was not until 1967 that

[98] DEA, "Threat Assessment: Middle East Heroin."

[99] McCoy, "Stimulus of Prohibition," 48–49.

[100] Memorandum Report, 22 October 1958; Turkey, 1957–59; FBN Files, 1916–70; DEA Records; RG 170, NAB.

[101] Charles Siragusa to Mr. H. J. Anslinger, 25 July 1950; Turkey, 1950; Subject Files of the Bureau of Narcotics and Dangerous Drugs, 1916–70; DEA Records, RG 170, NAB; Frank Sojat to Harry Anslinger, 5 February 1952, Turkey, 1951–52, FBN Files, 1916–70; DEA Records; RG 170, NAB.

the FBN finally devoted significant attention to the connection between the arms and heroin trades in Turkey.[102] Speaking shortly before the FBN's transformation into the BNDD, John Cusack reported to the State Department that the arms trade had served as a means to finance the narcotics trade in Turkey since the early 1950s. A Turkish trafficker, he estimated, accrued a 500 percent profit when he sold narcotics (presumably either heroin or morphine) in Europe. With the proceeds from drug sales, the same trafficker could buy arms (as well as cars, jewelry, and cosmetics) that were then smuggled back into Turkey, a transaction that then doubled his profits. Lebanese and Swiss banks, according to Cusack, were critical fixtures in this cycle of illicit trade, since much of the money a smuggler gleaned was often converted into stronger currencies than lira. He further stated that Turkish authorities were well aware of the existence of the drugs-for-arms trade but very rarely was action ever taken.[103]

Turkey in the mid-1960s, according to FBN sources, had become a "bridge" in the shipment of arms from Europe to Iraq, Syria, and Iran. As of 1967, between 2,000 and 3,000 handguns were smuggled into Turkey on a monthly basis. Much of these weapons, as well as ammunition, came from West German, Spanish, French, and Czechoslovak manufacturers. About three-quarters of the arms, according to the FBN, went to Kurdish resistance fighters loyal to Mustafa Barzani in northern Iraq. Kurds, it seems, were significant actors in the purchase of weapons for both domestic use and re-export, often paying in gold, as well as hard currency, for as many weapons as they could carry. Of all the weapons that entered Turkey during this period, the FBN posited that Bulgaria was the crucial wheel in the arms trade, with 70 percent of weapons smuggled out of Varna via fishing boat.[104]

Statistics from Turkey's urban police detachments and rural gendarmerie appear to speak to the growing availability of arms in Turkey's cities, small towns, and villages. While the records do not include tabulations for every month and do occasionally contains some discrepancies (thus making aggregate analysis impossible), we do get a good sense of the numbers of arms used in the course of violent crimes as well as the total of weapons uncovered as result of searches by law enforcement:

[102] According to Douglas Valentine, who interviewed Agent Richard Salmi, the CIA, with the FBN cooperation, had developed an interest in arms trafficking by 1967. Due to Bulgaria's connection to the Turkish arms trade, the CIA reportedly argued that domestic instability in Turkey was perhaps the work of the KGB. See Valentine, *Strength of the Wolf*, 401–404.

[103] American Embassy Ankara to Department of State, 18 December 1967, no file number, Subject Numeric Files, 1967–69; RG 59, NAB.

[104] American Embassy Ankara to Department of State, 18 December 1967, no file number, Subject Numeric Files, 1967–69; RG 59, NAB.

TURKISH NATIONAL POLICE STATISTICS: RIFLES AND HANDGUNS FOUND AS A RESULT OF CRIMES AND SEARCHES: 1964–1969[105]

	Jan.	Feb.	Mar.	Apr.	May	Jun.	Jul.	Aug.	Sept.	Oct.	Nov.	Dec.
1964												
Rifles in Crime	0		0									0
Rifles in Search	10		4									6
Handgun in Crime	36		92									51
Handgun Search	66		84									105
1965												
Rifles in Crime	0		0	0	13	2	0	1	0	1	0	0
Rifles Search	1		5	4	0	0	20	0	2	0	12	0
Handgun in Crime	27		50	41	71	46	64	66	72	57	156	57
Handgun Search	84		128	111	126	165	137	174	106	136	206	151
1966												
Rifles in Crime	0	0	0	0	2	1	0	0	0	0	9	0
Rifles Search	1	9	5	0	2	0	1	1	1	14	0	9
Handgun in Crime	60	90	60	98	90	81	91	79	86	59	95	49
Handgun Search	151	183	296	140	130	202	170	203	217	246	224	183
1967												
Rifles in Crime	0	0	5	0	0	0	1	0	2	0	1	0
Rifles Search	4	23	8	5	44	7	3	3	5	0	0	1
Handgun in Crime	78	68	83	116	331	107	99	108	115	116	126	7
Handgun Search	216	249	283	310	86	286	310	291	407	387	408	598
1968												
Rifles in Crime	0	1	0	1	1	0	1	1	1	1		0
Rifles Search	3	1	6	1	1	129	3	0	3	5		1
Handgun in Crime	100	85	95	144	149	153	137	133	156	112		7
Handgun Search	346	419	345	394	356	665	357	367	424	556		598
1969												
Rifles in Crime	0	0		0	2		0	1	0			
Rifles Search	3	4		40	11		0	1	1			
Handgun in Crime	123	132		158	151		191	209	243			
Handgun Search	496	336		581	402		533	585	506			

105 BCA 30.1.00.00.72.457.2, 11 March 1966; BCA 30.1.00.00.72.457.6, 20 May 1966; BCA 30.1.00.00.72.458.2, 7 February 1967; BCA 30.1.00.00.72.458.3, 4 March 1967; BCA 30.1.00.00.72.458.5, 4 April 1967; BCA 30.1.00.00.72.458.7, 7 June 1967; BCA 30.1.00.00.72.458.13, 17 July 1967; BCA 30.1.00.00.72.458.14, 7 August 1967; BCA 30.1.00.00.72.458.15, 9 September 1967; BCA 30.1.00.00.72.458.16, 16 October 1967; BCA 30.1.00.00.72.458.17, 10 November 1967; BCA 30.1.00.00.72.458.18, 6 December 1967; BCA 30.1.00.00.72.458.20, 9 January 1968; BCA 30.1.00.00.72.459.3, 7 December 1968; BCA 30.1.00.00.72.460.1, 8 February 1969; BCA 30.1.00.00.72.460.2, 11 March 1969; BCA 30.1.00.00.72.460.3, 8 April 1969; BCA 30.1.00.00.72.460.4, 5 June 1969; BCA 30.1.00.00.72.460.6, 3 July 1969; BCA 30.1.00.00.72.460.9, 5 September 1969; BCA 30.1.00.00.72.460.10, 3 October 1969; BCA 30.1.00.00.72.460.11, 8 November 1969.

TURKISH GENDARMERIE STATISTICS: RIFLES AND HANDGUNS FOUND AS A RESULT OF CRIMES AND SEARCHES: 1964–1969[106]

	Jan.	Feb.	Mar.	Apr.	May	Jun.	Jul.	Aug.	Sept.	Oct.	Nov.	Dec.
1964												
Rifles in Crime	11		18									15
Rifles Search	9		11									17
Handgun in Crime	101		183									159
Handgun Search	125		159									169
1965												
Rifles in Crime	10		12	0	21	28	6	21	20	17	0	17
Rifles Search	19		16	4	17	20	24	19	24	9	24	13
Handgun in Crime	124		142	41	269	215	209	182	22	135	167	140
Handgun Search	114		144	111	155	150	174	112	217	138	252	230
1966												
Rifles in Crime	4	41	12	0	25	26	19	38	29	17	12	12
Rifles Search	11	16	29	0	12	29	26	24	27	13	29	16
Handgun in Crime	119	190	228	98	234	177	219	276	254	283	222	163
Handgun Search	199	250	224	140	189	182	171	241	273	212	293	190
1967												
Rifles in Crime	8	3	15	14	22	26	90	19	21	15	18	9
Rifles Search	12	24	33	20	26	25	15	22	19	23	18	13
Handgun in Crime	158	143	225	267	215	258	247	265	306	239	196	198
Handgun Search	144	189	224	219	245	236	247	311	945	347	292	275
1968												
Rifles in Crime	3	12	14	10	12	26	22	23	22	13		12
Rifles Search	9	17	29	20	20	138	21	37	33	350		36
Handgun in Crime	240	204	274	278	289	329	227	349	270	281		238
Handgun Search	301	328	270	266	351	555	334	308	483	483		391
1969												
Rifles in Crime	15	3		19	14				14			
Rifles Search	11	24		14	38				27			
Handgun in Crime	266	143		276	291				205			
Handgun Search	512	189		306	336				306			

[106] BCA 30.1.00.00.72.457.2, 11 March 1966; BCA 30.1.00.00.72.457.6, 20 May 1966; BCA 30.1.00.00.72.458.2, 7 February 1967; BCA 30.1.00.00.72.458.3, 4 March 1967; BCA 30.1.00.00.72.458.5, 4 April 1967; BCA 30.1.00.00.72.458.7, 7 June 1967; BCA 30.1.00.00.72.458.13, 17 July 1967; BCA 30.1.00.00.72.458.14, 7 August 1967; BCA 30.1.00.00.72.458.15, 9 September 1967; BCA 30.1.00.00.72.458.16, 16 October 1967; BCA 30.1.00.00.72.458.17, 10 November 1967; BCA 30.1.00.00.72.458.18, 6 December 1967; BCA 30.1.00.00.72.458.20, 9 January 1968; BCA 30.1.00.00.72.459.3, 7 December 1968; BCA 30.1.00.00.72.460.1, 8 February 1969; BCA 30.1.00.00.72.460.2, 11 March 1969; BCA 30.1.00.00.72.460.3, 8 April 1969; BCA 30.1.00.00.72.460.4,

The growing significance of the arms trade from Europe (particularly West Germany) via Bulgaria points to another critical factor in the reorganization of the Turkish drug trade. For much of the history of the Turkish opiate trade, the role of Ottoman and Turkish nationals often began and ended within the borders of their native state. Even with the growing consolidation of the Istanbul wholesale market in the hands of Turkish Muslims in the 1950s, it appears that few Turkish nationals (save merchant sailors) were able to compete with foreign transnational smugglers of French or Italian origin. By the mid-1960s, this appears to have changed. One of the first allusions to this impending change came about in September 1966 in a meeting between Turkish Foreign Minister İhsan Çağlayangil and American Ambassador Martin. During the meeting, Çağlayangil mentioned to his counterpart that Turkish police had recently discovered a quantity of heroin hidden in a car carrying Turkish emigrants to central Europe. Interestingly, Ambassador Martin suggested that while the incident was representative of one pattern of illicit trade, far greater amounts of narcotics, he contended, passed across Turkey's border with Iran and Syria.[107]

As seen in the CIA and Justice Department reports cited earlier, the roles of Turkish immigrants living in Europe ultimately did usurp the prime positions once occupied by middlemen living in Aleppo or Beirut. Yet little is known about the first individuals who laid the foundation for Turkish heroin's rise within the central European marketplace. Official American studies only confirm the assumption that the first Turkish wholesalers and retailers were drawn from the increasing number of guest workers who came to live in Germany and elsewhere. A 1953 report submitted to the Arab League offers one interesting and provocative detail regarding the origins and character of some of the early trans-European smugglers from Turkey. In briefly surveying the state of drug trafficking in Turkey in contrast to the various states of the Middle East, Lewa Sawfat, director of the Bureau of Narcotics for the Arab League, made the following comment:

> This country is still a big source of raw opium and other white drugs in spite of the fact that the attention of the authorities had repeatedly been drawn to the activity of Turkish smugglers including some Albanian refugees.[108]

Sawfat's allusion to Albanian refugees strikes at a little-known, but ultimately deeply significant aspect of society and crime in Turkey. As mentioned earlier, over 180,000 Muslim citizens of Yugoslavia emigrated to Turkey between 1948 and 1970. As happened during previous eras of mass migrations out of the Balkans, the bulk of these immigrants and refugees were Albanian-speakers. Yet unlike the refugee crises of the late nineteenth and early twentieth centuries, this great wave of transplanted people did cause a kind of internal hysteria regarding security and

5 June 1969; BCA 30.1.00.00.72.460.6, 3 July 1969; BCA 30.1.00.00.72.460.9, 5 September 1969; BCA 30.1.00.00.72.460.10, 3 October 1969; BCA 30.1.00.00.72.460.11, 8 November 1969.

107 American Embassy Ankara to Department of State, 7 September 1966, Ankara 1186, Subject Numeric Files, 1970–73, RG 59, NAB.

108 "Report: Submitted to the Secretary General of the Arab League," 5 November 1953, Middle East File, 1930–67; Subject Files of the Bureau of Narcotics and Dangerous Drugs, 1916–70; DEA Records, RG 170, NAB.

crime within Turkey. These newcomers, by all accounts, did integrate readily and quickly into Turkish society. Some among these new citizens from Yugoslavia also retained personal and economic connections with their hometowns and relatives back in the Balkans. Others, it appears, also retained connections to family members and friends who joined the legions of foreign workers seeking opportunities for a better life in Europe and North America. By 1980, hundreds of thousands of individuals of Albanian descent came to settle in Germany, Switzerland, and the United States.[109] While American documents from the 1970s do not speak to the roles played by Albanians in the Turkish heroin trade, court cases and journalistic accounts from the 1980s and 1990s do shed some light upon the early development of Turkish-Albanian trafficking networks that, according to the Arab League, first came into existence as early as the mid-1950s.[110]

In 1984, federal prosecutors in New York brought drug trafficking and murder charges against several Albanian men from Yugoslavia. The men, prosecutors claimed, had started importing heroin into the New York City area in 1979. Over a brief period of time, the conspirators, Skender Fici and Xhevdet Lika, expanded their base of operations in the Lower Eastside of Manhattan to include distribution (a move that was accompanied with the killing of a rival in a downtown restaurant). Federal prosecutors (such as Rudolph Giuliani) upheld the Fici/Lika case as representative of an emerging threat of Albanian gangs operating in New York City. Central to the sudden ascendency of individuals like Xhevdet Lika were their personal connections to Turkish and Yugoslav heroin wholesalers. Lika, for example, was known to travel regularly back to Turkey and Yugoslavia to secure illicit shipments. The case, prosecutors claimed, was representative of a "Balkan Connection" of drug dealers of Albanian and Turkish origin that imported large amounts of heroin into the North America and Western Europe. By the opening years of the 1980s, the DEA contended that between 25 percent and 40 percent of the heroin sold within the United States came by way of Turkish Albanian smuggling networks.[111]

While Yugoslav and Turkish Albanian smugglers did appear to begin to enjoy greater influence within the transatlantic heroin trade, it was not until the breakup of Yugoslavia and the fall of Communism that outside observers came to recognize Albanian traffickers as a powerful force within the drug trade. An expansive exposé printed in *Der Spiegel* in 1999, for example, documented the degree to which both local Albanian street gangs, as well as major Albanian retailers, came to dominate the narcotics trade in Hamburg. According to Swiss officials, major drug

109 See e.g. Barbara Burri Sharani et. al., *Die kosovarische Bevölkerung in der Schweiz* (Bern: Bundesamt für Migration, 2010).

110 For further discussion of the origins of Albanian organized crime groups in Europe and North America, see Philippe Chassange and Kolë Gjeloshaj, "L'Emergence de la Criminalité Organisée Albanophone," *Cahiers D'Etudes sur La Méditerranée Orientale et le Monde Turco-Iranien* 32 (July–December 2001), 161–190.

111 Anthony DeStefano, "Balkan Connection: Brazen as the Mafia, Ethnic Albanian Thugs Specialize in Mayhem," *The Wall Street Journal* 9 September 1985.

wholesalers based in Turkey have historically relied heavily upon Turkish-born Albanians to distribute drugs in Europe.[112]

From the perspective of American officials in the 1970s, Kurdish traffickers, more than Albanians, reaped the greatest benefit from the various shifts that had occurred in the international heroin trade. As seen in earlier chapters, both Turkish and American observers were readily conscious of internal smuggling networks comprising of Kurds operating in Gaziantep and elsewhere in Anatolia. FBN and DPS agents also grasped and documented the prominence of Kurd smugglers operating along the Iranian/Turkish frontier. By the 1970s however, American officials took notice of two critical turns signaling a growing Kurdish influence within the transnational trade of Turkish heroin.

The impetus first leading to the increased visibility of Kurdish narcotics traffickers was the impact the arms trade had upon politics and the underground economy in eastern Anatolia. As mentioned earlier, weapons dealers and smugglers of Kurdish descent played critical roles in channeling guns to buyers in Iraq and elsewhere. Gun running in eastern Anatolia served to deepen the engagement of Turkish Kurds in the politics of resistance in Iraq. In 1963, an intense spate of "bandit attacks" and robberies swept the regions of Diyarbakir, Mardin, and Siirt. Turkish army commanders, in explaining the outbreak of violence to the State Department, claimed that many of the attackers were local Kurdish supporters of Mustafa Barzani who used theft and robbery as a means to finance the purchase of black market weaponry available throughout eastern Anatolia.[113]

The second, and more critical, factor leading to the ascendency of Kurdish trafficking networks occurred with the increasing availability of Afghan and Pakistani opium following Turkey's 1971 decision to prohibit poppy cultivation. In 1979, DEA officials reported that laboratories along the Turkish-Iranian border had proliferated in recent years. Clandestine processing centers, located particularly in Diyarbakir, appeared to have assumed the central role in processing raw opium from abroad and produced illicitly at home (thus replacing the functions once served by Syrian, Lebanese, and French traffickers).[114]

By the early 1970s, the confluence of the arms and heroin trade provided a springboard for Kurdish (and to some degree Albanian) traffickers to ascend to the heights of Turkey's smuggling underworld. Internal and external forces within the drug and arms trade do not explain one key element of the history of organized crime in Turkey during this era. When one looks beyond 1980 and towards the present, the names of the most prominent traffickers of the early postwar era, İhsan Sekban, Hüseyin Eminoğlu, Ahmet Soysal, and others, completely vanish from the public record. One may go so far as to say that the public, administrators, and scholars appear to have forgotten completely these men who first engineered Turkey's emergence as a key hub of international heroin trafficking. A select

[112] Ariane von Barth et al., "Sprache der Morde," *Der Spiegel* 2 August 1999.

[113] American Consulate Adana to Department of State, 31 October 1963, no document number, Subject Numeric Files, 1963; RG 59, NAB.

[114] DEA, "Threat Assessment: Middle East Heroin."

number of more contemporary and notorious individuals have since taken their place. More importantly, the individuals now considered the "first godfathers" of the so-called Turkish mafia, Dündar Kılıç, Abuzer Uğurlu, Behçet Cantürk and, arguably, Abdullah Çatlı, have gained equal notoriety as clandestine agents and provocateurs allied with (or, in Cantürk's case, against) the Turkish government. In previous chapters, we saw that American and Turkish sources did document those occasions when the interests of members of the Turkish government and the Istanbul underworld overlapped. Corruption, more than any other factor, seemed to have been the basis for these relationships (particularly during the Menderes years). The politics of the 1970s, coupled with the changes witnessed within Turkey's smuggling underworld, prompted a radical transformation in the relationships formed between politicians and traffickers.

It was during the 1970s that the Turkish and foreign public became increasingly aware of the blurred lines that bisected the machinations of the legitimate political overworld and narcotics underworld. While the cases concerning Nakiye Hıncal and Refik Can foreshadowed the degree to which politicians played active roles in the drug trade, a series of scandals that broke in the years immediately preceding and succeeding the 1980 military coup cast a spotlight upon the ties the drug traffickers shared with Turkey's influential radical right. It is also during this era that we see the first stages of a budding relationship formed between the underworld and Turkey's powerful National Intelligence Service (*Milli İstihbarat Teşkilatı*, or MİT). The crafting of this alliance, which was born out of the politics of the latter stages of the Cold War, was not entirely unprecedented. In securing the services of gangsters to serve as intelligence assets and assassins, MİT appears to have assumed the mantel of the Ottoman Special Organization. Like the *çetecis* of the Young Turk era before them, the gangsters of the 1970s, and beyond, became the instrument of a robust and paranoid government apparatus committed to the preservation of the state at all costs.

THE NEW *BABAS*: VIOLENCE, CLANDESTINE POLITICS, AND THE BIRTH OF THE "TURKISH MAFIA"

On 10 February 1969, the American Sixth Fleet steamed into the Bosphorus Straits and laid anchor across from Dolmabahçe Palace. The fleet's arrival, set against the context of the intensity of the Vietnam War and the left's surging fortunes on university campuses and other sectors of society, set off a wave of popular outrage in the city. On Sunday, 16 February, a crowd of 30,000 marched into Taksim Square, one of Istanbul's main thoroughfares. Most of the crowd comprised students carrying banners and signs denouncing American imperialism and the war in Vietnam. At the other end of the square, a separate, smaller crowd formed. Participants of this counter-demonstration, enraged by the suspected communist leanings of the marchers, carried sticks, knives, and bricks. Student demonstrators chanting slogans calling for an "independent Turkey" antagonized the smaller crowd on the opposite side of the square, who responded with shouts that Turkey was "Muslim." Riot police shadowing both groups then charged into the main demonstration. Counter-demonstrators aided their assault, leaving two dead and over a hundred people injured. As many as fifty-two leftist students were placed under arrest after the fighting ended. Newspapers the next day dubbed the event "Bloody Sunday."[115]

An official in the American Consulate in Istanbul, reflecting back upon the February 1969 demonstrations two years later, noted that Bloody Sunday had marked a profound sea change in public life and politics in Turkey. Violence had since spread "like a cancer" throughout the country, threatening the body politic of the state. University students appeared to be at the forefront of this rising tide of aggression. Militant leftist groups proliferated on university campuses, a movement undergirded by support from the children of affluent urban and notable Kurdish families from western and eastern Turkey, respectively.[116] Right wing groups, mostly comprising young people from low-income and rural backgrounds, also multiplied in the years following Bloody Sunday. Political forces more powerful than the students themselves bolstered the strength, vitality, and lethal potential of left and right wing groups. Conservative elements of the Justice Party (particularly those linked with small businesses and the country's religious establishment), as well as supporters within the newly established Nationalist Action Party (*Milliyetçi Hareket Partisi*, or MHP), provided financial and political support to the emerging power of right wing street gangs. State Department officials noted particularly the influence of Alparslan Türkeş, one of the leaders of the 1960 coup and founder of the MHP, as influential in forming "commando camps" used to train young men (thus becoming, in the words of one reporting agent, the right's "storm troops"). State Department sources were less certain as to the individuals or parties that stood behind the increasingly powerful leftist student groups such as the Revolutionary Youth (more commonly known as *Dev Genç*). While rumor had it that young leftists received financial support and training from the Eastern Bloc and Arab guerrillas, American sources deemed such claims to be "overstated." Nevertheless, some of the left's more militant leaders did receive training from "fedayeen" in Syria.[117]

Violent attacks and crimes committed by left and right wing militant groups claimed thousands of lives and left thousands more injured in the years between

[115] Ahmad, "The Special Relationship: The Committee of Union and Progress and the Ottoman Jewish Political Elite, 1908–1918," 381.

[116] American Consulate General Istanbul to Department of State, 30 April 1970, Subject Numeric Files, 1970–73, RG 59, NAB. In this report, the State Department further claimed that the children who came to join militant groups also derived from the families of Istanbul's intellectual elite, lesser government officials, Kurdish ağas, Çukorova's nouveau riche, Laz tea estate owners, and Aegean cotton farmers.

[117] American Consulate General Istanbul to Department of State, 30 April 1970, Subject Numeric Files, 1970–73, RG 59, NAB.

1969 and 1980. While leftist groups such as Dev Genç often gleaned the most notoriety during the early years in this struggle, it is clear that right wing ultranationalist organizations held the balance of power on the streets of Turkey by the military coup of 1980. From its humble origins in 1969, Türkeş's Grey Wolves (*Bozkurtlar*) ascended to become the decade's most fierce and violent faction. The militancy and extremism that defined the Grey Wolves' rise to power was displayed in its most violent terms in December 1977 when bands of ultranationalist supporters in Maraş attacked the homes and businesses belonging to the city's Alevi community (a non-Sunni religious group typically associated with leftist, secularist parties), leaving perhaps hundreds dead and injured.[118]

It is also during this era that diplomats and security officials first confronted the threat of international terrorism as a source of political violence. In January 1973, a lone gunman confronted the Turkish consul and vice consul at a suburban hotel in Los Angeles and shot them both dead. Before committing the act, the assailant, Gourgan Yanikian, posted a letter to a local Armenian newspaper, declaring that the killing of the two Turkish diplomats was an "act of war" in retaliation for the Ottoman Empire's genocidal policies towards its Armenian population during the First World War.[119] Yanikian's threats of war resounded two years later with the establishment of the Armenian Secret Army for the Liberation of Armenia. From its bases in Lebanon and France, ASALA (as it is better known) launched a bloody offensive against Turkey's diplomatic corps, killing multiple representatives in France, Austria, Greece, Spain, Switzerland, and France. In addition to the killing of forty-two Turkish diplomats, ASALA claimed responsibility for another 110 incidents over a ten-year period, including a brazen attack on Ankara's international airport.[120] While by no means posing the sort of existential threat leftist or rightist groups presented during this decade, ASALA's campaign of violence underscored fears in the capital that the state's survival was being called into question. From the perspective of the DEA, Ankara's heightened sensitivity towards the threat of terrorist violence served to undermine decades of collaboration between the United States and Turkey on counter-narcotics issues. DEA officers assigned to Turkey were increasingly prohibited from touring eastern Anatolia (where it was thought that trafficking syndicates were establishing large laboratories for processing raw opium into heroin).[121] In private, the DEA advocated that it was essential for Ankara to "raise the overall narcotics effort to the level currently exercised for terrorist activity."[122]

118 See Elise Massicard, *The Alevis in Turkey: Identity and Managing Territorial Diversity* (New York: Routledge, 2013), 30–32.

119 "Two Turkish L.A. Consulate Officials Slain," *Los Angeles Times* 28 January 1973; Richard West, "Armenian Held in 2 Slayings Urged War on Turk Envoys," *Los Angeles Times* 30 January 1973.

120 Andrew Mango, *Turkey and the War on Terror* (New York: Routledge, 2005), 11–12.

121 "Turkey [DEA memo?]," 1980, Subject Files of Attorney General Epstein, Southwest Asian Heroin, RG 60, NAB.

122 "Turkey [DEA memo?]," 1980, Subject Files of Attorney General Epstein, Southwest Asian Heroin, RG 60, NAB. For more discussion on party politics and violence in Turkey in the years preceding the 1980 coup, see Hamit Bozarlsan, *Violence in the Middle East: From Political Struggle to Self-Sacrifice* (Princeton, NJ: Markus Weiner Publishers, 2004), 66–77.

In this period of intense factional and communal violence, Turkish newspapers, more than in any other period previously, took active note of elected officials engaged in the heroin trade. The most famous case occurred in early March 1972 when French customs officials stopped and searched a Turkish vehicle arriving from Italy. A thorough search of the car revealed 146 kilos of morphine. One of the passengers apprehended in the seizure was Kudret Bayhan, an MHP senator from the central Anatolian province of Niğde. Bayhan, who had played a notable role in MHP's initial manifestation as a party (the Republican Villagers National Party), was accused of acting on behalf of three narcotics traffickers, Mehmet Çelik, Nuri Bostan, and Haydar Binicioğlu (who had also served in the national assembly until 1969).[123] After his return from French custody, he (along with his chauffeur) was sentenced to fifteen years in prison.[124] Cengiz Erdinç, in his research on this period, notes that Bayhan was not the only elected official to act as a "jockey" carrying morphine to illicit markets in Europe. Under the cover of diplomatic protection, three other representatives to the Turkish Grand National Assembly were arrested between 1970 and 1980 for attempting to smuggle narcotics outside of Turkey.[125]

The available archive evidence does not offer insights into how the State Department or the BNDD viewed the case of Kudret Bayhan (other than to trace the senator's opium source back to its point of origin in the province of Afyon).[126] Internal records from the State Department do, however, point to another case that achieved far less notoriety within the pages of the Turkish press. In the summer of 1972, BNDD officials arranged, through an informant, for the purchase of over two tons of opium from a trafficking suspect named "Özdemir." After an initial meeting, a second man, Abdullah Çilli, offered to sell an additional ton of opium from his own supply to the BNDD informant. Çilli also offered to sell an additional twenty-five kilos of morphine base as a part of separate transaction. While it is not clear from State Department records whether or not the BNDD ever completed the purchase of the drugs or apprehended anyone as a part of the case, a BNDD informant did suspect that Çilli suspected his potential clients to be "Interpol" officers. Çilli shared this suspicion with "Özdemir," who promptly ceased negotiations on the sale of the two tons of opium. It was even speculated that one associate in the deal may have plotted to kill the BNDD officer and his informant with the intent of stealing the "flash money" they carried with them for the deal. The suspect, who is identified as İbrahim Mengüllüoğlu, also feared that the men were Interpol

[123] "Fevzioğlu ve Erim Vekili Oldu," *Milliyet* 22 October 1965; "Kaçakçıların İstanbul Kolu Ele Geçti," *Milliyet* 15 March 1972; "Bostan ve Çelik 20'şer Yıl Hapse Mahkum Edildi," *Milliyet* 27 November 1974. While Bostan and Çelik were sentenced to long prison terms, an Istanbul court eventually cleared Binicioğlu of all charges.

[124] "Kudret Bayhan Bu Sabah Yargılanıyor," *Milliyet* 20 February 1973; "Senatör Kudret Bayan 15 Yıla Mahkum Oldu," *Milliyet* 28 February 1973.

[125] Erdinç, *Overdose Türkiye: Türkiye'de Eroin Kaçakçılığı, Bağımlılğı ve Politikalar*, 167–168.

[126] Izmir to Ankara, 8 October 1972, Ankara 7082, Subject Numeric Files, 1970–73, RG 59, NAB.

agents, a suspicion that was affirmed after police in Gaziantep refused to arrest the men after he informed them of their desire to buy narcotics.[127]

BNDD agents pursued the arrest of Abdullah Çilli knowing full well that he was a sitting member of the Turkish Grand National Assembly as representative from the province of Hatay.[128] Interestingly, Turkish narcotics officers in Istanbul, including Abdullah Pektaş, also endorsed the Çilli investigation.[129] The fact that Çilli was not arrested that summer did not, however, lead to an end to official suspicions of his activities. Eight months later, *Newsday*'s exposé on the Turkish heroin trade brought BNDD's revelations to the attention of their readers. In reacting to the paper's claim that he was the "one of the largest bosses [*patron*]" of the morphine trade in the province of Malatya, Çilli vowed to pursue his "legal rights" in defending himself from *Newsday*'s "baseless" accusations. The head of the DPS, Orhan Erbuğ, also came to his defense and called the news story a lie.[130]

Perhaps the most explosive allegation made against elected officials came from a disgraced assembly representative who accused Necmettin Erbakan of complicity in the heroin trade. Yiğit Kahraman, who was elected to the Grand National Assembly as a member of Erbakan's National Salvation Party, was arrested in Germany in 1978 in possession of three-and-a-half kilos of heroin. After having lost his bid for re-election, Kahraman claimed that Erbakan personally met with him in Ankara and asked him to transport the drugs to Germany and sell them there. Erbakan vehemently denied the accusation and was never charged with any criminal wrongdoing in either Turkey or Germany.[131]

The involvement of elected Turkish officials in the heroin trade occupied only a small number of Turkish journalists during this period of time. Even a cursory glance at the newspapers of this era suggests that journalists based in Turkey arrived at a new appreciation of the economic and political significance of the country's underworld. In this era which featured the release of the first two installments of the *Godfather* series, Turkish journalists and politicians readily began to adapt the terms of "mafia" and "godfather (*baba*)" to describe powerful criminal elements at work in Istanbul and elsewhere.[132] Before departing from the Directorate for Public Safety, Engin Giray, a DPS supervisor in Istanbul, suggested that there was

[127] American Embassy Ankara to Secrertary of State, 28 June 1972, Ankara 4583, Subject Numeric Files, 1970–73, RG 59, NAB.

[128] Abdullah Çilli was a veteran of the Turkish War of Independence and had served as a representative in the National Assembly from 1957 to 1977. During that time, he switched his party affiliation six times. See "Hatay Eski Milletvekili Abdullah Çilli Öldü," *Milliyet* 26 May 1991.

[129] American Embassy Ankara to BNDD, 12 June 1972, Ankara 4189, Subject Numeric Files, 1970–73, RG 59, NAB.

[130] "ABD'ye Soktukları İleri Sürülen 52 Türkün Adları Açıklandı," *Milliyet* 5 February 1973; "Çilli 'Baz Morfin Kaçakçılığı İddiası Yalandır' Dedi," *Milliyet* 6 February 1973.

[131] "Başbakanlık, MSP Eski Milletvekili Kahraman'ın Adının Uyuşturucu Madde Kaçakçılığına Karışmasını Doğruladı," *Milliyet* 25 March 1979: Uğur Mumcu, *Silah Kaçakçılığı ve Terör* (Istanbul: Tekin Yayınevi, 1981), 100–106.

[132] Bovenkerk and Yeşilgöz, *The Turkish Mafia: A History of the Heroin Godfathers*, 102. Both of these authors suggest that the term *baba* came into existence as a result of the impact of the first *Godfather* film in Turkey.

a "mafia organization" in Istanbul, one that influenced both the parliament and the DPS.[133] Precisely who made up this mafia, according to the contemporary observers, was not as straightforward, however, as it appeared in either installment of the *Godfather*.

The press attention given to Turkey's supposed mafia was manifested through its careful and lurid coverage of the activities of a new generation of *kabadayı* chieftains found in the city of Istanbul. This newfound fascination with this long-established criminal institution crystallized particularly around the violent outbursts and frequent arrests of Dündar Kılıç. Kılıç was born in 1935 in a village outside of Trabzon. Like many "Laz" families before them, his parents left Turkey's northeastern shores and relocated to Ankara. It was in Ankara that Dündar first entered into a life of crime as a petty ruffian. As a young man, he was accused of killing a noted Kurdish *kabadayı* by the name of Kürt Cemali (a crime he long denied any responsibility for).[134] Having earned the ire of Cemali's relatives and other Kurdish toughs, Kılıç relocated to Istanbul where he opened a gambling parlor in Beyoğlu. As a recent settler to the city in the mid-1960s, he established a lifelong friendship with another *kabadayı* with deeper roots in Istanbul, İdris Özbir. *Kürt* İdris, as he was more commonly known, became Kılıç's first partner in the gambling trade in spite of the accusations that he had killed a fellow Kurd back in Ankara.[135] From these humble roots, Dündar Kılıç became a prominent fixture of Istanbul's casino and gambling underworld. His frequent run-ins with the police, particularly after violent shootouts or personal squabbles, also made him an object of frequent media scrutiny.[136]

Unlike any other gangster before him, Kılıç did not shy away from the gaze of the press.[137] Until his death in 1999, he embraced opportunities to speak to journalists or appear on television. His disclosures to the press about life as an Istanbul *kabadayı* are among the few insider accounts available on the internal dynamics of the city's underworld. Kılıç revealed, for example, that there was little ethnic animosity between the powerful Laz and Kurdish crime bosses active in the city (a phenomenon affirmed by his partnership with İdris Özbir).[138] Despite his many arrests, he claimed to have held strong ties with local policemen and politicians.[139] Kılıç also did not shy away from the heated politics of the era. While in prison, he befriended young revolutionaries aligned with Turkey's radical left and

133 "İstifa Eden Ekipler Amiri 'İstanbulda Mafia Var' Dedi," *Milliyet* 6 June 1973. Interestingly, Giray supposedly befriended Dündar Kılıç as a young man. See Yurdakul, *Abi: Kabadayıler-Mafya Derin Devlet İlişkilsi*, 134.

134 Yurdakul, *Abi: Kabadayıler-Mafya Derin Devlet İlişkilsi*, 84.

135 Yurdakul, *Abi: Kabadayıler-Mafya Derin Devlet İlişkilsi*, 94.

136 Perhaps the most notorious incident involving Kılıç happened in 1969 when he attempted to shoot an individual after he was refused a room at the Hilton Hotel in Istanbul. See "Hilton'da Oda Verilmeyece Tabanca Çekti," *Milliyet* 11 April 1969.

137 Kılıç was probably the first underworld figure to embrace the media. Subsequent notable gangsters, such as Sedat Peker and Abdullah Çakıcı, shared a similar affection for newspaper and television coverage.

138 Yurdakul, *Abi: Kabadayıler-Mafya Derin Devlet İlişkilsi*, 97.

139 Yurdakul, *Abi: Kabadayıler-Mafya Derin Devlet İlişkilsi*, 130–135.

maintained friendly ties with İhsan Selçuk, the one-time outspoken publisher of *Cumhuriyet*.[140]

Dündar Kılıç's forthcoming nature did not extend to discussion of his personal involvement in illicit trafficking of narcotics or weapons.[141] Shortly after the military coup of 1980, authorities in Istanbul placed him, and seventy-five other suspects, under arrest on weapons smuggling charges.[142] Subsequent narcotics trafficking charges prolonged his stay in prison until he was cleared of any wrongdoing in 1985.[143] In denying any involvement in the smuggling trade, Kılıç later argued that two high-ranking security officials in the DPS and the National Intelligence Service had singled him out for his leftist associations.[144]

The 1980 crackdown carried out by the DPS brought to light the alleged smuggling activities of other prominent Istanbul *kabadayı* with close ties to Kılıç. DPS officials, who dubbed the round-up "Operation Godfather," also placed Kürt İdris under arrest for weapons smuggling. Unlike Kılıç, İdris did have a record and history as a smuggler. According to one account, he had worked in partnership with a band of smugglers in the Istanbul section of Beyoğlu, illegally importing cigarettes and electronic devices.[145] Within days of Turkey's military authorities taking him into custody, a German court in October 1980 sought Özbir for questioning after fifty kilos of opium resin and 2,400 kilos of hashish was uncovered in West Germany.[146] Charges of narcotics trafficking continued to dog İdris into the next year when he was taken into custody again after his brother-in-law, Maruf Eftim Veriopolos, was imprisoned after attempting to sell heroin to police in Elazığ.[147]

A second figure closely associated with Kılıç who attracted the attention of the press and Turkey's post-coup military government was his brother-in-law, İsmail Hacısüleymanoğlu (otherwise known as Oflu İsmail). İsmail's early criminal history differed somewhat from the likes of Dündar Kılıç and Kürt İdris. Before his involvement in the drugs or arms trade, he was arrested at the age of sixteen in 1959 for breaking into a series of apartments in the middle-class neighborhoods of Şişli, Cihangir, and Nişantaşı.[148] Eight years later he was imprisoned for shooting

140 Sefa Kaplan, "Solcu Yazar Solcu Baba'yı Yazdı," *Hürriyet* 21 July 2001.

141 While he was less than forthcoming about any dealings in narcotics or arms, he did admit in one interview to participating in the smuggling of cigarettes, coffee, and watches. Among his partners was Bekir Çelenk, a close associate of Abuzer Uğurlu. See Yurdakul, *Abi: Kabadayılar-Mafya Derin Devlet İlişkilsi*, 269.

142 "Silah Kaçakçılılğıyla İlgili 76 Kişi Gözatlında," *Milliyet* 11 October 1980.

143 "Dündar Kılıç Gözaltına Alında," *Milliyet* 1 January 1982; "Biz Çirikin Polisi Böcek Gibi Ezeceğiz," *Milliyet* 20 February 1985.

144 "Dündar Kılıç'tan Suçlama," *Milliyet* 20 March 1988. Dündar Kılıç particularly held Mehmet Eymür, head of the smuggling bureau of the National Intelligence Service, and Atilla Aytek, head of the smuggling bureau of the Directorate of Public Safety, responsible for his arrest and subsequent torture while in prison. In a later interview, he accused Atilla Aytek of being a "traitor to the state" and "Kirkuk Armenian."

145 "Nam-ı Diğer 'Kürt İdris,' " *Milliyet* 8 September 1983.

146 "Bir Alman Mahkemesi İdris Özbir İle Abuzer Uğurlu İçin Tutuklama Kararı Aldı," *Milliyet* 29 October 1980.

147 "Eroin Kaçakçılığına Adı Karışan Kürt İdris Gözaltına Alında," *Milliyet* 31 December 1981.

148 "50 Bin Liralık Eşya Çalan Üç Hırsız Yakalandı," *Milliyet* 8 April 1959.

two people in a brothel in Cihangir.[149] In 1979 he fled Turkey after his involvement in the shooting of a noted casino owner.[150] In 1980, authorities suspected that Turkish gangsters associated with arms smuggling in Bulgaria had harbored Oflu İsmail.[151] From Bulgaria he later passed through Hungary and Holland, all the while becoming more deeply intertwined with the weapons and narcotics trade. He remained on the run until 1987 when he was finally arrested in Amsterdam, by which time he had earned a reputation in the Netherlands and Italy as a wholesaler of heroin and arms.[152] İsmail, one trafficker later claimed, controlled all the heroin entering into Holland during much of the 1980s.[153]

Charges of illicit trafficking lodged against Oflu İsmail, Dündar Kılıç, and Kürt İdris represent only a portion of the activities carried out by Turkish traffickers during the 1970s. Notorious *kabaydayıs* like İdris and Kılıç (whether guilty or not) were not the only figures counted among the most influential heroin traders of the era. Equally powerful individuals within Turkey's drug trafficking underworld were found among a new generation of professional smugglers. Of all the men found within this new cohort of gangsters, one particular family from the region of Malatya attracted the most attention from the press and police.

Hüseyin Uğurlu, the founder and patriarch of this Kurdish crime family, first came to the attention of Turkish authorities in 1967. Born in the small town of Pötürge, he began his career as a low-ranking official within Turkey's Minisitry of Customs.[154] He was first arrested after police discovered thirteen tons of illegally imported coffee hidden on his chicken farm in Malatya.[155] He was arrested again in 1973 in a wide police sweep of suspected arms traffickers that resulted in the arrest of a total of twenty-six suspects.[156] Despite his police record, Hüseyin forged a close relationship with Rafet Küçüktiryaki, who served as governor of Malatya and head of the DPS as a member of the Justice Party during the 1970s.[157] The head of the Uğurlu household, like other major traffickers before him, was a noted philanthropist in his home province, building a mosque and an English-language school in his hometown of Pörtürge.[158]

[149] "Randevuevi Cinayeti İçin 2 Kişi Yakalandı," *Milliyet* 1 May 1967. According to another account, he was also placed in police custody after an attack on another brothel that did not pay him his protection money. See "9 Kara Prens," *Milliyet* 2 September 1988.

[150] "Gazinocular Çatıştı: Şişli'de bir Gazino Sahibi ile Garsonu Tabancayla Öldürüldü," *Milliyet* 1 April 1979.

[151] "Şehremini'de Bir Kuyumcuyu Soyan 3 Kişi Altınlarla Birlikte Yakalandı," *Milliyet* 8 November 1980.

[152] "Oflu İsmail Hollanda'da Yakalandı," *Milliyet* 24 February 1987; "Oflu İsmail'i Türk Polisi Sorgulayacak," *Milliyet* 1 March 1987.

[153] Yalçın, *Behçet Cantürk'ün Anıları*, 118.

[154] Uğur Mumcu, *Papa, Mafya, Ağca* (Istanbul: Tekin Yayınevi, 1984), 371.

[155] "Tavuk Çiftliğinden Kaçak Kahve Çıktı," *Milliyet* 22 October 1967.

[156] "Silah Kaçakçılarının Yargılaması Başladı, 22 September 1973

[157] Mumcu, *Papa, Mafya, Ağca*, 124; AP Hükümetinin Yeni Müdürleri Belli Oldu, 3 December 1979. Küçüktiryaki lost his position with the Justice Party administration after his connections to the Uğurlus were revealed. See "Genel Müdürü 'Bu Bir Bayrak Yarışıydı, Benimki Kısa Sürdü' Dedi," *Milliyet* 23 March 1980.

[158] Mumcu, *Papa, Mafya, Ağca*, 128.

Among those arrested with Hüseyin in 1973 were three of his sons, Abuzer, Mustafa, and Sabri. Of the three, Abuzer appeared to have been a particularly successful arms smuggler in his own right at the time of his capture. According to internal police records uncovered by famed investigative journalist Uğur Mumcu, Abuzer had been involved in the trafficking of thousands of handguns and vast amounts of ammunition between 1968 and 1973.[159] His operations further expanded to Germany in 1971.[160] While rarely dealing directly with individuals outside of his immediate family, Abuzer did appear to work alongside other individuals with closer ties to syndicates with a long history of heroin trafficking. Among one of his partners was Zihni İpek, a long time smuggler who often collaborated in the arms trade with Ali Bezal and Fahrettin Soysal, two men who represented the most notorious opiate smuggling families in Turkey.[161]

While the Uğurlu family may have moved in similar circles as such noted heroin traffickers as the Bezals and Soysals, it is not clear when Hüseyin and his sons first engaged in drug smuggling. It is probable that Abuzer Uğurlu was the first in the family to be officially suspected of narcotics dealing when he was wanted for questioning alongside İdris Özbir on trafficking charges in Germany in 1980.[162] Regardless of the year the family did ultimately enter the heroin trade, it is clear that the Uğurlus relied heavily upon contacts in Bulgaria to facilitate and expand their interests. *Cumhuriyet*'s coverage of Abuzer's arrest in 1973 on weapons smuggling charges mentions that he was already a Bulgarian citizen by that time.[163] According to a statement he later made before a Turkish court, Abuzer admitted that he first began working with Bulgaria's official import-export company, Kintex, in 1969. Court testimony in Italy, and DEA intelligence, later affirmed that Uğurlu entered into the drug trade in 1975 after establishing "a multi-billion dollar" contraband racket from his base in Sofia.[164] His influence over the European heroin market was in large measure indebted to ties he forged with members of Sicily's Cosa Nostra underworld. In 1975, men representing Abuzer's interests met with Sicilian gangsters and agreed to carve up the European market between them. For his part, Uğurlu allegedly established heroin refining labs in the Netherlands and West Germany (operated by chemists from Marseille) and arranged distribution networks in tandem with Cosa Nostra gangsters.[165]

Abuzer Uğurlu's rise to prominence within the European heroin trade, according to investigations in the 1970s and 1980s, was not purely the product of criminal cleverness or even raw political corruption. In the early 1970s, both American and Turkish officials were aware that smugglers like the Uğurlus received official

[159] Mumcu, *Silah Kaçakçılığı*, 56–61.

[160] Ferhat Ünlü, *Susurluk Gümrüğü: Kaçakçılık—Çete—Devlet* (Istanbul: Birey, 2000), 83.

[161] Ünlü, *Susurluk Gümrüğü: Kaçakçılık—Çete—Devlet*, 83.

[162] "Bir Alman Mahkemesi İdris Özbir İle Abuzer Uğurlu İçin Tutuklama Kararı Aldı," *Milliyet* 29 October 1980.

[163] "8 Yılda Yurda 60 Milyonluk Kaçak Silah ve Mermi Sokan 27 Sanık İçin 7-313 Yıl Hapis Cezası İstendi," *Cumhuriyet* 22 September 1973.

[164] Claire Sterling, *Octopus* (New York: Touchstone Books, 1990), 160.

[165] Sterling, *Octopus*, 165–166.

protection from the Bulgarian government. In undertaking their research of Turkey's heroin trade, *Newsday* reporters interviewed Galip Labernas about the role Kintex played in the arms and drug trade. Labernas, speaking on the record, stated only that he knew that the Bulgarian government gave "carte blanche" to Turkish morphine smugglers but he personally did not possess "many details."[166] Robert Greene, editor of the *Newsday* series, appears to have briefed the State Department of these revelations in October 1972, which resulted in an official BNDD request to interview suspects detained in Bulgaria.[167] Ironically, the connection between the Bulgarian government and Turkish arms and drug traffickers did not surface again in the press until 1981. When details of Kintex's support of the Uğurlus emerged, the circumstances and implications of this relationship appeared all the more convoluted, strange, and profound.

On 13 May 1981, Mehmet Ali Ağca opened fire on Pope John Paul II's motorcade in St. Peter's Square. After critically wounding the pope, bystanders and security officials tackled Ağca and wrestled him to the ground. During his subsequent trial, John Paul's would-be assassin spun a series of odd and shocking stories before the court. In addition to declaring the he was the second coming of Jesus Christ, Ağca claimed that Bulgarian officials knew of his plot to kill the pope. Journalists in Europe and the United States seized upon the confession and argued that the plot represented a larger Soviet conspiracy targeting Poland's Solidarity movement. Once his trial was complete and the furore had passed, official suspicions of a Soviet-Bulgarian plot gave way to a more complicated story concerning the interplay between state intelligence services in Turkey and Bulgaria and Turkish drug traffickers with radical right leanings.

Mehmet Ali Ağca had a reputation as a violent member of the Alparslan Türkeş's Grey Wolves before he attempted to kill John Paul II. As a student at Istanbul University in 1978, he had garnered a reputation as a militant aligned with the Grey Wolves.[168] In July 1979, authorities accused him of killing Abdi İpekçi, the outspoken editor of *Milliyet*.[169] Ağca denied the charge and argued before a Turkish court that he and his comrades in the Grey Wolves or the Nationalists Action Party were scapegoats for the crime. His incarceration proved brief when members of the Grey Wolves smuggled him out of prison and then out of the country. Among those who helped smuggle him out of prison, and perhaps aided in İpekçi's killing, was Abdullah Çatlı, a right wing militant who had also been accused of killing seven leftist students in Ankara in 1977.[170] The two men fled Turkey after Ağca's break from prison and sought support and protection from other right wing activitists

[166] Newsday, *The Heroin Trail*, 51.

[167] American Embassy Paris to Secretary of State, 10 October 1972, Paris 19138, Subject Numeric Files, 1970–73, RG 59, NAB; American Embassy Ankara to American Embassy Sofia, 3 October 1972, Ankara 7039, Subject Numeric Files, 1970–73, RG 59, NAB.

[168] Edward Herman and Frank Brodhead, *The Rise and Fall of the Bulgarian Connection* (New York: Sheridan Square Publications, 1986), 51–52.

[169] "İşte İpekçi'nin Katil Sanığı; Açıklama Bugün Yapılıyor," *Milliyet* 11 July 1979.

[170] Soner Yalçın and Doğan Yudakul, *Reis: Gladio'nun Türk Tetikçisi* (Istanbul: Doğan Kitapcılık, 2007), 57–69.

based in Europe and Iran. Among those who eventually came to harbor both these fugutives was Abuzer Uğurlu, who, like Ağca, was from Maltaya and possessed ties with right wing politicians in his home province.[171] During the course of his trial, Ağca maintained that Abuzer Uğurlu had provided him with money and a place to live in Sofia shortly before he came to Italy to kill the pope.[172] Although there is disagreement as to whether Ağca played any role in smuggling operations in Bulgaria, his allusions to Uğurlu opened a floodgate of interest in Bulgarian complicity in the heroin trade.[173] In the summer of 1984, the US House of Representatives convened hearings on the "Bulgarian-Turkish Narcotics Connection." The subcommittee's report of the hearings repeatedly painted Uğurlu as the "godfather of the Turkish mafia." Citing an official Turkish investigation, as well as various articles found in the American press, the committee held that Abuzer had ordered the assassination of Abdi İpekçi and that Kintex had helped facilitate Ağca's passage into Bulgaria.[174] All in all, Abuzer Uğurlu, with the complicity of the Bulgarian government, appeared to congressional investigators to be the ringleader in the plot to kill Pope John Paul II. While he was imprisoned on smuggling and corruption charges in Turkey in 1984, neither he nor any official in Bulgaria was ever held officially accountable for the attempt on the pope's life.[175]

In the three decades that have passed since Ağca's attack on John Paul II, subsequent investigations into Abuzer Uğurlu's political interests and clandestine ties appear even more opaque, complex, and difficult to verify. Uğur Mumcu, in his investigation of the attempt on the pope's life, claimed that Uğurlu worked on the behalf of the Bulgarian clandestine service (an accusation that seemed warranted given his association with Kintex).[176] In 2001, a letter published in the press claimed that he, along with Abdullah Çatlı, had in fact been employed at the same time by the Turkish intelligence service. Mehmet Eymür, MİT's one-time counter-terrorist chief, wrote in June 1984 that the intelligence service had retained Abuzer's services as early as 1974 as a double agent. Moreover, according to Eymür, MİT was aware that Uğurlu had "infiltrated" the Nationalists Action Party and that he, along with other right wing or nationalist (*ülkücü*) activists (such as Çatlı and Ağca), were employed in false flag operations aimed at impugning Turkey's radical right.[177]

171 Mumcu, *Silah Kaçakçılığı*, 50–53.

172 "Ağca Destekçilerinin İsimlerini Açıklandı," *Milliyet* 11 July 1982.

173 Herman and Broadhead, *The Rise and Fall of the Bulgarian Connection*, 59–60. Broadhead and Herman argue that Ağca may have had knowledge of Abuzer Uğurlu's operations in Bulgaria as a result of reading Uğur Mumcu's book, *Arms Smuggling and Terror* (*Silah Kaçakçılığı ve Terör*).

174 House of Representatives, *Bulgarian-Turkish Narcotics Connection: United States-Bulgarian Relations and International Drug Trafficking* (Washington DC: U.S. Government Printing Office, 1984), 47–48. These two specific charges were drawn from an article written by David Ignatius in the *Wall Street Journal* in 1984.

175 "Abuzer Uğurlu 15 Yıla Mahkum Oldu," *Milliyet* 14 March 1984.

176 Mumcu, *Papa, Mafya, Ağca*, 75.

177 "Eymür'den 'Şok' Metkup," *Milliyet* 27 July 2001; Soner Yalçin and Doğan Yurdakul, *Bay Pipo* (Istanbul: Doğan Kitapçilik, 2003), 394. For full text of the letter see <http://www.atin.org/detail.asp?cmd=articledetail&articleid=349> (accessed 18 December 2012).

The official investigations that followed Abdullah Çatlı's death in Susurluk brought forth the full extent to which Turkish security officials had clandestinely employed right wing sympathizers in the Turkish underworld. Çatlı's employment as an assassin in the Turkish Intelligence Service began as late as 1983. Up until that point, he had eluded incarceration in Europe (despite being apprehended with a fake passport). In Paris, he allegedly met with MİT officials who intended to deploy the long-time Grey Wolf against individuals associated with ASALA. His imprisonment in Paris and Switzerland on heroin trafficking charges did not end his career as a state assassin. After breaking out of prison in Switzerland in 1990, Çatlı, according to the Susurluk investigation, remained in contact with state handlers in Ankara. When his body was pulled from the wreckage of his Mercedes coupé in November 1996, a diplomatic passport, guns, money, drugs, and state weapons permit were found on his person. One of the fake passports found in Çatlı's possession bore the name Mehmet Özbay, one of the aliases used almost two decades earlier by Mehmet Ali Ağca.[178]

Many contemporary works published in Turkey in recent years have characterized the relationships formed between MİT and underworld figures like Uğurlu and Çatlı as manifestations of Turkey's participation in NATO's so-called "stay-behind" counter espionage/counter-insurgency program. This NATO initiative, often referred to as Operation Gladio, was first established in Turkey in 1952 under the auspices of the Turkish military's "Special Warfare Office" (*Özel Harp Dairesi*). Its existence was first brought to light during the administration of Bülent Ecevit in February 1973 in a letter addressed to him by the Turkish General Staff (*Genelkurmay*). With the assistance of the CIA and MİT, a series of irregular warfare units had been established with the intent of pre-empting "uprisings, psychological warfare and guerrilla attacks" in the event of a Soviet offensive.[179] While it is unclear if Abuzer Uğurlu played a direct role in Gladio operations in the 1970s, two journalists, Soner Yalçın and Doğan Yurdakal, have suggested that Gladio officers specifically employed Abdullah Çatlı to suppress or eliminate "subversive" leftists or dissidents living in various NATO member states. Çatlı, according to Yalçın and Yurdakal, visited Miami in 1982 in the company of a known Gladio agent (and Italian neo-Nazi) and was considered to be "under the protection" of the CIA.[180]

Other investigative reports undertaken by Soner Yalçın suggest that not every drug trafficker who engaged in clandestine politics in 1970s did so with the interests of the Turkish state at heart. In 1996, he published the "memoirs" of Behçet Cantürk, arguably the most notorious Kurdish heroin trafficker of the 1970s. Cantürk was born in Lice, a small municipality located outside of the southeastern Turkish city of Diyarbakir. As a young man, he and other members of his large

[178] For a short summary of Çatlı's life, see Belma Akçura, *Derin Devltet Oldu Devlet* (Istanbul: Güncel Yayıncılık, 2006), 222–224.

[179] Özkan, *MİT'in Gizli Tarihi*, 200–205.

[180] Soner Yalçın and Doğan Yudakul, *Reis: Gladio'nun Türk Tetikçisi* (Istanbul: Doğan Kitapcılık, 2007), 152–156.

extended family took to the hills outside of town after political disputes between rival local factions claimed the life of one of his relatives. It was as a member of this gang (*çete*) of extended family members that he was first exposed to the lucrative opium trade between Turkey and Iran.[181]

After the trade began to flag during the opium ban of 1971–74, Çantürk supplemented his trade as a construction contractor with personal investments into the arms trade between Turkey, Iran, and Iraq. As a patron of the local weapons smuggling industry, he came into contact with Black Sea gunrunners who brought their wares to market in Lice. A devastating earthquake in Lice in 1975 compelled him to move to Istanbul where he established himself among other migrants from his hometown. There he befriended Avni Karadurmuş (more commonly known as Sarı Avni), a "Laz" smuggler who had already established himself in the weapons and heroin trade.[182] The two struck up a close partnership in the drug trade. Like Uğurlu, Çantürk's success in the narcotics trade was in part due to his personal connection with Sicilian distributors based in Europe.[183]

While Avni reputedly moved in the same right wing political circles as Abuzer Uğurlu (and similarly did business with Uğurlu's Kintex connections), Behçet's political leanings were far more militantly leftist.[184] As a young man, he joined the Revolutionary Democratic Cultural Association (*Devrimci Demokratik Kültür Derneği*, or DDKD), an avowedly left-leaning group in favor of Kurdish independence.[185] While not engaging in direct political actions in the 1970s, Cantürk became synonymous with violent movements antithetical to the interests and aims of the Turkish state. In 1983, he helped to organize and execute the bombing of Istanbul's Covered Bazaar, an attack later attributed to ASALA. With the initiation of the Kurdish Workers' Party bloody insurgency against local security forces in 1986, Turkish authorities accused Cantürk of providing the guerrillas with money gleaned from the heroin trade. His involvement in Kurdish Workers' Party (PKK) activity fully came to light in 1992 when he allegedly helped to import six tons of hashish into Turkey via Pakistan. The proceeds of this shipment, authorities claimed, in part benefited the Kurdish rebels.[186]

From the perspective of the Turkish press, as well as from lawmakers and security officials, Cantürk's noterity as a mediator and fundraiser for the PKK embodied the degree to which Kurdish fighters relied upon the heroin trade to finance and maintain their war against Ankara. As early as 1984, officials speculated that ASALA worked hand in hand with the PKK within the drug trade.[187] Such conclusions may have come to the fore after Cantürk was taken into custody and and interrogated by

[181] Yalçın, *Behçet Cantürk'ün Anıları*, 22–26.
[182] Yalçın, *Behçet Cantürk'ün Anıları*, 33–46.
[183] Erdinç, *Overdose Türkiye: Türkiye'de Eroin Kaçakçılığı, Bağımlılğı ve Politikalar*, 224.
[184] "9 Kara Prens," *Milliyet* 2 September 1988.
[185] Yalçın, *Behçet Cantürk'ün Anıları*, 34–35.
[186] Human Rights Foundation of Turkey, "Human Rights Report 1998," (Ankara: HRFT Documentation Center, 2000).
[187] "PKK, ASALA ile İç, İçe," *Milliyet* 14 October 1984.

MİT agents. After forty-five days of interrogation and torture in 1984, he reportedly admitted to his MİT jailers that his ties with ASALA and the PKK predated the 1980 coup. In addition to these revelations, he is also alleged to have claimed that he had helped to supply weapons to Jalal Talabani's Kurdish fighters in Iraq and had used the profits from his heroin sales to provide financial aid to the DDKD.[188]

Cantürk's most shocking disclosure to Turkish intelligence officers did not relate to ties forged between heroin smugglers and domestic terrorists. According to his leaked testimony, a congress comprising many of Turkey's major narcotics traffickers was convened in the Vitosha Hotel in Sofia three to four months after the military's seizure of power in September 1980 (ironically, Mehmet Ali Ağca stayed at the same hotel later before undertaking his plot against the pope).[189] A number of luminaries of the Turkish narcotics trade, such as Ahmet Uğurlu and Oflu İsmail, were in attendence. While attendees also included representatives from Albania, Italy, and elsewhere, Oflu İsmail, who chaired the meeting, made a point of explicitly inviting other traffickers from the Black Sea (including Dündar Kılıç). According to the account Cantürk heard from others in attendance, Oflu İsmail declared that the Bulgarian government wished to extend to all those in attendance an invitation to live, trade, and invest in Sofia. Speaking as a self-proclaimed representative of the Communist Party, he beseeched his fellow smugglers to utilize Bulgaria's guarantees of protection, encouraging them to deposit their money in local banks without fear of prosecution. Oflu İsmail warned that those who did not accept Bulgaria's good graces would face the wrath of European law enforcement agencies alone. He cited the case of Sarı Avni, who despite threats of prosecution in Europe, chose not to attend.

Oflu İsmail, according to Cantürk, offered still more spoils and opportunities to those who attended the Sofia meeting. Participants spent a portion of the two-to-three-day conference discussing the expansion of smuggling opportunities in Middle Eastern countries (namely, Iraq and Iran) as well as seeking to establish a collective strategy in the wake of the September coup.[190] *Milliyet* later speculated that war broke out after the conclusion of the conference. A number of individuals who did not support Oflu İsmail's conclave, the paper claimed, were either found dead or arrested as a result of mysterious circumstances.[191] Cantürk, in his confession, affirms that Avni Karadurmuş was assaulted following the Sofia meeting.[192]

188 Ercan Gün, *Behçet Cantürk'ün MİT İtirafları* (Istanbul: Doğan Egmont Yayıncılık, 2009), 62–65. It should be noted that Cantürk, after his release from prison in the late 1980s, was more careful in forming alliances that preserved his personal safety (as well as his financial enterprises). Through bribes and other favors, he forged ties with generals within the Turkish military and noted politicians (he even gave a donation to Tansu Çiller's campaign for prime minister). See Hamit Bozarslan, *Network-Building, Ethnicity and Violence in Turkey* (Abu Dhabi: ECSSR, 1999), 15–16.

189 The Vitosha, it seemed, was a favorite local for multiple members of the Turkish underworld. See House of Representatives, *Bulgarian-Turkish Narcotics Connection: United States-Bulgarian Relations and International Drug Trafficking*, 64.

190 Gün, *Behçet Cantürk'ün MİT İtirafları*, 63; Yalçın, *Behçet Cantürk'ün Anıları*, 117–119.

191 "'Baba'lar Arasında Çatışma Başladı," *Milliyet* 30 October 1984.

192 Yalçın, *Behçet Cantürk'ün Anıları*, 119.

MAKING SENSE OF THE 1970S: CONCLUSIONS, SOURCES, AND COMPARISONS

Oflu İsmail's 1980 summit in Bulgaria is an illustrative and appropriate example of the lessons and challenges one confronts when assessing the evolution of organized crime and heroin trafficking in Turkey during the 1970s. Frank Bovenkerk and Yücel Yeşilgöz are correct in identifying the Sofia convention as a definitive turning point in the history of the "Turkish mafia." The Sofia meeting, as well as subsequent meetings that reportedly took place in 1983 and 1984, appear to conform to comparatively similar events that led to greater coordination between organized crime groups in the United States and Colombia (such as the infamous Appalachin and Cali congresses of 1957 and 1991, respectively).[193] Like the American mafia and the cartels of Colombia, Cantürk leads us to believe that the activities of drug trafficking and smuggling organizations grew more integrated after 1980. If this was indeed the result of the Sofia congress, then it may be argued that organized criminal activity in Turkey had definitively shifted away from the apparent precedents established by the major syndicates of the immediate postwar era. FBN records suggest that groups headed by İhsan Sekban, Hüseyin Eminoğlu, and others operated independently of one another, giving the impression that a laissez-faire system of ad hoc competition and alliances governed the Turkish opium market of the 1950s and 1960s. Moreover, Cantürk's revelations seem to suggest that the consolidation and coordination of drug dealing enterprises out of Turkey introduced a new culture of internecine violence within the Turkish underworld. There is no indication that the bosses (or *patronlar*) of the 1950s and 1960s used the threat of murder or violence to compel competitors and associates to comply with an overarching system of internal governance or order (remarkably, FBN records offer no evidence of "gang wars" between rival trafficking factions). In a sense, this new order, as dictated by Oflu İsmail and other allied bosses in Sofia, seems to suggest that new political (such as the 1980 coup) and economic (primarily the changes to the European and Amerian drug markets) realities had induced heroin traders to rationalize and streamline their endeavors in anticipation of an uncertain, but increasingly lucrative, future.

There are elements to Cantürk's story that do prompt the reader to approach its conclusions with some skepticism. In addition to the fact that he was not present at the Sofia meeting (nor any others that followed), MİT officials acquired Behçet's testimony through torture. Adding to the uncertainty of the story's veracity is *Milliyet*'s coverage of the congress in 1984 (which was printed, perhaps not incidentally, around the same time of his imprisonment). The article printed by *Milliyet* identifies no sources for the information it reveals about the 1980 meeting (a common trait of many articles on organized crime printed in the Turkish press). Even though it upholds and expands upon many elements of Cantürk's testimony,

193 Bovenkerk and Yeşilgöz, *The Turkish Mafia: A History of the Heroin Godfathers*, 111; Lupsha, "Transnational Crime versus Nation-State," 25.

it mentions the fact that Ahmet Uğurlu was in attendance at the meeting. If this was the case, it directly contradicts Behçet's claim that no Kurds were invited or allowed to participate in the proceedings.[194] While the implications of these contradictions may appear trivial in terms of the grander significance of the gathering, it does appear to affirm the historically inter-ethnic nature of cooperation and collusion within the Turkish underworld.[195]

Questions surrounding the veracity of what has been revealed about the Sofia meeting underscore the pitfalls that confront any historical investigation into the evolving nature of heroin trafficking in Turkey during the 1970s. In the absence of archival sources, journalists and investigators like Uğur Mumcu and Soner Yalçın often rely upon interviews with individuals connected to this period. The documentation for this period, whether found in the reporting of Mumcu, Yalçın, or others, often comes from uncited or unclear sources. The case of Behçet Cantürk's confession further suggests to us that factual inaccuracies or suspect circumstances (namely, in this case his imprisonment and torture) may belie the veracity of even direct testimony from this era. While fallacies and questionable sources may also beset our interpretation of archival sources, the advantage of reading contemporary documents (like those from the FBN or the DPS) at least provides a better feel for the historical limitations and insights of observers and investigators in real time. With that said, many of the conclusions and assertions submitted in this chapter must be read with a bit more caution and circumspection than those in previous chapters.

In spite of the challenges some of the sources pose to our reading of this period, the available archival and journalistic sources from the 1970s do allow us to safely arrive at several important conclusions. It is abundantly clear that a variety of forces stimulated a dramatic change in the nature of heroin trafficking in and out of Turkey. The forces that induced this shift were interdependently related and stemmed from rational decisions and, to some degree, organic trends occurring both inside and outside of the republic.

Perhaps the most important factor in initiating this transformation was the noticeable change in diplomatic relations between Washington and Ankara during the early 1970s. With backing of both the Nixon presidency and the Turkish military, officials from the State Department and the Turkish Minisitry of Foreign Affairs helped to categorically transform Turkey's role within both the legal and illicit international opium market. It should be noted that this negotiated transformation of Turkey's capacity to produce opium broke several precedents. The agreement forged between these two nations in 1971 marked a significant change in American and Turkish priorities with respect to narcotics trafficking. Nixon's election in 1968, coupled with his formal declaration of war upon narcotics one year later, elevated the status of narcotics trafficking within Turkish-American relations. As an issue now explicitly defined under the rubric of

[194] Yalçın, *Behçet Cantürk'ün Anıları*, 117–118.

[195] One Turkish drug trafficker declared that Abuzer Uğurlu (or Kürt Abuzer as he called him) was a member of the "Kurdish group" of southeastern Turkey. See Mumcu, *Papa Mafya Agca*, 329.

American national security interests, Nixon's inner circle utilized the full weight of the president's executive powers to force Ankara to take faster and more definitive steps to bring about a resolution to the "opium question." While the diplomatic record clearly indicates that the Demirel administration was sympathic to this change in priorities, decisive change ultimately occurred on the watch of the post-coup government of Nihat Erim. Erim, perhaps with the urging of the Turkish military, conceded to Washington's demands in the summer of 1971, a decision that, despite the reversal of Ankara's ban upon opium cultivation in 1974, brought about a final conclusion to US-Turkish negotiations over the country's status as an unbridled or unscrupulous producer of illicit opiates.

It should be noted that this new reckoning came at the expense of past cooperative initiatives undertaken by American and Turkish law enforcement officials during the previous two decades. With Nixon's personal intervention into negotiations over Turkey's status as an opium-producing nation, the officers employed by the BNDD and the DPS were cast in a supporting role within the crafting of a final settlement between Washington and Ankara. In historical terms, one cannot view the demotion of these two agencies too harshly. Without the investment of several decades' worth of time, money, and effort on the part of the FBN and DPS, much of the groundwork for Turkey's post-1971 approaches towards opium cultivation would not have existed. Even when one considers the troubled history of the relationship between these two departments, the combined efforts of Turkish and American law enforcement, as well as diplomatic, officials during this decade stands as a testament to the lasting impact the United States had upon the formation of Turkey's policies and institutions.

Yet in considering the actual implications of Ankara's changing approaches towards opiates after 1971 and 1974, it is clear that the imposition of a full or partial ban upon opium cultivation only modified how Turkish smugglers engaged in illicit drug trafficking. While Turkish organized crime figures may have lobbied against the 1971 ban (as British diplomats privately speculated), internal American correspondence and studies suggest that many Turkish syndicates had anticipated the change in policy and had begun to plot new courses of actions in advance of 1971.[196] The foundation for this change in practices and behavior of Turkish syndicates was perhaps first set in motion in the mid-1960s. In addition to stockpiling large amounts of morphine and opium in Turkey and Europe, it is clear that Turkish organizations capitalized upon the increasing availability of processed and unprocessed opiates outside of Turkey. In this respect Iran's decision to impose, and then abrogate, a similar ban upon opium production was critical. By the early 1970s, Turkish traffickers could rely upon available stocks of Afghan, and increasingly Iranian, opium to fulfill the demand for heroin trafficking syndicates

[196] From A. C. Goodson to R. A. Fyjia-Walker, PRO/FCO 9/2129, 16 July 1974. In addition to party pressure on Ecevit, national pride, and the influence of opium growers, British observers suspected that organized crime had an impact upon Ankara's decision in 1974 to reverse the opium ban. Quoting American sources, it was felt that the threat of financial losses compelled opium smugglers to start "pushing out cash to influence people, particularly in the press."

in Europe and North America. It also appears likely that other forms of illicit trafficking helped Turkish smugglers to profit from this era of market instability. The growth of the arms trade through Turkey seemed to provide a particularly essential lifeline to trafficking syndicates, allowing them to diversify their financial interests and further capitalize (through reinvestment) upon an increasingly lucrative heroin trade in Europe.

Other factors played a role in sustaining and expanding the interests and impact of Turkish trafficking magnates and syndicates. The sanctuary provided by Bulgaria (especially through the Kintex trading group) gave Turkish traffickers like Abuzer Uğurlu and Oflu İsmail a unique competitive edge within the European drug market and the Turkish arms trade. Hand in hand with the influence of officials in Sofia, dramatic shifts in demand for heroin and guns in Europe, North America, and Turkey created large numbers of buyers for illicit wares sold by Turkish smugglers. While it is difficult to definitively quantify the degree to which heroin use rose (or declined) in Western Europe and North America during the 1970s, the available statistics, coupled with the circumstantial attention American law enforcement devoted to the drug trade during the decade, suggests that the 1970s was a period of continued growth in the long history of the opium trade. The demand for small arms in Turkey, for use either by leftist or rightist factions or Kurdish rebels in Iraq, Iran, or Turkey, further fed the profits of narcotics smugglers and producers. American documents and investigative studies conducted by Turkish and American journalists equally corroborate the conclusion that the trade in weapons and drugs were deeply intertwined as early as the late 1960s, a phenomenon that elevated the financial status of Turkish drug traders to unprecedented levels.

One last feature of this shift in the nature of drug trafficking out of Turkey was the emergence of new trade routes and new smuggling connections utilized by Turkish syndicates. The development of an "over-land" route between Turkey and Western Europe was a process decades in the making. While direct shipment of morphine between Istanbul and Marseille was a strategy employed by major traffickers like Hüseyin Eminoğlu as early as the 1950s, it is clear that political instability in the Levant (namely, the outbreak of civil war in Lebanon) and the promise of increased profits compelled Turkish traffickers to deal directly and expressly with middlemen and retailers in Europe and North America. The establishment of larger and more entrenched diaspora networks in cities in Western Europe and the United States were critical in this transition. With the development of new European and North American "connections," Albanian and Kurdish traffickers first attracted the attention of police departments and courts outside of Turkey. As stated earlier, there remains much to be discovered about the individuals, impulses, and pressures that produced the so-called Albanian and Kurdish syndicates inside and outside of Turkey during the 1970s. Nevetheless, given the time and effort that law enforcement officials and journalists have invested in documenting and uncovering the activities of Kurdish and Albanian drug traffickers in the last twenty years, it is important to recognize the overall impact that Turkish society and politics had upon producing the the diasporas out of which many of the first traffickers emerged.

The rise of new kingpins and smuggling syndicates within the Turkish underworld is a vital element of another fundamental consequence of the history of the 1970s: the growing political significance and visibility of narcotics traffickers in the Republic of Turkey. While it may be said that individuals and groups with ties to criminal activity had exercised political influence at the local and national level before the 1970s, several factors suggest that relations between underworld and otherwise reputable figures did change dramatically in the decade preceding the 1980 coup. The most obvious symptom of this shift can be seen in the increased press coverage of drug traffickers and *kabadayıs* during this era. Large-scale police investigations and roundups of suspected smugglers (such as in 1973 and 1980) shed an unprecedented amount of light upon the dealings of illicit arms and drug traders. The apprehension of Kudret Bayhan, as well as other arrests and accusations levied against noted politicians, helped to reinforce the notion that the drug smuggling was a trade plied by individuals at various levels of Turkey's political establishment. Increasing press interest in the exploits of Istanbul's most notorious *kabadayıs* also seems to have contributed to the Turkish public's growing awareness of the culture and politics of the country's underworld. Turkish, European, and American press coverage of the attempted assassination of Pope John Paul II served to amplify and complicate this trend in the media's examination of the Turkish underworld. Abuzer Uğurlu's supposed involvement in Mehmet Ali Ağca's plot spurred journalists like Uğur Mumcu to delve deeper into the political interests and relations that bound together politicians and gangsters in Turkey. Despite the decades that have now passed, Mumcu's enterprising work remains the most definitive and expansive investigation into the connections between members of Turkey's political class and smugglers during this period.

The full extent to which gangsters like Uğurlu were intertwined with individuals and institutions within the Turkish state was not immediately clear before or after Kenan Evren and the military seized power in September 1980. Uğur Mumcu's investigation into the plot against John Paul II was one among many that attempted to highlight the possible connections between the Uğurlu and other traffickers and state intelligence agencies. Further disclosures in the Turkish press over the coming years, particularly following the Susurluk scandal, offered even stronger indications that members of the Turkish underworld served as provocateurs, killers, and intelligence sources for the country's National Intelligence Service.

The story of Behçet Cantürk further convolutes our understanding of the Turkish underworld's rising political fortunes during this period. It is now clear that individuals in the mold of Behçet Cantürk have played, and perhaps continue to play, important roles in the creation and preservation of the Kurdish Workers Party. His initiation into the arms and drug trade in the late 1970s is indicative of a general turn within both the illicit economy in southeastern Turkey as well as the growing capacity of Kurdish political dissidents to confront the Turkish state with violence. His confession to MİT agents in 1984 provides tantalizing insights into the increasing sophistication and interconnectedness of organized crime syndicates in Turkey. The fact that such an event as the Sofia meeting took place suggests that illicit sales of arms and drugs in and out of Turkey had grown to such a level that the trade's chief architects felt compelled to coordinate and mediate directly amongst themselves. Ironically, while the 1980 conclave at the Vitosha Hotel mostly drew together men with strong sympathies for Turkey's nationalist right, subsequent meetings would draw together individuals with more divergent political views and interests.[197]

To understand both how and why gangsters, politicians, and security officials came to cooperate with one another, one must contend with the volatile nature of politics in Turkey during the 1970s. The factional violence and upheaval seen in Turkey in this decade were not altogether unprecedented; going back to the late Ottoman period, intercommunal violence and government crackdowns (as well as more generalized or banal forms of lawlessness and crimes) frequently marked transitions in policies and administration in the Anatolian interior. However, from the perspective of civilian and military officials inside and outside of Ankara, the proliferation of violent left and right wing groups in Turkey in the 1970s appeared to undermine the credibility and stability of the state to an extent not seen since the foundation of the republic. ASALA's dramatic attacks upon diplomatic officials and other symbols of the Turkish government added still more tension within the country, creating a climate of crisis and dread. It is against this backdrop that one can deduce that political parties and security personnel revisited strategies once employed by officials of the late Ottoman Empire. Unlike other examples drawn from the Ottoman past, there appears to have been no guidebook (or *talimatname*) instructing or informing the alliances formed between gangsters, politicians, and security officials during the 1970s.[198] Yet like the Young Turk era, we see certain common threads that would lead to the formation of cooperative relationships between criminals and political operatives. Proceeds from the drug trade, like banditry at the turn of the century, served as a common glue that bound politicians and smugglers during this decade. Like Çerkes Reşit and Mehmet Reşit of the CUP era, the cases of Kudret Bayhan and Rafet Küçüktiryaki in particular represent the degree to which members of the political and security establishment did not remain immune from forming relationships with illicit trades as a whole. While perhaps nowhere near as profound as the challenges confronting Istanbul during the First World War, Turkey in the 1970s faced internal and external threats that were interpreted as existential threats to the state. These desperate times, more than anything, forged or further cemented

[197] While he did not attend the 1980 meeting, Dündar Kılıç did allegedly attend later conventions held by Oflu İsmail. This appears someone ironic since Kılıç's leftist leanings put him somewhat at odds with the right wing tendencies of the Uğurlu family and others. See Bovenkerk and Yeşilgöz, *The Turkish Mafia: A History of the Heroin Godfathers*, 113. Also see Gün, *Behçet Cantürk'ün MİT İtirafları*, 64–65.

[198] In 1919, the nascent Kemalist government issued a point by point guide to all regular military units on the use of "military detachments" in the defence of the empire. While making it clear that these units were explicitly not to employ brigands, revolutionaries, or individuals who had participated in bloodfeuds, many nationalist *çetes* knowingly and intentionally sought the aid of individuals involved in theft and violence. See Gingeras, *Sorrowful Shores*, 77.

relationships between outlaws and supposed officers of the peace. The methods and practices of the Ottoman Special Organization seem to echo in the recruitment of Abuzer Uğurlu and Abdullah Catlı into state service. Both men appear to have been been as willing, and disposable, instruments to further the interests of Turkey's national security.

Beyond these points, one is left on more uncertain ground in terms of understanding the reasoning and intentions behind the increasing political significance of powerful drug traffickers and syndicates during this era. As said previously, the limited and unverifiable nature of first hand accounts from this era, particularly from the press, places an enormous constraint upon contemporary scholars. However, examples from outside Turkey seem to affirm that narcotics smuggling and organized crime experienced similar patterns of transformation during this period. It is during this era that the likes of Fabio Ochoa, Pablo Escobar, Carlos Lehder, and other notorious cocaine barons first formed the Medellin cartel. Like the case of Turkey, the establishment of this powerful smuggling collective came about as a result of concomitant shifts in the nature of cocaine production in Chile and Bolivia and the collapse of Colombia's marijuana market (which had been the country's principal illicit commodity before the mid-1970s). Medellin's ascendency came at the expense of older smuggling networks, particularly those organized by Cuban-American groups in places like Miami and New York. The political weight of the cartel predated Pablo Escobar's election to the Colombian national assembly (based in part upon Ochao's influence as a prominent rancher). The political weight of the cartel assumed even greater significance with the establishment of *Muerte a Secuestraderos* (MAS, or Death to Kidnappers), Colombia's first right wing paramilitary organization. As a group established after the kidnapping of Fabio Ochao's daughter, MAS became an integral component of Colombia's war against left wing guerrillas. Like Turkey in the 1970s, one cannot fully interpret the rise of the Medellin cartel without taking into account the history of political instability and violence in Colombia (a culture that perhaps influenced the particularly violent nature of the Medellin and Cali cartels).[199]

Drug trafficking groups in Mexico similarly benefited from external and internal market shifts, as well as increasing amounts of political instability and political collusion.[200] Yet, as Paul Gootenberg argues, greater research is needed in order to understand exactly how and why cocaine assumed its preeminent place as a drug of choice for consumers and traffickers alike in North America. Moreover, it is unclear what effect the increase in cocaine use had upon Turkish heroin smugglers and refiners after 1980. Anecdotal evidence from the United States and elsewhere suggests that demand for heroin, regardless of its source, waned with the onset of the 1980s. Moreover, the rise of new trafficking syndicates in North America and Europe appeared to come at the expense of older, more established criminal

199 Gootenberg, *Andean Cocaine*, 291–324; Marco Palacios, *Between Legitimacy and Violence: A History of Colombia, 1875–2002* (Durham, NC: Duke University Press, 2006), 204–205.

200 Astorga, "Organized Crime."

milieus. Passage of the Racketeer Influenced and Corruption Organizations Act (or RICO laws) in 1970, as well as increased vigilance on the part of the FBI and local law enforcement, greatly undermined and, in some cases, destroyed the once powerful mafia families that held sway over cities like New York, Chicago, and Boston.[201] Yet while many of the Five Families of New York as well as other older North American partners in the Turkish drug trade may have suffered at the hands of this government crackdown, Turkish heroin dealers, as well as other drug traders, found new inroads in Western Europe (particularly in Holland, the United Kingdom, and West Germany). This chapter in the history of the drug trade, by all accounts, is one that is continuing to unfold.

[201] James Jacobs et al., *Gotham Unbound: How New York was Liberated from the Grip of Organized Crime* (New York: NYU Press, 1999).

Conclusion: The Deep State and Its Discontents: Heroin and Organized Crime in the Contemporary Age

The declaration of martial law in September 1980 brought about a violent end to the political instability and intense factional fighting of the preceding decade. With the establishment of a military junta under General Kenan Evren, each of the leading political figures of the 1970s, including Süleyman Demirel, Bülent Ecevit, Necmettin Erbakan, and Türkeş Alparslan, were banned from political life. Hundreds of thousands of others were arrested, with many imprisoned and tortured after the formation of hastily organized tribunals. Thousands more fled the country and were stripped of their citizenship. General elections were permitted in 1983 following the regime's passage of a new constitution that affirmed, in the eyes of the military, the country's ardent commitment to the Kemalist principles of nationalism and statism. The new constitution also provided the coup plotters with carte blanche for their actions; according to article fifteen, all those who had executed the coup, as well as those who were involved in the indiscriminate arrests and executions, were given amnesty preemptively from prosecution for any wrongdoing.[1]

The threat of a capricious return to authoritarian rule lingered into the new millennium. Political discussion in Turkey during the 1980s and 1990s, be it within the press or in academic forums, remained tightly controlled or self-censored in the face of military intervention and the rising tensions in the Kurdish regions of eastern Anatolia. Necmettin Erbakan's election to the post of prime minister in 1997, a turn that seemed to signal an emerging Islamist majority in the country, was forestalled after military officials issued an ultimatum suggesting the possibility of another intervention on the part of the armed forces. In hindsight, the principles and practices that undergirded the coup of 1980 embodied the Turkish military's role as "guardians of the state." Over the next quarter of a century, politicians of Turkey's left and right drew similar lessons from these events; cabals within the nation's armed forces were ever ready to resort to arbitrary military rule in order to maintain law and order, as well as to uphold Turkey's essential ideological underpinnings.[2]

[1] Kerem Öktem, *Angry Nation: Turkey Since 1989* (London: Zed Books, 2011), 58–66.

[2] The notion of a Turkish "guardian state" is one heavily employed most recently by Kerem Öktem in order to explain both the continuities within Ankara's approach towards governance as well as the oligarchical natüre of politics in Turkey. See Öktem, *Angry Nation: Turkey Since 1989*, xx.

A final moment of reckoning resolving the political impact of the 1980 coup now appears to have occurred. Following the discovery of a cache of arms in a suburban neighborhood of the Black Sea town of Trabzon in June 2007, Turkish police executed a series of high-profile arrests of military officers, businessmen, and activists. By the winter of 2008, reports in the press began to surface, each suggesting that the weapons uncovered in Trabzon were linked to terrorist attacks in various parts of the country. The individuals apprehended, media reports argued, were a part of an extensive network of individuals seeking to destabilize the current government of Tayyip Erdoğan, whose Justice and Development Party (*Adalet ve Kalkışma Partisi*, or AKP) had been re-elected to power after a landslide victory in July 2007. Since 2008, scores of individuals have been taken into custody and questioned on suspicion of belonging to Ergenekon, a vast organization, prosecutors claim, that was at the heart of a series of violent acts that undermined civilian rule over a twenty-year period.[3] The detention, questioning, and imprisonment of hundreds of individuals for their role in Ergenekon now seems to have reversed the political culture instilled by the 1980 coup. With each arrest and each judicial hearing, the air of secrecy that once concealed the actions and crimes of the post-coup era seems to dissipate, revealing an ever-more complex and ugly series of state-executed crimes.

Turkey's underworld has not been immune to this seismic shift within the country's political system. Since 2008, a number of notorious gangsters have been interrogated or brought up on charges of being a part of the Ergenekon conspiracy. The arrest of these prominent criminal figures, whose exploits generally date back to the 1980s and 1990s, has been interpreted as symptomatic of the changes wrought by the AKP's new hold on power. The discovery of Ergenekon, as many would have it, represents a general decline in the political influence once held by individuals and parties allied with the old "guardians of the state." The unveiling of this conspiracy appears to have definitively revealed a long-standing partnership between violent, undemocratic forces that have successfully bridled the Turkish state in the name of national security.

The inclusion of gangsters in the Ergenekon conspiracy seems to mark an unceremonious end to an age of extremes with respect to the political influence of organized crime in Turkey. In the two decades preceding the Ergenekon investigation, newspapers in Turkey featured a regular diet of stories discussing mafia-style killings, high-profile arrests, and fruitless criminal prosecutions into drug smuggling and governmental corruption. While the coup of 1980 had produced a number of conspicuous investigations against many of the prominent *baba*s of the 1970s (with several, including Dündar Kılıç, Abuzer Uğurlu, and Kürt İdris, receiving considerable prison sentences), the weight and influence of smugglers and racketeers appeared to grow as the 1980s progressed into the 1990s. An even younger generation of gangsters appeared to take the place of the notorious *baba*s

[3] For a general synopsis of the Ergenekon investigation, see Gareth Jenkins, "Between Fact and Fantasy: Turkey's Ergenekon Investigation," *Silk Road Papers* (Washington DC: Central Asia-Caucasus Institute and Silk Road Studies, 2009), 1–84.

of the pre-coup era. Like their predecessors in previous decades, this new breed of bosses, such as Sedat Peker and Alaattin Çakacı, made no secret of their political connections despite their reputation for violence and illicit dealings. The mysterious circumstances surrounding Abdullah Çatlı's death in 1996, in essence, gave further credence to the generally held opinion in Turkey that the country's underworld forms one of the pillars upon which the Turkish state rests. Democratic elections, constitutional law, and criminal courts provided, it seemed, only a thin veil obscuring the true sources of political authority in Ankara.

The discovery of the supposed Ergenekon conspiracy, coupled with the imprisonment of virtually all of Turkey's most notorious mobsters, appears to have produced an unprecedented reversal in the underworld's political fortunes. Journalists and commentators appear eager to greet the fall of these criminal figures as the hallmark of the new order that has resulted in criminal prosecutions of far more noted and powerful "guardians of the state." In an interview in 2011, Bülent Orakoğlu, a former intelligence officer within Turkey's national police, declared that while members of the "mafia" still held ties with the state, the age of a politically active and strong Turkish underworld was, for the time being, over. "These structures are currently asleep. However, they can become active again if they find a suitable political environment."[4]

The failing political fortunes of Turkey's more notorious gangsters has not impeded the illicit trafficking that helped to bring the Turkish underworld to life. Like many other countries since the end of the Cold War, narcotics trafficking in and out of Turkey has grown more diverse and ever-more lucrative. Continued illicit opium cultivation in Afghanistan, despite a brief dip in the late 1990s, remains a staple base for morphine and heroin production smuggled through Turkey. A vibrant "Balkan route" connecting Turkish wholesalers to retailers in Europe and elsewhere endures as a central conduit for heroin. According to Turkey's Department for Combating Smuggling and Organized Crime, 80 percent of drugs consumed in Europe is now trafficked through the southern Balkans.[5] Arrests and seizures in Turkey and elsewhere in the last decade testify to the fact that Turkish smugglers retain interests in the trade of other narcotics, including marijuana, ecstasy, and cocaine.[6]

The economic liberalization policies introduced by Turgut Özal in the 1980s have had a dramatic impact upon Turkey's black market. Ankara's adaptation to the norms of free trade has clearly been a boon for Turkish consumers who were previously prevented from purchasing higher quality foreign goods. The growth of Turkey's legitimate export industry appears to have had an equally mitigating effect upon such sectors as coffee and nut production (two products that were frequently

[4] Serkan Sağlam and Salih Sarıkaya, "Mafia now a Real Threat Only in the Movies," *Today's Zaman* 9 January 2011.

[5] Mahmut Cengiz, *Turkish Organized Crime: From Local to Global* (Saarbrücken, Germany: VDM Verlag Dr. Müller, 2011), 18.

[6] For the most recent statistics and analysis compiled by Turkey's Interior Ministry, see "Türkiye Uyuşturucu: 2012 Raporu" (Ankara: Kaçakçılık ve Örgüt Suçlarla Mücadele Daire Başkanlığı, 2012).

smuggled out of the country before the Özal era).[7] Yet other longtime black market commodities, such as cigarettes, currency, and weapons, continue to be plied alongside the region's growing human trafficking industry.[8]

It was during the 1980s that the Turkish press began to pay greater attention to the economic and geographical organization of major criminal syndicates in the country. Özal's reforms unleashed economic growth in major urban centers, creating, it seems, new opportunities for gangsters to participate in otherwise legitimate industries. *Milliyet*, in a feature investigation in 1998, surveyed the emergence of "land mafias" taking shape in the city of Istanbul. The city's rapidly growing suburbs along its western and eastern fringes offered opportunities for extortionists with friends in local government to sell and buy property (often under the threat of violence) as well as to contribute to the construction of new and often poorly built high-rises. The article further suggested that the city's suburbs had already been partitioned by a variety of gangs and notorious criminal figures. While Ali Yasak, more commonly known as Drej Ali, claimed ownership of the neighborhood of Zeytinburnu, close to the city's western Theodosian walls, Sedat Peker was known to haunt and influence neighborhood dealings in the Asian district of Maltepe. Meanwhile Kurdish mafia groups, Black Sea gangs, and Islamist syndicates asserted territorial claims to Ümraniye, Dudullu, and Sultanbeyli, respectively.[9]

Turkey's expanding policing apparatus has developed lockstep with the increasing number of illicit trades in the country. Months before the 1980 coup, the Interior Ministry created a special department (the Ministry's Department of Smuggling, or *Kaçakçılık Daire Başbakanlığı*) responsible for overseeing law enforcement issues (including intelligence) related to smuggling.[10] The office further expanded in 1995 and was renamed the Ministry's Department for Combatting Smuggling and Organized Crime (*Kaçakçılık ve Organize Suçlarla Mücadele Daire Başkanlığı* or KOM). In anticipation of the United Nation's first convention targeting the activities of "transnational organized crime" in 2000, the Turkish National Police, with the assistance of the United Nations Office of Drug Control (UNODC) established an international school tasked with training native and foreign officers on issues related to narcotics and organized crime.[11] As of 2011, TADOC (the Turkish Academy Against Drugs and Organized Crime) has trained thousands of officers from Turkey and thirty other countries in a variety of professional and academic topics including drug reduction techniques, criminal intelligence

[7] Interestingly there seems to be little analysis of how coffee smuggling came to an end as an illicit industry in Turkey. For example, Abuzer Uğurlu confessed in 1982 that he had begun smuggling coffee in 1968 but had abandoned this and other smuggling practices after the government issued a general amnesty to traffickers in 1974. See "Uğurlu 'Kaçakçılıkğın Her Türlüsünü Yaptım,'" *Milliyet* 16 December 1982.

[8] Cengiz, *Turkish Organized Crime: From Local to Global*, 20–24.

[9] Sevinç Yavuz, "İstanbul'un Taşı Toprağı Karapara," *Milliyet* 26 July 1998. For greater discussion of the various types of otherwise legal industries infiltrated by organized crime groups in Turkey see Adil Sedar Saçan, *Ak Baba Örgütü* (Istanbul: Toplumsal Dönüşüm Yayınları, 2004).

[10] Ünlü, *Susurluk Gümrüğü: Kaçakçılık—Çete—Devlet*, 19.

[11] See Cengiz, *Turkish Organized Crime: From Local to Global*, 95–96; <http://www.kom.gov.tr/Tr/KonuDetay.asp?id=0&BKey=21> (accessed 13 February 2013).

analysis, undercover training, and organized crime investigations.[12] The academy, which is located in Ankara, represents a broader push by Turkish law enforcement to engage transnational illicit trades on a multilateral plane. In addition to direct cooperation with individual states as well as multinational collectives such as OSCE and EUROPOL, KOM is a founding member of the Southeast European Law Enforcement Center (SELEC), a cooperative among Balkan states formed in 2009 in order to promote intelligence sharing and cross border logistical support for the region's national police departments.[13] Meanwhile, the American DEA remains active in its cooperative pursuits in Turkey. In addition to assisting and collaborating with Turkish customs officers, gendarmes, and policemen, the DEA's Ankara office serves as a center for investigations and cooperative activities in the states of Azerbaijan, Armenia, Iran, Iraq, Turkmenistan, and Georgia.[14]

It is somewhat difficult to reconcile organized crime's apparent political retreat in Turkey with the ongoing seriousness with which Ankara, as well as other international stakeholders, continues to regard heroin trafficking and other illicit trades in the region. The fall of major figures within Turkey's underworld seems to contrast with the outward resilience of the smuggling activities in the contemporary republic. How does one account for the supposed success with which contemporary prosecutors have dismantled organized crime's political clout in Ankara even though illicit trades remain more financially lucrative than ever? Are today's *baba*s simply "asleep" and waiting to reemerge as a political force? Or has the weight of new law enforcement techniques, coupled with the earnestness of the AKP's political will, brought about a new political environment free from the influence of gangsters?

In deciphering the current state of Turkish organized crime, many observers both inside and outside of Turkey have relied heavily upon a fairly new concept used to describe and interpret what many see as the historically clandestine and illicit nature of the country's governance. In the minds of many, the prosecution of gangsters alongside individuals likes Kenan Evren (who was arrested in January 2012 for spearheading the 1980 coup) epitomizes the notion that gangsters, most notably narcotics traffickers, composed a critical component of Turkey's so-called deep state (*derin devlet*).

The concept of the deep state entered popular speech following the Susurluk scandal.[15] Politicians (both current and retired), as well as army officers, journalists, and academics, have employed this term with even greater frequency in the years following the opening of the Ergenekon investigation. Opinions as to what constitutes Turkey's deep state vary radically even between those accused of being among its founders and participants. Speaking in 2005, Süleyman Demirel identified the deep state in the following way:

12 See "Annual TADOC Bulletin, Januaruy 2012" (Ankara: Kaçakçılık ve Örgüt Suçlarla Mücadele Daire Başkanlığı, 2012).

13 See <http://www.secicenter.org/m485/SELEC> (accessed 13 February 2013).

14 See <http://turkey.usembassy.gov/dea.html> (accessed 13 February 2013).

15 "'Derin Devlet' Sözlükte," *Milliyet* 8 February 2004.

> That evening [on 12 September 1980] . . . it was 3:59 am . . . the first decree was read on television: "The glorious Turkish nation . . ." Up until that minute there was no deep state. The administration was handed over and it became the state. The deep state is the military. The deep state is the state itself. They are not a state but in the times when the state was seized they became the deep state . . . Who are those inside of the deep state? You should look at the situation this way. Those who are inside of the deep state are, in normal times, certain authorities who want to become saviors (*kurtarıcı*). They feel that they are like this. However, someone did not give them this task.[16]

As cryptic as Demirel's explanation appears, Kenan Evren, when asked about the former prime minister's comments, agreed with the contention that the deep state and the military can be one and the same.[17] Speaking more recently, Prime Minister Tayyip Erdoğan has given further credence to the existence of the deep state as a political force in Turkey. Speaking on television in January 2007, Erdoğan expressed his belief that the deep state "had always been there" and was a phenomenon carried over from the Ottomans.[18]

Newspaper coverage of the Ergenekon trials has compelled observers and commentators in Turkey to use the term more expansively. If one accepts the Ergenekon investigation as quintessential confirmation of the deep state's existence, the current list of the conspiracy's suspects provides a sprawling exhibition of the diverse array of individuals and organizations at the core and periphery of Turkey's supposed deep state.

Generals, policemen, nationalist activists, journalists, television presenters, professors, lawyers, civil servants, spies, businessmen, entertainers, and, of course, gangsters have each been identified as playing major and minor roles in creating and perpetuating the Ergenekon organization. Regardless of how exactly one defines the contours of the deep state, the implications of its supposed existence are crystal clear: shadowy figures and factions, some without any official recognition or standing, have been the true arbiters of power in Turkey.

Current discourse on Turkey's supposed deep state provides some insights that are useful in bringing this study of narcotics trafficking and organized crime in Turkey to a close. More than anything, the disclosures that have emerged as a result of the Susurluk scandal, as well as even more recent revelations emanating from the Ergenekon investigation, provide a legitimate pretext for scholars and lay observers to contemplate the historical and political significance of organized crime in Turkey. Recent academic studies of the deep state paradigm outside of Turkey has also afforded some degree of context and comparative difference in assessing how and why criminal syndicates have helped to shape politics and the economy in the modern world.

[16] Akçura, *Derin Devltet Oldu Devlet*, 16.

[17] Merve Kavakci, "Turkey's Test with Its Deep State," *Mediterranean Quarterly* 20.4 (Fall 2009), 90.

[18] Mehmet Barlas, "Osmanlı'da Oyun Bitmez," *Sabah* (29 January 2007) <http://arsiv.sabah.com.tr/2007/01/29/yaz09-40-105.html> (accessed 1 February 2014).

However, there are certain pitfalls in utilizing the deep state as a prism of analysis when attempting to assess both the general history of Turkey, as well as organized crime's place in it. There is a general temptation to see essential or monolithic deep states firmly embedded within the late Ottoman Empire and the Republic of Turkey. Rather than analyze the social, economic, or political reasons for factionalism, violence, and secrecy found within the polies undertaken by Ankara or Istanbul, many attempt to isolate and identify the deep state as an enduring pattern or tradition of specific conspiratorial cabals. No particular facet of the Turkish state, overtly or covertly, has ever held absolute sway over the management of the country. Governance in Turkey, from its conception as a state, was hotly contested both at its center and its margins. Throughout Turkey's history (including the reign of the Ottomans), the parties and individuals involved in challenging and shaping the state's development have evolved considerably. If one had to pinpoint one element of continuity connecting the various regimes spanning the years between Enver, Atatürk, and Erdoğan, it is clear that the politics of national security have had a consistent bearing on who has assumed positions of power and how state policy has been acted upon in public and behind closed doors.

In thinking about organized crime within the framework of deep state politics, it is clear that the underworld's political significance is interconnected with the development of Turkish politics and society. A singular or unified underworld has never existed, at any level, within the Turkish Republic. Nevertheless, between the establishment of the Committee Union and Progress and the imposition of martial law in 1980, this *milieu*, now generally called the Turkish mafia, gained increasing economic and, consequently, political strength within the country at both local and national levels. In order to understand how handfuls of gangsters and smugglers gradually asserted themselves within Turkish political life, one must contend with a confluence of factors. The emergence of networks of Istanbul, Black Sea, or eastern Anatolian groups has depended largely on internal and external forces related to the migration of peoples, the flow of illicit commodities (particularly heroin), and the changing nature of state policies towards the economy. The development of criminal syndicates throughout Turkey was the product of the interaction between underworld figures and representatives of the Turkish state. A close inspection of sources spanning the twentieth century suggests that relations between gangsters, smugglers, officers, and politicians were simultaneously confrontational and cooperative. Like the imperial state before it, the Turkish Republic has continuously expanded its security apparatus. The desire to combat differing forms of organized criminal behavior, particularly banditry and smuggling, inspired this pattern of state development. In the case of narcotics trafficking, the United States played a major role in improving upon Ankara's capacity (and willingness) to address domestic criminal syndicates.

And yet, corruption or shared economic interests led elements of the Turkish state (or, if one wishes, the Turkish "deep state") to ally themselves or cooperate with smugglers or gangsters. Turkish, as well as American, desires to maintain a semblance of law and order was an equally common excuse for patronizing and abetting criminal networks. In its most extreme cases, a mutual aspiration to uphold the integrity of the Turkish state provided a potent incentive for forging ties between these otherwise adversarial actors.

FROM SUSURLUK TO ERGENEKON: REVELATIONS FROM TURKEY'S DEEP STATE

Dündar Kılıç did not live to see the trials that brought down many of his compatriots in the early twenty-first century. At the end of July 1999, he suffered a serious heart attack at his summer home in Selimpaşa, an upmarket seaside neighborhood in Istanbul. He was rushed into town to the American Hospital where he died after ten days in intensive care.[19] He was laid to rest shortly afterwards in Zincirlikuyu, a cemetery that houses the remains of such luminaries of Turkish politics and society as Ali Fethi Okyar, Sakıp Sabancı, Vehbi Koç, and Orhan Kemal. A diverse cast of mourners assembled to pay their final respects to Turkey's "last *kabadayı*." Counted among the more noted individuals present that day was shipping magnate Şadan Kalkavan, Süleyman Seba, a former soccer star and chairman of the Beşiktaş sporting club, and Yaşar Kemal, one of Turkey's most celebrated journalists and authors. When asked why he attended the funeral, Yaşar stated that "after years of journalism, [Dündar] had become my friend." The list of attendees also included prominent figures from the underworld. İdris Özbir, who had been Kılıç's main associate from his early days in Istanbul, joined in the burial but reportedly did not take part in the prayers offered up on his old partner's behalf. A second contemporary underworld figure paying his respects at the cemetery that day was Sami Hoştan.[20]

At the time of Dündar Kılıç's death, Sami Hoştan had become a household name in Turkey. Born in the Macedonian capital of Skopje in 1947, he arrived in Turkey at the age of seven and settled in the city of Istanbul (where he acquired the nickname *Arnavut* Sami, or Sami the Albanian). Over the course of his life he spent much of his time working in Europe, primarily in the Netherlands.[21] By the 1990s he had earned a reputation as a major investor and partner in several casinos in Istanbul as well as the Netherlands. His involvement in gambling, according to prosecutors in both Western Europe and Turkey, served to mask his involvement in the narcotics trade. In 1992, he was accused of smuggling close to 300 kilos of heroin into Holland and Germany.[22] In this case, as well as in a similar trial in Turkey in 2000, Sami was released due to the lack of evidence.[23]

The fallout of the Susurluk scandal, more than any other event, attracted the greatest amount of public scrutiny of Sami Hoştan's involvement in the Turkish

[19] Hakan Aslaneli, "Famous Mafia Godfather Dies of Heart Attack," *Hürriyet Daily News* 12 August 1999.
[20] "'Son Kabadayı' Toprağa Verildi," *Milliyet* 13 August 1999.
[21] "Dündar ve Hoştan'ın 'Garip' İlişkisi," *Haber 7* 15 October 2008.
[22] "Hoştan'ın 66 Yıl Hapsi İsteniyor," *Milliyet* 19 April 2000.
[23] "No Verdict for Sami Hoştan," *Hürriyet Daily News* 14 July 2000.

underworld. From 1996 onwards, a number of state inquiries, government reports, and newspaper exposés present a muddled picture of the individuals who formed Hoştan's social and personal circle. Although never convicted of any wrongdoing as a result of the scandal, government prosecutors have long maintained *Arnavut* Sami was one of a large cast of gangsters, politicians, and security personnel who helped to form a series of state-backed gangs (*çetes*) deployed against the PKK. Court proceedings and newspaper investigations have also suggested that these gangs exerted equal force within the Turkish underworld, a phenomenon that further blurred the line between the state and organized crime in the country.

The first indication of the complex and twisted web tying individuals like Sami to the Susurluk scandal came as a direct result of the car crash that killed Abdullah Çatlı in November 1996. Investigators who arrived at the scene discovered four passengers in the wreck of the car. Of the four, three individuals were found dead in the Mercedes: Çatlı, Hüseyin Kocadağ, the deputy chief of Istanbul's DPS office, and Çatlı's mistress, Gonca Us. The one passenger who survived the crash was soon identified as Sedat Bucak, a member of the National Assembly and head of a Kurdish tribe from the region of Urfa. The plot thickened when press reports got wind of the presence of both weapons and official passports bearing Çatlı's pictures and assumed aliases. The passports, which were reserved for special state employees, had been signed personally by the Minister of the Interior, Mehmet Ağar, a one time high-ranking DPS official who had recently been appointed to the Interior Ministry. The right to judicial immunity allowed Ağar and Bucak to evade harsh questioning after the crash. While Bucak initially claimed that his presence in the car that day was a mere coincidence, Ağar asserted that national security prevented him from revealing the full extent of his relationship with Abdullah Çatlı.[24] After the scandal broke, a commission formed in the Turkish Grand National Assembly, as well as the Turkish National Intelligence Service, offered their own interpretations of the events with the release of several general reports on the overlapping nature of what was referred to as the "state-mafia-politics connections."[25] MİT's third report, which was leaked to the press in February 1996, rendered no definitive judgement on the conspiracy formed by Ağar, Bucak, Çatlı, and others. No actual killings were ever definitively linked to the conspiracy formed by these men. Mehmet Ağar did stand trial in September 2011 and was found guilty of forming a criminal gang (even though this gang has never been implicated officially in any crime).[26]

[24] James Meyer, "Politics as Usual: Ciller, Refah and Susurluk: Turkey's Troubled Democracy," *Eastern European Quarterly* 32.4 (January 1999), 493–495.

[25] Human Rights Foundation of Turkey, *1998 Human Rights Report*, 565.

[26] "Mehmet Ağar Appeals Conviction in Susurluk Trial," *Today's Zaman* 16 September 2011; "High Court Upholds Five-Year Prison Sentence for Ex-Police Chief," *Today's Zaman* 15 April 2012. Ağar was sentenced to five years in prison on the following charges:

> …establishing an armed organization for the purpose of committing crimes, failing to inform authorities of the whereabouts of a suspect [Çatlı], granting firearms licenses to Çatlı and Yaşar Öz in violation of the law, ensuring the granting of senior public servant passports to Çatlı and Öz in violation of the law and dereliction of duty.

Much of MİT's third report deals with issues tangential to the activities of the principal figures directly connected to the Susurluk accident. The report examines an array of claims and accusations that had largely surfaced within the press (suggesting, for example, that further investigations should be made into suspected money-laundering activities conducted by former Prime Minister Tansu Çiller and exiled spiritual leader Fethullah Gülen).[27] Evidence marshaled for the report is scant. Nevertheless, Turkey's intelligence service did conclude that the Susurluk accident had clearly demonstrated that "an alliance" had been formed that was "hard to define and defend."[28]

Sami Hoştan is one of a number of individuals mentioned within an intricate and confusing web of possible participants or associates with the Susurluk gang. Two particular figures associated with Hoştan attracted the attention of official investigators: Veli Küçük, a general from the Turkish gendarmerie, and Ömer Lüftü Topal, a recently deceased operator of several large casinos in Turkey. Küçük, the reputed founder of the gendarmerie's secret intelligence unit, JİTEM, allegedly met Hoştan in 1986 while he served in a local gendarmerie headquarters in Edirne, west of Istanbul.[29] According to testimony given by an anonymous witness, the two continued to meet into the early 1990s while Küçük was the commander of the Kocaeli gendarme detachment.[30] In addition to these meetings, the two shared dealings with Topal, who partnered with Hoştan in establishing the Sheraton Casino in Istanbul in 1995.[31] Küçük refused to confirm his relationship with Hoştan throughout his examination during the Susurluk proceedings.[32]

Press reports since 1996 have often speculated that Veli Küçük served as a linchpin for JİTEM's effort to court prominent underworld figures and persuade them to take part in the fight against the PKK and ASALA. One crucial piece of evidence linking Küçük to top Turkish gangsters was a cell phone believed to belong to Mahmut Yıldırım, a shadowy figure frequently referred to as JİTEM's most feared assassin. Records from the phone, court officials argue, demonstrate that the device had been registered by Küçük and was frequently used to call Abdullah Çatlı as well as other reputed gangsters.[33]

Official interest in the connection between suspects involved in the Susurluk scandal and Ömer Topal underscores another side of the investigation, one completely divorced from Ankara's struggle with Kurdish rebels. Months before the crash, men armed with Kalashnikovs ambushed Topal in a suburban section of Istanbul, riddling his body with scores of bullets. In late 1996, three of Sedat Bucak's bodyguards (who were also members of the Turkish special forces) were arrested for

[27] Human Rights Foundation of Turkey, "*1998 Human Rights Report*," 571.
[28] Human Rights Foundation of Turkey, "*1998 Human Rights Report*," 573.
[29] "Dündar ve Hoştan'ın 'Garip' İlişkisi," *Haber 7* 15 October 2008.
[30] "Cem Tursan, Küçük, Hoştan'la Alayda Görüştü," *Hürriyet* 14 December 2011.
[31] "Dündar ve Hoştan'ın 'Garip' İlişkisi," *Haber 7* 15 October 2008.
[32] Erkan Acar and Büşra Erdal, "Cross Examination Silences Retired Gen. Veli Küçük," *Today's Zaman* 17 December 2008.
[33] Nuri İmre and Baran Taş, "Küçük Remains Obstinate Despite Clear-Cut Evidence," *Today's Zaman* 15 December 2008.

the shooting but were released upon the orders of then Interior Minister Mehmet Ağar.[34] Still other reports suggest that Abdullah Çatlı's fingerprints were discovered on one of the weapons found at the scene.[35] While no one has ever been charged with the killing, Susurluk investigators have made frequent note of Topal's historic dealings with organized crime as well as with state-employed assassins. His emergence as Turkey's "casino king" was premised upon his long and well-documented history as a heroin trafficker. After Belgian authorities imprisoned him in 1979 for importing almost seven kilos of heroin (for which he received a five-year sentence), he was arrested and imprisoned a second time in the United States on similar charges.[36] Topal, according to one official report, partnered with Çatlı in one of his casino ventures even though he (a Kurd from Malatya) had sympathies with the PKK.[37] Moreover, telephone records suggest that Topal frequently called both Hoştan (who, in addition to being his partner, was a childhood friend) and Küçük.[38]

The potential motives for the killing remain as elusive as the culprits of the crime. His interlocking relationship with the PKK, state assassins, and the underworld, many suspect, were perhaps the most likely triggers for his death. Years after Topal's death, newspaper reports suggested that Mahmut Yıldırım had extorted millions of dollars from the casino magnate. Often referred to in the press by his codename Green or *Yeşil*, Yıldırım was suspected of similar extortion plots while in the service of JİTEM and MİT.[39] It is also suggested that Topal was one of a number of Kurdish businessmen targeted for assassination by members of the Susurluk conspiracy (this list may also have included Behçet Cantürk, who was abducted and found murdered in 1993).[40] Regardless of who killed Topal or what precisely motivated his killers, the link between his murder and the Susurluk conspiracy seems to suggest that Çatlı and other gangsters used state protection to settle scores and expand their interests within the Turkish underworld.

Necmettin Erbakan, who had become prime minister in the summer of 1996, remained silent in the week after the crash was first reported. Meanwhile, his immediate predecessor, Mesut Yılmaz, declared that "the state was under the occupation of killers and thieves" and that the "mafia was intertwined, shoulder to shoulder, with the state." Erbakan's vice prime minister, Tansu Çiller, offered a tepid and callous response to the suspicious circumstances connecting the victims of the crash. She rejected such "slander" and argued that "we [be it her supporters or the government]" were not the ones who "went to casinos" or associated with

[34] "Turkey Still Coming to Grips with Susurluk Crash on 10th Anniversary," *Turkish Daily News* 3 November 2006.

[35] Bozarslan, *Network-Building*, 10.

[36] Esrar Kaçakçı, "2 Türk Belçika'da Hapse Mahkum Oldu," *Milliyet* 27 April 1979.

[37] Human Rights Foundation of Turkey, "1998 Human Rights Report," 533.

[38] "Bu Susurluk Bitmez," *Milliyet* 3 November 1999; Human Rights Foundation of Turkey, "1998 Human Rights Report," 538.

[39] "The Illusive Yeşil," *Hürriyet Daily News* 6 March 1998; "Her Taşın altı 'Yeşil'," *Milliyet* 3 November 1999.

[40] Bozarslan, *Network-Building*, 10.

the mafia but the ones who had prepared legislation countering money laundering.[41] Her comments became more combative one week later when she famously declared, with respect to Abdullah Çatlı, "those who shoot or take wounds on the behalf of the state are respected by us. For us, they are honorable men."[42] Deniz Baykal, then head of the Republican People's Party, called Çiller's sentiments a "false understanding" of the meaning of honorable. "The ones who are honorable are Abdi İpekçi and Uğur Mumcu [two journalists killed allegedly by members of organized crime]. Are those among our people (*halkımız*) who live modestly not honorable?"[43]

Confidence in the Turkish government plummeted with the many embarrassing disclosures that emerged after Susurluk. Matters grew worse after February 1997 when the Turkish general staff presented Erbakan with an ultimatum demanding that he take a harder line on fighting "political Islam." The ultimatum, which was clearly aimed at undermining the legitimacy and strength of Erbakan's religiously conservative base, ultimately led to his resignation in June. However, neither Erbakan's ousting, nor the continuing poor economic news in Turkey, displaced Susurluk from the media's attention.

Organized crime, meanwhile, appeared as deeply entrenched in the final years of the twentieth century as it did before the scandal. As Turkey entered the new century, four figures in particular achieved greater amounts of public notoriety. Of the four, three of them, Alaattin Çakıcı, Sedat Peker, and Ali Yasak, embodied the emergence of a particularly nationalist trend among gangsters first seen during the 1970s. These *ülkücü* mobsters, an epithet used in reference to their support of the politics of Alparslan Türkeş and the Nationalist Action Party, were uniformly indoctrinated at an early age within the confines of youth organizations such as the *Ülkü Ocakları Derneği*. Yet unlike their ideological predecessors within the Turkish underworld (such as Abuzer Uğurlu or Abdullah Çatlı) law enforcement officials inside and outside of the country never accused any of these men of involvement in Turkey's burgeoning heroin trade. The fourth figure found among this new elite, Hüseyin Baybaşin, typified trends first established by the rise of new Kurdish factions that had established themselves in both Turkey and western Europe in the 1970s. While often operating within the same political and criminal environment as his *ülkücü* counterparts, Baybaşin's political leanings reflected the escalating power and influence of the PKK as the focal point for dissident Kurds both within and exclusive of this new generation of *baba*s. While Baybaşin's support for the PKK may have put him at odds with the general consensus found among other politically active gangsters during the 1980s and 1990s, the Susurluk scandal, as well as the subsequent inquiries into the Ergenekon case, cast all four of these figures as critical actors within Turkey's unfolding deep state.

41 "Çiller: Demirel'de Belge Yok," *Milliyet* 14 November 1996.

42 "Çiller: Abdullah Çatlı Şerefli," *Milliyet* 27 November 1996. She also suggested that Mesut Yılmaz was also personally close to Abdullah Çatlı.

43 "Yılmaz: Çetenin Başı Vezirdir," *Milliyet* 19 December 1996.

Alaattin Çakıcı, like many other self-proclaimed Istanbul *kabadayıs* before him, was born (in 1953) along the Black Sea Coast in the town of Arsin, located close to Trabzon. His entrance into the Istanbul underworld during the 1980s came by the way of older criminal trades more fitting of a traditional *kabadayı*. By the late 1980s, he had achieved wide notoriety as an extortionist in both Istanbul and Ankara (often claiming 50 percent of the proceeds of the debts and bills he collected on the behalf of his clients). His earnings as a racketeer were later reinvested in casinos and hotels (although he reportedly left the gambling business after falling foul of one of his partners).[44] Arguably Çakıcı's greatest source of influence and power derived from his early involvement in *ülkücu* youth gangs. In June 1981, he was arrested and implicated along with fourteen other individuals in involvement in the murder of forty-one people during the height of Turkey's factional violence.[45] His status as an avowed right wing militant brought him into powerful circles. In addition to close ties with government ministers, Çakıcı, like Çatlı before him, entered into state service as a clandestine operative for executive actions abroad. According to Yavuz Ataç, who once served in MİT's Foreign Operations Department, as well as being Turkish representative to NATO, both Çakıcı and Çatlı were integral members of the Turkish military's Special Warfare Office's Gladio initiative.[46]

Despite having no direct connection to the crash, the Susurluk scandal heightened Çakıcı's significance within Turkey. Newspaper reporting, as well as official government inquiries, repeatedly mentioned his involvement in activities linked to Abdullah Çatlı's service as a state-backed contract killer. In August 1998, French police arrested him in Nice after he was accused of attempting to extort sums of money from bankers in the country. Police discovered an official passport in his possession at the time of his arrest, leading to suggestions that he, like Çatlı, was secretly employed by the elements of the Turkish state. A series of tape recordings of conversations between Çakıcı and an interior minister, also produced at the time of his arrest, gave further credence to this conclusion.[47] After a short extradition struggle, he was remanded to Turkish custody. In 2002, despite accusations and official inquiries into at least four other serious crimes (including the murder of Dündar Kılıç's daughter and his former wife, Uğur), Alaattin was released from prison after serving only three years.[48] He briefly escaped justice yet again in 2004 after fleeing the country when the news broke that he would be imprisoned for a raid on the Karagümrük soccer club in the Fatih section of Istanbul. It was later discovered that he obtained his visa to Greece with the help of officials from the

[44] "Alaatin Çakıcı'nın Gazinolardan Haraç İstediği Öne Sürülüyor," *Cumhuriyet* 15 November 1985; "Alaattin Çakıcı Kimdir?," *Sabah* <http://arsiv.sabah.com.tr/ozel/alaattin58/dosya_113.html> (accessed 17 February 2013); Soner Gürel, "'Baba'lar Banka Gibi," *Milliyet* 10 April 1988.

[45] "41 Kişiyi Öldüren Sağcı 15 Terörist Yakalandı," *Milliyet* 8 June 1981.

[46] Akçura, *Derin Devltet Oldu Devlet*, 34–55.

[47] Soner Arıkanoğlu, "Çakıcı Nice'te Yakalandı," *Radikal* 18 August 1998; Human Rights Foundation of Turkey, "1998 Human Rights Report," 79.

[48] Semra Pelek et al., "Üç Yılda Tahliye!. . ." *Milliyet* 30 November 2002.

Beşiktaş soccer club, who wrote a letter of recommendation on his behalf.[49] He was again captured in Austria and was returned to prison (where he is currently serving two lengthy jail sentences related to violent extortion schemes involving both the Karagümrük attack and an Istanbul stockbroker).[50]

A second, even younger, figure who encapsulated the spirit of organized crime in Turkey at the end of the twentieth century was Sedat Peker. Sedat was born in Sakarya (immediately east of Istanbul) in 1971. While he shared filial ties with the Black Sea (since his family had originally migrated to western Turkey from Rize), his childhood years were largely spent in Germany. Like Alaattin Çakıcı, extortion, as opposed to narcotics, served as the primary basis for his entry into a life of crime.[51] Sedat, who equally fancied himself a *kabadayı* in the traditional mold, explicitly derided those who profited from the drug trade (to the point that newspapers often referred to him as the "*baba* who struggles against narcotics").[52] He also shared Çakıcı's nationalist political leanings.[53] His stature as an *ülkücu* provided a reasonable basis for his inclusion in official investigations into the Susurluk scandal. In one report issued by the Turkish Grand National Assembly, Peker had telephoned Veli Küçük on numerous occasions, leading to further suspicions that he, like Abdullah Çatlı and Sami Hoştan, served as a "friend" of Turkey's gendarmerie.[54] In August 1998, prosecutors in Istanbul sought his arrest for a series of crimes related to his extortion activities.[55] Although convicted and imprisoned briefly, newspapers eagerly highlighted the many luxuries Peker had at his disposal while in the custody of the state.[56] Sedat's salacious exploits and high-profile relationships continued after his release in 1999. His relations with celebrities from Turkey's entertainment industry remain frequent fodder for newspaper tabloids.[57] In 2002, Istanbul police arrested him while he was sitting chatting with one of Turkey's most famous pop singers, İbrahim Tatlıses, in the city's most modern and opulent shopping center.[58] In a book published in 2004, journalist Ecevit Kılıç detailed Peker's long-standing influence over the teams, players, and officials of the Turkish Football Association. His work as both a player agent and gangster, according to Kılıç, led to his involvement in match-fixing, boardroom takeovers,

[49] Fatma Demirelli, "Beşiktaş Involvement in Çakıcı Escape Under Probe," *Hürriyet Daily News* 12 May 2004; "Futboldaki Susurluk," *Milliyet* 20 May 2004.

[50] "Çakıcı Gets 10 Years and 10 Months," *Hürriyet Daily News* 1 March 2006.

[51] "Lakabı Köroğlu," *Milliyet* 25 September 1999; Ömer Ülkü, "Sedat Peker Döndü," *Milliyet* 20 August 1998.

[52] "Sedat Peker Arslan Gibi Yaşarmış," *Radikal* 18 September 1999.

[53] He once stood accused of ordering the death of a barman who had tattooed the Word "Allah" on his arm. See Ömer Ülkü, "Sedat Peker Döndü," *Milliyet* 20 August 1998.

[54] "Yeşil'in 'Cep'I Küçük'ün," *Milliyet* 2 March 1998.

[55] Ömer Ülkü, "Sedat Peker Döndü," *Milliyet* 20 August 1998.

[56] Among the many comforts found in his possession in prison were washing machines, refrigerators, televisions, vases, and oil paintings. See "Peker's Luxurious Prison Life," *Hürriyet Daily News* 26 October 1998.

[57] See e.g. Lube Ayar, "Hepsi Reis'e Hayran," *Milliyet* 5 June 2005.

[58] "Police Detain Gang Leader Peker," *Hürriyet Daily News* 22 October 2002.

and the beating of the national team's star goalkeeper, Rüştü Reçber.[59] Journalists have also speculated that his relationship with actor Oktay Kaynarca, who played the character of Süleyman Çakır in the series *Valley of the Wolves*, may have influenced the decision to kill the character off in the first season.[60]

The third person on this list of preeminent characters from Turkey's late century underworld shared a similar pedigree to Peker and Çakıcı. Ali Yasak, better known as Drej (or tall in Kurdish) Ali, made his mark as a gangster in the late 1980s as an extortionist and debt collector in Istanbul (he too, it seems, was never arrested or accused of any complicity in Turkey's drug trade). Like Peker, his reputation for violence first catapulted him to national notoriety when he shot and wounded another infamous *kabadayı*, Nabi İnciler (more commonly known as İnci Baba) after a personal dispute.[61] Also like Çakıcı and Peker, Drej Ali was an active member of the *Ülkü Ocakları* as a youth in Urfa. His nationalist leanings appear all the more curious considering the fact that he, like Uğurlus, was raised as a Kurd.[62] In 1996, this self-proclaimed "large landowner" and "tea garden proprietor" became a name frequently mentioned in the context of the Susurluk scandal.[63] In addition to his direct association with Sedat Bucak (the two were seen leaving the politican's hospital that November), a secret tape recording of a conversation between Yasak and Mahmut Yıldırım affirmed that he too had been involved in "violence-for-hire" work in some official capacity.[64] Several months into the investigation, one MİT officer confirmed suspicions that the Special Warfare Office had employed Drej Ali alongside Abdullah Çatlı for clandestine operations against the PKK between 1987 and 1988.[65] The Susurluk investigation, while not resulting in any charges against him, did not end Yasak's legal troubles as the new century approached. In 2001, Turkish authorities placed him, as well as twenty state bureaucrats (including a relative of Sedat Bucak), under arrest for smuggling meat into the country (those

[59] Hakan Gülseven, "Futbolsever Mafyanın Halleri," *Radikal* 21 March 2004; Fatih Vural, "Journalist Ecevit Kılıç: Turkish Football Federation Scared of Aziz Yıldırım," *Today's Zaman* 12 August 2011. Peker's relationship with the soccer world first came to light when Sergen Yalçın, a star forward who played the majority of his career at Beşiktaş, was called to testify at a trial concerning his influence over the Trabzonspor soccer club. See Önder Şuşoğlu and Haluk Atalay, "Sergen'e Sedat Peker Sorgusu," *Milliyet* 14 December 1998.

[60] Kaynarca did not deny the relationship he had with members of Istanbul's underworld. In interviews, Kaynarca was open about the fact that Alaattin Çakıcı, who was the basis of the Süleyman Çakır character, was a childhood friend. See "Mafia Mania Grips Nation," *Hürriyet Daily News* 21 April 2004.

[61] "'İnci' Baba'ya Kurşun Yağmuru," *Milliyet* 8 February 1989. İnci Baba, like Yasak, was born in Urfa. In addition to being arrested for smuggling weapons and ammunition, İnciler was suspected of supplying money to Mehmet Ali Ağca. See "Ağca, Türkiye'de Bazı Tanınmış Kişilerden Para Yardımı Gördüğünü Öne Sürdü," *Milliyet* 28 May 1981; "İnci Baba'nın 48 Yıl Hapsi İsteniyor," *Milliyet* 12 March 1985.

[62] Melik Duvaklı, "Derin Kürtler," *Aksiyon* 25 January 2010 <http://www.aksiyon.com.tr/aksiyon/haber-25979-173-derin-kurtler.html> (accessed 24 February 2013).

[63] His claims to owning teahouses and land in Urfa can be found in Ercüment İşleyen, "İşte Drej Ali," *Milliyet* 9 February 1989.

[64] Bozarslan, *Network-Building*, 8; "Bucak Ankara'da," *Milliyet* 16 November 1996.

[65] Atilla Dişbudak, "Korkut Eken: Çatlı'yı MİT Kullandı," *Milliyet* 20 March 1997.

charges were later dismissed).[66] In late January 2008, he was convicted of a number of charges including theft, battery, and "forming a criminal gang" for which he was sentenced to fourteen years in prison.[67] One day after the court passed judgment, authorities in Istanbul named Drej Ali as a prime suspect involved in the formation of the Ergenekon conspiracy.[68]

A fourth figure who featured prominently in the press in the late 1990s was Hüseyin Baybaşın. Dubbed the "Pablo Escobar of heroin" by the *Observer* in London, Baybaşın's reliance upon the drug trade was in stark contrast to the stands Çakıcı and Peker took on the narcotics trade. He was born in Lice in 1956. Like Behçet Cantürk, who was six years his senior, the region's deep ties to the trade in smuggled opium and other illicit goods provided his first taste of criminal life. The devastating earthquake of 1975 compelled him, like Cantürk and many others in Lice, to seek a new life in Istanbul, where he similarly fell into smuggling circles in the city. After serving a term in prison in 1976 for possession of over ten kilos of hashish (which, he later claimed, resulted in the police approaching him as an informant and *agent provocateur*), Hüseyin made his first inroads into the heroin trade. With the help of a friend from Malatya, he contracted his first smuggling connections within both Turkey and Western Europe. His personal network, which began to take shape after his first trip to Western Europe in 1982, gradually encompassed points of distribution in Holland, Germany, and the United Kingdom.[69]

Heroin trafficking, by the mid-1980s, was an enterprise that occupied multiple members of the Baybaşın family. Along with his brothers and other family members (one of whom was a close associate of Behçet Cantürk), Hüseyin did face arrest, prosecution, and, at various points, torture, during his rise as a prominent narcotics trafficker.[70] In 1984, British police arrested him for possession of six kilos of heroin. After serving four years of a twelve-year sentence, he returned to Turkey only to be arrested a year later after police discovered him close to the Turkish-Bulgarian border in the custody of seventy-nine kilos of heroin.[71] The most notorious incident involving Baybaşın occurred in late 1992 when a ship, *Kismetim-1*, carrying a fortune in heroin was scuttled off the coast of Cyprus after police threatened to board the vessel. Turkish authorities issued an arrest warrant for him after the incident, prompting Baybaşın, then in Switzerland, to accuse a series of officials in Istanbul and Ankara, including Mehmet Ağar, of staging the shipment in the first place.[72]

[66] "Bufalo'da Susurluk İzi," *Radikal* 28 January 2001; "'Bufalo' Davasında 10 Tahliye Kararı," *Radikal* 14 July 2001.

[67] "Drej Ali Mahkum, Yeşil'in Oğlu Serbest," *Radikal* 26 May 2008.

[68] "More Neo-Nationalist Party Members Arrested in Ergenekon Probe," *Today's Zaman* 27 March 2008.

[69] Bovenkerk and Yeşilgöz, *The Turkish Mafia: A History of the Heroin Godfathers*, 222–236.

[70] "İhanet Bedeli," *Milliyet* 19 November 1986; Ercüment İşleyen and Ali Fuat Duatepe, "Ermeni Mafyası MİT Takıbinde," *Milliyet* 4 November 1988; Ali Fuat Duatepe, "Uyuşturucuda Kilit 'Aile,'" *Milliyet* 10 March 1989.

[71] Nevsal Elevli, "Baybaşın İkinci Escobar," *Milliyet* 18 November 2002.

[72] Bovenkerk and Yeşilgöz, *The Turkish Mafia: A History of the Heroin Godfathers*, 246–248; "'Büyük Baş' Kaçak Baybaşın Konuştu," *Milliyet* 24 January 1993.

The real reason for his repeated run-ins with the law during the 1980s and 1990s, in Baybaşın's estimation, had more to do with his political sympathies than with his illicit dealings. His support for Kurdish and left wing causes, he later admitted to Frank Bovenkerk and Yücel Yeşilgöz, started with the 1975 earthquake in Lice. As a result of the government's inaction in the wake of the earthquake's devastation, he, and many other Kurds from the region, drew closer to the gathering wave of resistance taking root in the region. Like Behçet Cantürk, he offered monetary support to the PKK from the proceeds of his drug transactions. His ties to the PKK, however, did not prevent him from seeking connections with members of Ankara political elite. With the commencement of the Susurluk scandal in 1996, Hüseyin's accusation that he had partnered Mehmet Ağar assumed greater relevance.[73] MİT's third report into Susurluk, for example, suggested that the government should apply "greater scrutiny" to the relationship between the Kurdish drug smuggler and the Interior Minister (who had already been directly implicated in employing Abdullah Çatlı).[74]

Since his arrest and imprisonment in Holland in 2001, Hüseyin Baybaşın has given many interviews about his dealings with the Turkish state and foreign intelligence agencies. Speaking with Bovenkerk and Yeşilgöz, he explained at length how the Turkish officials frequently interacted with conspicuous criminals like himself:

> Şükrü Balcı [head of Istanbul's DPS office in the early 1980s] came to talk to us himself. Our money came from the Netherlands and Germany via İşbank, but it was not recorded. We went to our man at the bank and he gave it to us. The same thing happened at Pamuk Bank. I didn't even realize it myself that it was also the state itself organising it, but in some cases we were told that the money was intended for development of the state. Half the money from every transaction went to the state. To us, it was a kind of tax, in exchange for which we received protection in all aspects. If the money was confiscated or we were arrested, then our contacts with the government came to fetch us and said that we worked for the state. They even protected us in Europe. When I made a second trip to Europe that year, I saw for myself how all the consulates were involved in the trafficking. There is a member of staff at each consulate for that purpose. That person is supposed to set up cultural centres and Turkish schools, for example. So we gave them money for that. The Turkish Cultural Association, for example, was entirely financed with money from drug trafficking. Practically no contribution came from Turkey itself. These officials organised meetings and produced posters in all the capital cities promoting Turkey.[75]

Baybaşın, in his discussion with Bovenkerk and Yeşilgöz, was somewhat coy in discussing the full intentions of the Turkish authorities who collaborated with him in his illicit enterprises. Yet, when his support for the PKK became more apparent, Baybaşın suggested that some of his political friends had hoped to employ him as an intelligence source.[76] When he declined, he claims that state authorities

[73] "Turkey's Drug Smuggling Counterattack," *Hürriyet Daily News* 19 March 1997.
[74] Human Rights Foundation of Turkey, "1998 Human Rights Report," 571.
[75] Bovenkerk and Yeşilgöz, *The Turkish Mafia: A History of the Heroin Godfathers*, 235–236.
[76] Bovenkerk and Yeşilgöz, *The Turkish Mafia: A History of the Heroin Godfathers*, 238–239.

attempted to kill him. It was after several failed attempts on his life that he was arrested as a result of the *Kismetim-1* incident.[77]

The opening of the Ergenekon investigation in 2006 cast the "state-mafia-politics connections" linking Baybaşın, Peker, Çakıcı, Yasak, and Hoştan to the Susurluk investigations in a new and more immediate light. In January 2008, an Istanbul court arraigned Veli Küçük, Sami Hoştan, and a number of former military officials on charges of "provoking armed rebellion against the state."[78] Alaattin Çakıcı and Sedat Peker, who had been arrested for "forming a criminal gang (*çete*)" and imprisoned for fourteen years in 2007, also drew suspicion from prosecutors investigating Ergenekon allegations.[79] When the two men appeared before Istanbul's Thirteenth Criminal Court, both of these veteran gangsters were subject to direct questioning on their role in the crimes and associations that comprised the Susurluk scandal. Çakıcı was repeatedly evasive during his official examination in July 2012. When asked if he knew Veli Küçük, he curtly replied that the prosecutor should "go ask him." Although he admitted to knowing Mehmet Ağar, Çakıcı was equally obstinate in explaining his relationship with the former Minister of Interior. "If you are going to hold someone responsible, ask Tansu Çiller. If you are going to hold someone responsible, ask Mesut Yılmaz."[80] Sami Hoştan was similarly hostile when questioned before an Ankara court in October 2011, saying that he had been imprisoned as a result of the Susurluk investigation for Ömer Lüftü Topal's death but had been cleared of all charges.[81]

Sedat Peker, who took the stand in the fall of 2011, was far more forthcoming in explaining his past dealings with high-ranking political officials and their connections to both Susurluk and Ergenekon. Before the court, Peker claimed to have intimate knowledge of the inner workings of the *milieu* that organized and executed the murders of several individuals in the 1990s. In his testimony (as well as in a public interview), he claimed that Hanefi Avcı, one-time DPS chief in Eskişehir and Diyarbakir, was "an Ergenekon administrator" tasked with extrajudicial killings and provocations.[82] Peker also claimed that an agent from MİT, Korkut Eken, had ordered and helped finance the killings of Kurdish businessmen with links to the PKK.[83]

Prosecutors compelled Veli Küçük to take the stand in December 2008 as part of the initial stages of the Ergenekon investigation. While not denying that he

77 Bovenkerk and Yeşilgöz, *The Turkish Mafia: A History of the Heroin Godfathers*, 242–245.

78 "'Untouchables' Nabbed in Raid," *Turkish Daily News* 28 January 2008.

79 "Sedat Peker 14 Yıl," *Sabah* 31 January 2007. Sedat Peker was also arrested within a day of Şami Hostan and Veli Küçük's arraignment. See "Sedat Peker Ergenekon'dan da Tutuklandı," *NTV-MSNBC* 27 January 2012 http://www.ntvmsnbc.com/id/25317554 (accessed 21 February 2012).

80 "Alaattin Çakıcı, Ergenekon'da Tanıklık Yaptı," *CNN Türk*, 26 July 2012 http://www.cnnturk.com/2012/turkiye/07/26/alaattin.cakici.ergenekonda.taniklik.yapti/670416.0/index.html (accessed 21 February 2013).

81 "Sami Hoştan İfade Verdi," *Zaman* 26 October 2011.

82 "Mustafa Turan, Peker Tells Prosecutors About Avcı's Links with Ergenekon," *Today's Zaman* 18 August 2011.

83 "Mesut Hasan Benli, Testimony Reveals Extrajudicial Killings," *Hürriyet Daily News* 3 November 2011.

had met with Sami Hoştan and Sedat Peker, he swore that he had never acted in the "interest" of leaders of organized crime. In addition to denying even the existence of JİTEM (which he considered an attack upon the Turkish armed forces), Küçük was resolute that he "had never thought of conspiring against the state."[84] Witnesses called to give testimony over the following years painted a very different picture of the former general of the nation's gendarmerie. One anonymous witness, identified only as Poyraz, claimed that Sedat Peker had commanded a death squad loyal to Küçük and was responsible for the killing of Behçet Cantürk.[85] Another witness, a convicted criminal and self-professed member of Ergenekon named Osman Yıldırım, described Peker as Küçük's personal errand-boy (*ayakçı*) and bagman (*çantacı*).[86] Perhaps the most explosive charge laid at Veli Küçük's feet came from another secret witness named Emrah Özdemir, who claimed that he had heard that Abdullah Çatlı had not died in the accident at Susurluk but was killed on the orders of the retired general.[87]

Hüseyin Baybaşın has yet to be called before any court in Turkey to answer questions related to either Susurluk or Ergenekon. Nevertheless, from his prison cell in Holland, he has freely given his own opinions on the significance of the trials that have compelled other underworld figures to give tesitmony on organized crime's relationship to elements of the Turkish state. On the one hand, he claims to have no knowledge of Veli Küçük's involvement in the *Kismetim-1* affair (even though he was adamant that the Turkish state had profited from heroin sales in the past).[88] On the other hand, he asserts that he received training from counter-guerrilla officers as early as 1970.[89] He has further quipped that to fully understand Ergenekon, one had to look beyond Turkey and analyze the connections of Germany, the United States, and other countries to narcotics trafficking and the Turkish state.[90] Referring to an interview he gave to the *Guardian* in London in 2006, Ian Cobain suggested that Baybaşın remained at risk from the wrath of parties close to Ankara. In addition to the confidential information he reputedly had regarding the alliances formed between state actors and elements of Turkish organized crime, the former Kurdish drug smuggler maintained ties with various intelligence services around Europe. In addition to aiding Britain's MI5's domestic surveillance of Kurdish activists in London, Cobain speculated that he had provided information to Spanish intelligence officials in the wake of the Madrid bombings of 2004 and had been approached by Russian spies seeking to assassinate two Chechens in an Istanbul hotel.[91]

84 "İşte Veli Küçük'ün Tam İfadesi," *Hürriyet* 15 December 2008.

85 "Gizli Tanık Poyraz: Sedat Peker, Küçük'ten Sonra İkini Adamdı," *Zaman* 24 January 2012.

86 " 'Sedat Peker, Veli Küçük'ün Ayakçısıdır,' " *Radikal* 22 November 2012.

87 "Çatlı ve Ersever'i Küçük Öldürttü," *Radikal* 18 September 2012.

88 "Fırat Alkaç, Silah Verir Eroin Alırdık," *Taraf* 5 January 2010.

89 "Hüseyin Baybaşın Taraf'a Konuştu," *Ajans Diyarbakir* 4 January 2010 http://www.ajansdiyarbakir.com/haber_detay.asp?haberID=1125 (accessed 22 February 2013).

90 Mahmut Övür, " 'Ergenekon'un Arakasında Almanya Var,' " *Sabah* 9 January 2010.

91 Ian Cobain, "Feared Clan Who Made Themselves a Home in Britain," *The Guardian* 27 March 2006.

The accusations and assertions levied by and against members of Turkey's underworld form only one chord within a cacophony of claims and official charges that have been made since 2006. Questions involving Sedat Peker, Sami Hoştan, and Alaattin Çakıcı's involvement in the "Ergenekon terrorist organization" have increasingly been overshadowed by other, seemingly more ominous conspiracy investigations orchestrated from Ankara. Following an explosive report released by the left-leaning *Taraf* newspaper in early 2010, prosecutors issued a sweeping indictment against scores of active and former military officers who, prosecutors claim, sought to incite a coup against Tayyip Erdoğan's AKP government in 2003. Investigations into the "Sledgehammer (*Balyoz*)" plot have resulted in the apprehension of over 200 military personnel (by 2011, over 10 percent of Turkey's generals and admirals had been detained and imprisoned).[92] Debate over the validity and legality of both the Ergenekon and Sledgehammer investigations has not prevented the opening of still more court cases against individuals suspected of having past or present affiliations with groups or conspiracies seeking to overthrow or undermine the Turkish state. In January 2012, prosecutors issued charges against two of the most powerful figures within the history of the Turkish military, İlker Başbuğ, former chief of the General Staff, and Kenan Evren. While Başbuğ's indictment echoed the charges issued in the Ergenekon and Sledgehammer investigations (namely, participation in a terrorist organization and attempting to overthrow Erdoğan's government), Evren's imprisonment and trial rests upon his actual participation in the coup of 1980.[93]

While prosecutors of the Sledgehammer trials have not drawn a direct connection between the alleged coup attempt of 2003 and organized crime, many within the Turkish media, and to some degree academia, have pointed to the apprehension of high-ranking military officers, including Başbuğ and Evren, as further evidence that the Turkish deep state was coming apart at the seams. The Susurluk scandal, in the eyes of some, primed the Turkish public for the kind of connections gangsters had formed with members of the political elite.[94] Prosecution of the Ergenekon conspirators not only helped to bring powerful criminal figures to justice (something that the Susurluk scandal failed to do), but served to highlight the existence and formidability of "the dark, subversive units set up to protect the state against the internal enemy."[95] While the capricious pattern of the investigations (not to mention the "secret" character of much of the witness testimony and evidence) has led many to question the current government's undemocratic motives, the trials of the last decade have cast an unfavorable light upon institutions many see as impediments to Turkish democracy.[96] The arraignment of gangsters alongside the

[92] Gareth Jenkins, "The Fading Masquerade: Ergenekon and the Politics of Justice in Turkey," *Turkey Analyst* 4.7 (4 April 2011) http://www.silkroadstudies.org/new/inside/turkey/2011/110404B.html (accessed 8 February 2013).

[93] Daniel Dombey, "Turkey Arrests Former Military Chief," *Financial Times* 6 January 2012.

[94] Mümtazer Türköne, "How Democracy Defeated the 'Deep State'" *Today's Zaman* 6 November 2011.

[95] Yavuz Baydar, "The 'Shadow State' Unfolding," *Today's Zaman* 24 January 2013.

[96] Mahtap Söyler, "The Deep State: Forms of Domination, Informal Institutions and Democracy," *Perspectives: Political Analysis and Commentary from Turkey* 3 (December 2012), 8–11.

likes of generals and policemen appears to represent a collective impeachment and debasement of Turkey's "guardians" within the security establishment (be it within the military, the intelligence service, or law enforcement).[97]

In historical terms, there are those who share in Tayyip Erdoğan's conclusion that the Ergenekon and Susurluk scandals are historically rooted in the Ottoman past. Considering the complex web of professional and personal ties binding its accused members, as well as its alleged violent policies, Ergenekon, in the opinion of some commentators, shares much in common with the Special Organization of the Young Turk era. The Democratic Society Party, the predecessor of the contemporary Peace and Democracy Party (a party with strong ties with Kurdish nationalist circles) declared in 2008 that Ergenekon is "the direct successor of the Ottoman Teşkilat-ı Mahsusa, which used state-sponsored assassins and carried out many deliberate acts of mass violence—most specifically against the Armenians during the early 20th century."[98] Still others have suggested that Ergenekon's existence reflects a historical mentality that also produced the Special Organization, a mentality that compelled both the Ottoman and Turkish states to undertake violent, extrajudicial actions against their own population.[99] Such sentiments have recently inspired a monograph length study analyzing continuities within a series of unsolved crimes associated with secret organizations in the mold of Ergenekon and the Special Organization.[100]

Discussion and debate on the significance of the Ergenekon investigation has spawned a host of questions within the pages of the Turkish press as well as within academic circles. Perhaps the most pertinent, and obvious, question revolves around its supposed relationship to Turkey's deep state. Is Ergenekon, as prosecutors claim, a centrally organized group linked to crimes undertaken in the name of Turkish national security? If so, is Ergenekon, itself as a unitary group, the deep state?[101] Or could Ergenekon, as well as Operation Sledgehammer, represent a "mode of domination," a *milieu* of powerful groups principally linked to members of the country's military (dating back to the establishment of Turkey's counter-guerrilla program)?[102] Or, is the deep state largely the product of a culture of paranoia and conspiracy? Are the crimes associated with Ergenekon, as Mustafa Akyol put it, "simply the results of hateful ideologies, angry masses and fanatical individuals"?[103]

There is some reason to be circumspect about the revelations the Ergenekon investigations have imparted regarding organized crime specifically. To date, no member of the Turkish underworld has been charged specifically with murder or

[97] Öktem, *Angry Nation: Turkey Since 1989*, 164.

[98] H. Akin Ünver, "Turkey's 'Deep State' and the Ergenekon Conundrum," *Middle East Institute Policy Brief*, 1 April 2009 http://www.mei.edu/content/turkeys-deep-state-and-ergenekon-conundrum#_ftn37 (accessed 23 February 2013).

[99] "Ergenekon Bir Zihniyettir," *Milliyet Blog* 28 July 2008 http://blog.milliyet.com.tr/Blog.aspx?BlogNo=122518 (accessed 23 February 2013).

[100] Gülçiçek Günel Tekin, *Teşkilat-ı Mahsusa'dan Ergenekon'a* (Istanbul: Belge Yayınları, 2012).

[101] For such a view, see "Indictment Says Gang Older Than the Republic," *Hürriyet Daily News* 16 July 2008.

[102] Söyler, "The Deep State: Forms of Domination, Informal Institutions and Democracy," 8.

[103] Mustafa Akyol, "It is the 'Deep Nation,' Not Deep State," *Hürriyet Daily News* 25 February 2013.

any other violent action (Peker, Hoştan, and Çakıcı, like other members of the Ergenekon conspiracy, have been charged with forming a criminal gang). Without the ability to cross-examine the state's secret witnesses, let alone independently analyze the documentary evidence put forward by the national intelligence service and various parliamentary commissions, it is difficult to fully and accurately ascertain how gangsters like Sedat Peker and Alaattin Çakıcı fit into the conspiratorial politics now alleged by Turkish prosecutors.

When considered against the wider backdrop of Turkish politics and history, analysis of the Ergenekon trials (as well as commentary on the Susurluk scandal) largely fails to address several key assumptions made about the relationship between the state, the mafia, and politics. Whether one accepts or denies the premise that a Turkish deep state exists, few question why gangsters, generals, and policemen came to collude with one another in the first place. To put it another way, why would Veli Küçük specifically seek the employment of Sami Hoştan or Sedat Peker? If he or others sought men to commit assassinations or other violent actions, why not rely solely upon individuals like the notorious Mahmut Yıldırım, who was already serving within the ranks of the state's security service?[104] In some sense, the answer to this question seems to be embedded within the social relationships gangsters and officials often shared exclusive of their political or criminal interests (mostly as evidenced through the dinners they enjoyed together).[105] Nevetheless, in recognizing the degree to which gangsters and officials may have mingled together socially and perhaps shared certain political views, how should one interpret the "Turkish mafia" relationship with various elements of the state? Is the Turkish underworld, as seen through the disclosures highlighted by the Susurluk and Ergenekon, an extension of state power? Are gangsters such as Hoştan and Çakıcı institutional sources of political authority in their own right? Or are they simple lackeys or henchmen for more individually powerful figures with greater claims to legitimacy?

In contemplating both the existence and meaning of the Turkish deep state, as well as organized crime's place within such a political system, it is fitting to examine how contemporary scholars have attempted to assess the interplay between organized crime and state governance outside of Turkey. Recent scholarship suggests that Turkey's deep state is symptomatic of a global pattern of state development in the twentieth and twenty-first centuries. In turn, the Turkish underworld has spawned a cast of political conspirators similar to the gangsters found elsewhere who have colluded with powerful, predominately conservative forces bent on protecting, consolidating, and insulating the authority of states from threat or duress.

[104] By all accounts, the infamous Yeşil held no direct connection with narcotics trafficking before entering the gendarmerie. However, according to one account, his entry into JİTEM was in part facilitated by his relationship with Abdullah Çatlı, who shared Yıldırım's right wing nationalist leanings (the two met when he was a youth member of the *Ülkü Ocakları*). See Çetin Agaşe, *Kod Adı: Yeşil* (Istanbul: Pencere Yayınları, 2000), 38.

[105] Human Rights Foundation of Turkey, "*1998 Human Rights Report*," 80.

THE DEEP STATE ABROAD: ORGANIZED CRIME WITHIN CONTEMPORARY "DEEP" POLITICAL DEBATES

What do you call a state that employs gangsters and smugglers to undertake illegal or clandestine actions? How should one interpret a political system that relies upon organized crime to fulfill the political goals of a governing elite? These are questions that have often been posed by scholars seeking to examine and explain a number of incidents exhibiting temporary or continuous alliances formed between underworld and official figures. While often seen as the grist for "conspiracy theory" literature, it is now undeniable that the twentieth century has produced a host of scandals revealing working relationships between politicians, intelligence agents, military officers, law enforcement personnel, prominent industrialists, and mobsters. It is only in recent years that scholars have attempted to describe and analyze the commonalities or the shared foundation that fuse such ties between the public and the criminal. In tackling the political and historical consequences of such alliances, the notion of the "deep state" appears to be gaining greater amounts of credibility and relevance.

The assassination of John F. Kennedy, more than any other event in American history, has evoked the greatest amount of debate on the structural relationships forged between elements of the American mafia and sources of political authority in the United States. Investigations into Jack Ruby's ties to the Chicago and Dallas underworlds gave immediate impetus for greater attention for the possible motives prominent mafiosi may have possessed in silencing the president's presumed killer. The findings of the House Select Committee on Assassinations, which raised the possibility of a mafia-led conspiracy organized against Kennedy, gave further encouragement for those who doubted the conclusions of the Warren Commission. More than offering an explanation for the Kennedy assassination, the House investigation shed light upon a host of other illicit ties between the United States government, elected officials, and organized crime. Chief among the committee's interests was the CIA's recruitment of gangsters such as John Roselli in assassination attempts targeting Cuba's Fidel Castro. In his documentary study of the JFK assassination, David Kaiser echoes the claims of the committee's chief counsel, Robert Blakey, in arguing in no uncertain terms that the president's death was the result of a mafia plot avenging Kennedy's abandonment of his Cuba gambit and his brother's crusade against organized crime.[106]

Although numerous detractors contest Kaiser and Blakey's thesis, few works seek to probe the representational significance of the mafia-state relationship their research unveils. Arguably the first work to broach the JFK assassination and the historical relevance of organized crime's collusion in state politics was Peter Dale

[106] George Robert Blakey, *The Plot to Kill the President* (New York: Times Books, 1981); Kaiser, *Road to Dallas*, 414.

Scott's *Deep Politics and the Death of JFK*. Scott's work, unlike other treatments of the assassination, is not a classic "whodunnit" focusing upon the mechanics of Kennedy's killing. Instead, in surveying some of the finer points of the official investigations into the crime, *Deep Politics* illuminates how official inquiries into JFK's death have shed light upon the formation of many "grey alliances" formed between elements of the state, organized crime, and sources of "private wealth." Scott speculates that the assassination was less the product of personal political aspirations or private vendettas; rather, in his words, it represents a "systemic adjustment" of deeply-rooted political forces found within the American state and society:

> ...most hypotheses of the Kennedy assassination, whether the designated culprits have been Communists or Minutemen, the CIA or the Mafia, have suffered from a common defect. This is to look for an external conspiracy violating a systemic political order from without... the forces behind the assassination no longer appear as extraneous, but deeply systemic; and the violation to the enlarged power system can be seen as coming from the Kennedys, with their policies of détente abroad and an attack on a CIA-sanctioned Hoffa-crime connection at home. From this perspective, the assassination was not a corrupt attack from outside an honest system. The assassination was a desperate, extraordinary defense, or adjustment, of a system that was itself corrupt.[107]

To explain both how and why the Kennedy assassination embodied the corrupt systemic relationships that may have resulted in the president's death, Scott coins the term "deep politics," a phrase he defines as "all those political practices and arrangements, deliberate or not, which are usually repressed rather than acknowledged."[108] Throughout the work's assessment of America's "deep political system," *Deep Politics* touches upon numerous cases, both actual and speculative, demonstrating organized crime's institutional relationship with power and governance in America, ranging from Lucky Luciano's employment by the Navy during the Second World War, labor leader Jimmy Hoffa's dealings with the Chicago Outfit, and Jack Ruby's possible service as a narcotics informant.

Inquiries into the attacks of 11 September 2001, as well as other extraordinary events in the last decade, have helped popularize Peter Dale Scott's writings and further legitimated the tacks of academic inquiry found in *Deep Politics*. In 2009, Eric Wilson edited the first collection of scholarly essays on the question of "criminal sovereignty" within regional and global politics and history. As a work intent upon describing and analyzing the cases when one finds "criminals behaving as sovereigns and sovereigns behaving as criminals in a systemic way," half of the book's essays examine how organized criminal groups have helped to contribute, in one way or another, to the making of state politics.[109] Henner Hess's analysis of Cosa Nostra affirms the observations of others in establishing how organized criminal

107 Scott, *Deep Politics*, 74.

108 Scott, *Deep Politics*, 7.

109 Robert Cribb, "Introduction: Parapolitics, Shadow Governanace and Criminal Sovereignty," in Eric Wilson (ed.), *Government of the Shadows: Parapolitics and Criminal Sovereignty* (New York: Pluto Books, 2009), 8.

gangs can coordinate closely with appendages of government in order to maintain the state's monopoly on power.[110] The corrupt practices of Italian politicians who rely upon the protection of gangsters is resonant in Alfred McCoy's depiction of the Philippines, where gambling proprietors and drug traffickers provide both the financial and electoral clout for aspiring elected officials.[111] The drug trade, more than any other source of illicit capital, provides for similar patterns of state collusion in Colombia and Afghanistan, two states faced with violent insurgencies that equally rely upon narcotics as a source of financial support for aspiring political actors.[112] Daniele Glaser and Ola Tunander extend this analysis specifically to the interests of state intelligences agencies, which, in the case of Italy, relied upon organized crime officials as willing, but disposable, agents assigned with operations targeting leftist political groups seeking to overturn the country's status quo.[113]

Where the contributors of Wilson's *Government of the Shadows* often differ in opinion and approach are in their elective use of terminology. In describing the political systems in which criminal syndicates are allotted some portion of state power, authors mostly rely upon the concept of "parapolitics" as the most serviceable and applicable term for academic usage. What parapolitics exactly entails, in terms of its breadth of application, is not uniformly applied throughout the book. While Rensselaer W. Lee finds the term denoting "state activity in collaboration with international organized crime," Peter Dale Scott and Eric Wilson opt for a broader definition that emphasizes the clandestine nature of the illegal activities of national intelligence services.[114] McCoy settles upon his own nomenclature, "covert netherworld," to describe the criminal-state alliances shaping the Phillipines, arguing that terms like "deep politics" are "fraught with undertones of conspiracy theory" associated with Scott's *Deep Politics* and Oliver Stone's film *JFK*.[115] Interesting, neither Hess's contribution on Sicily nor Thoumi's survey of Colombia contain any reference or critique of the meaning or appropriate use of "parapolitics" or any other terms.

110 Henner Hess, "The Sicilian Mafia: Parastate and Adventure Capitalism," in Eric Wilson (ed.), *Government of the Shadows: Parapolitics and Criminal Sovereignty* (New York: Pluto Books, 2009), 153–172.

111 Alfred McCoy, "Covert Netherworld: Clandestine Services and Criminal Syndicates in Shaping the Philippine State," in Eric Wilson (ed.), *Government of the Shadows: Parapolitics and Criminal Sovereignty* (New York: Pluto Books, 2009), 226–255.

112 Rensselaer W. Lee III, "Parapolitics and Afghanistan," in Eric Wilson (ed.), *Government of the Shadows: Parapolitics and Criminal Sovereignty* (New York: Pluto Books, 2009), 195–204; Francisco Thoumi, "From Drug Lords to Warlords: Illegal Drugs and the 'Unintended' Consequences of Drug Policies in Colombia," in Eric Wilson (ed.), *Government of the Shadows: Parapolitics and Criminal Sovereignty* (New York: Pluto Books, 2009), 205–225.

113 Daniele Ganser, "Beyond Democratic Checks and Balances: The 'Propaganda Due' Masonic Lodge and the CIA in Italy's First Republic," in Eric Wilson (ed.), *Government of the Shadows: Parapolitics and Criminal Sovereignty* (New York: Pluto Books, 2009), 256–276; Ola Tunander, "Democratic State vs. Deep State: Approaching the Dual State of the West," in Eric Wilson (ed.), *Government of the Shadows: Parapolitics and Criminal Sovereignty* (New York: Pluto Books, 2009), 56–72.

114 Lee, "Parapolitics and Afghanistan," 195; Wilson, *Government of the Shadows*, 30.

115 McCoy, "Covert Netherworld" 228.

Ola Tunander's contribution stands as the sole essay within the collection in adopting and analyzing the concept of the "deep state." Tunander, in his reading of a wave of terrorist attacks staged by members of the Italian clandestine service during the height of the Cold War, argues that the deep state is in fact one function of what Hans Morgenthau had earlier called the modern "dual state." As an entity separate from the transparent, officially recognized "democratic" state, the deep state, or security state, represents coalitions within the government that work to "veto" or "fine tune" policies related to national security. When actions undertaken by the democratic state places the nation's domestic or international security at risk (such as when the Italian Communist Party threatened to take power in the late 1960s), actors aligned with the deep state (such as members of the military, the clandestine service, the mafia, and fascist politicians) employ any means to reverse the state's political course (to the point of killing innocent civilians in order to frame unsuspecting leftists).[116] Peter Dale Scott, while not making specific reference to the term in his contribution to Wilson's edited volume, similarly adopts the concept of the deep state in some of his recent writings, labeling it "that part of a state driven by top-down policy making, often by small cabals."[117]

Many of the trends referenced by the authors of Wilson's collection, particularly those centering upon alliances formed between officials, gangsters, and intelligence agencies, can be readily found in a plethora of works that do not seek to label or classify the political systems that harbor or cultivate such relationships. Nonetheless, *Government of the Shadows* does signify an important step in attempting to historicize and universalize the study of organized crime as a force in shaping the formation of modern states. Mehtap Söyler, in her recent appraisal of the phenomenon in Turkey, is correct in seeing the deep state as a mode of "dual domination," a force that acts as a formal and informal impediment to democracy. But if we accept the conclusions of Ola Tunander, as well as the collective conclusions of the other authors of Wilson's study, it comprises more than just the legitimate and illicit power invoked by the Turkish military (as Söyler contends).[118] In seeking some sort of unanimity among those who have struggled with the meaning and implications of what scholars have alternatively labeled the "deep state," "parapolitics," or "deep politics," perhaps it is best to think about the collaborative activities of criminals and statesmen in broader terms.

The deep state, if one must employ the term, is an eclectic, ever evolving political theater of competition and cooperation, one that includes elements both explicitly legal and illegal in nature. It is not, as some contend in the case of the Ergenekon investigation, a single organization. The studies cited earlier, as well as many others cited throughout this book, suggest that the forces that comprise "parapolitical"

[116] Tunander, "Democratic State vs. Deep State: Approaching the Dual State of the West," 156–159.

[117] Peter Dale Scott, *The Road to 9/11: Wealth, Empire and the Future of America* (Berkeley: University of California Press, 2007), xvi.

[118] Söyler, "The Deep State: Forms of Domination, Informal Institutions and Democracy," 8–11.

or "deep state" coalitions evolve in conjuction with the political economy and political cultures of regions, countries, and transnational spaces. To put it another way, in the case of organized crime, changes in how states are governed and how economies are regulated have a strong influence over the political and social complexion of criminal syndicates. These shifts have a direct effect upon the ability of a gangster to access and influence sources of political power.[119]

If one accepts some of the comparisons drawn throughout this book from such disparate cases as China, Mexico, the United States, Italy, and Russia, it is reasonable to suggest that state security and the survival of reigning governing elites (be they elected or unelected) is critical in initiating, perpetuating, and severing the relationships formed between gangsters and state officials. A shared commitment to a political or economic status quo (be it democratic or authoritarian in nature) is what most often binds and breaks such alliances. From their conception, "state-mafia-politics connections" often begin as coalitions between local actors. Law enforcement agents and provincial politicians are commonly the initial arbiters of the ties formed with gangsters and smugglers. Bigger criminal syndicates capitalize on such relations at the expense of smaller organizations and gangs. Be it in the case of Tammany Hall, interwar Shanghai, postwar Sicily, or post-revolutionary Baja California, a shared desire to uphold an oligarchical political order, as well as a mutual need to maintain and divide the profits of specific trades, bridges the interests of these otherwise diverging bedfellows. Threats to this "Chicago-style" working arrangement, either from political dissidents (such as leftist or nationalist factions) or more authoritative, "corrective" governing sources (such as the intervention of national governments into local affairs), do often prompt violent reactions, either resulting in the collapse of the coalition or acts of illicit (and often bloody) subterfuge targeting those seeking to bring about political change. Such coalitions can take on national (and even international) dimensions depending upon the economic clout of a given underworld or *milieu*. A gangster's ability to intermingle with individuals at the heights of power requires large sums of capital, thereby reserving such a right to a select few. Nevertheless many of the provincial dynamics of "state-mafia" relations have equally been factored into patterns of collusion at a national level. The degree to which military officers, business magnates, or elected officials in Bogota, Moscow, and Tokyo shared ties with the Medellin cartel, the *vory-v-zakhone*, and the Yakuza depended upon the corrupt proceeds they gleaned from the criminals they may have known socially or professionally. As seen time and again, powerful criminal syndicates, in exchange for protection, may offer a variety of services outside the reach or ability of those in power (the mobilization or suppression of votes, the extraction of information, or the application of muscle or violence). Still, trends in global history tell us that such national alliances are as fleeting as they are at the local level. Shifts in the political economy of crime (such as fluctuations in the demand, flow, or availability of illicit goods)

[119] Howard Dick, "The Shadow Economy: Markets, Crime and the State," in Eric Wilson (ed.), *Government of the Shadows: Parapolitics and Criminal Sovereignty* (New York: Pluto Books, 2009), 97–116.

as well as sudden changes to a political regime may promptly dissolve liaisons between criminals and political actors (or worse, result in violent internal fighting or bloody repression).

Eric Hobsbawm's work on banditry underscores the fact that government complicity in criminal enterprises is a practice that is both old and universal. States, big and small, strong or weak, "open" or "closed," confront organized criminal *milieus* on their physical and economic peripheries. Modern policing practices, no matter how rigid, measured or widespread, have been proven to have only limited success in suppressing such centers of crime and illicit trades. Historical case studies dating back into the classical era demonstrate a recurring utilization of bandits, smugglers, and thugs as allies in endeavors tailored to the state's interests. Criminals connected to lucrative illicit trades and violent criminal rackets often filled the ranks of pre-modern and modern armies, supplied needed intelligence, and helped to "manage" provincial and urban crime. In developing or peripheral economies, one must also recognize the fact that what one calls organized crime today often was, and still is, the life blood of local and national economies. Whether it was trading in slaves, prostitutes, tobacco, alcohol, ivory, gold, tea, or opium, smugglers in the early modern and modern eras challenged state authority while at the same time conferring financial gains upon politically invested individuals and groups. In short, in historical terms, there is nothing new, monolithic, or culturally specific about what one may now call the "deep state," "deep politics," or "parapolitics."

Tayyip Erdoğan, from at least one perspective, is correct in his appraisal of the Turkish deep state's imperial roots. The power of the *ayan* (and their bandit retainers), as well as the CUP's mobilization of provincial *çetes*, resembles contemporary state-criminal alliances similar to those seen in the wake of the Susurluk scandal. Ankara's recent need to recruit members of Turkey's underworld for service against ASALA and the PKK resonate strongly in the assistance rendered by kidnappers, brigands, and killers as frontline troops and policemen (in the case of the seventeenth, eighteenth, and nineteenth centuries) or clandestine assassins and storm troopers (as in the *çetes* of the Special Organization). A select number of outlaws in the Ottoman Empire and Turkey have benefited from such patronage, resulting in the marginalization of competing criminal interests and the entrenchment of illicit syndicates within the provincial and national political system (particularly in times of crisis).

The rise of the opiate trade in the late Ottoman Empire marks an important juncture in terms of the evolution of the relationship between gangs and the state. Since the nineteenth century, opium, morphine, and heroin have become staple products critical to Anatolia's economy. The proceeds from this trade have sustained the livelihoods of agricultural workers, merchants, politicians, and criminals alike for over two centuries now. After several decades of foreign dominance, Ankara has fought very hard, in one form or another, to maintain this industry in both its legal and (arguably) illicit forms. Shifts in the value, availability, and legality of opium-based products have forced Turkish producers and dealers to evolve with the conditions of the times. Even with Anatolia's transformation from a center of opium production to a transit point in the global heroin market, the trafficking industry has remained and grown more entrenched and complex. The ever-increasing proceeds harnessed from the heroin trade intensified the strength, organization, and lethality of Turkish criminal syndicates over the course of the twentieth century, making them more self-sustaining and international in size and authority.

Unlike the *çetes* of the pre-1923 era, whose economic livelihood depended greatly upon more tenuous illicit marketplaces (such as animal theft or extortion), the individuals and gangs associated with the postwar heroin trade realized previously unachievable and seemingly unimaginable amounts of wealth. As a consequence of the stability and expansiveness of the drug trade, a chosen number of *patrons* and *babas* (İhsan Sekban, Hüseyin Eminoğlu, Ahmet Soysal, and others) demonstrated an impressive degree of resilience over the course of the twentieth century. Through their influence among local and national political figures (such as Ali Eren and Kemal Aygün), they proved themselves to be relatively successful in marginalizing competitors and insulating themselves from prosecution. Prominent gangsters from the late twentieth century, such as Abuzer Uğurlu, Oflu İsmail, and Behçet Cantürk, while enjoying similarly durable careers in the Turkish underworld, held even greater sway than their predecessors as ideological and tactical allies of actors wishing to promote or contest state policy (be they within the Turkish gendarmerie, the Nationalist Action Party, or the PKK). Considering the degree to which *ülkücu* gangsters played a role in Ankara's policies towards Kurdish and Armenian militants (as well as the degree to which individuals like Cantürk and Baybaşin helped to support ASALA and the PKK), it is important not to dismiss this generation of *babas* as simple-minded lackeys of the state and its detractors. Their personal wealth, ideological inclinations, reputations, and personal connections empowered them to become both conductors as well as tools of political change.

The deep state paradigm may be helpful in labeling and explaining the structural relationships undergirding centers of power and influence committed to the security of the state. In addition to contextualizing the degree to which gangsters may collude with state officials and officers, the notion of the deep state may provide an appropriate starting point in investigations of how both foreign and domestic industrial magnates, bankers, intellectuals, and social activists engage and negotiate with bureaucratic and military agents seeking to overtly or covertly suppress dissent and promote the interests of governing regimes. What the deep state paradigm does not adequately address in the case of organized crime are the more mundane factors that facilitate its existence, determine its construction, and help to promote, or limit, its influence. There are several factors examined in this book that are critical to comprehending how Turkish narcotics groups came into being. These factors equally reflect important contributing elements to the making of modern Turkish politics, economy, and society. In looking at the history of heroin syndicates in Turkey over the course of the twentieth century, one is reminded of the dramatic and didactic elements that often inform many of the acclaimed films depicting organized crime in America. Movies like *The Godfather, Goodfellas*, or *Scarface* (both the 1932 and 1983 versions) are not simply crime dramas; they are, at multiple levels, meditations on urban life, capitalism, immigrant culture, materialism, and corruption in the United States in the modern era.

Organized crime, as noted in the introduction of this book, is equally employed to identify and describe both illicit trades as well as the individuals who undertake them. When thinking about the production, trafficking, and sale of opiates as an organized criminal activity, one must appreciate, first and foremost, that its birth and continued relevance is a product of both Turkish and transnational political and economic forces. The story of heroin trafficking out of Asia Minor is, in the grand scheme of things, a testament to the steady integration of the Ottoman Empire and the Republic of Turkey into the global economy. Increasing foreign demand, beginning in the early nineteenth century, first brought about the development of mass opiate cultivation and transshipment in Anatolia. Demand for Turkish opium continued to grow throughout the twentieth century despite (or because of) the prohibitions placed upon the use of its derivatives. Similar limits placed upon production and economic exchange in Turkey (such as the sale of firearms, nuts, and nylons) gave rise to other forms of illicit smuggling in the country. Old imperial trade networks, ones dominated by Western shippers and refiners, provided a foundation for the first smuggling syndicates operating out of Turkey. By the end of the twentieth century, newly fabricated transnational cooperatives (such as those with Iranian producers, Italian wholesalers, or Albanian retailers) allowed Turkish underworld syndicates greater autonomy and control over the heroin trade. In last forty years, Turkish trafficking groups have adapted to a number of challenges. The evidence available to us suggests that the ability of some smuggling outfits to exert political influence and diversify their economic interests as well as capitalize on new resources (such as the utilization of large Turkish diaspora networks) have helped the most recent generation of Turkish traffickers to overcome both the instability of the liberalizing Turkish economy and the ongoing shifts in the global narcotics trade.

While the growth of illicit trades and Ankara's statist policies may help to explain the historic contours of organized crime as an aspect of Turkey's economy, it does not fully account for who participated in such crimes. Like the discussion of many underworlds throughout the world, understanding the origins of the "Turkish mafia" compels one to gauge the significance of migration and ethnicity among the gangsters who populate this history. Ethnic tropes are found throughout discussions and analysis of crime in Ottoman and Turkish history. Contemporary sources frequently identified the most likely participants of organized crime in the empire and the republic as members of foreign and domestic immigrant groups and minorities. From the Young Turk period to the present, the ethnicity of characters associated with narcotics trafficking (as well as other criminal enterprises) has changed to some degree. The prewar smugglers and producers of Greek and Jewish descent eventually gave way to new generations of Muslim traffickers and refiners within a few years of the conclusion of the Second World War. One sees some degree of ethnic continuity between the Muslim heroin syndicates and the historical "bête noir" found within the criminal trades of the Ottoman Empire. One important factor that may have perpetuated official perceptions and actual associations of Laz, Kurdish, and Albanian gangsters of the pre- and post-imperial eras is the continuing pattern of migration and economic marginalization found among these three groups. While the causes may have changed, the migration of Albanians, Kurds, and Laz across the Ottoman countryside or into Turkish cities produced diasporas that imperial and republican officials often associated with crime. A closer examination of the case files of the FBN suggests, however, that Laz or Kurdish wings of the "Turkish mafia" may never have existed in entirely pure forms. Greeks, Armenians, Arabs, Circassians, and, for that matter, Turks contributed to these otherwise Laz or Kurdish syndicates. Moreover, the records of the FBN, as well as the careers of Dündar Kılıç and Kürt İdris, attest to the fact that ethnicity did not form barriers to cooperation between gangs.

Turkish and American approaches to policing have had an inordinate impact upon both the perceptions and the realities of the twentieth century Turkish underworld. In addition to helping to inspire and pilot the modern prohibition on narcotics, the United States provided the conceptual and practical framework for delineating and describing organized crime in Turkey and a host of other countries. Agents of the Federal Bureau of Narcotics, in cooperation with Turkish officers and in keeping with their experiences back at home, seized upon the Laz and Kurdish character of the syndicates they confronted. They described them and ranked them much like the crime families of New York or Chicago. More importantly, the FBN gradually utilized their own devices to attract the "special employees" who identified the key traffickers and informed them as to the structure and modus operandi of the syndicates of Turkey (a practice also rooted in the American experience). The Directorate of Public Security, in addition to bringing prominent and marginal opiate traffickers to trial, informed the construction of organized crime (again both real and imagined) in other ways. The restrictions the DPS placed upon the FBN tended to steer law enforcement efforts away from the major wholesalers of Istanbul towards the rural, and less significant, smugglers of the Anatolian interior. American agents suspected, and indeed witnessed, that DPS policies were in part influenced by official collusion with major traffickers. Whether it was sheltering major figures like İhsan Sekban from prosecution, or cracking down on Christian smugglers in favor of Muslim ones, the DPS, and elements of the Ankara and regional governments, was as much a part of organized crime in Istanbul and elsewhere as the traffickers themselves.

In completing this study, it is important to bear in mind the limitations of the available sources used to construct this history of drug trafficking and organized crime in Turkey. Archival documents do provide timely and informative insights into the history of the movement of narcotics in Turkey and the gangsters that controlled this trade. However, it is clear that both Turkish and American officials often relied upon duplicitous or unknowing informants who supplied them with information. Bureaucratic and personal priorities within the FBN and DPS also compelled agents to inflate or misconstrue trends and incidents they supposedly witnessed. We have some reason to doubt, for example, the official estimates of the amount of Turkish heroin imported into the United States during the twentieth century (let alone what percentage of the overall traffic it may have comprised). Personal accounts provided by investigating agents and newspaper reporters, while at times helpful, are also fraught with errors and omissions. In looking at the state of organized crime in Turkey over the last thirty years, it is difficult to explain, for example, why gangsters such as Sedat Peker or Alaattin Çakıcı attained such power and wealth without resorting to the drug trade. Depending on what future examination of internal governmental records or documentary sources tells us, it is possible that there were other figures within the Istanbul underworld with influence and financial clout surpassing the likes of Peker, Çakıcı or Drej Ali. Perhaps of greatest importance, the contemporary political climate, particularly within the Turkish press, may not allow for a full evaluation of the veracity of the many claims that have emerged as a result of the Susurluk and Ergenkon investigations. So much of what has been said about the state of organized crime, heroin, and politics in Turkey, now as well as in the past, appears to be an approximation of the truth.

Bibliography

ARCHIVAL SOURCES

Başbakanlık Cumhuriyet Arşivi
- Bakanlar Kurulu Karaları
- Başbakanlık Özel Kalem Müdürlüğü

Başbakanlık Osmanlı Arşivi
- Dahiliye Nezareti
  - Kalem-i Mahsus

Central Intelligence Agency
- CIA Records Search Tool (CREST)
- Declassified, unorganized files (where cited)

George H. White Papers, Special Collections Department, Stanford University

National Archives and Records Administration
- State Department Central Decimal Files (RG 59)
- Records of the Drug Enforcement Administration (RG 170)

National Archives, Great Britain
- Public Records Office
  - Foreign Office
  - Foreign and Commonwealth Office

Richard Nixon Presidential Library and Museum, Yorba Linda, California
- White House Special Files, Staff Member and Office Files: Egil Krogh, 1969–73
- National Security Council (NSC) Files, Country Files—Middle East

NEWSPAPERS

Akşam
Ajans Diyarbakir
CNN Türk
Cumhuriyet
Der Spiegel
Financial Times
The Guardian
Haber
Hürriyet
Hürriyet Daily News
Milliyet
Los Angeles Times
New York Times
NTV-MSNBC
Radikal
Sabah

Taraf
Today's Zaman
Turkish Daily News
The Wall Street Journal
The Washington Post
Zaman

BOOKS

Akcam-Ahmad, Feroz. The Making of Modern Turkey. London: Routledge, 2002.

Abadinsky, Howard. *Organized Crime*. Belmont, CA: Wadsworth Publishing, 2009.

Adanır, Fikret. *Die Makedonische Frage: Ihre Entstehung und Entwicklung bis 1908*. Wiesbaden: Steiner Verlag, 1979.

Adanir, Fikret. "Semi-Autonomous Provincial Forces in the Balkans and Anatolia," in Suraiya Faroqhi (ed.), *The Cambridge History of Turkey: Volume 3, The Later Ottoman Empire, 1603–1839*. Cambridge: Cambridge University Press, 2006, 157–185.

Afetinan, Ayşe. *Medeni Bilgiler ve M. K. Atatürk El Yazıları*. Ankara: Türk Tarih Kurumu, 1968.

Agaşe, Çetin. *Kod Adı: Yeşil*. Istanbul: Pencere Yayınları, 2000.

Ahmad, Feroz. "War and Society under the Young Turks, 1908–1918," *Review* 11.2 (1988), 265–286.

Ahmad, Feroz. "The Special Relationship: The Committee of Union and Progress and the Ottoman Jewish Political Elite, 1908–1918," in Avigdor Levy (ed.), *Jews, Turks, Ottomans: A Shared History, Fifteenth Through the Twentieth Century*. Syracuse: Syracuse University Press, 2002, 212–230.

Akçam, Taner. *Armenien und der Völkermord: Die Istanbuler Prozesse und die türkische Nationalbewegung*. Hamburg: Hamburger Edition, 1996.

Akçura, Belma. *Derin Devltet Oldu Devlet*. Istanbul: Güncel Yayıncılık, 2006.

Akkuş, Turgay. "Bir İktisadi Siyasa Projesi: Milli İktisat ve Bursa," *Çağdaş Türkiye Tarihi Araştırmaları Dergisi*. 8.16–17 (2008), 103–141.

Aksan, Virginia. "War and Peace," in Suraiya Faroqhi (ed.), *The Cambridge History of Turkey: Volume 3, The Later Ottoman Empire, 1603–1839*. Cambridge: Cambridge University Press, 2006, 81–117.

Aktar, Ayhan. *Varlık Vergisi ve "Türkleştirme" Politikaları*. Istanbul: İletişim Yayınları, 2001.

Al-Jabarti's Chronicle of the First Seven Months of the French Occupation of Egypt, June-December 1798/Muharram-Rajab 1213. Princeton, New Jersey: Markus Wiener Publishing, 1993, 19–48.

Albanese, Jay. *Organized Crime in Our Time*. Burlington, MA: Elsevier, 2011.

Albanese, Jay. *Transnational Crime and the 21st Century*. Oxford: Oxford University Press, 2011.

Alonso, Ana Maria. *Thread of Blood: Colonialism, Revolution, and Gender on Mexico's Northern Frontier*. Tucson: University of Arizona Press, 1997.

Andreas, Peter and Ethan Nadelmann. *Policing the Globe: Criminalization and Crime Control in International Relations*. Oxford: Oxford University Press, 2006.

Anscombe, Fredrick. "Albanians and 'Mountain Bandits'," in Fredrick Anscombe (ed.), *The Ottoman Balkans, 1750–1830*. Princeton, New Jersey: Markus Wiener Publications, 2006, 87–113.

Anscombe, Frederick. "Islam and the Age of Ottoman Reform," *Past & Present*. 208 (August 2010), 159–189.

Anslinger, Harry J. and Will Oursler, *The Murderers: The Story of the Narcotics Gang*. New York: Farrar, Straus and Cudahy, 1961.

Anthony, Robert. "Demons, Gangsters and Secret Societies in Early Modern China," *East Asian History*. 27 (June 2004), 71–98.

Asbury, Herbert. *Barbary Coast: An Informal History of the San Francisco Underworld*. New York: Basic Books, 2002.

Asbury, Herbert. *Gangs of Chicago: An Informal History of the Chicago Underworld*. New York: Basic Books, 2002.

Asbury, Herbert. *The French Quarter: An Informal History of the New Orleans Underworld*. New York: Basic Books, 2003.

Asbury, Herbert. *Gangs of New York*. New York: Vintage, 2008.

Astorga, Luis. "Organized Crime and the Organization of Crime," in John Bailey and Roy Godson (eds.), *Organized Crime and Democratic Governability*. Pittsburgh: University of Pittsburgh Press, 2001, 58–82.

Astorga, Luis. *Drogas Sin Fronteras*. Mexico City: Grijalbo, 2003.

Ateş, Sabri. "Empire at the Margins: Towards a History of the Ottoman-Iranian Borderland and the Borderland Peoples," Ph.D. Dissertation: New York University, 2006.

Avagyan, Arsen. *Osmanlı İmparatorluğu ve Kemalist Türkiye'nin Devlet-İktidar Sisteminde Çerkesler*. Istanbul: Belge Yayınları 2004.

Bahar, İlhan. *Teşkilat-ı Mahsusa, MİT ve İstihbarat Örgütleri*. Istanbul: Kum Saati Yayıncılık, 2009.

Barkey, Karen. *Bandits and Bureaucrats: The Ottoman Route to State Centralization* Ithaca, NY: Cornell University Press, 1994.

Baum, Dan. *Smoke and Mirrors: The War on Drugs and the Politics of Failure*. New York: Little, Brown and Company, 1997.

Bayat, Kaveh. "Riza Shah and the Tribes: An Overview," in Patricia Cronin (ed.), *The Making of Modern Iran: State and Society under Riza Shah, 1921–1941*. London: Routledge, 2003, 213–219.

Bein, Amit. *Ottoman Ulema, Turkish Republic: Agents of Change and Guardians of Tradition*. Palo Alto CA: Stanford University Press, 2011.

Bernstein, Lee. "The Greatest Menace: Organized Crime in U.S. Culture and Politics, 1946–1961," Ph.D. Dissertation: University of Minnesota, 1997

Bernstein, Lee. *Greatest Menace*. Boston: University of Massachusetts Press, 2009.

Billingsley, Phil. "Bandits, Bosses and Bare Sticks: Beneath the Surface of Local Control in Early Republican China," *Modern China*. 7.3 (July 1981), 235–288.

Billingsley, Phil. *Bandits in Republican China*. Stanford: Stanford University Press, 1988.

Bingsong, He. "Organized Crime: A Perspective from China," in Jay Albanese et al. (eds.), *Organized Crime: World Perspectives*. Upper Saddle River, NJ: Prentice Hall, 2003, 279–297.

Bıyıklıoğlu, Tevfik. *Trakya'da Milli Müdadele*. Ankara: Türk Tarıh Kurumu, 1992.

Blakey, George Robert. *The Plot to Kill the President*. New York: Times Books, 1981.

Block, Alan. "European Drug Traffic and Traffickers between the Wars: The Policy of Suppression and its Consequences," *Journal of Social History*. 23.2 (Winter 1989), 315–337.

Block, Alan. *East Side West Side: Organizing Crime in New York: 1930–1950*. New Brunswick, NJ: Transaction Publishers, 1999.

Blok, Anton, "The Peasant and the Brigand: Social Banditry Reconsidered," *Comparative Studies in Society and History*. 14.4. (September 1972), 494–503.

Bloxham, Donald. "Terrorism and Imperial Decline: The Ottoman-Armenian Case," *European Review of History*. 14.3 (2007), 301–324.

Blue, Gregory. "Opium for China: The British Connection," in Timothy Brook and Bob Tadashi Wakabayashi (eds.), *Opium Regimes: China, Britain and Japan, 1839–1952.* Berkeley: University of California Press, 2000, 31–54.

Blumi, Isa. "Contesting the Edges of the Ottoman Empire: Rethinking Ethnic and Sectarian Boundaries in the Malësore, 1878–1912," *International Journal of Middle East Studies.* 35.2 (May 2003), 237–256.

Blumi, Isa. "Illicit Trade and the Emergence of Albania and Yemen," in I. William Zartman, *Understanding Life in the Borderlands.* Atlnta: Georgia State Press, 2010, 58–84.

Booth, Martin. *Opium: A History.* New York: St. Martin's Press, 1999.

Booth, Martin. *Cannabis: A History.* New York: St. Martin's Press, 2003.

Bonnano, Joseph with Sergio Lalli, *Man of Honor: The Autobiography of Joseph Bonanno.* New York: Simon and Schuster, 1983.

Bovenkerk, Frank and Yücel Yeşilgöz. *The Turkish Mafia: A History of the Heroin Godfathers.* Lancs, United Kingdom: Milo Books Ltd., 2007.

Bozarslan, Hamit. *Network-Building, Ethnicity and Violence in Turkey.* Abu Dhabi: ECSSR, 1999.

Bozarslan, Hamit. "Türkiye'de Devlet, Komitacılık, Cuntacılık ve Cetecilik Konusunda Fikret Birkaç Hipotez," in Başkaya (ed.), *Resmi Tarih Tartışmaları, Cilt I.* Ankara: Türkiye ve Ortadoğu Forumu Vakfı/Özgür Üniversite Kitaplığı, 173–190.

Bozarslan, Hamit. *Violence in the Middle East: From Political Struggle to Self-Sacrifice.* Princeton, NJ: Markus Weiner Publishers, 2004.

Brailsford, Henry Noel. *Macedonia: Its Races and their Future.* London: Methuen & Co., 1906.

Bresler, Fenton. *Interpol.* New York: Penguin Books, 1993.

Burri Sharani, Barbara et al. *Die kosovarische Bevölkerung in der Schweiz.* Bern: Bundesamt für Migration, 2010.

Çagaptay, Soner. "Crafting the Turkish Nation: Kemalism and Turkish Nationalism in the 1930s," Ph.D. Dissertation: Yale University, 2003.

Cagaptay, Soner. *Islam, Secularism and Nationalism in Modern Turkey: Who is a Turk?* Abingdon: Routledge, 2006.

Çantay, Hasan Basri. *Kara Günler ve İbret Levhaları.* Istanbul: Ahmet Said Matbaası, 1964.

Carey, Elaine. "'Selling is more of a Habit than Using': Narcotraficante Lola la Chata and Her Threat to Civilization," *Journal of Women's History.* 21.2 (2009), 62–89.

Castillo, Elias and Peter Unsinger, "Mexican Drug Syndicates in California," in John Baily and Roy Godson (eds.), *Organized Crime and Democratic Governability: Mexico and the U.S.–Mexico Borderlands.* Pittsburgh: University of Pittsburgh Press, 2000, 199–216.

Çelikpala, Mitat. "From Immigrants to Diaspora: Influence of the North Caucasian Diaspora in Turkey," *Middle East Studies.* 42.3 (2006), 423–446.

Cem, Hasan. *Türkiye'de Babalar ve Mafya.* Istanbul: Geçit Kitabevi, 2004.

Cengiz, Mahmut. *Turkish Organized Crime: From Local to Global.* Saarbrücken, Germany: VDM Verlag Dr. Müller, 2011.

Chassange, Philippe and Kolë Gjeloshaj, "L'Emergence de la Criminalité Organisée Albanophone," *Cahiers D'Etudes sur La Méditerranée Orientale et le Monde Turco-Iranien.* 32 (July–December 2001), 161–190.

Chin, Ko-Lin. *Chinatown Gangs: Extortion, Enterprise and Ethnicity.* Oxford: Oxford University Press, 2000.

Clark, Norman. *Deliver Us From Evil: An Interpretation of American Prohibition.* New York: W.W. Norton Press, 1976.

Colombie Thierry. *La French Connection: Les Entreprises Criminelles en France.* Nantes: Obervatoire Geopolitique des Criminalites Editions, 2012.

Courtwright, David T. "The Hidden Epidemic: Opiate Addiction and Cocaine Use in the South, 1860–1920," *The Journal of Southern History*. 49.1 (February 1983), 57–72.

Creechan, James and Jorge de la Herran Garcia, "Without God or Law: Narcoculture and Belief in Jesus Malverde," *Religious Studies and Theology*. 24.2 (2005), 5–57.

Cribb, Robert. "Introduction: Parapolitics, Shadow Governanace and Criminal Sovereignty," in Eric Wilson (ed.), *Government of the Shadows: Parapolitics and Criminal Sovereignty*. New York: Pluto Books, 2009, 1–12.

Cuthell, David. "The Muhacirin Komisyonu: An Agent in the Transformation of Ottoman Anatolia, 1860–1866," Ph.D. Dissertation: Columbia University, 2005.

Czitrom, Daniel. "Underworlds and Underdogs: Big Tim Sullivan and Metropolitan Politics in New York, 1889–1913," *The Journal of American History*. 78.2 (September 1991), 536–558.

Dadrian, Vahakn N. *The History of the Armenian Genocide: Ethnic Conflict from the Balkans to the Caucasus*. Providence, RI: Berghahn Books, 1995.

D'Agostino, Peter. "Craniums, Criminals, and the 'Cursed Race': Italian Anthropology in American Racial Thought, 1861–1924," *Comparative Studies in Society and History*. 44.2 (April 2002), 319–343.

Dakin, Douglas. *The Greek Struggle in Macedonia, 1897–1913*. Thessaloniki: Institute for Balkan Studies, 1966.

Darling, Linda. "Public Finance: The Role of the Ottoman Center," in Suraiya Faroqhi (ed.), *The Cambridge History of Turkey: Volume 3, The Later Ottoman Empire, 1603–1839*. Cambridge: Cambridge University Press, 2006, 118–131.

Davenport-Hines, Richard. *The Pursuit of Oblivion: A Global History of Narcotics*. New York: W. W. Norton Company, 2004.

Deal, Roger. "The Kabadayis of Istanbul," Masters Thesis: University of Utah, 2000.

Demirtaş, Mehmet. "XVIII Yüzyılda Osmanlıda Bir Zümrenin Alt-Kültür Grubuna Dönüşmesi: Külhanbeyleri," *OTAM*. 19–20 (January 2006), 113–141.

Der Matossian, Bedross. "The Taboo within the Taboo: The Fate of 'Armenian Capital' at the End of the Ottoman Empire," *European Journal of Turkish Studies* (2011).

Dick, Howard. "The Shadow Economy: Markets, Crime and the State," in Eric Wilson (ed.), *Government of the Shadows: Parapolitics and Criminal Sovereignty*. New York: Pluto Books, 2009, 97–116.

Dickie, John. *Cosa Nostra: A History of the Sicilian Mafia*. New York: Palgrave Macmillan, 2004.

Dikici, Ali. *"Demokrat Parti Döneminde İç Güvenlik ve Türk Polis Teşkilatı"*, *Akademik Bakış* 3.5 (Winter 2009), 61–94.

Dimeski, Dimitar. *Makedonskoto Nacionalnooslobodítelno Dvizhenje vo Bitolskiot Vilaet (1893–1903)*. Skopje: Studentski Zbor, 1981.

Dündar, Fuat. *İttihat ve Terakki'nin Müslümanları İskan Politikası (1913–1918)*. Istanbul: İlestişim Yayınları, 2001.

Dunn, Wie Tsain. *The Opium Traffic in its International Aspects*. New York: Columbia University Press, 1920.

Egmond, Florike. "Multiple Underworlds in the Dutch Republic of the Seventeenth and Eighteenth Century," in Cyrille Fijnaut and Letizia Paoli (eds.), *Organised Crime in Europe*. Dodrecht, The Netherlands: Springer, 2004, 77–109.

Eichenberg, Julia. "The Dark Side of Independence: Paramilitary Violence in Ireland and Poland after the First World War," *Journal of Contemporary European History*. 19.3 (2010), 231–248.

Eldem, Edhem. "Capitulations and Western Trade," in Suraiya Faroqhi (ed.), *The Cambridge History of Turkey: Volume 3, The Later Ottoman Empire, 1603–1839.* Cambridge: Cambridge University Press, 2006, 283–325.

Epstein, Edward Jay. *Agency of Fear: Opiates and Political Power in America.* New York: G. P. Putnam's Sons, 1977.

Erdinç, F. Cengiz. *Overdose Türkiye: Türkiye'de Eroin Kaçakçılığı, Bağımlılğı ve Politikalar.* Istanbul: İletişim Yayınları, 2004.

Ergut, Ferdan. "State and Social Control: The Police in the Late Ottoman Empire and the Early Republican Turkey, 1839–1939," Ph.D. Dissertation: New School for Social Research, 1999.

Erhan, Çağrı. *Beyaz Savaş: Türk-Amerikan İlişkilerinde Afyon Sorunu.* Ankara: Bilgi Yayınevi, 1996.

Eymür, Mehmet. *Çeteler, Mafya ve Siyaset.* Istanbul: Birey Yayıncılık, 2001.

Faroqhi, Suraiya. *The Ottoman Empire and the World Around It.* London: I.B. Tauris, 2006.

Findley, Carter Vaughn. *Bureaucratic Reform in the Ottoman Empire: The Sublime Porte, 1789–1922.* Princeton: Princeton University Press, 1980.

Findley, Carter Vaughn. "The Tanzimat," in Reşat Kasaba (ed.), *The Cambridge History of Turkey, Volume 4: Turkey in the Modern World.* Cambridge: Cambridge University Press, 2008, 11–37.

Fleming, Katherine. *The Muslim Bonaparte.* Princeton: Princeton University Press, 1999.

Foreign Relations of the United States, 1952–1954. Vol. VIII: Eastern Europe; Soviet Union; Eastern Mediterranean. Washington DC: Government Printing Office, 1988.

Foreign Relations of the United States, 1969–1976. Vol. XXIX: Eastern Europe; Eastern Mediterranean, 1969–1972. Washington DC: Government Printing Office, 2007.

Foreign Relations of the United States, 1969–1976. Vol. XXX: Greece; Cyprus; Turkey, 1973–1976. Washington DC: Government Printing Office, 2007.

Foster, Anne. "Prohibiting Opium in the Philippines and the United States: The Creation of an Interventionist State," in Alfred McCoy and Francisco Scarano (eds.), *Colonial Crucible: Empire in the Making of the Modern American State.* Madison: University of Wisconsin Press, 2009, 95–105.

Fox, Stephen. *Power and Blood.* New York: William Morrow and Company, 1989.

Fraser, Chris. *Bandit Nation: A History of Outlaws and Cultural Struggle in Mexico, 1810–1920.* Lincoln: University of Nebraska Press, 2006, 20–57.

Fulvetti, Gianluca. "The Mafia and the 'Problem of the Mafia': Organised Crime in Italy, 1820–1970," in Cyrille Fijnaut and Letizia Paoli (eds.), *Organised Crime in Europe.* Dodrecht, The Netherlands: Springer, 2004, 47–76.

Galante, Abraham. *Türkler ve Yahudiler: Tarihî, Siyasî Tetkik.* Istanbul: Tan Matbaası, 1947.

Galante, Pierre and Louis Sapin. *The Marseilles Mafia: The Truth Behind the World of Drug Trafficking.* London: W.H. Allen, 1979.

Galeotti, Mark. "Brotherhoods and Associates: Chechen Networks of Crime and Resistance," *Networks, Terrorism and Global Insurgency.* 1 (2005), 171–182.

Galleotti, Mark. *Organized Crime in History.* New York: Routledge, 2009.

Ganser, Daniele. "Beyond Democratic Checks and Balances: The 'Propaganda Due' Masonic Lodge and the CIA in Italy's First Republic," in Eric Wilson (ed.), *Government of the Shadows: Parapolitics and Criminal Sovereignty.* New York: Pluto Books, 2009, 256–276.

Gaskill, Malcolm. "The Displacement of Providence: Policing and Prosecution in Seventeenth- and Eighteenth-Century England," *Continuity and Change.* 11.3 (1996), 341–374.

Gaunt, David. *Massacres, Resistance, Protectors: Muslim-Christian Relations in Eastern Anatolia During World War I.* Piscatway, NJ: Gorgias, 2006.

Gawrych, George. "The Culture of Violence in Turkish Society, 1903–1914," *Middle Eastern Studies*. 22.3 (1986), 307–330.

Gellner, Ernest. *Nations and Nationalism*. Ithaca, NY: Cornell University Press, 1983.

Gerwarth, Robert and John Horne, "The Great War and Paramilitarism, 1917–1923," *Journal of Contemporary European History*. 19.3 (2010), 267–273.

Geyikdağı, Necia. *Foreign Investment in the Ottoman Empire*. London: I.B. Tauris, 2011.

Gilinski, Yakov and Yakov Kostjukovsky, "From Thievish Artel to Criminal Corporation: The History of Organised Crime in Russia," in Cyrille Fijnaut and Letizia Paoli (eds.), *Organised Crime in Europe*. Dodrecht, The Netherlands: Springer, 2004, 181–202.

Gingeras, Ryan. *Sorrowful Shores: Violence, Ethnicity and the End of the Ottoman Empire*. Oxford: Oxford University Press, 2009.

Gingeras, Ryan. "'Scores Dead in Smerdesh': Communal Violence and International Intrigue in Ottoman Macedonia," *Balkanistika*. 25 (2012), 75–98.

Ginio, Eyal. "Migrants and Workers in an Ottoman Port: Ottoman Salonica in the Eighteenth Century," in Eugene Rogan (ed.), *Outside In: On the Margins of the Modern Middle East*. London: I.B. Taurus, 2002, 126–148.

Göçek, Fatma Müge. *Rise of Bourgeoisie, Demise of Empire: Ottoman Westernization and Social Change*. New York: Oxford University Press, 1996.

Goffman, Daniel. *The Ottoman Empire and Early Modern Europe*. Cambridge: Cambridge University Press, 2002.

Göksu, Saime and Edward Timms, *Romantic Communist: The Life and Work of Nazım Hikmet*. New York: Palgrave Macmillan, 1999.

Gootenberg, Paul. "The 'Pre-Colombian' Era of Drug Trafficking in the Americas: Cocaine, 1945–1965," *The Americas*. 64.2 (October 2007), 133–176.

Gootenberg, Paul. *Andean Cocaine: The Making of a Global Drug*. Chapel Hill: University of North Carolina Press, 2008.

Gordon, Leland James. *American Relations with Turkey, 1830–1930*. Philadelphia: University of Pennsylvania Press, 1932.

Gül, Murat. *The Emergence of Modern Istanbul*. London: I.B. Tauris Publishers, 2009.

Gültekin, Zeynep. "Irak'dan Önce: Kurtlar Vadisi Dizisi," *İletişim Kuram ve Araştırma Dergisi*. 22 (Winter 2006), 9–36.

Gün, Ercan. *Behçet Cantürk'ün MİT İtirafları*. Istanbul: Doğan Egmont Yayıncılık, 2009.

Güven, Zühtü. *Anzavur İsyan: İstiklâl Savaşı Hatıralarından Acı Bir Safha*. Ankara: Türkiye Iş Bankası, 1965.

Hale, William. *Turkish Foreign Policy, 1774–2000*. London: Routledge, 2012.

Hall, William H. *Reconstruction in Turkey*. New York: American Committee of Armenian and Syrian Relief, 1918.

Haller, Mark. "Organized Crime in Urban Society: Chicago in the Twentieth Century," *Journal of Social History*. 5.2 (Winter 1971–1972), 210–234.

Hanioğlu, Şükrü. *Preparation for a Revolution: The Young Turks, 1902–1908*. Oxford: Oxford University Press, 2001.

Hansen, Bradley. "Learning to Tax: The Political Economy of the Opium Trade in Iran, 1921–1941," *The Journal of Economic History*. 16.1 (March 2001), 95–113.

Hanssen, Jens. *Fin de Siecle Beirut: The Making of an Ottoman Provincial Capital*. Oxford: Oxford University Press, 2005.

Harris, George S. "Turkey and United States," in Kemal Karpat (ed.), *Turkey's Foreign Policy in Transition, 1950–1974*. Leiden: E.J. Brill, 1975, 51–72.

Herman, Edward and Frank Brodhead, *The Rise and Fall of the Bulgarian Connection*. New York: Sheridan Square Publications, 1986.

Hersh, Burton. *Bobby and J. Edgar*. New York: Carroll & Graf Publishers, 2007.

Herzog, Christoph. "Migration and the State: On Ottoman Regulations Concerning Migration Since the Age of Mahmud II," in Ulrike Freitag et al. (eds.), *The City in the Ottoman Empire: Migration and the Making of Urban Modernity*. New York: Routledge, 2011, 117–134.

Hess, Henner. "The Sicilian Mafia: Parastate and Adventure Capitalism, in Eric Wilson (ed.), *Government of the Shadows: Parapolitics and Criminal Sovereignty*. New York: Pluto Books, 2009, 153–172.

Hill, Peter. "The Changing Face of the Yakuza," in Mark Galeotti (ed.), *Global Crime Today: The Changing Face of Organised Crime*. London: Routledge, 2005, 97–117.

Hill, Peter. *The Japanese Mafia: Yakuza, Law, and the State*. Oxford: Oxford University Press, 2003.

Hobsbawm, Eric. *Bandits*. London: Abacus, 2007.

Hoffman, Elizabeth Cobbs. "Decolonization, the Cold War, and the Foreign Policy of the Peace Corps," in Peter Hahn and Mary Ann Heiss (eds.), *Empire and Revolution: the United States and the Third World Since 1945*. Columbus: Ohio State University, 2001, 123–153.

Holquist, Peter. "To Count, to Extract, and to Exterminate: Population Statistics and Population Politics in Late Imperial and Soviet Russia," in Ronald Grigor Suny and Terry Martin (eds.), *A State of Nations: Empire and Nation Making in the Age of Lenin and Stalin*. New York: Oxford University Press, 2001, 111–144.

Hopwood, Keith (ed.). *Organised Crime in Antiquity*. London: The Classical Press of Wales, 1998.

House of Representatives, *Bulgarian-Turkish Narcotics Connection: United States-Bulgarian Relations and International Drug Trafficking*. Washington DC: U.S. Government Printing Office, 1984.

Hughes, Steven. "Brigands, Mafiosi and Others: Italy," in Clime Emsley and Louis A. Knafla (eds.), *Crime History and Histories of Crime*. Westport, CT: Greenwood Press, 1996, 139–159.

Human Rights Foundation of Turkey, "*1998 Human Rights Report* Ankara: Human Rights Foundation of Turkey Publications, 2000.

İnalcık, Halil. "The Yürüks: Their Origins, Expansion and Economic Role," in Halil Inalcik (ed.), *The Middle East and the Balkans under the Ottoman Empire: Essays on Economy and Society*. Bloomington: Indiana University Press, 1993, 97–136.

Inalcik, Halil and Donald Quataert. *Economic and Social History of the Ottoman Empire, Volume I*. Cambridge: Cambridge University Press, 1997.

İpek, Nedim. *Rumeli'den Anadolu'ya Türk Göçleri (1877–1890)*. Ankara: Türk Tarih Kurumu, 1994.

Jacobs, James et al., *Gotham Unbound: How New York was Liberated from the Grip of Organized Crime*. New York: NYU Press, 1999.

Jamieson, Alison. "Mafia and Political Power 1943–1989," *International Relations*. 10.13 (1990), 13–30.

Jelavich, Barbara. *History of the Balkans: Volume I*. Cambridge: Cambridge University Press, 1983.

Jenkins, Gareth. "Between Fact and Fantasy: Turkey's Ergenekon Investigation," *Silk Road Papers*. Washington DC: Central Asia-Caucasus Institute and Silk Road Studies, 2009, 1–84.

Jones, Howard. *The Bay of Pigs*. Oxford: Oxford University Press, 2008.

Jonnes, Jill. *Hep-cats, Narcs and Pipe Dreams: A History of America's Romance with Illegal Drugs*. Baltimore: Johns Hopkins University Press, 1999.

Kafadar, Cemal. *Between Two Worlds*. Cambridge, MA: Harvard University Press, 1996.

Kaiser, David. *Road to Dallas*. Cambridge, MA: Harvard University Press, 2009.
Kaligian, Dikran. *Armenian Organization and Ideology Under Ottoman Rule, 1908–1914* New Brunswick, NJ: Transaction Publishers, 2011.
Kaplan, David E. and Alec Dubro. *Yakuza: Japan's Criminal Underworld*. Berkeley: University of California Press, 2003.
Karpat, Kemal. "The Military and Politics in Turkey, 1960–64: A Socio-Cultural Analysis of a Revolution," *American Historical Review*. 75.6 (October 1970), 1654–1683.
Karpat, Kemal. *Ottoman Population, 1830–1914: Demographic and Social Characteristics*. Madison: University of Wisconsin Press, 1985.
Karras, Alan. *Smuggling: Contraband and Corruption in World History*. Lanham, MD: Rowman & Littlefield, 2011.
Kasaba, Resat. "Migrants, Refugees and Smugglers: The Impact on Border-Crossers," *Turkish Studies Association Bulletin*. 17 (1993), 88–91.
Kasaba, Reşat. *A Moveable Empire: Ottoman Nomads, Migrants & Refugees*. Seattle: University of Washington Press, 2009.
Kavakci, Merve. "Turkey's Test with Its Deep State," *Mediterranean Quarterly*. 20.4 (Fall 2009), 83–97.
Kayaalp, Ebru. "From Seed to Smoke: The Re-Making of the Tobacco Market in Turkey," PhD Dissertation: Rice University, 2009.
Kefauver Committee Report on Organized Crime, Volume 5. Washington DC: United States Congress, 1951.
Kieser, Hans-Lukas. *Der Verpasste Friede: Mission, Ethnie und Staat in den Ostprovinzen der Türkei*. Zurich: Chronos Verlag, 2000.
Kieser, Hans-Lukas. "Dr. Mehmed Reshid (1873–1919): A Political Doctor," in Hans-Lukas Kieser and Dominik J. Schaller (eds.), *Der Völkermord an den Armeniern und die Shoah/The Armenian Genocide and the Holocaust*. Zurich: Chronos, 2003, 245–280.
Kinder, Douglas Clark. "Shutting Out the Evil: Nativism and Narcotics Control in the United States," in William O. Walker III (ed.), *Drug Control Policy: Essays in Historical and Comparative Perspective*. University Park: Pennsylvania State University Press, 1992, 117–142.
Kırımlı, Hakan. *National Movements and National Identity Among the Crimean Tatars, 1905–1916*. Leiden: E.J. Brill Press, 1996.
Kitson, Simon. "Police and Politics in Marseille, 1936–8," *European History Quarterly*. 37:81 (2007), 81–108.
Klein, Janet. *Power in the Periphery: The Margins of Empire*. Palo Alto, CA: Stanford University Press, 2011.
Kolars, John. "The Integration of the Villager into the National Life of Turkey," in Kemal Karpat et al. (eds.), *Social Change and Politics in Turkey: A Structural-Historical Analysis*. Leiden: E.J. Brill, 1973, 182–202.
Koraltan, Refik. *Bir Politkacının Anıları*. Ankara: Hacettepe-Taş Yayınevi, 1999.
Kostanick, Huey Louis. "Turkish Resettlement of Bulgarian Refugees, 1950–1953," *Middle East Journal*. 9.1 (1955), 41–52.
Lamothe, Lee and Adrian Humphreys. *The Sixth Family: The Collapse of the New York Mafia and the Rise of Vito Rizzuto*. Mississauga, Ontario: Wiley, 2008.
Landau, Jacob. *Radical Politics in Turkey*. Leiden: Brill, 1974.
Lange-Akhund, Nadine. *The Macedonian Question, 1893–1908: From Western Sources*. Boulder, CO: East European Monographs, 1998.
Lange, Katrin. "'Many a Lord is Guilty, Indeed for Many a Poor Man's Dishonest Deed': Gangs of Robbers in Early Modern Germany," in Cyrille Fijnaut and Letizia Paoli (eds.), *Organised Crime in Europe*. Dodrecht, The Netherlands: Springer, 2004, 109–150.

Lee, Rensselaer W., III. "Parapolitics and Afghanistan," in Eric Wilson (ed.), *Government of the Shadows: Parapolitics and Criminal Sovereignty*. New York: Pluto Books, 2009, 195–204.

Lee, Wayne (ed.), *Empires and Indigenes: Intercultural Alliance, Imperial Expansion and Warfare in the Early Modern World*. New York: NYU Press, 2011.

Levy, Noemi. "Une Institution en Formation: La Police Ottomane a l'époque d' Abdülhamid II," *European Journal of Turkish Studies*. 8 (2008).

Levy, Rene. "Crime, the Judicial System and Punishment in Modern France," in Clime Emsley and Louis A. Knafla (eds.), *Crime History and Histories of Crime*. Westport, CT: Greenwood Press, 1996, 87–108.

Lewis, Bernard. *The Emergence of Modern Turkey*. Oxford: Oxford University Press, 1968.

Lewis, Geoffrey. "Political Change in Turkey Since 1960," in William Hale (ed.), *Aspects of Modern Turkey*. London: Bowker, 1976, 15–19.

Lewis, Mary. *The Boundaries of the Republic*. Palo Alto, CA: Stanford University Press, 2007.

Lintner, Bertil. "Heroin and Highland Insurgency in the Golden Triangle," in Alfred McCoy and Alan Block (eds.), *War on Drugs: Studies in the Failure of U.S. Narcotics Policy*. Boulder, CO: Westview Press, 1992, 281–317.

Lodhi, Abdul Qaiyum and Charles Tilly. "Urbanization, Crime, and Collective Violence in 19th-Century France," *The American Journal of Sociology*. 79.2 (September 1973), 296–318.

Lopez Restrepo, Andres and Alvaro Camacho Guizado. "From Smugglers to Warlords: Twentieth Century Colombian Drug Traffickers," *Canadian Journal of Latin American & Caribbean Studies*. 28.55–56 (2003), 249–263.

Lüdke, Alf and Herbert Reinke. "Crime, Police and the 'Good Order': Germany," in Clime Emsley and Louis A. Knafla (eds.), *Crime History and Histories of Crime*. Westport, CT: Greenwood Press, 1996, 109–138.

Lupsha, Peter. "Transnational Crime versus Nation-State," *Transnational Organized Crime*. 2.1 (Spring 1996), 21–48.

Lyman, Michael and Gary Potter, *Organized Crime*. New York: Prentice Hall, 2010.

Maas, Peter. *The Valachi Papers*. New York: Harper Paperback, 2003.

Makdisi, Ussama. *Artillery of Heaven: American Missionaries and the Failed Conversion of the Middle East*. Ithaca, NY: Cornell University Press, 2009.

Mallory, Stephan. *Understanding Organized Crime*. Boston, MA: Jones and Bartlett Publishers, 2011.

Mandel, Maud S. *In the Aftermath of Genocide: Armenians and Jews in Twentieth-Century France* (Durham, NC: Duke University Press, 2003).

Marshall, Jonathan. *Drug Wars: Corruption, Counterinsurgency and Covert Operations in the Third World*. Forestville, CA: Cohan & Cohen Press, 1991.

Marshall, Jonathan. "CIA Assets and the Rise of the Guadalajara Connection," in Alfred McCoy and Alan Block (eds.), *War on Drugs: Studies in the Failure of U.S. Narcotics Policy* Boulder, CO: Westview Press, 1992, 197–208.

Marshall, Jonathan. *The Lebanese Connection*. Palo Alto, CA: Stanford University Press, 2012.

Marshall, Jonathan. "Opium, Tungsten, and the Search for National Security, 1940–1952," in William O. Walker III (ed.), *Drug Control Policy: Essays in Historical and Comparative Perspective*. University Park: Pennsylvania State University Press, 1992, 89–116.

Martin, Brian. "The Green Gang and the Guomindang State: Du Yuesheng and the Politics of Shanghai," *The Journal of Asian Studies*. 54.1. (February 1995), 64–92.

Massicard, Elise. *The Alevis in Turkey: Identity and Managing Territorial Diversity.* New York: Routledge, 2013.

Matthee, Rudi. *The Pursuit of Pleasure: Drugs and Stimulants in Iranian History 1500–1900.* Princeton, NY: Princeton University Press, 2005, 207–218.

McAllister, William. *Drug Diplomacy in the Twentieth Century.* London: Routledge, 2000.

McCarthy, Justin. *Ölüm ve Sürgün: Osmanlı Müslümanlarına Karşı Yürülten Ulus Olarack Temizleme İşlemi.* Istanbul: İnkılap Kitapevi, 1998.

McCoy, Alfred. "Heroin as a Global Commodity: A History of Southeast Asia's Opium Trade," in Alfred McCoy and Alan Block (eds.), *War on Drugs: Studies in the Failure of U.S. Narcotics Policy.* Boulder, CO: Westview Press, 1992, 237–280.

McCoy, Alfred. *The Politics of Heroin: CIA Complicity in the Global Drug Trade.* Chicago, IL: Lawrence Hill Books, 2003.

McCoy, Alfred. "The Stimulus of Prohibition: A Critical History of the Global Narcotics Trade," in Michael K. Steinberg et al. (eds.), *Dangerous Harvest: Drug Plants and the Transformation of Indigenous Landscapes.* New York: Oxford University Press, 2004, 24–99.

McCoy, Alfred. "Covert Netherworld: Clandestine Services and Criminal Syndicates in Shaping the Philippine State," in Eric Wilson (ed.), *Government of the Shadows: Parapolitics and Criminal Sovereignty.* New York: Pluto Books, 2009, 226–255.

McIllwain, Jeffrey Scott. "Organizing Crime in Chinatown: New York City's Chinatown and the Social System of Organized Crime during the Progressive Era," Ph.D. Dissertation: Pennsylvania State University, 1997.

McMullan, John. "Organization in Sixteenth and Seventeenth Century London," *Social Problems.* 29.3 (February 1982), 311–323.

McWilliams, John. *The Protectors: Harry J. Anslinger and the Federal Bureau of Narcotics, 1930–1962.* Newark: University of Delaware Press, 1990.

McWilliams, John. "Through the Past Darkly: The Politics and Policies of America's Drug War," in William O. Walker III (ed.), *Drug Control Policy.* University Park: Pennsylvania State University Press, 1992, 5–41.

Meeker, Michael. *A Nation of Empire: The Ottoman Legacy of Turkish Modernity.* Berkeley: University of California Press, 2002.

Meyer, James. "Politics as Usual: Ciller, Refah and Susurluk: Turkey's Troubled Democracy," *Eastern European Quarterly.* 32.4 (January 1999), 489–502.

Meyer, Kathryn and Terry Parssinen. *Web of Smoke: Smugglers, Warlords, Spies and the History of the International Drug Trade.* Lanham, MD: Rowman and Littlefield Publishers, 1998.

Moore, Robin. *The French Connection.* Guilford, CT: Lyons Press, 2003.

Moscow, Alvin. *Merchants of Heroin.* New York: Dial Press, 1968.

Mottier, Nicole. "Drug Gangs and Politics in Ciudad Juarez: 1928–1936," *Mexican Studies.* 25.1 (Winter 2009), 19–46.

Mumcu, Ugur. *Silah Kaçakçılığı ve Terör.* Istanbul: Tekin Yayınevi, 1981.

Mumcu, Uğur. *Papa, Mafya, Ağca.* Istanbul: Tekin Yayınevi, 1984.

Nasiali, Minayo. "Native Republic: Negotiating Citizenship and Social Welfare in Marseille "Immigrant" Neighborhoods Since 1945," Ph.D. Dissertation: University of Michigan, 2010.

Newark, Tim. *Lucky Luciano: The Real and the Fake Gangster.* New York: St. Martin's Press, 2010.

Newman, John Paul. "Post-Imperial and Post-war Violence in the South Slav Lands, 1917–1923," *Journal of Contemporary European History.* 19.3 (2010), 249–265.

Newsday. *The Heroin Trail.* New York: New American Library, 1973.

Oğuz, İsmail. *Babalar Vadisi.* Istanbul: Ares Kitap, 2006.

Öktem, Kerem. *Angry Nation: Turkey Since 1989.* London: Zed Books, 2011.
The Opium Trade, 1910–1941, Volume 5—1922–1926. Wilmington, Delaware: Scholarly Resources, Inc., 1974.
Özbek, Nadir. "Policing the Countryside: Gendarmes of the Late 19th Century Ottoman Empire (1876–1908)," *International Journal of Middle East Studies.* 40 (2008), 47–67.
Özgür-Baklacıoğlu, Nurcan. "Devletlerin Dış Politikaları Açısından Göç Olgusu: Balkanlar'dan Türkiye'ye Arnavut Göçleri (1920–1990)," Ph.D. Dissertation: Istanbul University, 2003.
Özkan, Tuncay. *MİT'in Gizli Tarihi.* Istanbul: Afla, 2003.
Özyürek, Esra. *Nostalgia for the Modern: State Secularism and Everyday Politics in Turkey.* Chapel Hill, NC: Duke University Press, 2006.
Palacios, Marco. *Between Legitimacy and Violence: A History of Columbia, 1875–2002.* Durham, NC: Duke University Press, 2006.
Paoli, Letizia. *Mafia Brotherhoods: Organized Crime, Italian Style.* Oxford: Oxford University Press, 2008.
Paoli, Letizia and Cyrille Fijnaut, "Introduction to Part I: The History of the Concept," in Cyrille Fijnaut and Letizia Paoli (eds.), *Organised Crime in Europe.* Dodrecht, The Netherlands: Springer, 2004, 21–46.
Park, Geoffrey. "Crisis and Catastrophe: The Global Crisis of the Seventeenth Century Reconsidered," *American Historical Review.* 113.4 (October 2008), 1053–1079.
Pearson, John. *The Life of Ian Fleming.* London: Jonathan Cape, 1966.
Perry, Duncan. *The Politics of Terror: The Macedonian Liberation Movement 1893–1903.* Durham, NC: Duke University Press, 1988.
Jerome Pierrat, *Une Histoire du Milieu.* Paris: Denoel, 2003.
Pietrusza, David. *Rothstein: The Life, Times and Murder of the Criminal Genius Who Fixed the 1919 World Series.* New York: Basic Books, 2004.
Poroy, İbrahim İhsan. "Expansion of Opium Production in Turkey and the State Monopoly of 1828–1839," *International Journal of Middle East Studies.* 13.2 (May 1981), 191–211.
Quataert, Donald. "Ottoman Resistance to European Economic Penetration: Tobacco Smugglers, the Regie and the Ottoman Government," *Turkish Studies Association Bulletin.* 7.1 (1983), 25–27.
Raab, Selwyn. *Five Families: The Rise, Decline and Resurgence of America's Most Powerful Mafia Empires.* New York: St. Martins Griffin, 2006.
Reece, Jack. "Fascism, the Mafia and the Emergence of Sicilian Separatism, 1919–1943," *The Journal of Modern History.* 45.2 (June 1973), 261–276.
Rice, Robert. *The Business of Crime.* New York: Farrar, Straus & Cudahy, 1956.
Rogan, Eugene. *Frontiers of the State in the Late Ottoman Empire: Transjordan 1850–1921.* Cambridge: Cambridge University Press, 1999.
Ruff, Julius. *Violence in Early Modern Europe, 1500–1800.* Cambridge: Cambridge University Press, 2001, 216–247.
Russell, Thomas. *Egyptian Service 1902–1946.* London: John Murray, 1949.
Saçan, Adil Sedar. *Ak Baba Örgütü.* Istanbul: Toplumsal Dönüşüm Yayınları, 2004.
Saenz Rovner, Eduardo. *The Cuban Connection: Drug Trafficking, Smuggling and Gambling in Cuba from the 1920s to the Revolution.* Chapel Hill: University of North Carolina Press, 2008.
Sandos, James A. "Northern Separatism during the Mexican Revolution: An Inquiry into the Role of Drug Trafficking, 1910–1920," *The Americas.* 41.2 (Oct. 1984), 191–214.
Schatzberg, Rufus and Robert Kelly, *African American Organized Crime.* New Brunswick, NJ: Rutgers University Press, 1997.

Schayegh, Cyrus. "The Many Worlds of 'Abud Yasin; or, What Narcotics Trafficking in the Interwar Middle East Can Tell Us about Territorialization," *American Historical Review*. 116.2 (April 2011), 273–306.

Schneider, Eric. *Smack: Heroin and the American City*. Philadelphia: University of Pennsylvania Press, 2008.

Scott, Peter Dale. *Deep Politics and the Death of JFK*. Berkeley: University of California Press, 1996.

Scott, Peter Dale. *The Road to 9/11: Wealth, Empire and the Future of America*. Berkeley: University of California Press, 2007.

Shaw, Stanford. *History of the Ottoman Empire and Modern Turkey Volume II*. Cambridge: Cambridge University Press, 1977.

Siniawer, Eiko Maruko. *Ruffians, Yakuza, Nationalists: The Violent Politics of Modern Japan, 1860–1960*. Ithaca, NY: Cornell University Press, 2008.

Siragusa, Charles and Robert Wiedrich. *Trail of the Poppy*. Englewood Cliffs, NJ: Prentice Hall Inc., 1966.

Slack, Edward R. *Opium, State and Society: China's Narco-Economy and the Guomindang, 1924–1937*. Honolulu: University of Hawaii Press, 2001.

Sofuoğlu, Adnan. *Kuva-yı Milliye Döneminde Kuzeybatı Anadolu, 1919–1921*. Ankara: Genelkurmay Basım Evi, 1994.

Sowards, Steven. *Austria's Policy of Macedonian Reform*. Boulder, CO: East European Monographs, 1989.

Söyler, Mehtap. "The Deep State: Forms of Domination, Informal Institutions and Democracy," *Perspectives: Political Analysis and Commentary from Turkey*. 3 (December 2012), 8–11.

Sterling, Claire. *Octopus*. New York: Touchstone Books, 1990.

Steward, Douglas. *Creating the National Security State*. Princeton: Princeton University Press, 2008.

Stoddard, Philip Hendrick. "The Ottoman Government and the Arabs, 1911 to 1918: A Preliminary Study of the Teşkilat-ı Mahsusa," Ph.D. Dissertation: Princeton University, 1963.

Streatfeild, Dominic. *Cocaine*. London: Virgin Limited Books, 2002.

Suny, Ronald Grigor. *Looking Towards Ararat: Armenia in Modern History*. Bloomington: Indiana University Press, 1993.

Tanilli, Sever. "Geçen Yüzyılda İstanbul'de Kabadayılar ve Külhanbeyleri," in François Georgeon and Paul Dumont (eds.), *Osmanlı İmparatorluğunda Yaşamak*. Istanbul: İletişim, 2003, 137–146.

Taylor, Arnold H. *American Diplomacy and the Narcotics Traffic, 1900–1939*. Durham, NC: Duke University Press, 1969.

Thoumi, Francisco. "From Drug Lords to Warlords: Illegal Drugs and the 'Unintended' Consequences of Drug Policies in Colombia," in Eric Wilson (ed.), *Government of the Shadows: Parapolitics and Criminal Sovereignty*. New York: Pluto Books, 2009, 205–225.

Tilly, Charles. "War Making and State Making as Organized Crime," in Peter Evans et al. (eds.), *Bringing the State Back In*. Cambridge: Cambridge University Press, 1985, 169–187.

Üngör, Uğur Ümit. *The Making of Modern Turkey*. Oxford: Oxford University Press, 2011.

Toledano, Ehud R. *Slavery and Abolition in the Ottoman Middle East*. Seattle: University of Washington Press, 1998.

Toprak, Zafer. *İttihad-Terakki ve Cihan Harbi: Savaş Ekonomisi ve Türkiye'de Devletçilik* Istanbul: Homer Kitabevi, 2003.

Toumarkine, Alexandre. "Kafkas ve Balkan Göçmen Dernekleri: Sivil Toplum ve Milliyetçilik," in Stefanos Yerasimos et al. (eds.), *Türkiye'de Sivil Toplum ve Milliyetçilik*. Istanbul: İletişm Yayınları, 2001, 425–450.

Traffic in Opium and Other Dangerous Drugs for the Year Ended December 31, 1942. Washington DC: U.S. Treasury Department, Bureau of Narcotics, 1943.
Traffic in Opium and Other Dangerous Drugs for the Year Ended December 31, 1944. Washington DC: U.S. Treasury Department, Bureau of Narcotics, 1945.
Traffic in Opium and Other Dangerous Drugs for the Year Ended December 31, 1945. Washington DC: U.S. Treasury Department, Bureau of Narcotics, 1946.
Traffic in Opium and Other Dangerous Drugs for the Year Ended December 31, 1946. Washington DC: U.S. Treasury Department, Bureau of Narcotics, 1947.
Traffic in Opium and Other Dangerous Drugs for the Year Ended December 31, 1947. Washington DC: U.S. Treasury Department, Bureau of Narcotics, 1948.
Traffic in Opium and Other Dangerous Drugs for the Year Ended December 31, 1951. Washington DC: U.S. Treasury Department, Bureau of Narcotics, 1952.
Traffic in Opium and Other Dangerous Drugs for the Year Ended December 31, 1952. Washington DC: U.S. Treasury Department, Bureau of Narcotics, 1953.
Traffic in Opium and Other Dangerous Drugs for the Year Ended December 31, 1955. Washington DC: U.S. Treasury Department, Bureau of Narcotics, 1956.
Traffic in Opium and Other Dangerous Drugs for the Year Ended December 31, 1956. Washington DC: U.S. Treasury Department, Bureau of Narcotics, 1957.
Traffic in Opium and Other Dangerous Drugs for the Year Ended December 31, 1958. Washington DC: U.S. Treasury Department, Bureau of Narcotics, 1959.
Traffic in Opium and Other Dangerous Drugs for the Year Ended December 31, 1959. Washington DC: U.S. Treasury Department, Bureau of Narcotics, 1960.
Traffic in Opium and Other Dangerous Drugs for the Year Ended December 31, 1960. Washington DC: U.S. Treasury Department, Bureau of Narcotics, 1961.
Traffic in Opium and Other Dangerous Drugs for the Year Ended December 31, 1961. Washington DC: U.S. Treasury Department, Bureau of Narcotics, 1962.
Traffic in Opium and Other Dangerous Drugs for the Year Ended December 31, 1962. Washington DC: U.S. Treasury Department, Bureau of Narcotics, 1963.
Traffic in Opium and Other Dangerous Drugs for the Year Ended December 31, 1963. Washington DC: U.S. Treasury Department, Bureau of Narcotics, 1964.
Traffic in Opium and Other Dangerous Drugs for the Year Ended December 31, 1964. Washington DC: U.S. Treasury Department, Bureau of Narcotics, 1965.
Traffic in Opium and Other Dangerous Drugs for the Year Ended December 31, 1965. Washington DC: U.S. Treasury Department, Bureau of Narcotics, 1966.
Traffic in Opium and Other Dangerous Drugs for the Year Ended December 31, 1966. Washington DC: U.S. Treasury Department, Bureau of Narcotics, 1967.
Traffic in Opium and Other Dangerous Drugs for the Year Ended December 31, 1967. Washington DC: U.S. Treasury Department, Bureau of Narcotics, 1968.
Tunander, Ola. "Democratic State vs. Deep State: Approaching the Dual State of the West," in Eric Wilson (ed.), *Government of the Shadows: Parapolitics and Criminal Sovereignty.* New York: Pluto Books, 2009, 56–72.
Turgay, A. Üner. "The Nineteenth Century Golden Triangle: Chinese Consumption, Ottoman Production, and the American Connection, II," *International Journal of Turkish Studies.* 3.1 (1984–1985), 65–93.
"Türkiye Uyuşturucu: 2012 Raporu." Ankara: Kaçakçılık ve Örgüt Suçlarla Mücadele Daire Başkanlığı, 2012.
United Nations Office on Drugs and Crime. *United Nations Convention Against Transnational Organized Crime and the Protocols Thereto.* New York: United Nations, 2004.
Ünlü, Ferhat. *Susurluk Gümrüğü: Kaçakçılık—Çete—Devlet.* Istanbul: Birey, 2000.

Ünver, H. Akin. "Turkey's 'Deep State' and the Ergenekon Conundrum," *Middle East Institute Policy Brief.* 1 April 2009.
Ural, Gültekin. *Teşkilat-ı Mahsusa'dan MİT'e: Abdullah Çatlı ve Susurluk Olayı.* Istanbul: Kamer Yayınları, 1997.
US Senate, Permanent Subcommittee on Investigations. *Organized Crime and Illicit Traffic in Narcotics, Part 3.* Washington DC: U.S. Government Printing Office, 1964.
Valentine, Douglas. *The Strength of the Wolf.* London: Verso, 2004.
Valentine, Douglas. *The Strength of the Pack.* Walterville, OR: Trine Day, 2009.
Vander Lippe, John. "Forgotten Brigade of the Forgotten War: Turkey's Participation in the Korean War," *Middle East Studies.* 36.1 (January 2000), 92–102.
Vanderwood, Paul. *Disorder and Progress: Bandits, Police, and Mexican Development.* Wilmington, DE: A Scholarly Resources Inc., 1992.
Vızzını, Sal et al. *Vizzini: The Secret Lives of America's Most Successful Undercover Agent.* New York: Arbor House, 1972.
Vyronis, Speros. *The Mechanism of Catastrophe: The Turkish Pogrom of September 6–7, 1955, and the Destruction of the Greek Community of Istanbul.* Greekworks.com, 2008.
Wagner, Kim A. "The Deconstructed Stranglers: A Reassessment of Thuggee," *Modern Asian Studies.* 38.4 (2004), 931–963.
Wakeman, Fredric. "Licensing Leisure: The Chinese Nationalists' Attempt to Regulate Shanghai, 1927–1949," *The Journal of Asian Studies.* 54.1 (February 1995), 19–42.
Walker III, William O. *Opium and Foreign Policy: The Anglo-American Search for Order in Asia, 1912–1954.* Chapel Hill: University of North Carolina Press, 1991.
Wallerstein, Immanuel et al. "The Incorporation of the Ottoman Empire into the World Economy," in Huri Islamoglu-Inan (ed.), *The Ottoman Empire and the World Economy.* Cambridge: Cambridge University Press, 1987, 88–100.
Walston, James. "See Naples and Die: Organized Crime in Campania," in Robert Kelly (ed.), *Organized Crime: A Global Perspective.* Totawa, NJ: Rowman & Littlefield, 1986, 134–158.
Wang, W. C. "Tu Yueh-Sheng (1888–1951): A Tentative Political Biography," *Journal of Asian Studies.* 26.3 (May 1967), 433–455.
Wasserman, Mark. *Persistent Oligarchs: Elites and Politics in Chihuahua, Mexico 1910–1940.* Durham, NC: Duke University Press, 1993.
Weissman Joselit, Jenna. *Our Gang: Jewish Crime and the New York Jewish Community, 1900–1940.* Bloomington: Indiana University Press, 1983.
White, Joshua. "Easy Targets: The Illegal Enslavement of Ottoman Subjects in the Aegean (Late 16th C.)," paper presented at New York University Ottoman Studies Workshop on Violence in Anatolia (4–5 March 2011).
White, Richard. "Outlaw Gangs of the Middle Border: American Social Bandits," *The Western Historical Quarterly.* 12.4 (October 1981), 387–408.
White, Sam. *The Climate of Rebellion in the Early Ottoman Empire.* Cambridge: Cambridge University Press, 2011.
Wighton, Charles. *Dope International.* London: Frederick Muller Limited, 1960.
Wilson, Stephen. "Banditry in Corsica: The Eighteenth to Twentieth Centuries," in Cyrille Fijnaut and Letizia Paoli (eds.), *Organised Crime in Europe.* Dodrecht, The Netherlands: Springer, 2004, 151–180.
Woodiwiss, Michael. "Organized Crime—The Dumbing of Discourse," *The British Criminology Conference: Selected Proceedings.* Volume 3. Papers from the British Society of Criminology Conference, Liverpool (July 1999), 1–10.

Woodiwiss, Michael. *Organized Crime and American Power: A History*. Toronto: University of Toronto Press, 2001.

Woodiwiss, Michael. *Gangster Capitalism: The United States and the Globalization of Organized Crime*. New York: Basic Books, 2005.

Yalcun, Soner. *Efendi: Beyaz Türklerin Büyük Sırrı*. Istanbul: Doğan Kitapçilik, 2004.

Yalçın, Soner. *Behçet Cantürk'ün Anıları*. Istanbul: Doğan Kitap, 2007.

Yalman, Ahmed Emin. *Turkey in the World War*. New Haven, CT: Yale University Press, 1930.

Yasmanoğlu, İpek. "The Priest's Robe and the Rebel's Rifle: Communal Conflict and the Construction of National Identity in Ottoman Macedonia, 1878–1908," Ph.D. Dissertation: Princeton University, 2005.

Yavuz, Hakan. *Islamic Political Identity in Turkey*. Oxford: Oxford University Press, 2005.

Yavuz, Hakan. *Secularism and Muslim Democracy*. Cambridge: Cambridge University Press, 2009.

Yetkin, Sabri. *Ege'de Eşkıyalar*. Istanbul: Tarih Vakfı Yurt Yayınları, 2003.

Yongming, Zhou. "Nationalism, Identity and State-Building: The Antidrug Crusade in the People's Republic, 1949–1952," in Timothy Brook and Bob Tadashi Wakabayashi (eds.), *Opium Regimes: China, Britain and Japan, 1839–1952*. Berkeley: University of California Press, 2000, 380–403.

Yurdakul, Doğan. *Abi: Kabadayıler-Mafya Derin Devlet İlişkilsi*. Istanbul: Positif Yayınları, 2007.

Zurcher, Erik Jan. *The Unionist Factor: The Role of the Committee of Union and Progress in the Turkish Nationalist Movement, 1905–1926*. Leiden: Brill, 1984.

Zürcher, Erik Jan. "The Ottoman Legacy of the Turkish Republic: An Attempt at a New Periodization," *Die Welt des Islams*. 32 (1992), 237–253.

Zurcher, Erik Jan. *Turkey: A Modern History*. London & New York: I.B. Tauris, 1993.

Zurcher, Erik Jan. "Young Turks—Children of the Borderlands?," in Kemal Karpat and Robert W. Zens (eds.), *Ottoman Borderlands: Issues, Personalities and Political Changes*. Madison: University of Wisconsin Press, 2003, 275–286.

Zurcher, Erik Jan. "Young Turks, Ottoman Muslims and Turkish Nationalists: Identity Politics 1908–1938," in Erik Jan Zürcher (ed.), *The Young Turk Legacy and Nation Building: From the Ottoman Empire to Atatürk's Turkey*. London: I.B. Tauris, 2010, 213–235.

Index

Made in the USA
Middletown, DE
19 September 2020

20046237R00177